Pawns of Yalta

J. Thiel's *Group of Russian Prisoners*, 1945.

Soviet Refugees and
America's Role
in Their Repatriation

MARK R. ELLIOTT

PAWNS
OF
YALTA

UNIVERSITY OF ILLINOIS PRESS   Urbana Chicago London

Library of Congress Cataloging in Publication Data

Elliott, Mark, 1947–
  Pawns of Yalta.

  Includes index.
  1. World War, 1939–1945—Forced repatriation.
2. World War, 1939–1945—Refugees. 3. Refugees—
Soviet Union. I. Title. II. Title: Soviet
refugees and America's role in their repatriation.
D809.S65E44   940.53'159   81-7599
ISBN 0-252-00897-9   AACR2

In Memory of a Refugee Gone Home

Loc Ba Tran
1972–1980

Contents

Acknowledgments

THE WRITTEN APPRECIATIONS HISTORIANS EMPLOY to acknowledge their indebtedness to secretaries, librarians, archivists, and colleagues are frequently predictable, but a great deal more heartfelt than the repetitive quality of the thanks might indicate. Words seem inadequate to acknowledge others' help, but between two covers words are all that an author can employ.

A number of secretaries and student assistants at Asbury College helped with typing and bibliographical work, including Lydia Joly, Nancy Harrison, Marilyn Neff, Tillie Moore, Dorothy Smith, Crystal Barham, Glenn Spann, and Mark Goode. Beth Gardner, besides typing several drafts of several chapters, provided expert critical review and editorial assistance.

Among the many librarians and archivists who came to my aid, two in particular deserve thanks: Lois Luesing, reference librarian at Asbury College, who secured innumerable books and articles for me on interlibrary loan; and John Taylor, Modern Military Records, the National Archives, who not only supplied an array of documents I requested, but provided me with invaluable leads to materials that previously had escaped my attention.

I wish to express my gratitude also to my doctoral adviser, Dr. Robert Warth of the University of Kentucky, who directed my original investigation of repatriation. Dr. Ralph T. Fisher, Jr., director of the Russian and East European Center of the University of Illinois, Dr. George Herring, University of Kentucky, and Dr. Robert Slusser, Michigan State University, provided me with encouragement, valuable advice, and helpful critiques of my manuscript.

The author is grateful for financial support provided by the University of Illinois Russian and East European Center's Summer Workshops, the Southern Regional Education Board, and the Kennan Institute for Advanced Russian Studies, Washington, D.C. Also, I wish to acknowledge the generous assistance of the Asbury College Board of Trustees, President Dennis Kinlaw, and former Vice-President Roger Kusche who, through Asbury's Faculty Research and Development Committee, provided me with a work leave for the fall of 1979.

My wife and daughter deserve awards for outstanding patience and understanding in the face of a seriously distracted husband and father.

Finally, and ultimately, I wish to give thanks to God—as Paul says, "To the only wise God, through Jesus Christ, be the glory forever." It is a certainty this book would never have been, but for a quickening of the Spirit of God within, which, among other things, awakened me to the sanctity of time and the preciousness of each of our fleeting moments.

List of Abbreviations and Acronyms

ACNS	American Council for Nationalities Service
ACS	Assistant Chief of Staff
AFHQ	Allied Forces Headquarters (Italy)
AGWAR	Adjutant General, War Department
AP	Associated Press
APC	Allied Polish Commission
BBC	British Broadcasting Corporation
CAD	Civil Affairs Division
CCAC	Combined Civil Affairs Committee
CCS	Combined Chiefs of Staff
CDPX	Combined Displaced Persons Executive
CFM	Council of Foreign Ministers
CIA	Central Intelligence Agency
COMGENUSFA	Commanding General, U.S. Forces, Austria
C(POW)PC	Combined (Prisoners of War) Planning Committee
CS	Chief of Staff
df	decimal file
DP	displaced person
EAC	European Advisory Commission
EUCOM	European Command
FR	*Foreign Relations of the United States, Diplomatic Papers*
G1	Personnel Section of the U.S. Army General Staff

G5	Civil Affairs Section of the U.S. Army General Staff
GSC	General Staff Corps
GUKR	Glavnoe Upravlenie Kontrrazvedkoi (Main Administration for Counterintelligence)
HDQ	headquarters
Hiwi	Hilfswilligen (Auxiliary Volunteers)
IRO	International Refugee Organization
JCS	Joint Chiefs of Staff
JLC	Joint Logistics Committee
JPRS	Joint Publications Research Service
KGB	Komitet Gosudarstvennoi Bezopasnosti (Committee on State Security)
KONR	Komitet Osvobozhdeniia Narodov Rossii (Committee for the Liberation of the Peoples of Russia)
M.P.	Member of Parliament
MR	Map Room
MTOUSA	Mediterranean Theater of Operations, U.S. Army
NA	National Archives
NAS	National Archives, Suitland Branch
NKGB	Narodnyi Komissariat Gosudarstvennoi Bezopasnosti (People's Commissariat of State Security)
NKVD	Narodnyi Komissariat Vnutrennikh Del (People's Commissariat of Internal Affairs)
OCH	Office of the Chief Historian
OCMH	Office of the Chief of Military History
OKH	Oberkommando des Heeres (High Command of the Army)
OKW	Oberkommando der Wehrmacht (Armed Forces High Command)
OMGUS	Office of Military Government, U.S. Zone
OPD	Operations Division
OSS	Office of Strategic Services
PCIRO	Preparatory Commission of the International Refugee Organization

PFK	Proverochno-Fil'trovochnye Komissii (Vetting and Screening Commission)
PMGO	Provost Marshal General's Office
POW	prisoner of war
RAMP	Recovered Allied Military Personnel
RG	Record Group
ROA	Russkaia Osvoboditel'naia Armiia (Russian Liberation Army)
ROD	Russkoe Osvoboditel'noe Dvizhenie (Russian Liberation Movement)
SACMED	Supreme Allied Command, Mediterranean Theater
SACS	Special Assistant to the Chief of Staff
SANACC	State-Army-Navy Coordinating Committee
SD	State Department
sf	subject file
SHAEF	Supreme Headquarters Allied Expeditionary Force
SMERSH	"Smert' shpionam!" ("Death to Spies!")
SWNCC	State-War-Navy Coordinating Committee
UNRRA	United Nations Relief and Rehabilitation Administration
UPI	United Press International
USAFE	U.S. Army Forces Europe
USFET	U.S. Forces, European Theater
USMMM	U.S. Military Mission Moscow
USSBS	U.S. Strategic Bombing Survey
UUARC	United Ukrainian American Relief Committee
WD	War Department
WDGSS	War Department General and Special Staffs

INTRODUCTION

"The Desperate Amuses Man"

IN A SMALL CEMETERY AT FORT MOTT STATE PARK, New Jersey, lies the mute evidence of a wartime tragedy. Three graves there contain the remains of a Red Army private and two second lieutenants who took their own lives rather than submit to repatriation to Russia. Each died at Fort Dix, New Jersey, on 29 June 1945, the only "successful" participants in a mass suicide attempted by 154 Soviet citizens captured in German uniform.[1] American military police brought the macabre demonstration under control with the use of tear gas, but only after the three now buried at Fort Mott had hanged themselves. At Moscow's insistence the United States repatriated the rest amid Soviet charges that American guards had wounded and teargassed Red Army soldiers to prevent their return home.[2]

Seven months later the *New York Times* reported that Dachau, Germany, already infamous for Nazi atrocities, had once again become the scene of a "frenzy of terror": on 19 January 1946, American soldiers forced their Soviet charges from the concentration camp barracks with tear gas. Collapsing in the snow from wounds of their own making, the Russians begged to be shot by their American guards, preferring death to repatriation. The toll for one day of forced repatriation was eleven dead, twenty-one wounded.[3]

The following month U.S. Army translator William Sloane Coffin, Jr., witnessed a repetition of the carnage at Plattling, Germany. Under the pretext of gathering information about the men's reasons for leaving the Soviet Union, he helped sort out several thousand displaced persons (DPs) subject to forced extradition. His part in the deception came to haunt him, especially the memory of those so fearful of their homeland that death seemed preferable: "Despite the fact that there were three GIs to every returning Russian, I saw several men commit suicide. Two rammed their heads through windows sawing their necks on the broken glass until they cut their jugular veins. Another took his leather bootstraps, tied a loop to the top of his triple-decker bunk, put his head through the noose and did a back flip over the edge which broke his neck."[4] Frosty-breathed GIs, one in sunglasses, forced one sobbing, suicidal Russian to bare his self-inflicted chest wounds to an Army Signal Corps cameraman before his departure for the Soviet zone. The footage has to be among the grimmest treasures at the National Archives.[5]

World War II was a desperate time for the peoples of Europe, and for the millions of Soviet DPs it was doubly cruel: having endured immense suffering in German hands, these hapless pawns of war were, in turn, effectively condemned by the United States as well as by the Soviet government for having tolerated Nazi captivity. In cold statistics roughly 5,600,000 of 8,350,000 displaced Soviet nationals survived World War II. The Red Army took custody of some 3 million of these unfortunates outright. Under an agreement signed at Yalta, the United States bound itself to repatriate better than 2 million Soviet refugees, many against their will. And by various ploys maybe 500,000 "nonreturners" evaded forced return.

The mortal terror that accompanied repatriation merely perplexed General Dwight D. Eisenhower, who lamely recalled "a number of suicides among individuals who preferred to die rather than return to their native land."[6] Other Americans have been more upset. Besides Yale and the Central Intelligence Agency, archetypal conservative William F. Buckley, Jr., and liberal William Sloane Coffin, Jr., have little in common save a loathing for America's role in repatriation after World War II. Speaking on the Dick Cavett show, Buckley has decried the act as "most inexcusable."[7] And for Coffin, "The memory . . . is so painful that it's almost impossible for me to write about it. . . . My part . . . left me a burden of guilt I am sure to carry the rest of my life."[8]

Why did Soviet refugees not want to go home? Why did Russia demand their return? Why did the United States force their homegoing, even when that led to suicides? And why are emotions still triggered by an affair now behind us a third of a century? These questions, central to an understanding of repatriation, finally can receive full answers now that all relevant U.S. archives have been opened and can supplement unofficial sources. But for decades the tragic tale has been for most Americans, as *Newsweek* put it, "buried history."[9]

To be sure, nothing approaching a candid exposition of wartime displacement and repatriation has appeared in the Soviet Union—and never will as long as the Politburo holds sway. But during the early postwar period the Western news media also largely ignored the subject. The U.S. Army came to abhor its task of mass extradition and naturally did not want to publicize its distasteful role. Then, too, the unhappy saga of So-

viet citizens abroad had to compete with the even more horrendous revelations of Nazi atrocities. The enormity of the German crime against the
Jews eclipsed even the massive mistreatment and starvation of Soviet
prisoners of war (POWs) and slave laborers. Reports of their being forcibly transported home and their suicidal protests did not arouse the sen-
sitivities of a world deadened by years of exposure to monumental human
misery and depravity. Repatriation could hardly be expected to move
people still trying to comprehend the enormous dimensions of a cata-
strophic world war. It was true that eleven Russians took their own lives
at Dachau, Germany, rather than return home, but under the Nazis, this,
the first German concentration camp, had claimed the lives of a minimum
of 32,000 inmates.[10]

A great many communications concerning repatriation passed between Washington and Moscow, but diplomatic histories of Cold War
origins have given scant attention to repatriation, if indeed they mention
it at all.[11] Supreme Headquarters Allied Expeditionary Force (SHAEF)
publicly admitted the use of force in returning displaced Soviet nationals
at least by 30 May 1945, but it was not until the early 1970s that historians
began gaining access to a substantial portion of the voluminous archives
documenting that fact.[12]

Even in more specialized monographic literature the topic was slighted
for decades. True, the related Vlasov movement received the attention of
many, including Robert B. Burton, Alexander Dallin, George Fischer,
Sven Steenberg, and Juergen Thorwald.[13] (Andrei Vlasov was a Soviet
general who, after his capture by the Germans, headed a largely phantom
Russian Liberation Army recruited from Russian POWs.) But *The East
Came West* by Peter J. Huxley-Blythe, the only secondary account devoted exclusively to repatriation until the 1970s, focused solely on the
trials and tribulations of "Cossackhood."[14] Although covering much
more than Soviet-American repatriation, Malcolm Proudfoot's *European Refugees, 1939–52* stood for years as the best single secondary account of the topic. Here was a coherent analysis of the Yalta repatriation
agreement that made judicious use of available government documents.[15]

The tremendous volume of U.S. repatriation records released in the
1970s, however, severely dated Proudfoot's work and stimulated renewed interest in the topic. Besides Buckley and Coffin, newspapers, radio, and documentary filmmakers all recently have found repatriation
newsworthy.[16] And the subject has come to attract not only the press and
the electronic media but also writers as well. Three studies on repatriation have appeared in the past eight years. In *Operation Keelhaul* Julius
Epstein tackled the topic with enthusiasm, pouring passionate indignation not only on Soviet but also Western leaders for their part in the af-

fair.[17] More recently, two well-researched studies, Nicholas Bethell's *The Last Secret* and Nikolai Tolstoy's *The Secret Betrayal*, have appeared, dealing in detail with British involvement in repatriation.[18] Also in the last eight years two bitter antagonists, the Soviet establishment and Alexander Solzhenitsyn, have aired their own caustic and very different opinions on the subject: the former in an account that in times past would have been considered an unprintable advertisement of political infidelity, the treason trial of the collaborator-general Vlasov;[19] the latter in the three volumes of *Gulag Archipelago.*[20]

The strongest argument for a fresh examination of repatriation is, quite simply, the availability of many hitherto untapped archival records: some, previously off limits to private researchers; others, until now overlooked. In the first category are a host of government records opened to historians in the past few years, including the recently declassified "Operation Keelhaul" papers. In the latter category are the data collected by the Harvard Project on the Soviet Social System, an undertaking jointly sponsored from 1950 to 1954 by Harvard University and the Human Resources Research Institute of the U.S. Air Force. This ambitious and sophisticated sociological investigation based upon tests and interviews of more than 3,000 Soviet refugees sought to lay bare contemporary Soviet society by means of the recollections of recent émigrés. The information, whether representative of the general Soviet population or not, provided numerous and valuable insights into the thinking of those subject to repatriation. The various unpublished project reports were especially helpful in analyzing the motives of the *nevozvrashchentsy*, the nonreturners who successfully evaded forced repatriation.

Besides documenting the repatriation of Soviet nationals and related Soviet-American negotiations, the present study also deals with the phenomenon of the nonreturner; the repatriation of American servicemen liberated by the Red Army; the Kremlin's harsh reception of its wayward millions; and the evolution of the party line on Soviet citizens abroad over three decades.

Repatriation, fully and incontrovertibly documented, can now take a prominent position in the gallery of the cruel by-products of World War II, second only to Jewish genocide in its dimensions. At the end of the war officialdom, East and West, proved oblivious to the suffering this massive extradition entailed. But for those not involved, the saga somehow becomes curiously fascinating. People find unpleasantness—such as repatriation—compelling because they continually seem attracted by the torment and despair of others. The success of NBC's *Holocaust* and the never-ending parade of Hitler biographies demonstrate that. *Before Winter Comes*, a superb British film on repatriation and the human condition in general, well illustrates this fascination with agony. Here Russian DPs bound for extradition while away their time tying fleas to miniature carts. The cruel harnesses that kill inside a week disturb an onlooker, the able DP translator Janovic, whose Russian will prove to be too good to spare him repatriation. He says of the scene—and by implication, of the film audience—"The desperate amuses man. Funny creatures we are."[21]

NOTES

1. Joseph Grew to Robert Murphy, 11 July 1945, U.S. Department of State, *Foreign Relations of the United States, 1945* (hereafter cited as *FR*), V: 1099; *New York Times*, 14 May 1946; Frederic N. Smith, "The American Role in the Repatriation of Certain Soviet Citizens, Forcible and Otherwise, to the USSR Following World War II" (Ph.D. diss., Georgetown University, 1970), 113-14. The Russian graves are at Finn's Point National Cemetery.

2. Grew to George Kennan, 27 July 1945, *FR, 1945*, V: 1100-1. Annex to memorandum by Soviet delegation at meeting of Foreign Ministers, 13 Sept. 1945, ibid., II: 154.

3. 20 Jan. 1946; Murphy to Robert Byrnes, 14 Feb. 1946, *FR, 1946*, V: 141. Nikolai Tolstoy, *The Secret Betrayal: 1944-1947* (New York, 1978), 355.

4. *Once to Every Man: A Memoir* (New York, 1977), 73, 76-77. Coffin is mistaken in dating the Plattling incident in mid-May.

5. Army Signal Corps Film no. 5824, National Archives, Record Group (hereafter NA RG) 111.

6. *Crusade in Europe* (Garden City, N.Y., 1948), 439.

7. 12 June 1978.

8. *Once*, 72, 77.

9. S. K. Oberbeck, "Their Unfinest Hour," review of *The Last Secret*, by Nicholas Bethell, *Newsweek*, 85 (20 Jan. 1975), 76.

10. *New York Times*, 20 Jan. 1946.

11. Those not mentioning repatriation are: Diane Clemens, *Yalta* (New York, 1970); Gabriel Kolko, *The Politics of War: The World and United States Foreign Policy, 1943-1945* (New York, 1968); John L. Snell, ed., *The Meaning of Yalta: Big Three Diplomacy and the New Balance of Power* (Baton Rouge, La., 1956); and William A. Williams, *American Russian Relations, 1781-1947* (New York, 1952). Those that treat the question in fleeting fashion are: Herbert Feis, *Churchill, Roosevelt, Stalin: The War They Waged and the Peace They Sought* (Princeton, N.J., 1967), 521, 598; John L. Gaddis, *The United States and the Origins of the Cold War, 1941-1947* (New York, 1972), 84; William Hardy McNeill, *America, Britain and Russia: Their Cooperation and Conflict, 1941-1946* (London, 1953), 543; and Adam B. Ulam, *Expansion and Coexistence: The History of Soviet Foreign Policy, 1917-67* (New York, 1968), 380, 534.

12. *New York Times*, 30 May 1945; author's correspondence with the State Department and National Archives, in his possession; and Carol M. Barker and Matthew H. Fox, *Classified Files: The Yellowing Pages; a Report on Scholars' Access to Government Documents* (New York, 1972), 39-40.

13. Robert B. Burton, "The Vlasov Movement of World War II: An Ap-

praisal" (Ph.D. diss., American University, 1963); Alexander Dallin, *German Rule in Russia, 1941-1945* (New York, 1957); George Fischer, *Soviet Opposition to Stalin: A Case Study in World War II* (Cambridge, Mass., 1952); Sven Steenberg, *Vlasov* (New York, 1970); Juergen Thorwald, *The Illusion: Soviet Soldiers in Hitler's Army* (New York, 1975).

14. (Caldwell, Idaho, 1964).

15. (Evanston, Ill., 1956). Parts of this book cannot be classified as a secondary source, since the author himself was a Western repatriation official. Nevertheless, Proudfoot's documentation goes well beyond firsthand experience.

16. In April 1978 UPI and AP dispatches on newly declassified repatriation documents led to a flurry of newspaper articles, for example, the *Ann Arbor News*, 23 Apr. 1978; interview with author on "As It Happens," Canadian Broadcasting Corporation, 18 Apr. 1978; British Broadcasting Corporation, *Orders from Above*.

17. (Old Greenwich, Conn., 1973); Mark Elliott, review of *Operation Keelhaul* by Julius Epstein, in *Canadian-American Slavic Studies*, 9 (Spring 1975): 125-26; "Skonchalsia Dzhulius Epstein," *Novoe Russkoe Slovo*, 10 July 1975, 10.

18. Bethell, *The Last Secret: The Delivery to Stalin of over Two Million Russians by Britain and the United States* (New York, 1974); Tolstoy, *Secret*.

19. A. V. Tishkov, "Predatel' pered sovetskim sudom," *Sovetskoe gosudarstvo i pravo*, no. 2 (Feb. 1973), 89-98.

20. (New York, 1973, 1974, 1978).

21. Windward Film Productions, 1969. The film was based on Frederick L. Keefe, "The Interpreter," *New Yorker*, 62 (10 Dec. 1966), 178-96. For a film synopsis see *Before Winter Comes* in *American Film Institute Catalogue, Feature Films, 1961-70*, 76.

1

IN THE SERVICE OF THE REICH:

"Subhumans," "Slaves," and the "Army of the Damned"

WORLD WAR II, WITH ITS 30 MILLION FATALITIES, exacted the largest human toll of any military conflict in history. The fighting also scattered nations to the wind as never before: estimates of civilians made homeless—40 million—are greater than for any other war. In Europe alone the fighting made refugees of 30 million persons. The Soviet Union, with 20 million of its citizens displaced, witnessed the largest human upheaval of any country. While Siberia and Central Asia received 12 million civilians fleeing European Russia, Germany took better than 8 million Soviet POWs and forced laborers in the opposite direction.[1]

The size of the captive population stemmed in part from the speed with which motorized Wehrmacht divisions devoured Soviet territory. The German Blitzkrieg advanced from the frontier in late June to the suburbs of Moscow by December 1941 and benefited from Stalin's self-defeating standfast orders, which contributed to the needless capture of millions of Soviet soldiers. "Divers," those who surrendered voluntarily, could be found among the masses of captives. In addition, Red Army defensive measures in the early months of the invasion proved disorganized and supremely inadequate, contributing to the breakneck pace at which Germany engulfed Soviet territory and troops.[2] The Wehrmacht simply overwhelmed the Red Army in the first months of fighting, taking hundreds of thousands of prisoners at a time: 320,000 in the Bialystok and Minsk sectors from June 29 to July 7; 300,000 in the battle for Smolensk in mid-July; an astounding 650,000 in the Kiev encirclement in late September.[3] In 1941 the Germans captured 3 to 4 million members of the Red Army; for the entire war, they captured some 5.75 million. Every fourth Soviet soldier became a German POW.[4]

Although a Soviet demographer claims Red Army personnel "perished by the thousands," in reality the deaths ran into the millions. Alfred Rosenberg, German commissioner for the East European region,

complained to Field Marshal Wilhelm Keitel as early as February 1942
that of 3.6 million Soviet prisoners "only several hundred thousand are
fully capable of working. The overwhelming majority perished."[5] More
trustworthy sources have confirmed the appalling dimensions of this
tragedy. Belated, grudging improvements in prisoner treatment ultimately saved some souls from extinction, but fatalities in this "Lost Russian Army of POWs," mostly in the winter of 1941–42, still numbered at
least 2 million, more likely closer to 3 million men.[6]

Germany's inhumane treatment of millions of Soviet POWs ranks
among the worst atrocities of a war replete with them. The disaster resulted from deliberate, systematic destruction, intentional and unintentional neglect, and the lack of international protection for prisoners on
the Eastern front. The Nazis methodically singled out special categories
for extinction. The most certain to perish were Communist party members, military commissars, Jews, and the ill-defined category of intellectuals. The Soviet novelist, Mikhail Sholokhov, has painted a picture of
Hitler's threat to Soviet Jewry with candor uncommon among Kremlin
favorites. His *Fate of a Man*, a moving vignette on war's brutality,
describes German screening of Russian POWs: "Three SS officers started
picking out the ones among us they thought were dangerous. They asked
who were Communists, who were officers, who were commissars . . . .
some Russians landed in trouble because they were all dark and had curly
hair. The SS men just came up to them and said: 'Jude?' The one they
asked would say he was a Russian, but they wouldn't even listen. 'Step
out!' and that was that. They shot the poor devils."[7] Not only Russians,
but darker skinned, circumcised Moslems of Central Asia were mistaken
for Jews.[8]

Given Nazi loathing of Slavs, being Russian or Ukrainian offered little
protection. Alexander Solzhenitsyn relates the story of an artillery officer
that could be repeated innumerable times: the Germans captured him
near Luga and drove him to a Soviet officers' compound near Vilnius.
"Two years in that camp shook Uri up once and for all. It is impossible to
catch with words or to circumvent with syllogisms what that camp was.
That was a camp to die in."[9] Air force commander Hermann Goering
found humor in the situation in conversation with Count Ciano,
Mussolini's son-in-law: "After having eaten everything possible, including the soles of their boots, they have begun to eat each other and, what is
more serious, have eaten a German sentry."[10] Only 4,700 of 23,500 Soviet citizens doomed to Buchenwald survived. And of 10,000 Soviet POWs
sent to Auschwitz in October 1941, the camp roster showed 910 still alive
in March 1942; 163 in August 1942; 96 in January 1945.[11]

The most charitable explanation for the wholesale deaths among Red

Army captives would be that the Wehrmacht did not anticipate the masses of POWs and, therefore, did not have the means to handle three to four times the number captured in the Battle of France. If these unfortunates did not die from overt German actions, their end might come through neglect, sometimes unintentional, sometimes calculated. The refusal of the majority of camp commandants to allow civilian donations of food to starving prisoners and the primitive conditions in POW compounds came as the first great shock to the population of the occupied regions. If starvation did not overcome the hapless captive, lack of protection from the elements, physical abuse, or epidemics might prove lethal. Short on supplies for its own troops, the Wehrmacht made no special arrangements to see the unexpected millions of Soviet POWs safely through the first winter. In the first year, therefore, almost all prisoner compounds suffered at least 30 percent fatalities, and in some the rate of attrition approached 95 percent.[12]

The lack of legal protection under existing international agreements contributed to the plight of Soviet POWs. The U.S.S.R. had not signed the 1929 Geneva Prisoner of War Convention, nor had it formally ratified the 1899 and 1907 Hague Conventions on Land Warfare. Soviet spokesmen have claimed Moscow's adherence to the turn-of-the-century treaties and have invoked all three in arguing German criminal responsibility for POW and civilian atrocities—but without mentioning the awkward lack of official accession in every case.[13] For most of the war the Soviet government took no interest in those who did not die fighting, which is reflected in the absence of any diplomatic effort to ameliorate POW conditions. Moscow, Solzhenitsyn rightly states, "did not recognize its own soldiers of the day before."[14]

How much Soviet adherence to the Hague and Geneva conventions would have helped the POWs is highly questionable. By 1941 Hitler had amply demonstrated his willingness to disregard inconvenient treaties. Besides, Russians were not reckoned to be much superior to Jews. "As for the ridiculous hundred million Slavs," Hitler declared, "we will mold the best of them to the shape that suits us, and we will isolate the rest of them in their own pigsties, and anyone who talks about cherishing the local inhabitant and civilizing him goes straight off into a concentration camp!" He dismissed the "non-Aryans" of the East as "a mass of born slaves, who feel the need of a Master"—and if not slaves, then colonial natives for whom "scarves" and "glass beads" would suffice.[15] The Fuehrer considered the struggle on the Eastern front to be a "war of extermination. If we do not grasp this, we will still beat the enemy but thirty years later we will again have to fight the Communist foe. We do not wage war to preserve the enemy."[16] This was not idle chatter; Hitler's secret orders of 17 May 1941 had bluntly warned the Wehrmacht command that fighting in the East could not be conducted in "chivalrous" fashion but "must be waged with unprecedented, ruthless, merciless harshness."[17] And once the fighting began, he frequently intervened to prevent the "coddling" of Russians. Hitler so distrusted the army on this score that he assigned a member of his Party Chancellery to the Wehrmacht High Command (OKH) to keep close watch on POW affairs.[18]

Heinrich Himmler, powerful chief of Nazi elite troops (SS), shared the Fuehrer's racial convictions. In October 1943 he told an assemblage of SS officers that if 10,000 Russian females dropped dead from exhaustion preparing German defenses, it concerned him only to the extent that the fortifications were completed.[19] *Der Untermensch* [The Subhuman], a pamphlet partially written by Himmler, gives a plain statement of Nazi opinion of Slavs: "Whether under the Tartars, or Peter, or Stalin, this people is born for the yoke." Published by the SS in 1942, the tract bore marked resemblance to a comic book, with as much scientific credibility. Photographs purported to demonstrate the difference between subhumans and Aryans. The text backed up this thesis of racially inferior types with biological arguments amounting to nothing more than crude, perverse extrapolations of nineteenth-century social Darwinism. The subhuman, it was explained, resembled a human in certain anatomical respects, but was in reality more closely related to lower orders of the animal kingdom. And his natural habitat was the swamp![20]

Given the Nazis' jaundiced thinking, it is no wonder that Soviet captives consistently fared worse than other prisoners: less and inferior food, poorer shelter and clothing, and no succor from the International Red Cross. Solzhenitsyn relates, "Wherever there were Allied POW camps next door, their prisoners, out of kindness, threw our men handouts over the fence, and our prisoners jumped on these gifts like a pack of dogs on a bone." One Red Army POW, now in the West, recalled with gratitude American black prisoners who shared their cakes and chocolates with him.[21]

The Germans hindered their own war effort by treating Russians so much worse than other POWs. The Wehrmacht developed elaborate propaganda to encourage desertion from the Red Army, but the prevailing *untermensch* philosophy frequently prevented preferential treatment being accorded to deserters over ordinary POWs. Knowing what capture could mean, Soviet soldiers came to dread it like death.[22] Had it not been for substantial covert opposition to the destruction of Soviet captives, the death rate would have been higher. Some German officials looked upon the question of decent treatment from a utilitarian perspective. Propaganda chief Joseph Goebbels and some of his coterie, for example, realized that Himmler's crudity in pamphlets like *Der Untermensch* would deeply insult Soviet captives and cripple Wehrmacht recruitment in POW camps. Consequently, Goebbels relied less on the theme of Slavic inferiority than other Nazi stalwarts. The *untermensch* policy also alarmed intelligence specialist General Reinhard Gehlen. In November 1942 he argued that unless there was an end to the "subhuman" approach to Soviet civilians and POWs, partisan warfare could not be controlled.[23]

Many commanders saved Soviet captives from the harsher regimen of POW camps and Nazi labor drafts by quietly diverting them into auxiliary units. Generally, the greater the distance from Hitler, the greater the likelihood that German officials would regard the Soviet population under their control as a potential source of labor rather than as an expendable waste product of total war. Thus some of the field officers saw Russians not so much as implacable ideological foes but as potential allies: "Whoever among the indigenous population participates in the struggle against Bolshevism . . . is not our enemy but our fellow fighter and fellow worker in the struggle against the world foe."[24]

Rarely did a person of high rank openly admit such sentiments. One outspoken general, Ernst Koestring, did denounce Nazi notions of a master race and fought energetically for a more enlightened policy toward occupied Eastern territories. Born near Moscow in 1876 and educated in Russia, this son of a German publisher and landowner accepted a commission in the Kaiser's army in 1900. Koestring brought an understanding of Russian affairs to his military calling that few of his peers possessed, which figured prominently in his subsequent career. Retained in the hundred-thousand-man Reichswehr after World War I, he became military attaché to Moscow in 1931. Not sufficiently cowed for Hitler, Koestring temporarily lost his job in 1933, only to be reinstated before the year was out, remaining at his post until the outbreak of war in June 1941. This Russian-born German tendered sharp and, therefore, unappreciated criticisms of Hitler's Eastern policies. He foresaw no prospect for ultimate success in a war against the Soviet Union and afterward mercilessly derided those who had felt a quick warm-weather Blitzkrieg would eliminate the Red Army: "One doesn't go to the toilet without paper and one doesn't go to Russia without a fur coat."[25]

Because his views clashed so sharply with prevailing sentiments, Koestring spent most of the war in oblivion: commissioner for Caucasian Affairs, Army Group A—1942, and OKH inspector of Turkoman units—1943. Finally, in January 1944, Major Klaus Von Stauffenberg, chief of the Organization Division of the OKH General Staff and eventual leader of the abortive conspiracy against Hitler, appointed him general of Eastern Troops, or *Osttruppen*. He replaced Lieutenant General Heinz

Hellmich, who was glad to be relieved of this assignment. (Depressed by German reverses and personal losses in the war, he wondered aloud to Koestring, "Perhaps I shall follow my two sons." Hellmich died in an air raid while commanding a division in France.)[26]

Koestring came to a position of genuine authority too late to make more than cosmetic reforms in German treatment of Eastern units. He demanded that discipline be the same as for German troops; he had the pejorative Osttruppen patch removed from volunteer uniforms; he secured leave centers in Germany, France, Italy, and Denmark and twenty-one hospitals with 25,000 beds for Eastern troops; and he permitted Orthodox chaplains, mostly old émigrés, to work with the men. But these modest improvements counted for less than practical considerations by ordinary German commanders in the field. Even if they were cocky about defeating Russia, many Wehrmacht officers still saw in Soviet POWs a tremendous military resource that ought not be squandered. Millions of POWs perished, but the fraction who did survive benefited from individual captors sprinkled throughout the Wehrmacht who were more utilitarian than racist.[27]

Appalling conditions in the camps no doubt simplified matters for Wehrmacht recruiters, since the dangerous step of joining enemy ranks could appeal only to persons in the most hopeless of predicaments. On other occasions the semblance of voluntary enlistment gave way to conscription, the captors simply handing out German uniforms, even weapons, with only the foolhardy refusing.[28]

Nazi *untermensch* philosophy, which coldly anticipated POW mistreatment and starvation, was not the only official position accelerating the rate of enlistment among Soviet captives. The Kremlin itself contributed to the movement by washing its hands of yesterday's fighters. Not only were POW conditions ignored, but an ill-conceived Soviet decree branded all captives as traitors simply for having been taken alive. That information only made POWs more susceptible to German suggestions that they take up arms against Stalin.[29]

The employment of substantial numbers of Soviet prisoners in the German war effort began almost immediately after the surprise attack on Russia, 22 June 1941. German troop strength did not equal the Soviet, even at the outset of hostilities, and the Wehrmacht's dramatic advances could not change the fact that early losses were costly even if Red Army losses were costlier. The invader's casualties took on dimensions incomparably greater than in earlier campaigns. From 22 June to 26 September 1941, Hitler's forces suffered 534,000 dead and wounded, or 15 percent of total troop strength in the East. Up to the Battle of Moscow in December

1941, Wehrmacht progress went unchecked, and victories were sweeping, but German losses for the summer and fall soared to 800,000. Always short of manpower, the Wehrmacht had good reason to tap the huge Soviet POW labor pool, which increased with each mammoth encirclement. Hilfswillige (auxiliary volunteers) quickly became indispensable, constituting up to 40 percent of some support formations. [30]

At first the Germans utilized these auxiliaries, or Hiwis for short, in noncombat roles: in paramilitary maintenance, supply, transport, engineer, and labor battalions. But before the summer was out, Russian volunteers began to appear in regular Wehrmacht combat formations, even in small all-Russian units under German command. Also in 1941 the Abwehr, or military intelligence service, began organizing several one- to two-hundred man companies of Russian scouts. These grew so rapidly that they soon lost their reconnaissance character and took on regular, antipartisan combat assignments. [31]

All this movement from POW compounds into Wehrmacht ranks had to be done discreetly, for Hitler's proscriptions were explicit. Commanders bent on circumventing early prohibitions against arming Soviet nationals took care to mislead headquarters. Rather than report all captured enemy personnel, shorthanded officers recruited a portion of their catch on the spot, concealed them among their troops, and bypassed prisoner compounds altogether. Some "all German" units quietly admitted Soviet POWs up to the level of 10 or 15 percent. In 1942 Hitler reluctantly recognized the presence of ex–Red Army prisoners in German uniforms as a *fait accompli*. Wary of racial contamination, and even more so of redefection, he did, however, prohibit the formation of any large-scale Russian forces. Osttruppen, as Red Army men in Wehrmacht ranks were called, could not exceed battalion strength and front-line volunteer units could not be placed side by side. [32] The German Armed Forces High Command (OKW), parroting Hitler, turned down requests from Koestring and others for larger non-German formations. The rationale was clear: "We will never permit the bringing up of our own executioners." [33]

This viewpoint prevailed until Nazi advances turned into retreats; and when the Germans began to ignore the original restrictions, they turned first to units of Soviet minority nationalities, thought to be more trustworthy than Great Russians. At least three such formations, all under German leadership, achieved division size: a Cossack Division within the regular army but supplied by the SS, a Turkish Division, and a Galician/Ukrainian SS Division. Curiously, the Nazis exempted Cossacks, Russian frontier warriors of mixed ancestry, from *untermensch* classification. Pulled from Soviet POW camps, they saw action in German ranks as early as 1941. The Wehrmacht deployed some Cossacks in front-line action, but more often assigned them to antipartisan operations. The majority served in that capacity until well past the war's midpoint.[34]

In the spring of 1943, Hitler authorized the formation of the 1st Cossack Division under General Helmut Von Pannwitz. Combat training at Mlawa (Mielau), Poland, for existing cavalry units and POW "recruits" occupied mid-May to late August 1943. The division's six regiments, numbering 20,000 men by June 1944, represented all the major Cossack hosts: two Don, two Kuban, one Terek, and one Siberian. In his Wehrmacht division Pannwitz had five Cossack officers: three old émigrés out of the tsar's army via Belgrade exile and two ex–Red Army men out of POW camps. The general's personal bodyguard of old Cossacks, with their imposing if antiquated uniforms, crisscrossed with munition belts, added a novel, even bizarre touch to twentieth-century total war. But the natives of Croatia, where the division first served, saw nothing quaint in the Cossacks' time-honored ravaging of war zones. Achieving moderate success battling Tito's partisans, they seem to have been even more adept at plundering and pillaging.[35]

Unlike the 1st Cossack Division, the 162nd Turkish Infantry Division maintained a fifty-fifty German-Osttruppen personnel ratio, an experiment that worked better than most. Major General Ralph Von Heygendorff, already experienced in leading Eastern legions, took command of the nascent 162nd in late 1942. Troop-training took place at Neuhammer, Germany, instead of occupied Russia, since the Wehrmacht knew that ready knowledge of German mistreatment of the civilian population damaged Osttruppen morale. Primarily engaged in antipartisan activity, the Turkish Division, with some Azerbaidzhani as well as many Germans, saw action from June 1943 in Croatia, Istria, and northern Italy.[36]

The Wehrmacht's use of ex-Soviet Ukrainians included the 10,000-man Sumy division, which fought at Khar'kov and disintegrated at Stalingrad in 1942–43. More is known about the SS Division Halychyna (Galicia) organized in April 1943 in occupied Poland. Soviet forces badly mauled this formation of 16,000 Ukrainians in German uniform at the Battle of Brody, July 1944. After further serious losses near L'vov, a desperate Himmler permitted the unit's reorganization in the fall of 1944 as the First Ukrainian Division. After a stint in Slovakia it made its way to northern Italy by the war's end.[37]

The Cossack, Turkish, and Ukrainian divisions accounted for only a fraction of the Soviet Union's national minorities in German uniform and not even all of these groups in enemy ranks. At least a score of other ethnic populations of the U.S.S.R. could be found dispersed in smaller units throughout the Wehrmacht: Finns, Estonians, Latvians, Lithuanians, Belorussians, Crimean and Volga Tatars, Kalmyks, North Caucasians, Georgians, Armenians, and Azerbaidzhani (Table 1).

Table 1. Major Soviet Nationalities in Osttruppen Formations, December 1942

Ethnic Population in U.S.S.R.	Number
Russians	310,000 [1]
Estonians	10,000
Latvians	104,000
Lithuanians	36,800
Crimean Tatars	10,000
Kalmyks	5,000
North Caucasians	15,000
Georgians	19,000
Armenians	7,000
Azerbaidzhani	36,500
Turks	20,550 [2]
Total	573,850

SOURCE: Gehlen, *Service*, 86; Gordon, "Partisan Warfare," 66, 77; Thorwald, *Illusion*, 73; OSS, "Reichswehr," 6.

[1] This figure undoubtedly includes Ukrainians and probably Belorussians as well.
[2] This figure includes Volga Tatars, Kazakhs, Turkmen, and Tadzhiks.

Russian collaborators did not play as large a role in German ranks as the above figures suggest. First, the large number of Russians in the table is misleading, since the figure of 310,000 includes unknown but surely substantial numbers of Ukrainians; for the war, probably less than half of the total of 1 million Soviet military collaborators were Great Russians.[38] Second, because of the Germans' special fear and loathing of them, Russian "volunteers" were recruited in quantity later than other Soviet nationalities and were relegated to the least responsible positions. From 1941 until well into 1944 their slots were usually support roles; when Russian combat units were formed, the Wehrmacht carefully scattered them throughout the ranks. When a German-sponsored Russian Liberation Army under ex–Red Army General Andrei Vlasov finally did appear, it barely reached division strength by the war's end.

Vlasov's eleventh hour army was inconsequential, but Russians in strength did play an important role in the German military effort—not in the front lines, to be sure— but in antipartisan warfare. Here their help was enlisted early and amounted to something. Vlasov was fond of saying it takes a Russian to beat a Russian. He never got a fair chance to prove it, but a goodly number of Germans appreciated the sentiment, as demonstrated by their liberal recruitment of Russian POWs to fight Soviet partisans. The Soviet territory Germany conquered proved too vast for effective occupation, especially with the forests and swamps of the western Ukraine and Belorussia serving as perfect guerrilla bases. The Wehrmacht quickly turned to native collaborators to help counter Soviet resistance behind the lines. By the end of 1942 the Wehrmacht employed about 500,000 ex–Red Army men in its antiguerrilla operations, most of them apparently Russian.[39] They varied enormously in education, in political persuasion, and in temperament; but they detested the Soviet regime and had resigned themselves to their dangerous profession only with the realization that the war's cruel circumstances offered few choices.

In Belorussia a Graukopf Battalion—for the Russian commander's gray hair—numbered 10,000 men at one point. Zuev of the Old Believer sect ruled his "republic" in the Polotsk region from the summer of 1941 until the summer of 1944.[40] One Petukhov directed a similar operation near Vitebsk. The Germans found an especially efficient collaborator in engineer Voskoboinikov, who ran Lokot'—a town of 6,000 and region of 100,000. His territory between Orel and Kursk ultimately encompassed 1.7 million inhabitants, which he controlled with 20,000 men and twenty-four tanks. In exchange for local autonomy he killed partisans, collected taxes, and paid regular tribute in provisions. Moscow so feared the experiment that parachutists were sent in to kill him, which they did in January 1942.[41]

After Voskoboinikov's death the Kaminskii Brigade, most notorious of all antipartisan units, commandeered the Lokot' base. In the next nineteen months Bronislav Kaminskii, an engineer like his predecessor, expanded operations into the Pripet Marshes and the forests along the Berezina River, finally commanding 10,000 men with as many camp followers.[42] Widely known for his brutal treatment of captured partisans, he vied in cruelty with the German SS in suppressing the 1944 Warsaw uprising. An émigré wrote, "The Kaminsky brigade had the most sinister reputation among the Russians and was highly valued by Himmler."[43] Somehow the brutality of his brigands exceeded what even the Germans would tolerate. Kaminskii, heavily laden with jewels—and crimes—from the Warsaw ghetto, was shot by the SS in August 1944. The remnants of the 50,000 who had fled with him from Russia were sent to Germany to help fill the ranks of Vlasov's first division. Officers arrived at Camp Munsingen sporting three, four, and five wrist watches apiece while women camp followers came replete with Warsaw finery.[44]

Troops under Gil'-Blazhevich, alias Rodionov, were nearly as infamous. Poles and Jews especially had reason to dread the appearance of Rodionovites. But one act set Rodionov apart from Kaminskii in notoriety: his redefection in 1943, after the tide had turned against the Germans. Given his followers' paltry human credentials, compound duplicity is not surprising; the stupidity of the move is. Moscow rewarded this erstwhile traitor with the Order of the Red Star for the overnight creation of a "partisan region" in northeast Belorussia. It has not, however, advertised the postwar fate of Rodionovites, which was imprisonment at best.[45]

Line-crossing was no isolated phenomenon. Soviet redefectors, either unaware of the harsh reception awaiting them, or dreading it less than remaining in Wehrmacht ranks, multiplied in proportion to German defeats. Hitler viewed the large-scale defection, even revolts of 1942-43, as confirmation of his low opinion of Eastern nationalities and ordered Osttruppen units disbanded or transferred to another front. Fritz Sauckel, chief Nazi labor scavenger in the East, greedily anticipated the swelling of his labor shipments to German factories. Wehrmacht commanders, however, protected their auxiliaries, allowing very few to fall into his hands. Some collaborators, especially Hiwis, remained on the Eastern front scattered throughout the German army up to twelve per company, but the great majority moved to other parts of occupied Europe in the early fall of 1943.[46] They were transferred hither and yon, literally from the fjords of Norway to the islands of Greece. Earlier, Russians in German uniform had seen service even farther south in Libya. The tides of war now split the Osttruppen in every direction: into Norway, Denmark, Holland, Belgium, Luxemburg, and France; into Yugoslavia, Greece, and Crete; and as the war concluded, into Italy, Austria, and Germany.[47]

In 1943 southwestern France replaced Poland as the center for Soviet POW recruit-training. German preparations against the anticipated Anglo-American invasion spurred the demand for troops and workers, and France became the destination for more Osttruppen than any other single country: sixteen battalions by November 1943, close to one hundred shortly after the Allied landings of 6 June 1944. The Wehrmacht placed each of these units, 1,000 to 1,200 strong, in German divisions and concentrated over half of them along France's Atlantic and Mediterranean coastlines (Table 2).

Table 2. Osttruppen in France as of 16 June 1944

Region	Number
English Channel coast	36,500
Bay of Biscay coast	11,500
Mediterranean coast	17,500
French interior	50,000
Total	115,500

SOURCE: OSS, "Reichswehr," 7, 9, 12; OSS Intelligence Report 52267, NA RG 226.

Almost immediately after D-Day Allied forces were dismayed to find former Soviet soldiers among captured Germans. American intelligence had amassed voluminous data on the Osttruppen—not only head counts but precise knowledge of unit movements, current locations, even troop morale—but this information rarely filtered down to front line units, who were stumped by German POWs who could not speak German.[48]

If American and British officers knew anything at all about the "volunteer" units, they mistakenly labeled them part of Vlasov's army. That phantom force became more than a contrivance of German propaganda only fleetingly at the close of the war, and not on the Western front. Vlasov's army received the most publicity and the least combat experience, boasted of more and amounted to less, than most ex-Soviet contingents in Wehrmacht ranks. Throughout most of the war Nazis of influence viewed this movement merely as propaganda. Serious consideration for anti-Stalinist Russians in a viable military capacity came only as a last-minute act of desperation.[49]

General Andrei Andreevich Vlasov, who in 1941 fought his way out of encirclement twice and who received decorations and promotions for his part in the successful defense of Moscow, fell captive to the Germans in 1942. Personally chosen by Stalin to save the Second Shock Army, trapped by German troops along the Volkhov River, Vlasov flew into the cauldron in March 1942. The hero of the Battle of Moscow immediately concluded that only an immediate breakthrough eastward could save the situation. But for months Stalin refused to agree to a retreat from the Volkhov swamps, thereby sealing the doom of the Second Shock Army. Organized resistance ended in late June. This time Stalin's intractability cost him nine divisions, seven brigades, and Vlasov, taken prisoner 11–12 July 1942.[50]

Disillusioned with Communism and Stalin in particular, Vlasov quickly became the figurehead of a German-sponsored Russian collaborator movement, but a genuine military role eluded him until the waning months of the war. Most Nazis valued Stalin's darling-turned-traitor solely as "recruiting bait." In reality, Russian "volunteers" served where Germany placed them and under German command, but if Vlasov's speeches about the ROD (Russian Liberation Movement) and the ROA (Russian Liberation Army) could increase the enlistment of Soviet POWs in Wehrmacht ranks, he could have his letterheads.[51]

In the winter of 1942–43 ROA insignia and shoulder patches appeared, but the Nazis' chief Soviet collaborator did not command the scattered troops who wore them. Nevertheless, the publicity surrounding the Nazis' most celebrated defector became so intense that almost everyone, regardless of nationality or ideology, came to equate Vlasov and collaboration, from its most innocent to its most heinous dimensions.[52] Outside Germany few recognized how impotent Vlasov was and therefore how inappropriate it was to blame him for excesses committed by troops who were his men in name only. During the war at least, U.S. intelligence made this important distinction, which was lost on most: "He became so thoroughly identified with former Soviet elements in the German army that they are occasionally referred to, even at present, as 'Vlasov's' troops. However, Vlasov appears never to have been anything more than the Russian head of the Russian Army of Liberation."[53]

The organization and training of Russian forces under Vlasov's authority did not begin until November 1944, and only one division ever became operational. Pieced together from odd Russian battalions, recent POW recruits, and the remnants of Kaminskii's guerrillas, the 15,000-man formation fought briefly and ineffectively along the Oder River in mid-April 1945, then moved south against German orders. In a bizarre ending too incredible for fiction, these Vlasovites helped Czech partisans drive the Nazis out of Prague (6–8 May) and then surrendered to the U.S. Third Army (starting 10 May).[54]

Soviet collaborator forces under Vlasov then were inconsequential, but at the same time no nation in Hitler's path provided the Wehrmacht with as many recruits as did the Soviet Union. Certainly its citizens did not find the black logic of Nazism any more appealing than other Europeans. On the contrary, the Slavs, whom Hitler dismissed as subhumans, had more to fear from Germany's berserk racial determinism than any group save the Jews. Rather than any positive attraction to Wehrmacht enlistment, large-scale military collaboration on the Eastern front stemmed from the size of the Soviet POW pool to begin with, the absolute wretchedness and brutality of their incarceration, and the grievances of many who had suffered under Stalin's rule.

If all the diverse auxiliary and fighting formations are included, about 1 million Soviet soldiers served in German ranks in World War II.[55] This "Army of the Damned," as an American documentary styled it, amounted to the largest military defection in history.[56] But was it mainly Red Army troops betraying their homeland, or was it rather more a case of Stalin's forsaking his own countrymen by military blundering and by ignoring the POWs' plight? Solzhenitsyn would lay the blame squarely at the feet of the "Great Strategist": "Was there ever so multimillioned foul a deed as this: to betray one's own soldiers and proclaim them as traitors?"[57]

The Soviet Union never has softened its appraisal of the collaborator phenomenon: treason is treason whether committed by General Vlasov or the lowliest Hiwi boot polisher; and no predicament, no matter how desperate, can excuse it.[58] In this instance, Moscow's propaganda apparatus does not have to conjure up popular indignation toward those who aided the enemy because the Soviet population, which suffered so terribly in World War II, genuinely loathes them, particularly those detailed to neutralize resistance in occupied Russia. Vlasov, the most widely known defector, had no part in the antipartisan campaigns that terrorized occupied Soviet territory, but his name has been indelibly linked with them because Fascist and Communist propaganda attributed powers to him that he never possessed. Collaborator crimes, popularly though inaccurately linked to the erstwhile defender of Moscow, gave the term Vlasovite, Solzhenitsyn says, "the same force as the word 'sewage.' We feel we are dirtying our mouths merely by pronouncing it."[59] The famous Russian writer ultimately shed himself of the notion, but these words accurately reflect not only the party line but the mass sentiment.

Dramatic as their story is, Red Army POWs in Wehrmacht formations together accounted for only a small portion of Soviet nationals caught up in the German war effort. Millions more—civilians as well as soldiers— had no choice but to work in the Reich's factories and fields. Not only did many more Soviet nationals work than fight for the Third Reich, but Germany used them in great numbers almost from the start of the war. Following the invasion of Russia, and no doubt in good measure because of it, an acute labor shortage developed. Hitler and Nazi purists harbored grave fears of racial contamination, but expediency won out. As early as September 1941, German economic planners were meeting to discuss the utilization of Soviet workers in the Reich; at the same time Goering was busy figuring where Red Army POWs could be used to best effect. Hitler did spell out that no Mongolian or Asiatic prisoners were to be brought in and that only Russian-speaking POWs could be drafted—to prevent the spread of Communist ideas to other workers.[60] Still, 1942 saw Russia's invaders marshal 2 million Soviet nationals to work in German-occupied Europe.[61]

In the East, recruiting drives quickly degenerated into forced labor drafts: threats replaced appeals; primitive coercion replaced voluntary quotas. German troops shortly laid all pretenses aside, cordoned off villages—more frequently, whole city blocks—and simply dispatched westward every last able-bodied soul caught in the net. Recruiting took on particularly heinous dimensions in the Ukraine, where Erich Koch ran a fiefdom in gleeful disdain of his nominal superior, Ostminister Alfred Rosenberg. This would-be lord of the Steppes indiscriminately rounded up civilians for Labor Minister Fritz Sauckel "in part out of sheer spite for Rosenberg. The more Rosenberg complained about the inhuman recruitment in the Ukraine, the more Koch enjoyed it."[62]

Here forty Ukrainian school girls were taken straight from their gymnasium to Germany, with their parents being informed only after the fact; there a group was whisked straight from hoeing potatoes to a factory in the Reich. Those who survived often recalled "a mother, a father, a brother or a sister killed or hung before their eyes because the person refused to go to work for the 'New Order.' "[63] Such actions, officials in Rosenberg's East Ministry vainly argued, fueled the resistance movement in occupied territories as nothing else could. The Wehrmacht, which also deplored these self-defeating recruiting tactics, documented the senseless rapine as a means of protest; "the executing agencies have committed errors which should have been avoided: de-lousing of Russian girls by men, taking nude photographs in forced positions, locking female doctors in cars in order to make them available to the transport leaders, transporting of shackled girls in nightshirts through Russian towns to the railroad, etc."[64]

The transport to Germany proved more harrowing than recruitment. Primitive conditions—little or no food, sanitary facilities, or heat—led to much illness and death en route. Of 500 Soviet POWs arriving at one I. G. Farben plant in January 1942, only 185 or 37 percent were well enough to work. By February only 158 could work, 200 were sick, and 107 were dead. That same month a German doctor complained, "It is insane to transport these laborers in open or closed unheated box cars, merely to unload corpses at the destination." By 1942 millions of Soviet captives, Rosenberg lamented, regarded the Third Reich as another Siberia.[65]

Soviet conscripts worked at every conceivable task in every conceivable corner of the continent. Sholokhov's hero in *Fate of a Man* reckoned he had seen half of Germany in his two years of captivity: "I was in Saxony, at a silicate plant, in the Ruhr, hauling coal in a mine. I sweated away with a shovel in Bavaria, I had a spell in Thuringen, and the devil knows what German soil I didn't have to tread."[66] On this the Soviet novelist does not exaggerate: eight months after Germany attacked Russia, 32,000 Soviet nationals worked in Norway building railroads and fortifications; 7,000 in Belgian mines; 35,000 on Rumanian farms; and an unknown number on Greek coastal defenses. By March 1943 the majority of Danzig dockworkers were Russian.[67]

For the war as a whole, most Ostarbeiter, or Eastern workers as the Nazis contemptuously styled them, ended up in Germany proper and most in agriculture or industry. All other occupations including transportation, distribution, administration, manual labor, and domestic service accounted for less than a quarter of the total. As time passed foreign workers, with Soviet nationals the most numerous, became more and more vital to the German economy. Between 1941 and 1944 the proportion of alien laborers in the Third Reich increased from 9 to 20 percent, in the crucial industrial sector, from 9 to 29.[68] By 1944 Ostarbeiter were particularly numerous in mining, the chemical industry, and armaments production. The Germans assigned large contingents of Soviet POWs and laborers to massive combines such as I. G. Farben and the Hermann Goering Works because of the close connections of these industrial empires with high Nazi officials and their priority classification for labor allotments; Berlin assigned many to newer factories, since these lost more German youths to the Wehrmacht than the older plants with workers of all ages, and the Germans assigned many to industries that could absorb large numbers of unskilled laborers, such as aircraft assembly centers.[69]

Treatment for Ostarbeiter was barely better than that meted out to Red Army men in POW cages. It was not enough that the German population regarded them with suspicion and open contempt. Nazi propaganda placed these unfortunates in a category little higher than Jews, a point ever impressed upon the Easterners by the Ost patch, a mandatory humiliation worn over the left breast. Seeing such measures as counterproductive, the Eastern Ministry, General Koestring, and Munitions Minister Albert Speer, among others, worked energetically for the elimination of this needless indignity. Strict enforcement of the Ost badge regulation ended in April 1944, despite the opposition of the more doctrinaire racists—including the German Housewives' Association, anxious over the prospect of unlabelled Russian women running loose. There were other signs of the Germans' growing desperation—enlightenment would be a wrong conclusion. Labor lord Sauckel's "subhuman" of 1941 became his "guest worker" of 1944. And the war years saw SS Chief Heinrich Himmler manage the conversion of Vlasov from a "swine" to a "friend and ally." Toward the end of the war Eastern workers made a host of gains over the more than 600 pages of Ostarbeiter regulations, but the benefits rarely budged from the printed page. And the theoretical improvements could hardly compensate for the increase in the work week to sixty hours (March 1944) and an arrest rate among foreign workers that was fifteen times that of Germans (January–June 1944).[70]

Meanwhile, living conditions had long since permanently embittered Ostarbeiter against Hitler's "New Order." As early as the fall of 1942 Eastern workers suffered from grossly inadequate clothing. Standard issue consisted of low-quality uniforms made of rags or a cellulose material and wooden clogs that injured the feet so badly that many Soviet conscripts went barefoot rather than wear them. And that was it: Goering claimed Russians were unacquainted with underwear. A staple of the Ostarbeiter diet was Russian bread, German style: 50 percent rye husks, 20 percent sugar beet chips, 20 percent flour, and 10 percent ground straw or leaves. Better-fed Western conscripts commonly sold or bartered their gift parcels to starving Eastern workers for whom the Red Cross did not exist.[71]

Housing, sanitary, and medical conditions were likewise inadequate. One Krupp camp in Essen had hundreds of Ostarbeiter jammed into a former elementary school. Even before air raids took their toll, 1,200 adults had to make do with ten children's toilets. Worse than that, terrible suffering and death awaited many Soviet conscripts in Essen for want of doctors, medicine, and bandages. The Nazis discriminated against the hapless Ostarbeiter even in death. The Reich Minister of Labor refused transport to send Russian bodies home for burial, and public cemeteries segregated their remains from German graves. Poorly clothed, fed, and sheltered, ill-treated, unfamiliar with the German language or modern machinery, and scarcely motivated, should it come as any surprise that a Regensburg factory would report Russian workers producing at a third or half of normal German capacity?[72]

By 1944 recruiters in occupied Soviet territory had deported an estimated 1.8 percent of the rural and 17.8 percent of the urban population. For the war as a whole Germany mobilized between 2.8 and 7 million Soviet forced laborers, close to 6 million being a likely figure.[73] These conscripts from Russia along with another 6 million from the rest of occupied Europe provided substantial even if unwilling assistance to the Reich war effort. After the war American military intelligence judged Germany's ability to integrate large numbers of alien laborers into its labor force as "*the* main factor in the maintenance of the German war economy during the last years of the conflict."[74] This involuntary aid, however, came at great personal cost to the Ostarbeiter. Dragged to Germany by force, humiliated and mistreated at every turn, given unfamiliar work under wretched conditions, it is little wonder that some 600,000 Eastern workers were dead by September 1944, some 750,000 to 800,000 by the end of the war.[75]

In the Nazis' thinking, contradictions abounded. Their notion of Aryan superiority contributed to that exalted self-confidence that helped make the Blitzkrieg invincible—until 1942 anyway. But this blind racial hubris that drove them to surprising successes also led them to defeat. Once in possession of the continent's human resources, the Nazis' brutal, race-inspired mistreatment of captive populations fired resistance—and nothing more than forced labor drafts and nowhere more than in Russia. The shortsighted Sauckels, Kochs, and Himmlers found it impossible to extract workers for the Reich without simultaneously driving reluctant conscripts into the arms of the partisans.

Not only were the Nazis the "victims of their own propaganda," but their use of Ostarbeiter and Osttruppen undermined some of their most cherished prejudices. [76] One of the greatest ironies of the Third Reich has to be that the nation so obsessed with racial purity forced the intermingling of the peoples of Europe on a scale unparalleled in the continent's history.

NOTES

1. Andrei Amalrik, "Victims of Yalta," *Harper's*, 258 (May 1979), 91-92; Boris L. Dvinov, *Politics of the Russian Emigration* (Santa Monica, Calif., 1955), 5; Mark Elliott, "The Repatriation Issue in Soviet-American Relations, 1944-1947" (Ph.D. diss., University of Kentucky, 1974), 10-21; Nancy Eubank, *The Russians in America* (Minneapolis, Minn., 1973), 74; Edward A. Raymond, "The Juridical Status of Persons Displaced from Soviet and Soviet-dominated Territory" (Ph.D. diss., American University, 1952), 172.

2. Mikhail M. Koriakov, *I'll Never Go Back: A Red Army Officer Talks* (New York, 1948), 128-29. A powerful Soviet novel depicting these disasters is Konstantin Simonov's *The Living and the Dead* (New York, 1962).

3. Dallin, *German Rule*, 69; Albert Seaton, *The Russo-German War, 1941-45* (London, 1971), 125, 130; Boris Shub, *The Choice* (New York, 1950), 50; Steenberg, *Vlasov*, 4.

4. Amalrik, "Victims," 91; V. P. Artiemev, "Crime and Punishment in the Soviet Armed Forces," *Military Review*, 42 (Nov. 1962), 73; Dallin, *German Rule*, 69, 417, 427; Dvinov, *Politics*, 38; Eugene Kulischer, *The Displacement of Population in Europe* (Montreal, 1943), 152; Norman Luxenburg, "Solzhenitsyn, Soviet Literature and the Returned P.O.W.'s Issue" (paper presented at the Midwest Slavic Conference, Cleveland, Ohio, 2 May 1975), 4; Vladimir Petrov, *My Retreat from Russia* (New Haven, Conn., 1950), 274-75; Shub, *Choice*, 50.

5. Boris Urlanis, *Wars and Population* (Moscow, 1971), 172, 176. See also Dallin, *German Rule*, 417; Shub, *Choice*, 63.

6. Jay Warren Baird, "German Home Propaganda, 1941-1945, and the Russian Front" (Ph.D. diss., University of Colorado, 1966), 27; Patricia Blake, "Solzhenitsyn: An Artist Becomes an Exile," *Time*, 103 (25 Feb. 1974), 39; Dallin, *German Rule*, 426; Edward L. Homze, *Foreign Labor in Nazi Germany* (Princeton, N.J., 1967), 80; Petrov, *Retreat*, 274-75; Janusz Sawczuk, *Hitlerowskie Obozy Jenieckie W Lambinowicach W Latach 1939-1945* (Cieszyn, 1974), 226-27; Alexander Werth, *Russia at War, 1941-1945* (New York, 1964), 703.

7. *The Fate of a Man* (Moscow, 1957), 25-26.

8. Dallin, *German Rule*, 418.

9. Solzhenitsyn, *Gulag*, I: 217-18.

10. Quoted in Alan Clark, *Barbarossa. The Russian-German Conflict, 1941-45* (New York, 1965), 207.

11. Rudolf Hoess, *Commandant of Auschwitz, the Autobiography of Rudolf Hoess* (Cleveland, 1959), 133-34; Jan Sehn, *Oswiecim-Brzezinka (Auschwitz-Birkenau) Concentration Camp* (Warsaw, 1961), 96; Mikhail I. Semiriaga, *Sovetskie liudi v evropeiskom soprotivlenii* (Moscow, 1970), 293.

12. Oleg Animisov, *The German Occupation in Northern Russia during World War II: Political and Administrative Aspects* (New York, 1954), 28-29; Dallin, *German Rule,* 418.

13. Heinz L. Ansbacher, "The Problem of Interpreting Attitude Survey Data: A Case Study of the Attitude of Russian Workers in Wartime Germany," *Public Opinion Quarterly,* 14 (Spring 1950), 126; Dallin, *German Rule,* 445; George Ginsburgs, "Laws of War and War Crimes on the Russian Front during World War II: The Soviet View," *Soviet Studies,* 11 (Jan. 1960), 254; Alexander Pronin, "Guerrilla Warfare in the German-Occupied Soviet Territories, 1941-1944" (Ph.D. diss., Georgetown University, 1965), 36-37; Aron N. Trainin, *Hitlerite Responsibility under Criminal Law* (London, n.d. [1945]), 34-35, 47. The Nazi perspective is at least as self-serving: see Albrecht, "The Legal Situation Existing between Germany and the Soviet Union," Appendix I of "German Camps for Russian and Polish War Prisoners," by Adolph Westhoff, NA RG 338, Foreign Military Studies, P-046. Albrecht was chief of the legal branch of the German foreign office.

14. Solzhenitsyn, *Gulag,* I: 219. See also ibid., 240; Koriakov, *I'll Never Go Back,* 130.

15. Quoted in Baird, "Home Propaganda," 25-30. See also Homze, *Foreign Labor,* 79.

16. U.S. Office of the United States Chief of Counsel for the Prosecution of Axis Criminality, *Nazi Conspiracy and Aggression,* 8 (Washington, D.C., 1946), 646. See also EUCOM, Historical Division, "Displaced Persons" (Carlisle Barracks, Pa., Military Historical Research Collection, 1947), 6.

17. Quoted in Thorwald, *Illusion,* 32-33.

18. Westhoff, "German Camps," 9.

19. International Military Tribunal, *Trial of the Major War Criminals,* 29 (Nuremberg, 1949), 122.

20. Baird, "Home Propaganda," 40-41; Clark, *Barbarossa,* 205.

21. Sawczuk, *Hitlerowskie Obozy Jenieckie,* 227; Solzhenitsyn, *Gulag,* I: 219; Koriakov, *I'll Never Go Back,* 128.

22. John Buchsbaum, "German Psychological Warfare on the Eastern Front: 1941-1945" (Ph.D. diss., Georgetown University, 1960), 97-98; Shub, *Choice,* 63-64. For more on German attitudes toward Russians, see "The German Concept of the Russian Mind" in Buchsbaum, "Psychological Warfare," 73-85; Francis Sampson, "Paratrooper Padre," *American Ecclesiastical Review,* 116 (Feb. 1947), 118.

23. Baird, "Home Propaganda," 29, 39-41.

24. Quoted by Baird, ibid., 28. See also Interrogation Report of General Ernst Koestring, 30-31 Aug. 1945, p. 9, NA RG 165, Shuster Mission. For a description of these interrogations, see Oron J. Hale, "World War II Documents and Interrogations," *Social Science,* 47 (Spring 1972), 75-81.

25. Koestring Interrogation, 7. See also Viacheslav Naumenko, *Velikoe predatel'stvo,* II (New York, 1970), 381.

26. Thorwald, *Illusion,* 181-82. See also OSS, "Use of Soviet Citizens in the Reichswehr," 5, NA RG 59, no. 2297, 13 Dec. 1944.

27. Hans von Herwarth, "Memoirs: 1904-1945" (unpublished manuscript), 229, 231-34; Koestring, "The People of the Soviet Union," 20-21, NA RG 338, C-035; Koestring Interrogation, 9; OSS, "Reichswehr," 1, 9, 11; Hans Seraphim, "Eastern Nationals as Volunteers in the German Army," iv, 95, NA RG 338, C-

043; Maj. Gen. Alfred Toppe *et al.*, "Political Indoctrination of War Prisoners," 64, NA RG 338, P-018d.

28. George Fischer, "The New Soviet Emigration," *Russian Review*, 8 (Jan. 1949), 11; Roy A. Medvedev, *Let History Judge: The Origins and Consequences of Stalinism* (New York, 1971), 467; OSS, "Reichswehr," 17-18.

29. Burton, "The Vlasov Movement," 14; Dvinov, *Politics*, 51; Ft. Dix Interviews, NA RG 59, 711.62114/8-1045.

30. Anisimov, *German Occupation*, 26; OSS, "Reichswehr," 12; Seaton, *Russo-German War*, 175.

31. Baird, "Home Propaganda," 29; Alexander Dallin, "Portrait of a Collaborator: Oktan," *Survey*, no. 35 (Jan.-Mar. 1961), 117; Alexander Dallin and Ralph Mavrogordato, "Rodionov: A Case-Study of Wartime Redefection," *American Slavic and East European Review*, 18 (Feb. 1959), 25; Reinhard Gehlen, *The Service: The Memoirs of Reinhard Gehlen* (New York, 1972), 73-92; Koestring Interrogation, 8; OSS, "Reichswehr," 9; Wladimir W. Posdnjakoff, "German Counterintelligence Activities in Occupied Soviet Union 1941/45," 63, NA RG 338, P-122; Toppe *et al.*, "Indoctrination," 22.

32. Gary Howard Gordon, "Soviet Partisan Warfare, 1941-1944: The German Perspective" (Ph.D. diss., University of Iowa, 1972), 63; Koestring Interrogation, 7-8; Koestring, "People"; OSS, "Reichswehr," 1; Posdnjakoff, "German Counterintelligence," 179.

33. Quoted in Seraphim, "Eastern Nationals," 97.

34. Ibid., 92; Gordon, "Partisan Warfare," 62; Herwarth, "Memoirs," 235.

35. Alexander von Bosse, "The Cossack Corps," 6, 8, 17, NA RG 338, P-064; Koestring, "People," 12; OSS, "Reichswehr," 17; Steenberg, *Vlasov*, 116-18, 124; Toppe *et al.*, "Indoctrination," 63.

36. Koestring Interrogation, 8; Seraphim, "Eastern Nationals," iii, 36-37, 41; Thorwald, *Illusion*, 77.

37. Yaroslav J. Chyz, "Ukrainians in America, Political Attitudes and Activities," 1953, 10, American Council for Nationalities Service, Box 5, University of Minnesota Immigration History Research Center, Minneapolis; Koestring Interrogation, 8; Volodymyr Kubijovych, ed., *Ukraine: A Concise Encyclopedia*, II (Toronto, 1971), 1087-88; Steenberg, *Vlasov*, 163; Thorwald, *Illusion*, 233-34.

38. Thorwald, *Illusion*, 228.

39. Gordon, "Partisan Warfare," 66, 148.

40. Ibid., 64; Steenberg, *Vlasov*, 55-62; V. Volzhanin, "Zuyev's Republic," NA RG 338, P-124. Old Believers separated from the Russian Orthodox Church in the seventeenth century.

41. Posdnjakoff, "German Counterintelligence," 81; Steenberg, *Vlasov*, 76-77; Donald B. Vought, "An Inquiry into Certain Aspects of the Soviet Partisan Movement 1941-1944" (M.A. thesis, University of Louisville, 1963), 148.

42. Alexander Dallin, "The Kaminsky Brigade: A Case-Study of Soviet Disaffection" in *Revolution and Politics in Russia: Essays in Memory of B. I. Nicolaevsky*, ed. by Alexander and Janet Rabinowitch (Bloomington, Ind., 1972), 227; " 'Haunted Forests': Enemy Partisans behind the Front," 11, NA RG 338, C-037; Vladimir D. Samarin, *Civilian Life under the German Occupation, 1942-1944* (New York, 1954), 58; John J. Stephan, *The Russian Fascists: Tragedy and Farce in Exile, 1925-1945* (New York, 1978), 27; Vought, "Inquiry," 149.

43. Dvinov, *Politics*, 57.

44. Clark, *Barbarossa*, 394; Paul Petelchuk, "The National Alliance of Rus-

sian Solidarists—A Study of a Russian Freedom Movement Group" (Ph.D. diss., Syracuse University, 1970), 76-77; Seaton, *Russo-German War*, 456; Steenberg, *Vlasov*, 79-80, 170-71; Thorwald, *Illusion*, 243.

45. Aleksei I. Briukhanov, *Vot kak eto bylo; o rabote misii po repatriatsii sovetskikh grazhdan; vospominaniia sovetskogo ofitsera* (Moscow, 1958), 12-13; Dallin and Mavrogordato, "Rodionov"; Col. P. Z. Kalinin, "Uchastie sovetskikh voinov v partizanskom dvizhenii Belorussii," *Voenno-istoricheskii zhurnal*, no. 10 (Oct. 1962), 34-37; Solzhenitsyn, *Gulag*, I: 257; Steenberg, *Vlasov*, 106-10.

46. Dallin and Mavrogordato, "Rodionov," 30; Dallin and Mavrogordato, "The Soviet Reaction to Vlasov," *World Politics*, 8 (Apr. 1956), 320; Kalinin, "Uchastie," 347; Koestring Interrogation, 8-9; OSS, "Reichswehr," 1, 9, 13, 16; Seraphim, "Eastern Nationals," 93-96; Wilfried Strik-Strikfeldt, *Against Stalin and Hitler: Memoir of the Russian Liberation Movement, 1941-5* (London, 1970), 174; Tishkov, "Predatel'," 93; Toppe *et al.*, "Indoctrination," 66. Herwarth unconvincingly downplays the defections as a cause for the transfers: "Memoirs," 267.

47. OSS, "Reichswehr," 11-12; Seraphim, "Eastern Nationals," 91; Solzhenitsyn, *Gulag*, I: 246.

48. OSS files, NA RG 226 and 59. See for example OSS, "Reichswehr," 4.

49. Dvinov, *Politics*, 82.

50. John Erickson, *The Road to Stalingrad* (New York, 1975), 322, 331; George Fischer, "General Vlasov's Official Biography," *Russian Review*, 8 (Oct. 1949), 299; Albert Seaton, *The Battle for Moscow, 1941-1942* (New York, 1971), 167, 204; Steenberg, *Vlasov*, 21-28. For Vlasov's biography also consult: Paul Carrell, *Hitler Moves East 1941-1943* (London, 1964), 430-31, 439-41; Mark Elliott, "Andrei Vlasov: Red Army General in Hitler's Service," *Military Affairs*, in press; Institute for the Study of the USSR, *Who Was Who in the USSR* (Metuchen, N.J., 1972), 588; B. Osokin, *Andrei Andreevich Vlasov, kratkaia biografiia* (New York, 1966); Petrov, *Retreat*, 274-300; Michael Schatoff [sic], *Bibliografiia osvoboditel'nogo dvizheniia narodov Rossii v gody vtoroi mirovoi voiny (1941-1945)* (New York, 1961); Strik-Strikfeldt, *Against Stalin and Hitler*; Thorwald, *Illusion*. For hostile Soviet accounts of Vlasov's career, see Yuri Bondarev, "A Russian View," *The Last Circle* (Moscow, 1974), 66; Jean Taratuta, "Tell Me Who Your Friend Is. . .," ibid., 114; P. A. Zhilin, "How A. Solzhenitsyn Sang of the Vlasovites' Betrayal," ibid., 104-7; Tishkov, "Predatel'," 91-92.

51. Dvinov, *Politics*, 82.

52. Ibid., 363-64.

53. OSS, "Reichswehr," 6.

54. Dallin, "Kaminsky," 227; Dvinov, *Politics*, 109; Koestring Interrogation, 11; Petelchuk, "National Alliance," 86; Solzhenitsyn, *Gulag*, I: 258-59; Tishkov, "Predatel'," 95-96.

55. All but a few estimates, and the great majority of the most believable ones, run between 0.75 and 1 million. Furthermore, two Germans intimately involved in Osttruppen activites, Vlasov's interpreter, Capt. Wilfred Strik-Strikfeldt, and Koestring, both set the number at 1 million. Some figures probably include old tsarist émigrés and Baltic nationals, whose homelands were independent prior to World War II. But these minor sources of inflated calculations cannot be compared to Germany's systematic, wholesale underestimates, which the Wehrmacht used to hide the extent of Soviet collaboration from a wary Hitler and

which makes many approximations conservative. Fischer, *Soviet Opposition*, 108, cites 0.5 to 1.0 million; Toppe *et al., "*Indoctrination," 33, cites 0.75 million; Eugene Lyons, *Our Secret Allies, the Peoples of Russia* (New York, 1953), 243, claims 0.8 million, as do David Footman in his introduction to Strik-Strikfeldt, *Against Stalin and Hitler,* 4, Kubijovych, *Ukraine*, II: 1986-87, Gerald Reitlinger, *The House Built on Sand: The Conflicts of German Policy in Russia, 1939-1945* (New York, 1960), 99; Frederick Wyle, "Memorandum on Statistical Data on Soviet Displaced Persons," Harvard Project on the Soviet Social System, cites 0.8 to 1 million; Thorwald, *Illusion*, 228, records 0.9 to 1 million; *Army of the Damned* (CBS, 1962), Hans deWeerd, "Operation Keelhaul," *Ukrainian Review*, 2 (Dec. 1955), 26, A. I. Romanov, *Nights Are Longest There: Smersh from the Inside* (Boston, 1972), 127, Steenberg, *Vlasov*, 104, and Strik-Strikfeldt, *Against Stalin and Hitler*, 49, all say 1 million; Burton, "Vlasov," iv, and Posdnjakoff, "German Counterintelligence," 179-80, both say more than 1 million; Ernst Koestring, *General Ernst Koestring* (Frankfurt-am-Main, 1966), 324, says at least 1 million.

56. CBS, 1962. Audio-Brandon Co. rental.

57. Solzhenitsyn, *Gulag*, I: 240-41.

58. Tishkov, "Predatel'," 89.

59. Solzhenitsyn, *Gulag*, I: 261.

60. Homze, *Foreign Labor*, 74, 76.

61. E. A. Brodskii, *Vo imia pobedy nad fashizmom: antifashistskaia bor'ba sovetskikh liudei v gitlerovskoi Germanii (1941-1945)* (Moscow, 1970), 10; G. A. Kumanev, "Sovetskaia istoriografiia ob uchastii grazhdan SSR v antifashistskom dvizhenii soprotivleniia v Evrope" in *Vtoraia mirovaia voina i sovremenost'*, ed. by P. A. Zhilin (Moscow, 1972), 262.

62. Homze, *Foreign Labor*, 159.

63. B. Panchuk to President Walter Gallan of the Ukrainian American Relief Committee, 10 June 1945, Panchuk Papers, folder 5, Immigration History Research Center.

64. Homze, *Foreign Labor*, 157, 165. See also M. M. Zagorul'ko and A. F. Iugenkov, *Krakh ekonomicheskikh planov fashistskoi Germanii na vremenno okkupirovannoi territorii SSSR* (Moscow, 1970), 226-27.

65. Homze, *Foreign Labor*, 81-82, 157, 272.

66. Sholokhov, *Fate*, 27.

67. Kulischer, *Displacement*, 153.

68. Homze, *Foreign Labor*, 235; OSS, "An Estimate of Russian Workers Removed from Axis Europe (Based upon Russian Charges)," NA RG 59, no. 2173, 12 June 1944, 11. See also E. A. Brodskii, "Geroicheskaia bor'ba sovetskikh patriotov v fashistskoi Germanii," *Vtoraia mirovaia voina,* vol. 3, *Dvizhenie soprotivleniia v Evrope*, ed. by E. A. Boltin (Moscow, 1966), 139.

69. Homze, *Foreign Labor*, 237-38; Max Seydewitz, *Civil Life in Wartime Germany* (New York, 1945), 251; William Raymond Vizzard, "Prisoner of War Policy in Relation to Changing Concepts of War" (Ph.D. diss., University of California, Berkeley, 1961), 262-63.

70. Alfred Joachim Fischer, "A Russian Quisling," *Contemporary Review*, 167 (Feb. 1945), 119; Homze, *Foreign Labor*, 169, 172-73, 256-57, 264, 287; Koestring Interrogation, 11.

71. Homze, *Foreign Labor*, 78, 278-79.

72. Ibid., 78, 82, 262, 268, 273, 276, 283-84.

73. Baird, "Home Propaganda," 30, claims 2.8 million; Werth, *Russia at War*, 701, cites "nearly 3 million"; International Military Tribunal, *Major*, 41: 186, and Petrov, *Retreat*, 274-75, both say 5 million; Kumanev, "Sovetskaia istoriografiia," 262, claims almost 6 million by 1944; Thorwald, *Illusion*, 216, gives 6 million; Steenberg, *Vlasov*, 174, reports 6 to 7 million.

74. Homze, *Foreign Labor*, 237-38. See also ibid., 263; Daniel Lerner, *Sykewar. Psychological Warfare against Nazi Germany, D-Day to VE-Day* (New York, 1949), 150; Ia. Shmel'tser, "Soprotivlenie inostrannykh rabochikh, ugnannykh v gitlerovskuiu Germaniiu," *Novaia i noveishaia istoriia*, no. 2 (Mar.-Apr. 1962), 131.

75. Amalrik, "Victims," 94; Dallin, *German Rule*, 451-52.

76. Homze, *Foreign Labor*, 175.

2

NEGOTIATING REPATRIATION:

Toward a "Tightly Drawn Contract"

A SOVIET-AMERICAN REPATRIATION AGREEMENT helped to redress the demographic chaos of Hitler's New Order, but not without much mutual recrimination. Signed on 11 February 1945, at the conclusion of the Yalta Conference, this convention guaranteed the return of displaced Allied nationals on a reciprocal basis. The Soviet Union did not think each DP should be free to decide whether to return home, and disagreements over the handling of Allied DPs and POWs resulted largely from this Soviet insistence upon forced repatriation, a position that affected the negotiation of the Yalta accord from beginning to end.

The Kremlin had not always maintained that international law required every nation to return all DPs and liberated POWs to their homeland. Prior to World War II the U.S.S.R. had concluded many POW conventions that explicitly affirmed the principle of voluntary repatriation. From the Treaty of Brest-Litovsk in March 1918 through 1921 the Kremlin concluded fifteen such agreements.[1] Much later, the Red Army offered to make repatriation optional for those Germans voluntarily laying down their arms at Stalingrad and, subsequently, for Nazi forces in Hungary.[2]

In World War II the Kremlin reversed itself and pressed insistently for the return of all its citizens abroad. But initially American officials did not know what position Moscow would take on the question. Nor did U.S. authorities perceive how strongly the Soviet Union would oppose any Allied limitations upon repatriation. By December 1943 the State Department had decided to permit Red Army personnel captured in German uniform and confined within U.S. borders to rejoin Soviet armed forces voluntarily. A trickle did board Soviet ships without coercion.[3] In 1943 and 1944 the United States also returned a number of Soviet nationals discovered among German POWs in the North African, Sicilian, and Italian campaigns, although the degree to which this was voluntary is questionable. Solzhenitsyn relates that Lend-Lease Studebakers took unhappy Hiwis captured with Rommel's Afrika Corps back home by way of Egypt, Iraq, and Iran. After screening in desert detention camps along the Caspian Sea, it was off to hard labor in the cooler climates of Siberia.[4]

Throughout the planning stages of Operation Overlord SHAEF recognized the possibility that some liberated persons would be reluctant to return home. Even before the invasion of Normandy, General Eisenhower's staff queried the Russians regarding the treatment to be accorded Soviet citizens captured in German uniform. Even though the United States had already repatriated Red Army men found in Wehrmacht formations, Moscow replied that there were no Russians in German ranks and therefore the problem would not arise. Nevertheless, four months after the invasion of France the Western Allies held some 28,000 Soviet nationals captured in German uniform.[5] Since the Kremlin at first sought to ignore the fact that large numbers of Red Army soldiers had collaborated with the enemy, SHAEF decided not to screen them out from among German POWs. As a result some ended up in camps for Axis captives scattered all across the United States: in New Jersey, Pennsylvania, Virginia, Alabama, Mississippi, Arkansas, and Idaho.[6]

Between 4,000 and 10,000 of the 400,000 German POWs within U.S. borders turned out to be Soviet citizens.[7] That ratio of 5 to 10 percent held true for all Wehrmacht formations surrendering in the West.[8] And figures of that magnitude moved Soviet authorities in a mighty way. Their indifference to Red Army men in German custody underwent a curious metamorphosis once these same pawns of war turned up in British and American POW camps. Disinterest rapidly gave way to solicitude: in late May 1942 V. M. Molotov had sharply rejected Franklin D. Roosevelt's suggestion that Russia negotiate the POW issue with Germany; yet in the fall of 1944 Ambassador Andrei Gromyko fired off trenchant complaints about poor U.S. treatment of citizens of an Allied power, i.e., Soviet nationals captured in German ranks.[9] On 1 December 1944, Charles Bohlen, State Department adviser on Eastern Europe, informed Gromyko that within a week the War Department would begin segregating these Soviet citizens at Camp Rupert, Idaho.[10]

Prior to VE-Day, the United States based its treatment of Soviet citizens captured in German uniform upon the 1929 Geneva Prisoner of War Convention—despite increasing Soviet objections. This agreement required that the capturing army not "look behind the uniform" of the prisoner, that is, not differentiate among captives according to any standards other than rank, and certainly not according to nationality. Before the war ended, officials in Washington refused to repatriate by force Soviet citizens found in Wehrmacht formations in order to avoid giving the Germans any reason to retaliate against captured U.S. servicemen. The possibility of mistreatment of Americans of German, Italian, Japanese, or Czech origin caused particular concern.[11]

The United States did make one exception to this rule. Individuals who claimed Soviet citizenship received different treatment from those who claimed the protection of the Geneva Convention. The United States forcibly repatriated anyone freely acknowledging Soviet nationality.[12] Presumably Washington considered persons voluntarily admitting their Soviet citizenship to be simultaneously forgoing the rights guaranteed them as German POWs under the Geneva Convention. Still, since the United States did not care to advertise this approach, International Red Cross inquiries concerning the disposition of Soviet nationals found among stateside Wehrmacht POWs went unanswered. The segregation of German POWs of Soviet origin at Camp Rupert in no way satisfied Red Army representatives, whose attitude the American War Department described as "far from amiable." They insisted that Camp Rupert officials give their men captured in German ranks "full freedom." But when it became obvious that "full freedom" would permit many reluctant returners to flee to the hills, overweening concern for the welfare of hapless prisoners turned into angry demands for the forced repatriation of miserable traitors to the motherland.[13]

The American reading of the Geneva Prisoner of War Convention did nothing to improve the atmosphere at Rupert. On 21 December 1944, General B. M. Bryan of the Provost Marshal General's Office in Washington explained American policy to authorities in Idaho by telephone:

Camp Rupert: If they do not claim Russian citizenship, they do not go back.
Bryan: They do not have to at this moment. . . . In other words, if a
                fellow is smart, he will say "no, I'm a German." He is a German then.[14]

Moscow's representatives at Rupert bitterly protested this interpretation and made the task of screening out "German claimants" and "Soviet claimants" extraordinarily difficult. A Colonel Rodionov complained about his camp quarters until hotel accommodations were arranged; for his rounds he demanded a sedan that had to be brought from Fort Douglas, Utah; and Camp Rupert authorities complained that his deputy's penchant for belittling American officers in front of their subordinates got "under the skin." The tension in Idaho mounted so that an investigator from the Office of the Inspector General in Washington visited the camp in hopes of resolving differences.[15] In the end the United States turned over 2,100 "Soviet claimants" at dockside in Portland, Oregon, 28–29 December 1944. At least three attempted suicide. At least two others succeeded: their bodies turned up in the Columbia River after debarkation. Back at Rupert, 118 Soviet soldiers captured in Wehrmacht ranks staved off repatriation for awhile by insisting upon their status as German POWs. Amidst elaborate precautions they were transported to Camp Ruston, Louisiana, for the duration of the war.[16]

From the start American policy was more than a trifle inconsistent. The forcible repatriation of German POWs admitting Soviet citizenship violated the spirit if not the letter of the Geneva Convention. But out of consideration for its obligations under the same treaty, the United States temporarily spared German "claimants" the tribulations of an unhappy homecoming. But whatever the shortcomings of U.S. policy regarding stateside Soviet nationals, they pale before Moscow's ludicrous accusations regarding their predicament. Well after the Camp Rupert incident, Acting Secretary of State Joseph Grew still had to rebut Russian charges that the United States was preventing the return home of POWs claiming Soviet citizenship. Although it did not satisfy Moscow, Grew explained that since 1943 those admitting Soviet citizenship were allowed, indeed were forced, to repatriate. But those claiming the protection of the Geneva Convention were treated as Germans, even if they clearly were not. This was not to frustrate repatriation, the acting secretary reiterated, but to safeguard captive Americans whom the Nazis might abuse in retaliation for any disregard of the Geneva accord by the United States. The Russians' strained parallel between Soviet citizens in enemy formations and Americans freed from German POW camps especially peeved Grew: "They were not captured by American forces while they were detained in German prisoner of war camps but were serving Germany in German military formations in German uniforms. They are not, therefore, to be compared with American or Soviet military personnel who may be liberated from German prisoner of war camps."[17]

The repatriation of stateside Soviet nationals accounted for only a small fraction of the millions dealt with in Europe. And concern over the disposition of those millions heightened as victory grew closer. Early initiatives, best described as lackadaisical, gave way in short order to intense bureaucratic and diplomatic maneuvering. By mid-January 1944, almost a year before the Camp Rupert incident, the United States and Britain began talks on repatriation, which led to the creation of a Combined (Prisoners of War) Planning Committee in the spring of 1944—but without Soviet participation.[18] Then the London-based European Advisory Commission (EAC), responsible for some military and postwar planning, started debating the issue. By late November 1944 British, French, and Russian delegations had all voiced a willingness to proceed with talks through the EAC.[19]

The American delegation, headed by U.S. Ambassador to Britain John Winant, could not pry instructions out of Washington, which was still undecided as to repatriation policy. Furthermore, Roosevelt declined to give the EAC any important responsibility. George Kennan recalled that most everyone in Washington felt "a lively concern lest the new body should at some point and by some mischance, actually do something."[20] A frustrated Winant complained, "The subcommittee was unable to meet since I was left totally without instructions. Other delegations were naturally unwilling to treat with an American Delegation which could only sit and listen." The ambassador, whose own son was among American POWs in Eastern Europe soon to be freed by the Red Army, reminded the State Department, "I have cabled repeatedly, trying to get some action in a matter which has such great humanitarian importance and which may deeply affect our relations with our allies."[21]

In the end, Allied military missions in Moscow served as the conduit for discussions that ultimately led to signed agreements. The administration of American Lend-Lease aid was the greatest responsibility for General John Deane as head of the United States Military Mission in Moscow (USMMM), but his greatest headache, he readily admits, was the mutual repatriation of Soviet and American citizens. The winter of 1944–45, the period of greatest debate over the POW issue, he called his "darkest days in Russia." Deane, in conjunction with the British Military Mission, first broached the subject on 11 June 1944. After talking with Major General N. V. Slavin about American and British POWs in the Balkans, he figured the question "had not occurred to the General Staff and that no plans had been made to meet it."[22]

The way Deane first heard about a thousand American POWs stranded in Rumania convinced him this was the case: the U.S. Middle East Command relayed word of these men to Moscow from an Air Force liaison officer in Bucharest. Getting no response on a request to send American contact teams into Eastern Europe further exasperated Deane. He did not know whether the lack of close military cooperation should be blamed on bureaucratic inefficiency or design, but he knew he needed help with POWs. And Ambassador W. Averell Harriman provided it. On 30 August 1944, the two proposed to Soviet Foreign Minister Molotov and Chief of the Red Army General Staff General A. E. Antonov procedures for the handling and "prompt return" of Allied POWs. They asked for an exchange of information regarding recovered Allied personnel, reciprocal camp privileges for U.S. and Red Army officers, and administration of camps by countrymen prior to repatriation.[23] Molotov did not reply for three months—and even then his cautious endorsement was only "in principle."[24] Possibly the Kremlin's dawdling stemmed from the knowledge that many of the considerations Washington asked for were being granted Soviet officials already.

While ignoring the U.S. proposal, the Soviet government made the first of many accusations concerning American treatment of Soviet citizens. The purpose seemed to be to put the West on the defensive at the negotiating table and to fortify the myth of the unqualified wartime devotion of all Soviet nationals. Ambassador Gromyko informed Secretary of State Cordell Hull on 23 September 1944 that the Soviet government expected all its liberated citizens to be treated as free men, not as POWs. The secretary responded that they were treated as POWs because they had in fact fought in German ranks. But the West's alleged recruitment of Red Army POWs was the charge that really amazed Hull: "I said to him that my country had twelve million men of its own enlisted and had no earthly use for any additional soldiers."[25]

Early in November, about six weeks after Gromyko chastised Hull, *Pravda* carried an article by Colonel General Filip Golikov that castigated the United States and Britain for their handling of liberated Russians. The piece emphasized that Soviet nationals captured in German uniform had served against their will and had sabotaged German military operations at every opportunity.[26] Having lost his patience after months of programmed invective, General Deane sarcastically remarked: "It was the old question of Russians captured in German uniforms while in the act of shooting at American soldiers. We could hardly be expected to put them up at the Ritz in Paris or the Mayflower in Washington."[27] Not only did Deane have to contend with Moscow's fusillade of complaints about Western treatment of Soviet POWs, he had to convince Russian authorities that his own criticisms of their handling of liberated American servicemen were more substantive.

That November also witnessed the first Soviet requests for the admission of its contact teams into the Western theater of operations. On the twentieth Gromyko asked Acting Secretary of State Edward Stettinius to accredit to General Eisenhower's staff about forty Red Army repatriation officers under General V. N. Dragun. Quite anxious about Moscow's treatment of American servicemen being liberated by the Red Army, SHAEF had Dragun and party installed in Paris in less than three weeks.[28] Indicative of Washington's accommodating posture, the Joint Chiefs of Staff (JCS) advised Eisenhower on 22 November to relax drastically restrictions on Soviet nationals captured in German ranks and to give Moscow's representatives ready access to them.[29]

By 1 December 1944, the Red Army was nearing two prison camps in Hungary known to contain Americans. An anxious Deane requested that American diplomats again approach Molotov on the POW issue. Despite this renewed pressure, not until 29 December—six months and eighteen days after the first request for discussions on reciprocal repatriation—did Deputy Commissar for Foreign Affairs A. Y. Vyshinskii finally accredit Lieutenant General K. D. Golubev and Major General Slavin to negotiate with Allied military representatives in Moscow.[30] Golubev, the political commissar and therefore Slavin's superior, amazed Deane with his diplomatic incapacity: he had "the largest body and the lowest I.Q. of any human being I have ever encountered."[31] Nonetheless, negotiations began to move rapidly, too rapidly for the United States to secure adequate safeguards for American repatriates. On 9 January 1945, at the very first meeting, Golubev and Slavin presented a draft agreement on repatriation. Despite his relief at finally having a Soviet proposal in hand, Deane seized the opportunity to vent his spleen: he was sure "if the Red Army functioned the same way the Russians function with foreigners [in Moscow], with all the negotiations and delays involved, they would never have gotten even to Kiev, but would more likely be somewhere back in the Urals." General Slavin, unperturbed, replied cleverly that, as the West should know from its lengthy preparations for the second front, these things take time.[32]

In spite of the rancorous exchanges, Deane still viewed the Soviet draft for a repatriation agreement as a positive development. The brief text seemed innocuous enough with its specifications for the care and handling of Allied DPs and POWs, but, significantly, it offered no alternative for refugees other than repatriation. It did not dawn on Deane at the time that, between the lines, this Soviet proposal entailed forcible repatriation: "It was a reasonable plan and with a few minor changes it embodied exactly what we hoped to accomplish." Anxious about American servicemen in Eastern Europe, he declared it to be a "good one" in order to get some kind of agreement signed soon.[33] By 9 January Deane regarded the POW situation as "very acute" and wanted something concrete before leaving Moscow on the sixteenth. This very well may explain why he waited twelve days to relay even minor criticisms of the Soviet draft to Washington.[34]

Deane, however, could not reach a settlement before Yalta because of dissension over repatriation policy with the federal bureaucracy. This dispute, centering at first in the War Department, was the same one that had aborted Ambassador Winant's attempt to negotiate a treaty through EAC.[35] No archival or published records provide details of the infighting, but this much is known: Secretary of War Henry L. Stimson temporarily won out against forced repatriation, at least, but alas only, in his own bailiwick. Stimson adamantly and repeatedly objected "to turning over German prisoners of Russian origin to the Russians. First thing you know we will be responsible for a big killing by the Russians. . . . Let the Russians catch their own Russians."[36] The secretary of war disliked the Soviet draft proposal not only because it required wholesale forced repatriation but also because it placed American servicemen captured by the Germans and liberated by the Red Army in the same category with ex-Soviet soldiers captured by American forces while fighting for the Germans.[37]

Stimson found an ally in Attorney General Francis Biddle, who questioned whether anyone had the lawful right to remove Soviet citizens from U.S. territory by force. On 5 January 1945, he wrote Stimson that U.S. authorities were repatriating Russians

> without fulfilling the requirements of either the deportation provisions of the immigration laws or the provisions of any extradition treaties. . . . I gravely question the legal basis or authority for surrendering the objecting individuals to representatives of the Soviet Government. . . . Even if these men should be technically traitors to their own government, I think the time-honored rule of asylum should be applied. . . . It has been so applied in many cases of men who were firmly regarded as traitors or otherwise political criminals in their own country.

Stimson agreed, at least regarding those *"who object to being transferred to Russian Government* [his emphasis]. Before we deliver any to the Soviets I think we should be sure that we are not delivering them to execution or punishment." At least regarding stateside POWs admitting their Soviet origin, the secretary did concede that "to refuse to return those. . . even against their express desires, might result in the retention of our released prisoners of war in Russian custody."[38]

But on the main issue of wholesale repatriation Stimson would not budge. On 16 January at a meeting with Navy Secretary James Forrestal, Undersecretary of State Joseph Grew, Undersecretary of War Robert Patterson, and Assistant Secretary of War John McCloy, the secretary of war reiterated his objections to the indiscriminate use of coercion in returning Soviet citizens to Russia:

> The Russians are making some awkward demands on us. They wish to have turned over to them German prisoners that we have taken who are of Russian citizenship, and the State Department has consented to this in spite of the fact that it seems very likely that the Russians will execute them when they get them. I pointed out that that was contrary to the traditions of sanctuary . . . and besides it violated the rules of the Geneva protocol toward prisoners of war. . . . I refused to sign the letter which McCloy had drawn [up] for me consenting to [forced repatriation for all Soviet POWs].[39]

In countering Soviet insistence upon forced repatriation Stimson and others of like mind had to contend with officials of opposite views not only in Washington but in London. Alarming reports of stranded Allied servicemen hitchhiking about Eastern Europe made British Foreign Secretary Anthony Eden as anxious as Deane: "I attach great importance to reaching final agreement between the three Governments as soon as possible," he advised Washington, "and I consider this must be done at impending conference." Aiming at a speedy settlement, London had its own draft ready by 27 January. It differed in no significant way from the Soviet original, thus undercutting the position of U.S. officials like Stimson and Biddle who held out against forced repatriation.[40]

The State-War-Navy Coordinating Committee (SWNCC), created in December 1944 to resolve interdepartmental disputes, tried to reach a consensus on the handling of displaced Soviet nationals before U.S. negotiators took up the subject at Yalta. With time running short and amidst myriad pressures—from the British, from the USMMM, from the Pentagon, and from the federal bureaucracy—SWNCC met on 29 January to formulate *one* American repatriation policy.[41] The committee had before it a counterproposal to the Soviet and British drafts prepared by its own staff and the War Department's Joint Logistics Committee (JLC). At important points it differed sharply from the earlier formulas.[42] In particular, this proposal specified that repatriation would be mandatory only for civilian "claimants" and captured Red Army soldiers who did *not* fight for the Germans. Civilians not admitting Soviet citizenship and collaborating soldiers would be spared.[43] The committee's curious categorization of those who could stay and those who had to go reflected the contradictory advice pouring in from all quarters. But that does not explain why America's counterproposal singled out ordinary Soviet POWs for mandatory repatriation. Possibly SWNCC sought to draft these innocents as the minimum sacrifice necessary to insure the good treatment and repatriation of American POWs in Soviet hands. To be sure, the uncompromised POW would dread repatriation less than collaborators, and conveniently, would be less likely to cause an embarrassing fuss.

In choosing the phrase, "claimants to U.S.S.R. or U.S. citizenship," the drafters explained that they meant to: (1) exclude from consideration any Poles or Balts from territory recently annexed by the Soviet Union; (2) avoid the necessity of setting up screening boards to rule on thorny citizenship cases; and (3) "avoid any U.S. assumption of obligation to repatriate to U.S.S.R. any person not himself affirmatively asserting U.S.S.R. citizenship."[44] Now it seems not even ordinary Red Army POWs would be subject to repatriation.

No less puzzling is another record of the 29 January SWNCC meeting giving McCloy's opinion on forced repatriation for Soviet civilians. Inexplicably, he reiterated Stimson's support for the traditional American concept of political asylum, even though the argument failed to move Mc-Cloy personally. Equally mystifying, and with no rationale offered, the committee agreed that repatriation should apply to civilians as well as POWs—right in the face of objections raised and left unanswered that very day. SWNCC was proposing a great expansion of the number subject to repatriation immediately after having catalogued objections to that course of action. On second thought, ready to put distance between itself and its own creation, the committee lamely argued that the returning civilians were not a military matter; they should be left to the State and Justice departments.[45] Not knowing for sure what SWNCC intended in its recommendations to the Yalta delegation matters little; those Americans who went to the conference ignored the committee's counterproposal altogether—just as they ignored all advice on repatriation coming from anyone left behind in Washington.

Ambassador Harriman, Secretary of State Stettinius, and General Deane for the United States, Foreign Secretary Eden and General W. B. Burrows for Britain, and Foreign Minister V. M. Molotov and General A. A. Gryzlov for the U.S.S.R. all had a hand in two separate repatriation accords worked out while Winston Churchill, Roosevelt, and Joseph Stalin held their more famous discussions. Negotiators came to an understanding on liberated Allied personnel with little fuss because no one in the U.S. delegation would support any significant provision in the American draft. Because SHAEF was an integrated British-American command, JLC recommended a tripartite accord for administrative reasons, but Deane reported that the Russians "do not seem receptive to the idea." Two similar bilateral agreements were the result.[46] Also, the American counterproposal would have obligated the signatories to reimburse each other for expenses incurred in caring for Allied nationals, a provision aimed at apportioning the cost of repatriation equitably by obligating the Western Allies to underwrite the approximately 60,000 American and British servicemen in Eastern Europe rather than the mass of displaced Soviet citizens. This article of the American draft, which even Deane supported, never saw the light of day. As a result the Western Allies paid the bill for the care and repatriation of over 2 million Soviet nationals.[47] And the U.S. proposal exempting Soviet citizens captured in German uniform never even came up for discussion.

U.S. negotiators not only ignored the draft agreement prepared for them by SWNCC and JLC, but they also dismissed all counsel to which Britain or the Soviet Union would have taken exception. On 7 February, for instance, the American and British chiefs of staff conferred on the subject of repatriation but "did not pay overmuch attention to the views of Mr. Grew [the undersecretary of state, who opposed indiscrimi-

use of force], thinking these to be essentially diplomatic rather than practical considerations for military leaders."[48] The single tripartite session
on repatriation, which took place only two days before the signing on 11
February, saw only one point hotly debated: proposed DP and POW calorie allotments! In contrast, Article One, which would later occasion bitter disagreements, elicited no comment whatsoever.[49] The wording as it
stood then, and as it would appear in the final text, allowed that "all Soviet citizens . . . and all United States citizens . . . will, without
delay . . . be separated from enemy prisoners of war and maintained
separately . . . until they have been handed over." The last six words
proved to be critical in subsequent debate over the treaty's requirements,
yet neither side at Yalta attempted to clarify the meaning of this crucial
phrasing. That same day Churchill and Stalin briefly touched on the question of repatriation, but managed to skirt the unpleasant issue of the use
of force. Roosevelt was not a party to this, the only recorded top-level
discussion of the topic.[50]

Article Two of the repatriation accord, which accrued solely to the
Russians' benefit, also went uncontested by the U.S. delegation: "Repatriation representatives will have the right of immediate access into the
camps and points of concentration where their citizens are located" and
the right to oversee "the internal discipline and management."[51] As this
worked out in practice, the Western Allies allowed Soviet officials to
carve out extraterritorial islands throughout the Western occupation
zones of Germany and Austria. Yet Generals Deane and Burrows had
extreme difficulty getting a single repatriation team into Poland; and
1,400 miles separated the one and only camp under Western control from
the closest point of liberation for British and American POWs.[52]

The ambiguity of the treaty, especially on the crucial question of what
the United States was obligating itself to in Article One, permits two
quite disparate interpretations. Sven Steenberg, Vlasov's biographer,
and Eugene Kulischer, eminent authority on population movements,
read it as a prescription for forced repatriation. In contrast, journalist-
historian Julius Epstein and Congressional aide Frederic Smith adamantly maintain that Article One does not sanction the use of force.[53]
While in a strictly semantic sense Epstein and Smith have a point—force
is never mentioned—Steenberg and Kulischer are correct in seeing the
agreement as coercive in intent. Western signators recognized that Soviet
authorities would assume the use of force, unless it was specifically proscribed; they did not press for the use of the phrase "claimants to
U.S.S.R. and U.S. citizenship"; and they made no provision for any
course of action other than repatriation. With that sort of passive assent,
Moscow could hardly be blamed for assuming that all Soviet nationals

would be returned.[54] And for seven crucial months, from 11 February to 4 September 1945, the Kremlin managed the indiscriminate repatriation of civilians as well as military personnel.

Actually, what the text said mattered little next to what Allied officials thought it said: Washington's changing views of its obligations counted for more than the agreement itself. Before Yalta, the United States already had decided upon a policy of forced repatriation for stateside Wehrmacht POWs admitting Soviet citizenship. Similarly, Washington would adopt important policies regarding other categories of Soviet nationals well after the Crimean Conference. Since America's administration of repatriation fluctuated both before and after Yalta, the agreement itself mattered less than the changing interpretations given it by policy makers and policy implementers.

How did the United States obligate itself to repatriate millions of Soviet refugees by force—knowing full well that the task would be difficult and extremely onerous and that it would violate traditional American principles of liberty and justice? More than any other factor, keen fear for the well-being of U.S. servicemen in territory overrun by the Red Army is the reason. Diplomatic correspondence bears this out, for the subject of the West's liberated POWs figured prominently in communications dealing with Russian repatriation.[55] Specifically, those present at a SWNCC meeting on 5 January 1945 believed the Soviet Union would tie Western handling of its citizens to Red Army treatment of Americans in its custody. That same day Attorney General Biddle told Secretary of War Stimson point blank that "the Russians have already threatened to refuse to turn over to us American prisoners of war whom they may get possession of in German internment camps."[56]

More than thirty years after the war, former State Department official Elbridge Durbrow still feels that the United States had no choice but to acquiesce in forced repatriation, as much as it galled him. He had been stationed in Moscow during the purge trials of the 1930s and knew "how tough [Soviet leaders] were to their own citizens." Clearly aware of the retribution awaiting returning Vlasovites and sympathizing with their plight, he nevertheless was haunted more by the prospect of Soviet retaliation against stranded American servicemen should Washington not sign an exchange agreement to Russia's liking. Durbrow has no difficulty summing up reciprocal repatriation: "The Russians blackmailed us in that."[57]

For its part SHAEF considered mandatory repatriation the only basis for productive negotiations. Supreme Headquarters felt quick action on an agreement imperative "due to urgent need . . . to send U.S. and British PW camp contact teams to Russian armies without delay."[58] An aide to Eisenhower later explained, "The point of concern about U.S.

prisoners in Soviet hands was real and well based. . . . Nothing in Solzhenitsyn's *Archipelag Gulag* was unknown to us by 1944—and it horrified our command, much as the facts of German slave labor and the gas chambers did."[59]

General Deane, who was anxious to finish the negotiations, noted the possibility of German reprisals against American POWs if the United States repatriated Russians in German uniform. But this did not alarm General George C. Marshall or Secretary of State Stettinius en route to Yalta. "As to the question of reprisals by Germans on U.S. POWs of Slavic origin," the general cabled Washington, "State Department [meaning here, Stettinius] believes the greater danger lies in the possibility of Soviet reprisals against such nationals in U.S. uniform if we exercise undue discrimination in determination of Soviet citizenship."[60]

Charles E. Bohlen, Roosevelt's interpreter at Yalta, also felt the POW questions interrelated. At confirmation hearings before his appointment as ambassador to Moscow, Senator Homer Ferguson of the Senate Foreign Relations Committee asked him, "Even after we knew that these people were committing suicide rather than go back, we forced them to go back. . . .How do you account for the fact that we did not sense what was going on and refuse to carry out an agreement that not only enslaved these people but took their lives?" "There were," Bohlen pointed out, "60,000 [*sic*] American prisoners in Poland and Eastern Germany under the control of or about to be under the control of the Red Army, and the purpose was to get those prisoners back."[61]

Moscow's lackadaisical approach to POW negotiations and its guilty-till-proven-innocent attitude toward soldiers taken alive by the enemy made Western diplomats especially edgy.[62] Month after month of Russian inaction reinforced Washington's fears for its POWs and contributed to American acquiescence in mandatory repatriation. Soviet negotiating delays may have been calculated, or they may have been the result of the normal, ponderous workings of Russian bureaucracy. Still, even if Moscow's diplomats were not purposefully dilatory, they were plainly stubborn. For example, they did not have to take into consideration public opinion, which might have necessitated compromise. Furthermore, they were trained to follow instructions to the letter. For safety's sake, Soviet diplomats put absolutely no store in initiative. In most cases they served as little more than messengers, those with spunk and spark having been winnowed out long since in the purges. By 1941 few were left who had much knowledge of the West and as few who spoke a foreign language with facility. Soviet negotiators in World War II exhibited exasperating inflexibility because of their strict adherence to the chain of command and because stalemate troubled them far less than progress, if that entailed compromise. "When every foreign initiative was viewed as a threat and every concession . . . as an ideological defeat, deadlock could be quite satisfactory." Facts could be denied, unrelated issues connected, and arguments endlessly repeated: no wonder the proverbial "stoutness" of Soviet diplomats.[63]

A steady flow of grievances, real or imagined, put U.S. officials on the defensive, and by implication, provided Moscow with a rationale for delay. It was what Philip Mosely of the State Department called their "treasuring of grievances . . . within a cycle of themes for negotiation."[64] One ludicrous verbal assault had it that the Americans were poisoning Soviet citizens. Investigation revealed that Russian DPs had broken into a tank car of methyl alcohol and had consumed quantities, which proved fatal despite the energetic efforts of American doctors to save them.[65] The Soviet barrage grew to such proportions that the State Department had to ignore repeated dispatches bearing the same complaint; one answer per charge became the policy. SHAEF issued "blanket replies."[66] Western officials dealing with repatriation could readily empathize with the distraught British negotiator of 1933 who complained of Russian diplomats' inability "to see themselves in any other light than that of an aggrieved Power."[67]

After concern for American POWs in Soviet hands, accentuated by Moscow's complaints and negotiating delays, London's support for repatriation probably affected U.S. policy more than anything else. The British precedent of forcibly returning Soviet citizens to Russia made it very difficult to avoid a settlement that did not continue this policy. Since at least the fall of 1942, London had been giving the occasional Soviet nationals uncovered in the course of British guerrilla activity in Greece no choice in their future. Churchill's war cabinet formally adopted a policy of mandatory repatriation late in August 1944, the overriding consideration being to give Moscow absolutely no cause to obstruct the homecoming of British POWs liberated by the Red Army.[68] On the eve of Yalta, after the English already had sent home 17,500 Soviet citizens, British Foreign Secretary Eden reiterated his conviction that compulsory return was "the only real solution." That decided the issue for Admiral William Leahy, Roosevelt's chief of staff: "Since the British War Office, with Foreign Office concurrence, has agreed that all captured Soviet citizens should be returned to Soviet authorities without exception . . . it is not advisable for the United States Government to proceed otherwise."[69]

Initially, the military's nearly universal desire to be rid of its DP charges also expedited the movement. In December 1944, General Eisenhower, expressing a sentiment widely shared by American commanders at the time, complained that "Russians [are] a considerable charge against the resources of this theater."[70] The headaches and expenses incurred in caring for millions of displaced Soviet nationals led Eisenhower to advise Washington that "the only complete solution to this problem from all points of view is the early repatriation of these Russians."[71] *Before Winter Comes*, a strikingly perceptive feature film on the DP problem, has DP camp administrator Burnside declare, after almost forcibly extraditing a legally exempt refugee, "With all those thousands there had to be one or two mistakes. The point was to get them sorted out quickly."[72]

In 1945 military opinions counted, not just because of the war, but because Roosevelt often took the advice of generals over that of diplomats. The president met almost every day with the JCS but frequently neglected to consult the State Department even in military matters with obvious political ramifications.[73] And when it came to Soviet refugees, military supporters of unconditional repatriation, including Generals Deane, Eisenhower, and Marshall, worked their will over the objections not only of State Department officials but also over the opposition of the civilian head of the armed forces, Secretary of War Stimson. In February 1945 there were those familiar with the Geneva Convention and sensitive to the principle of political asylum; these officials, including Stimson, Grew, and Biddle, remained in Washington. Then there were the credulous who, with the exception of Deane and Harriman, knew little of the intricacies of the repatriation question; these officials, including Leahy, Marshall, and Stettinius, went to Yalta.

The State Department, most of whose second echelon officers opposed unqualified mandatory return, lost clout through the war years in part due to Roosevelt's penchant for sending his own personal emissaries on important overseas missions, rather than professional diplomats. It was part of Roosevelt's political credo to avoid challenges to his authority by obscuring the divisions of authority among his subordinates. Since he was the only arbiter of jurisdictional disputes, the resulting administrative confusion checked the growth of independent power bases and kept his lieutenants constantly beholden. This is not to say that the president had any reason to distrust his secretaries of state. On the contrary, Cordell Hull and Edward Stettinius were, if anything, loyal to a fault. Nevertheless, Roosevelt carried over into diplomacy his penchant for "dispersing a common set of functions among disparate agencies."[74]

The army, rather than the State Department, negotiated the repatriation agreement, illustrating both Roosevelt's control mechanism and the military's invasion of State Department prerogatives in the formulation of foreign policy. Whereas Eden and Molotov, the civilian foreign ministers, signed the Anglo-Soviet repatriation accord, two generals initialed its Soviet-American counterpart. To demonstrate the divergent perspectives, General Deane naively commented that the Soviet draft of 9 January 1945 "with a few minor amendments was exactly what we wanted." In contrast, career diplomat Bohlen noted that "State Department people" in Washington had misgivings about parts of the agreement as soon as they saw it. The sentiment of one junior-level diplomat speaks for many: It was a "hell of a thing. I fought that with all I could but I couldn't do much." The Combined Chiefs of Staff (CCS) felt repatriation should be a "military commitment . . . handled independently of any civil machinery."[75] And so it was.

The White House Map Room symbolized Roosevelt's "personal diplomacy" and the army's new ascendancy in foreign affairs. The campaign maps could not reveal that this was the nerve center for the entire U.S. war effort. Because of White House fears of State Department leaks, Roosevelt had the navy set up a communications network here to handle diplomatic as well as military messages. The Map Room was a military show from beginning to end, and Secretary of State Hull seems never to have known its true function. Ambassador Harriman, nominally Hull's subordinate, frequently communicated directly with Roosevelt using this facility, thereby short circuiting the State Department altogether.[76]

Given the general demoralization of the State Department and the president's partiality toward military advisers, it was a matter of course that Edward R. Stettinius, who replaced Hull as secretary of state on 27 November 1944, carried little clout with him to the Yalta Conference and injudiciously spurned the cautionary advice on repatriation offered by his more experienced subordinates. James F. Byrnes, the next occupant of the post under Harry Truman, said Stettinius's appointment merely confirmed that the president had chosen to continue as "his own Secretary of State."[77] Recognizing his new superior for the diplomatic novice that he was, Acting Secretary of State Grew cabled Yalta, advising against forced repatriation. Concerned about stranded American POWs, swayed by British pressure, and being malleable to start with, Stettinius responded, "The consensus here is that it would be unwise to include questions relative to the protection of the Geneva Convention." Particularly keen on winning Soviet support for a United Nations, Stettinius husbanded his meagre influence to that end, following the path of least resistance elsewhere.[78]

Allied propaganda, responsible for forging a pro-Soviet climate of opinion by 1944–45, made it easier for negotiators to effect a repatriation agreement requiring the use of force. To be sure, few who had direct dealings with Soviet officials shared the public's naive wartime assumption of basic Russian-American compatibility. Indeed, Deane, Eisenhower, and

Marshall agreed to Moscow's insistence upon forced repatriation *because* they had no illusions about Russian ruthlessness and *because* they feared for the safe return of GIs stranded in Eastern Europe. Nevertheless, the stateside, pro-Soviet climate of opinion certainly made it easier for them to seal an accord so skewed to Moscow's advantage. Elbridge Durbrow, in recalling how Washington "bent over backwards to make our Soviet allies happy," emphasizes that this atmosphere contributed to the decision of the United States to repatriate all displaced Soviet nationals including civilians.[79]

The popular attitude in America that heaped indiscriminate praise upon wartorn Russia grew out of German aggression and an ideological truce between East and West. Much of the media hammered at the necessity and correctness of the wartime alliance: for eighty minutes *The Battle of Russia* in the army's *Why We Fight* film series managed to relate Soviet life and history as well as the war effort without a single use of the word *Communist*; Stalin's brutal industrialization became a necessary Russian version of the New Deal; and "Uncle Joe," though a little eccentric, was one of the family.[80] *Life* magazine admired the Russians as "one hell of a people," said they "looked, dressed and thought like Americans," and gullibly compared the Soviet secret police to the Federal Bureau of Investigation. The Allies' marriage of convenience, based solely upon opposition to Hitler, came to be heralded as a harbinger of the millennium. In pursuit of a postwar peacekeeping alliance, Soviet goodwill was to be cherished and energetically nourished.[81]

U.S. citizens could develop as jaundiced a view of repatriation as they did of the Soviet Union. The term itself was formidable; if it were not confused with reparations, the economic term it resembled, Americans usually felt more comfortable calling it "bringing the boys home." That seemed so natural that any other course of action was inconceivable. To the uninformed, and misinformed, repatriation sounded like "the kind of hurry-up humanitarianism in which Americans excel."[82] Those in a position to know better did not always act like it. Assuming that a speedy return home would be uppermost in every soldier's mind, the U.S. Army's Psychological Warfare Division airdropped leaflets and aimed sound truck broadcasts across enemy lines that made the incredible blunder of promising speedy repatriation to Soviet military collaborators.[83] No more effective damper to defection could have been devised. Other times the inept gave way to the deceptive. One flier prepared for ROA troops guaranteed a "free and independent life" for those laying down their arms.[84] Yet American military intelligence had specifically warned: "No definite promises can be made since nothing is known definitely about Soviet plans for the ultimate disposition of these men."[85] The left hand was a stranger to the right.

At first people having to be made to go home left GIs merely perplexed. The commonest desire of millions of American soldiers who missed their family and friends and everything familiar was to go home. To imagine that Soviet citizens in large numbers would not share this sentiment confounded many U.S. servicemen. It was as if GIs captured at Bataan or pilots downed over Germany had pleaded or even fought with the Axis powers to forestall their homegoing. And when their fearful charges resisted repatriation it was just as hard for U.S. soldiers to fathom a native land that could induce such anxieties among its citizens abroad. Again, it was as if Americans formerly in German hands were arriving to a stateside reception not of ticker tape but of more barbed wire—until their dispatch like convicts to the Alaskan tundra.[86] Who could comprehend such a thing?

In 1945 the only plausible explanation seemed to be that reluctant returners must have something to hide. At the very least SWNCC concluded that ex–Red Army POWs not eager to go home must have been deserters.[87] Even worse, the Soviet Union, always, and the United States, frequently, concluded that only Fascists would hesitate to return to their homeland. As the *New York Times* put it: "The overwhelming majority desire nothing more ardently than to go home. Of the pre-1939 Russians who do not, most were collaborationists who have no claim on the sympathies of Russia's Western allies."[88] The director of the United Nations Relief and Rehabilitation Administration (UNRRA) for the American occupation zone in Germany also took a dim view of nonreturners: "These anti-repatriation groups are not the product of democratic processes but are rather the remnants of pre-war regimes that reflect Nazi and fascist concepts."[89] In the first flush of victory, the United States had no sympathy for any Russian who had aided Germany even under compulsion. Compassion was especially lacking for followers of General Vlasov. Despite his movement's considerable success in resisting the racist doctrines of its Nazi patrons, there was no place in 1945 for the "proud Western principle of political asylum" in a black-and-white world that was "blissfully pro-Soviet and passionately anti-German."[90]

So the United States acquiesced in forced repatriation out of concern for American servicemen stranded in Eastern Europe, a concern greatly heightened by Soviet accusations and delays on POW matters. A British precedent of involuntary return, the military's obsession to dispose of its DP albatross, a disjointed, disheveled diplomatic apparatus (Roosevelt's own doing), and a pro-Soviet climate of opinion did not help. Still, the forces opposed to indiscriminate repatriation represented an impressive array of powerful Washingtonians, certainly in the collective. Individuals included Secretary of War Stimson, Attorney General Biddle, and Acting Secretary of State Grew. In particular, the absence from Yalta of

Stimson, the ranking opponent of mandatory repatriation, weakened the chances of the United States signing an exchange agreement facilitating rather than forcing the return of Soviet nationals abroad. Not just individuals but important segments of various bureaucracies and commands also objected to forced repatriation from the start: the departments of State, War, and Justice; SWNCC; JLC; the War Refugee Board; and Allied Forces Headquarters (AFHQ-Italy).[91]

Other persons close to Roosevelt—and all important, with him at Yalta—were oblivious to the future difficulties that force would entail or actively supported mandatory repatriation as America's only alternative. At Malta and Yalta Roosevelt had the company of Churchill, Eden, Deane, Harriman, Leahy, and Marshall—all willing to agree to the compulsory return of all Soviet citizens to Russia. Stettinius would wash with the tide. And at the Crimean Conference in February 1945 the diplomatic tide obliterated all trace of the proud Western tradition of political asylum.

And what of Roosevelt? On repatriation policy he was, at best, ill-prepared, at worst, almost totally ignorant. At Malta on the eve of the conference, if future Secretary of State Byrnes is to be believed—not always a safe assumption—the president had not yet looked at his Yalta briefing books. Churchill, too, was disturbed: by Roosevelt's fragility in part, but even more by his seeming indifference to British briefing papers offered him at Malta.[92] In mid-January FDR had made a suggestion on logistics—using Italian ships to repatriate Soviet citizens captured in German ranks—which at least showed he knew there were displaced Russians to be dealt with.[93] But without question he never contributed to the formulation of American policy on repatriation. "Chip" Bohlen, his translator, later testified that the president had no part in the repatriation agreement signed at Yalta; Harriman says that he "never saw the document."[94]

Before and during the Crimean Conference this issue did not receive the sort of attention that took into account the onerous responsibility mandatory repatriation would entail. And when certain negotiators at Yalta did address the issue, they ignored all reservations that might delay agreement. The price paid has to be calculated not only in terms of a tarnished principle of political asylum, but also in terms of lives forfeited, or at the least wrecked a second time, by return to a hostile homeland; and in terms of a country breaking one treaty to fulfill another—the United States could not abide by the sense of the Geneva Convention and the Yalta Repatriation Agreement simultaneously. Malcolm Proudfoot, a SHAEF repatriation official who had to live with the agreement, put it bluntly: "What properly should have been a flexible working arrange-

tions to individual documents and published materials, one source has proven invaluable in providing a clear understanding of the work of the USMMM. It is a nineteen-page memorandum prepared by the Mission for Ambassador Harriman, dated 23 Mar. 1945, which summarizes American efforts regarding liberated POWs. Because of its constant relevance in this chapter, it will not be repeatedly footnoted except for direct quotations. NA RG 334, USMMM-POWs, 13 Mar. 1945–26 Mar. 1945.

23. "History of U.S. Military Mission to Moscow," 91-92, NA RG 165, OPD 336, case 233 part I; Proudfoot, *European Refugees*, 153.

24. Kennan to Stettinius, 27 Nov. 1944, *FR, 1944*, IV: 1265.

25. Gromyko to Hull, 23 Sept. 1944, ibid., 1252-53; Hull Memorandum of Conversation, 24 Sept. 1944, ibid., 1251. Grateful letters of appreciation to Western repatriation authorities from individual liberated Russians lend credence to the view that much of the Soviet outcry over mistreatment of Soviet nationals was feigned. Lt. Colonel Zapozin and Maj. Berizofski to Eisenhower, 9 Apr. 1945, in Alfred D. Chandler, ed., *The Papers of Dwight David Eisenhower: The War Years* (Baltimore, 1970), IV: 2603; *New York Times*, 1 May 1945.

26. Dennett and Johnson, eds., *Negotiating*, 12; Proudfoot, *European Refugees*, 154.

27. Deane, *Strange Alliance*, 188. See also Forrest C. Pogue, *The Supreme Command* (Washington, D.C., 1954), 521-22.

28. Gromyko to Stettinius, 20 Nov. 1944, and to Eisenhower, 22 Nov. 1944, and SHAEF to SD (London base, 6 Dec. 1944), NA RG 218, CCS 383.6 (7-4-44) (2) Sec. 2; CS to SHAEF, 28 Nov. 1944, Map Room Files, MR 330 (2) POWs, Refugees, July-Dec. 1944, box 110, Franklin D. Roosevelt Library, Hyde Park, N.Y.

29. JCS to Eisenhower, 22 Nov. 1944, NA RG 218, CCS 383.6 (7-4-44) (2) Sec. 2.

30. Kennan to Stettinius, 5 Dec. 1944, *FR, 1944*, IV: 1270; Harriman to Stettinius, 29 Dec. 1944, ibid., 1272. Slightly altered circumstances very easily could have made Golubev one of the objects of negotiation—he had barely escaped German encirclement in the Bialystok pocket at the war's outset. And in another curious twist of fate, he commanded the Forty-Third Army in the defense of Moscow, sharing the front with Vlasov, later the prize catch of the Soviet repatriation campaign. Seaton, *Moscow*, 114, 118; Georgii I. Zhukov, *The Memoirs of Marshal Zhukov* (New York, 1971), 252.

31. Dennett and Johnson, eds., *Negotiating*, 13. Concerning "the curious second . . . party who invariably accompanied Soviet negotiators," see Alfred R. Hupp, Jr., "The Technique of Soviet Diplomatic Negotiation," National Technical Information Service, AD 728773, 1971, 64.

32. Memo of Deane-Slavin meeting, 9 Jan. 1945, NA RG 334, USMMM-POWs, Oct. 1943–Oct. 1945.

33. Dennett and Johnson, eds., *Negotiating*, 14.

34. Deane to SHAEF, 21 Jan. 1945, NA RG 334, USMMM-POWs, Oct. 1943–Oct. 1945. See also Proudfoot, *European Refugees*, 154.

35. Winant to Stettinius, 28 Jan. 1945, *FR, Yalta*, 419.

36. Memo of the Office of the Secretary of War to Henry, undated [filed next to a document dated Jan. 1945], NAS RG 165, G1 383.6 (8 May 1942) (1) Sec. 6.

37. WD memo, 24 Jan. 1945, NAS RG 165, WDGSS, ACS 383.6 (8 May 1942) (1) Sec. 6.

38. Biddle to Stimson, 5 Jan. 1945, NA RG 107, "Russia-Safe File," and NAS RG 165, WDGSS ACS 383.6 (8 May 1942) Sec. 6, Part 1; Stimson memorandum, 5 Jan. 1945, ibid; Stimson to Biddle, 11 Jan. 1945, ibid.

39. Stimson diary, 16 Jan. 1945, L, 48, Henry L. Stimson Papers, Yale University Library, New Haven, Conn. Before Yalta the State Department recommended forced repatriation only for the small number of Red Army personnel who voluntarily acknowledged Soviet citizenship.

40. Eden to British Embassy in Washington, 27 Jan. 1945, NA RG 218, CCS 383.6 (7-4-44) (2) Sec. 2; British redraft, 21 Jan. 1945, NA RG 334, USMMM-POWs, Oct. 1943–Oct. 1945.

41. George Curry, *James F. Byrnes* (New York, 1965), 141; interview with Elbridge Durbrow, Washington, D.C., 6 July 1977; Gaddis, *Origins*, 126.

42. Grew to Harriman, 27 Jan. 1945, NA RG 334, USMMM-POWs, Oct. 1943–Oct. 1945; Grew [Elbridge Durbrow] to U.S. Embassy in London, 27 Jan. 1945, *FR, Yalta*, 418; JLC report, between 9 Jan. and 3 Feb. 1945, NA RG 218, CCS 383.6 (7-4-44) (2) Sec. 2. Set up in August 1943, the JLC, consisting of three army and three navy representatives, coordinated WD planning staffs and served the JSC in an advisory capacity. Robert W. Coakley and Richard M. Leighton, *Global Logistics and Strategy, 1943-1945* (Washington, D.C., 1968), 95.

43. JLC and SWNCC draft counterproposals to Yalta delegation, 29 Jan. 1945, NA RG 218, CCS 383.6 (4-4-44) (2) Sec. 2.

44. Draft counterproposals and JLC Corrigendum to JLC 203/10, 29 Jan. 1945, ibid.

45. Eighth SWNCC meeting, 29 Jan. 1945, NA RG 218, CCS 334 SANACC (12-19-44) (1) Sec. 1 and 2.

46. JLC report on repatriation counterproposal, approximately 27 Jan. 1945, NA RG 218, CCS 383.6 (7-4-44) (2) Sec. 2; Deane to SHAEF, 21 Jan. 1945, NA RG 334, USMMM-POWs, Oct. 1943–Oct. 1945.

47. JLC and SWNCC draft counterproposals to Yalta delegation, 29 Jan. 1945, NA RG 218, CCS 383.6 (7-4-44) (2) Sec. 2; Deane to SHAEF, 21 Jan. 1945, NA RG 334, USMMM-POWs, Oct. 1943–Oct. 1945.

48. deWeerd, "Operation Keelhaul," 27. It is a mystery how deWeerd came upon his surprisingly accurate data years before the State Department published the relevant volumes of the *Foreign Relations* series or opened its archives for this period.

49. Memo of meeting attended by Archer, Deane, and Novikov, 9 Feb. 1945, NA RG 334, USMMM-POWs, Oct. 1943–Oct. 1945; minutes of tripartite meeting, 9 Feb. 1945, *FR, Yalta*, 864, 866; Bethell, *Secret*, 31. The negotiators made plans for a second meeting to be held the next day, but neither the *Foreign Relations* editors nor this researcher found any documentation in the archives to indicate that it took place.

50. "Soviet Citizenship Law," 457; U.S. Dept. of State, *Liberated Prisoners of War and Civilians Agreement between United States and Union of Soviet Socialist Republics, signed at Crimea February 11, 1945*, Executive Agreement Series 505, Pubn. No. 2530 (1946), 1; Bethell, *Secret*, 31.

51. Dept. of State, *Liberated Prisoners*, 1.

52. F. S. V. Donnison, *Civil Affairs and Military Government, North-West Europe, 1944-46* (London, 1961), 344; Epstein, "American Forced Repatriation," 357.

53. Steenberg, *Vlasov*, 219; Kulischer, "Displaced Persons in the Modern

World," *Annals of the American Academy of Political and Social Science*, 262 (Mar. 1949), 170; Julius Epstein, review of *Wlassow, Verrater oder Patriot* by Sven Steenberg, *Russian Review*, 28 (July 1969), 367-68; Epstein, "American Forced Repatriation," 357; Epstein, "An American Crime," *National Review*, 1 (21 Dec. 1955), 20; Epstein, "Forced Repatriation: Some Unanswered Questions," *Russian Review*, 19 (Apr. 1970), 209-10; Smith, "American Role," 76. Gillett Griswold and deWeerd side with Steenberg and Kulischer: Griswold, "The Recovery and Repatriation of Liberated Prisoners of War, Occupation Forces in Europe 1945-1946," Military History Research Collection, Carlisle Barracks, Pa., 64; deWeerd, "Operation Keelhaul," 28.

54. Briukhanov, *Vot kak eto bylo*, 9. See also Bethell, *Secret*, 33.

55. Paul H. Gore-Booth, First Secretary of the British Embassy in Washington, to Bernard Gufler, 26 Sept. 1944, *FR, 1944*, IV: 1254; Byrnes (H. Freeman Matthews) to Murphy, 29 Aug. 1945, *FR, 1945*, V: 1105. See also Bethell, *Secret*, 9, 27, 40; Don Cook, "On Revealing the 'Last Secret,' " *Encounter*, 45 (July 1975), 81.

56. SWNCC minutes, 5 Jan. 1945, NA RG 218, CCS 334 SANACC (12-19-44) (1) Sec. 1; Biddle to Stimson, 5 Jan. 1945, "Russia-Safe File," NA RG 107, Sec. of War (Stimson) sf 1940-45.

57. Interview, 29 July 1977, Washington, D.C. See also Maurice Bernard Conway, "The Intellectual Origins of the Cold War: American Policy Makers and Policy, 1933-1945" (Ph.D. diss., University of California, Santa Barbara, 1974), 265-66.

58. JLC appendix: SHAEF to Marshall, 26 Jan. 1945, NA RG 218, CCS 383.6 (7-4-44) (2) Sec. 2.

59. Demitrii Shimkin to author, 17 Aug. 1976. See also W. Averell Harriman and Elie Abel, *Special Envoy to Churchill and Stalin, 1941-1946* (New York, 1975), 416-17.

60. Deane to SHAEF, 21 Jan. 1945, NA RG 334, USMMM-POWs, Oct. 1943–Oct. 1945; Argonaut (Yalta delegation) to WD, 2 Feb. 1945, NA RG 218, CCS 383.6 (7-4-44) (2) Sec. 3. See also Holowka, "Development," 29.

61. U.S. Senate, Committee on Foreign Relations, *Nomination of Charles E. Bohlen, Hearings . . .*, 83d Cong., 1st sess., 1953, 57. See also Charles E. Bohlen, *Witness to History, 1929-1969* (New York,1973), 199.

62. Dennett and Johnson, eds., *Negotiating*, 9; Fischer, *Soviet Opposition*, 112.

63. Hupp, "Technique," 67-68; Gordon A. Craig, "Techniques of Negotiation," in *Russian Foreign Policy: Essays in Historical Perspective*, ed. by Ivo J. Lederer (New Haven, Conn., 1962), 366. See also ibid., 55-56, 62-63, 66, 68; Larry I. Bland, "W. Averell Harriman: Businessman and Diplomat, 1891-1945" (Ph.D. diss., University of Wisconsin, 1972), 243; Stephen D. Kertesz, "Reflections on Soviet and American Negotiating Behavior," *Review of Politics*, 19 (Jan. 1957), 11-13.

64. Dennett and Johnson, eds., *Negotiating*, 282. See also Proudfoot, *European Refugees*, 213.

65. Dennett and Johnson, eds., *Negotiating*, 18. Eisenhower informed Truman that by October 1945 2,000 Soviet DPs had died from consumption of methylated alcohol and other poisonous liquors. Frank Lorimer, *The Population of the Soviet Union: History and Prospects* (Geneva, 1946), 26. See also Alexander Solzhenitsyn, *The First Circle* (New York, 1968), 462.

66. Grew to Kennan, 27 July 1945, *FR, 1945*, V: 1100. See also Proudfoot, *European Refugees*, 213.

67. Craig, "Techniques," 365.

68. Donnison, *Central Organization and Planning*, 199, 202; Alexander C. Kirk to Hull, 16 Sept. 1944, *FR, 1944*, IV: 1250. From June to October 1944, the British worked out a definitive position, acquiescing in forced repatriation but, contrary to what Bethell (*Secret*, 7-8, 12-13, 21) implies, their use of force began much earlier.

69. 5 Feb. 1945, NA RG 59, 740.00114 EW/2-545; Leahy to Hull, 2 Nov. 1944, *FR, 1944*, IV: 1262. The present study treats British repatriation diplomacy only as it bears upon the formation and evolution of American repatriation policy. In keeping with this approach, the author makes no claims to having exhausted British sources on the subject nor to having covered all aspects of London's role in returning Soviet citizens to Russia.

70. Eisenhower to JCS, 8 Dec. 1944, quoted in Holowka, "Development," 18.

71. Tolstoy, *Secret*, 94. See also ibid., 311-12; Bethell, *Secret*, 63.

72. Windward Productions.

73. Harold Zink, "American Civil-Military Relations in the Occupation of Germany," in *Total War and Cold War: Problems in Civilian Control of the Military*, ed. by Harry L. Coles (Columbus, Ohio, 1962), 231.

74. Oscar William Perlmutter, "Dean Acheson and the Diplomacy of World War II," *Western Political Quarterly*, 14 (Dec. 1961), 901, 906. See also Charles J. Jefferson, "Bureaucracy, Diplomacy, and the Origins of the Cold War" (Ph.D. diss., Claremont Graduate School, 1975), 74-75.

75. Deane, *Strange Alliance*, 189; U.S. Senate, *Bohlen Hearings*, 57; July 1977, confidential interview, Washington, D.C.; CCS Report, 18 Jan. 1944, NA RG 218, CCS 472 CCAC file (2-25-44) Sec. 1.

76. Richard L. Walker, *E. R. Stettinius, Jr.* (New York, 1965), 12-13. See also Perlmutter, "Dean Acheson," 897-98.

77. Quoted in Robert Louis Messer, "The Making of a Cold Warrior: James F. Byrnes and American-Soviet Relations, 1945-1946" (Ph.D. diss., University of California, Berkeley, 1975), 116; see also pp. 115, 135; Walker, *Stettinius*, 1.

78. Stettinius to Grew, 9 Feb. 1945, *FR, Yalta*, 757; Walker, *Stettinius*, 37.

79. Interview with Durbrow, Washington, D.C., 6 July 1977. See also Melvin Small, "Buffoons and Brave Hearts: Hollywood Portrays the Russians, 1939-1944," *California Historical Quarterly*, 52 (Winter 1973), 335.

80. Roger Manvell, *Films and the Second World War* (New York, 1974), 168-71; Roman Il'nytz'kyi, *The Free Press of the Suppressed Nations* (Augsburg, Germany, 1950), 14; Warren Walsh, "What the American People Think of Russia," *Public Opinion Quarterly*, 8 (Winter 1944), 513-22.

81. "The Peoples of the U.S.S.R.," *Life*, 14 (29 Mar. 1943), 23; "Red Leaders: They Are Tough, Loyal, Capable Administrators," ibid., 40. See also McNeill, *America, Britain, and Russia*, 747-48, 760; Gaddis, *Origins*, 36-39; Ralph B. Levering, *American Opinion and the Russian Alliance, 1939-1945* (Chapel Hill, N.C., 1976), 50, 54-55, 58, 71, 113, 115-16, 194, 204; Small, "Buffoons," 330, 333-34; Small, "How We Learned to Love the Russians: American Media and the Soviet Union during World War II," *The Historian*, 36 (May 1974), 458, 460-61, 463-65; James S. Twohey, "U.S. Opinion on Russia," *Fortune*, 32 (Sept. 1945), 233.

82. Carl J. Friedrich *et al.*, *American Experiences in Military Government in World War II* (New York, 1948), 180.

83. Epstein, "American Forced Repatriation," 360; Fischer, *Soviet Opposition*, 116; Harriman and Abel, *Special Envoy*, 416; John H. Hilldring, "Position on Resettlement of Displaced Persons," *Department of State Bulletin*, 16 (15 June 1947), 1163; Strik-Strikfeldt, *Against Stalin and Hitler*, 200-1; Thorwald, *Illusion*, 220.

84. Enclosure to a letter from the San Francisco Branch Russian-American Union for Protection and Aid to Russians to Secretary of War Patterson, 19 Mar. 1946, NA RG 165, CAD WDSCA 383.7, 1 Mar. 46, Sec. 3.

85. OSS, "Reichswehr," 23.

86. Lyons, *Secret*, 255; Shub, *Choice*, 46; Smith, "American Role," 111.

87. Report of SWNCC Subcommittee for Europe, 21 Nov. 1945, 27, NA RG 353, SWNCC, 45 Series, 383.6 POW, Russia, SWNCC 46/8. See also Fischer, *Soviet Opposition*, 114.

88. 24 Jan. 1945, 4. See also George Fischer, "The Soviet 'Non-Returners,' " *New Republic*, 120 (13 June 1949), 13; William D. Leahy, *I Was There* (New York, 1950), 425.

89. Quoted by David Martin, "Not 'Displaced Persons'—But Refugees," *Ukrainian Quarterly*, 4 (Spring 1948), 112-14.

90. Fischer, *Soviet Opposition*, 114. See also Reitlinger, *House Built on Sand*, 395. On the general subject of the climate of opinion, in addition to the above, consult Burton, "The Vlasov Movement," 120; Levering, *American Opinion*; Clarence A. Manning, "Significance of the Soviet Refugees," *Ukrainian Quarterly*, 2 (Autumn 1945), 14; Small, "Buffoons"; Small, "How We Learned"; Wyle, "Memorandum," 8.

91. Holowka, "Development," 21, 28-29; Grew to American Embassy (Moscow), 4 Feb. 1945, NA RG 334, USMMM-POWs, Oct. 1943–Oct. 1945; American Embassy (Paris) to Secretary of State, 14 Dec. 1944, NA RG 353, SWNCC 091-Russia file; Col. T. R. Henn, Act. Asst. CS, G5, to Dep. CS, 5 Jan. 1945, NAS RG 331, AFHQ, Roll 227-B, Sacs 400-7, Russian Matters.

92. Messer, "Cold Warrior," 135; Daniel Newton Keck, "Designs for the Postwar World: Anglo-American Diplomacy, 1941-1945" (Ph.D. diss., University of Connecticut, 1967), 180-81.

93. Holowka, "Development," 16.

94. U.S. Senate, *Bohlen Hearings,* 57-58; Harriman and Abel, *Special Envoy*, 416.

95. Proudfoot, *European Refugees*, 155.

3

REPATRIATION OF AMERICAN PRISONERS OF WAR:

"The Difficulties . . . Would Fill a Book"

AT THE CRIMEAN CONFERENCE THE UNITED STATES and the Soviet Union agreed to an exchange of Allied liberated personnel, meaning that repatriation involved two directions. In the thinking of American officials, the movement of thousands of U.S. POWs westward loomed every bit as large as the dispatch of millions of Soviet citizens eastward. While the course of the streams might seem independent, in fact the flow of each directly affected the flow of the other. More specifically, one can speculate that the retrieval of American POWs might have been jeopardized if Washington had not complied with Moscow in returning the vast majority of Soviet nationals abroad. Certainly, the U.S. government feared as much, and acted accordingly. Nevertheless, to the chagrin of American officials, their concessions in the Yalta repatriation accord did not secure the desired level of Soviet cooperation in returning U.S. POWs. On the contrary, the USMMM considered the plight of American POWs "one of the most difficult problems which it had to contend with during the entire period of its existence." Next to the problem of Poland, Ambassador Averell Harriman considered it his "most pressing concern."[1]

Well before controversy developed over Soviet treatment of liberated American servicemen, U.S. military representatives in Moscow had prepared plans for their repatriation. On 4 September 1944, General John Deane appointed Colonel James C. Crockett as senior member of a newly created board of officers charged specifically with this assignment. Simultaneously, SHAEF headquarters in London questioned Soviet officials there about plans for handling liberated Americans. By 3 November Red Army liaison officers had given General Walter Bedell Smith, a ranking member of Eisenhower's staff in London, a number of assurances but no action.[2] Military planners continued their work undaunted, despite uncertainty whether many of their proposals would meet with Soviet approval.

Toward the end of the war the Wehrmacht held about 75,000 U.S.

POWs, most of whom were deliberately concentrated away from the Western front in eastern Germany and western Poland.[3] In December 1944 and January 1945, as the Red Army began to overrun camps holding American servicemen, Nazi commanders resorted to forced marches westward in a futile attempt to hold on to their captives.[4]

By late 1944 U.S. military authorities felt genuine alarm at the prospect of defenseless POWs strung out across the East European countryside: might they make easy targets for reprisals from the Gestapo or German civilians, even after the war ended? To avert this possibility JCS considered asking Moscow to permit the dispatch of armed airborne units to eastern Germany and Poland. JCS estimated that after the German surrender U.S. ex-POWs in Eastern Europe could be airlifted out in four or five days with the use of 400 heavy bombers, "if no Soviet objection is raised."[5] However, that single qualification, Washington came to conclude, would render such a request a waste of time. The fact was the Kremlin very rarely allowed representatives of the Western powers into Eastern Europe, and then only under the strictest controls.

Moscow's close supervision of Allied shuttle-bombing operations in the East convinced Washington it was pointless to propose an American-administered airlift for its POWs in Red Army zones. Cross-continent bombing flights between England or Italy and Soviet-held territory began in June 1944 as a means of increasing the effective range of Allied air raids over German-held territory. The Kremlin felt discomfort over the presence of American and British pilots at air facilities behind Soviet lines and, therefore, only reluctantly agreed to shuttle bombing. The Red Army much preferred to carry out its military and occupation assignments without the inhibiting factor of outside observers, even if they were allies. That being the case, Soviet authorities determined to isolate Western fliers and ground crews as much as possible. Moscow not only segregated these airmen and support personnel from the local inhabitants, but would not let them aid in the repatriation of their liberated countrymen who were wandering about the countryside. U.S. pilots had trouble even communicating with ex-POWs, Soviet restrictions were so pervasive.[6]

One wandering serviceman, Colonel G. V. Millet, Jr., did succeed in locating Americans at a shuttle-bombing base at Thorn, Poland. Red Army officers, however, watched his every move lest he stow away on a plane. The normal evacuation procedure for liberated POWs consisted of rail travel to Odessa, and from there, by U.S. or British transport home. One enterprising ex-POW, Private David J. Nagle, engineered a speedier repatriation home by posing as a pilot who had bailed out over eastern Germany. Only under such false pretenses would Soviet officials agree to airborne evacuation.[7] For twelve months in 1944–45 George Fischer, later an authority on repatriation, served at Poltava, a U.S. shuttle-bombing base in the Ukraine. There he saw Soviet-American friction over the handling of ex-POWs lead to more "sharp disagreements, curt measures, and mutual suspicion" than any other issue.[8]

At least one high-ranking United States official decided, independently of Soviet objections, that a repatriation airlift might not be the best approach. On second thought General Deane felt that air evacuation might create more problems than it solved: what if large Red Army contingents were to come into Western occupation zones on a reciprocal basis? "The total number of Soviet citizens now in the hands of the Germans is variously estimated from two to five million persons. To permit Soviet troops to move into American or British controlled zones for the purpose of protecting Soviet citizens on this scale may cause administrative difficulties that would be undesirable." Consequently, the expectation of Soviet opposition and American misgivings meant that neither an airlift nor protective units would ease the repatriation of stranded Western servicemen in Eastern Europe.[9]

Liberated POWs had to fend for themselves, not only due to aborted U.S. plans, but also due to Moscow's belated attention to the problem. As often as not, the presence of Americans in Eastern Europe befuddled the Red Army. A band of ex-POWs under a Major Dobson had to convince suspicious Soviet troops that they were not German paratroopers in disguise. That hurdle crossed, the Russians became very cordial. The liberators treated the liberated to a small feast and provided them with more vodka than they could stomach. (The Americans compared the Soviet brew to ethyl alcohol.) Russian hospitality impressed the American major, but not nearly as much as did the lack of Soviet planning. Not only Dobson, but most repatriated U.S. servicemen reported that their presence in Eastern Europe surprised the Red Army: "It was a new problem to them . . . and they were most anxious that the Americans should not learn that they'd been caught unprepared."[10]

The Red Army's "loose administrative system," as one War Department colonel put it, contributed mightily to Soviet shortcomings in the reporting and care of ex-POWs.[11] Then, too, the Soviet bureaucracy might not answer American requests for information because of inadequate staffing, as well as general secretiveness: "The Russians kept far fewer records than the British or the Americans, but pride kept them from admitting this."[12] The Soviet military support apparatus, relatively unsophisticated by Western standards, partly explains why Deane found K. D. Golubev's POW briefings so unsatisfactory. As the Moscow Mission chief phrased it, this Soviet general's "continued uncertainty was ample evidence of the ineffectiveness of his organization and the lack of foresight in planning to meet problems which were certain to arise."[13]

After escaping or after being liberated by Red Army units, the freed servicemen thought of little else but going home. Understandably, time-consuming, indirect routes held little appeal. One ex-POW, liberated by Red Army troops south of Potsdam, related that Soviet plans for their evacuation eastward to Odessa meant that "day after day more of us left camp to find our own lines, which we did and they took care of us. I think if we went back to Odessa I would not be writing this letter now."[14] But most GIs liberated in Eastern Europe were not that near Western lines and could only work their way eastward, usually on their own. They tended to move in that direction because it was away from the front and because they expected to receive aid from American repatriation teams in the Soviet rear. Most definitely needed assistance because Soviet provisions proved to be erratic or nonexistent. One group of repatriates reported their first Russian rations came twenty-nine days after liberation. Despite the Poles' terrible suffering during the war, they generously assisted destitute American servicemen. Former American POWs often praised the simple Polish peasant's hospitality when they could find nothing else positive to say about their post-liberation ordeal.[15]

To the great surprise of U.S. and Soviet authorities, a number of liberated POWs turned up in Moscow, some having covered close to 1,000 miles from as far as Szubin, Poland. The first three of at least eighteen of these hitchhikers arrived in the Soviet capital on 7 February 1945, twenty-eight days after their liberation at Szubin. "I don't think any officer," Deane figured, "ever had a more sincere welcome than those first three bedraggled ex-prisoners did when they came into our headquarters."[16]

The general and Ambassador Harriman, starved for firsthand information on the condition of stranded American servicemen, listened intently to the story these men had to tell. After their liberation the Red Army had paid no attention to the three, telling them only to "go East." They first had contact with Soviet DP officials at Wegheim, a repatriation camp near Exin, East Prussia, present day Kcynia, Poland. Finding conditions there "intolerable," they escaped, determining from then on to avoid Soviet-run camps at all costs. As they moved eastward, they met other Americans, but decided against forming large parties. Because of its reputation for "indescribable filth," the ex-POWs purposefully passed up Rembertow, a collection point near Warsaw where earlier four Osttruppen legions had trained.[17] Moving on, the men caught rides on Red Army supply trains and frequently put up at night with accommodating Polish peasants. They finally arrived in Moscow, undetected by any government authorities, much to the chagrin of the Soviet secret police who made sure that that did not happen again—subsequent American arrivals would be held by the NKVD for several days' interrogation before being turned over to Deane.[18]

Additional information about Russian treatment of U.S. servicemen came from Captain Richard Rossbach, nephew of former New York governor Herbert H. Lehman. When this ex-POW turned up at Odessa, Ambassador Harriman had him flown to Moscow. According to Rossbach the Russians had made no preparations for the care and evacuation of liberated Allied personnel; Soviet troops relieved them of their watches; some ex-POWs had been greeted in Odessa with fixed bayonets.[19]

Repatriates' early, consistently negative testimony on Soviet treatment gave way eventually to more mixed evaluations, which fluctuated erratically between angry denunciation and enthusiastic praise. One American recalled a warm Soviet reception: they "greeted me by shaking hands and being as happy about it as though I was a long lost brother." Another ex-POW, in this case British, related Allied prisoners rushing out "to greet the Russian tanks waving their arms in welcome. . . . the Russians thinking they were Germans had mown them down with machine gun fire and then run over them with their tanks."[20] Two repatriated officers wrote General Marshall, "Even liberated Russian prisoners who had suffered amputations of both legs were not shown as much consideration as the American officers"; but two other officers complained to War Department interrogators that Americans never received food or lodging as good as Russians and that they had trouble hitching rides on U.S. Lend-Lease Dodges or begging Lend-Lease Russian rations.[21]

On the one hand, Indiana Congressman Earl C. Wilson returned from a European tour demanding that the House Foreign Affairs Committee investigate Soviet handling of American ex-POWs who, he reported, "were stripped by their 'Russian Allies' of clothing, watches, wallets and other personal effects."[22] On the other hand, reports surfaced stating that Americans alone of all the Allied refugees in Soviet custody could write letters that would be flown to U.S. lines.[23] In describing Russians, for every "liar" and "failure to live up to any of the terms of the [repatriation] agreement," there were an equal number of reports of "sincere goodwill" and "treatment . . . above reproach."[24] Without question, Soviet handling of liberated Western servicemen varied widely from circumstance to circumstance, and the Red Army had no clear knowledge of or effective control over Americans stranded in Eastern Europe.

Before the German capitulation, the Soviet evacuation of liberated Allied personnel depended primarily upon the Black Sea route. Although west of Lublin, Poland, transportation was happenstance, once in this

Polish city, ex-POWs (not only American and British, but French, Dutch, and Belgian) generally could count on a train to Odessa.[25] But owing to the destruction in the war zone and the mammoth Soviet offensive that had hardly halted since 1943, first-class transportation eastward was nonexistent. One British repatriate recalled:

> The engine was something out of Stephenson's era—but for all that it was a game one! We would come to a small incline and the engine would . . . try to get to the top and sometimes it wouldn't make it and would roll all the way back again. The trouble was we had no coal and the poor thing had to be stoked up on wood. . . . when we stopped for any length of time to allow the engine to recuperate and cool down we would wander off in search of a Russian village to see if we could barter anything. In this way we got meat, milk, bread and eggs, usually for chocolate or cigarettes. There was never any animosity shown to us, if anything quite the reverse.

From Lublin to Odessa took five to six days for a very modest average of eighty to one hundred miles per day by rail.[26] Many returning Americans complained that they had to make the trip in unheated boxcars without proper sanitary facilities. Although arrangements were primitive by Western standards, they were not unusual in wartorn Russia. For the most part, Red Army rank and file traveled no better.[27]

The U.S. officers charged with the responsibility for liberated servicemen arrived in Odessa on 26 February. But they had little time to prepare for their task because several hundred ex-POWs began arriving almost immediately. This circumstance did not matter much, since Soviet officials severely restricted the scope of American activities. The Russians claimed that U.S. and British personnel were in charge of the Odessa camp.[28] However, not only were Western repatriation officials prohibited from living in the same quarters with the ex-POWs, they were not allowed to set up the internal administration of the compound—a clear violation of the Yalta agreement. In addition, Major Paul Hall, who coordinated U.S. relief operations in Odessa, considered Soviet accommodations, food, and medical care for American ex-POWs wholly inadequate.[29] Having the shell of a bombed-out school building collapse, killing two British and four U.S. soldiers, did nothing to reassure officials like Hall.[30]

Higher-ups, however, found more to their liking—at least in Odessa. Deane considered conditions there "as good as might have been expected." And Harriman agreed, even though Soviet handling of repatriation obligations in general deeply disturbed him. The ex-POWs, at any rate, had no strong complaints about their reception at Odessa. And whatever opinion they may have had of Soviet repatriation officials there, they had nothing but the highest praise for the job done by members of the American Military Mission stationed at the Black Sea port.[31] Perhaps the best summary of conditions comes from the first batch of interrogation reports of Odessa repatriates: U.S. investigators concluded that Soviet treatment of ex-POWs had been "good by Russian standards, indifferent by British, barbaric by American."[32]

The Soviet attempt at hospitality in Odessa comes to life best in Sam Kydd's colorful reminiscence, *for* You *the War is Over.* Stories of communal baths, concerts, evenings at the ballet, and Soviet propaganda films, yes, but above all, this irreverent yet believable ex-POW recollected olympian drinking bouts: "After one to two speeches we would toast and drink the health of Joseph Stalin—Marshal Zhukov—Rokossovsky—Churchill—Rooshvelt—and Ruskian sholgiers the Brisssh soljershhs and anybody else you can shink of—if you're still standing up that is!" Souvenirs of the sojourn included hand-painted Russian soupbowls and hammer-and-sickle helmets. "Wearing the hats we marched proudly to the harbour as near in step as those Russian Steppes would allow, led by a Soviet Military Band and watched with awe and envy by the Germansky prisoners working on the roads—poor devils. We'd done our stint."[33]

By the time the Allies had joined forces in Germany and direct overland repatriation between occupation zones had become the rule, only 2,800 to 3,000 U.S. military personnel had been repatriated through Odessa.[34] Most Americans freed by the Red Army passed undramatically from Soviet to U.S. control in Germany after VE-Day: from April to July, between 23,554 and 28,662 men. Thus, about 90 percent returned home via the shorter, less publicized route.[35]

The logistics of repatriating Americans proved to be a simple matter compared to the East-West diplomatic sparring over the issue. The leisurely pace of the ponderous Soviet bureaucracy particularly distressed Western officials anxious about POWs recently freed from German captivity. In late January 1945, Ambassador John Winant, whose own son was wandering about Eastern Europe, cabled Secretary of State Stettinius from London that twenty U.S. repatriation officers could not budge for lack of Soviet visas. The ambassador added that Molotov ought to hear about this at Yalta. On 18 February, a week after the close of the Big Three meeting, Deputy Foreign Minister Andrei Vyshinskii finally informed Harriman that the visas were approved.[36]

Success in obtaining travel documents could occasion no elation on the part of the American diplomats, however, for reaching Soviet territory was one thing and reaching POW liberation points was quite another. Realizing this, Harriman had written V. M. Molotov two days earlier, detailing specific U.S. proposals for expediting the repatriation of ex-

POWs. Among other things, the ambassador suggested that : (1) a contact team under Colonel James D. Wilmeth be permitted to go to Lublin; (2) this party be allowed to use American aircraft in its work; (3) U.S. personnel be permitted to evacuate ex-POWs by air; and (4) American officers be given immediate authority to contact ex-POWs at other locations.[37] Being extremely reluctant to allow U.S. repatriation officials into Poland and Eastern Germany, the Kremlin flatly refused requests 2 and 3 and approved, but then circumvented by restrictions and repeated postponements, requests 1 and 4.

Meanwhile, Deane had become concerned because the Moscow-sponsored Polish Provisional Government (commonly referred to as the Lublin Committee) proved more diligent in reporting the recovery of American ex-POWs than Soviet authorities.[38] Having correctly guessed that Molotov would not respond quickly to Harriman's suggestions, Deane emphatically voiced his displeasure at a meeting on 17 February with General N. V. Slavin. He stressed that the Yalta agreement was effective from the date of signature, expressed disappointment over the failure of Soviet authorities to permit U.S. contact teams in Poland, and reiterated his desire to be promptly notified when American POWs were liberated.

General Slavin, after stating that he could not reply to Deane's assertions at that time, countered with complaints of his own. He also made it clear that he expected the chief of the American Military Mission to report to him in answering Soviet repatriation grievances. By this time Deane could barely control his temper. It was not his responsibility to answer Soviet complaints, he tartly replied. That was Eisenhower's and Joseph McNarney's job. An exasperated Deane concluded by telling Slavin he wished to end their futile discussion and intended to report back to Washington that "in his opinion, the repatriation agreement was not being effectively carried out." As far as he was concerned, "Negotiations looking toward a new and more effective agreement ought to be worked out between the two governments."[39]

Two days later, on 19 February, Golubev announced to Deane Moscow's approval for an American contact team in Lublin. It would be difficult to say whether the timing resulted from Deane's outburst or the largely unfathomable workings of Soviet bureaucracy. This much is certain: the Kremlin's modest step toward compliance with the repatriation accord did not mollify Deane. The rest of his meeting with Golubev was, as usual, stormy. First, they could not agree on the number of American servicemen in Eastern Europe. The Soviet general considered any approximation based on the testimony of POWs who had hitchhiked to Moscow to be as unreliable as "inflated" Polish estimates. Then, Golubev claimed he had not had a chance to study the POW agreement, having just received his copy that day. But why did he have to study a document he had helped formulate? Even more inexplicable was his bizarre suggestion that a POW transit camp be established at Murmansk. American repatriation officers interested in flying ex-POWs directly out of Poland and eastern Germany had difficulty getting excited about an exchange point on the Arctic Ocean. [40]

Despite the Kremlin's permission for Colonel Wilmeth's contact team to go to Lublin, gaining final clearance proved to be a difficult task. As late as 25 February frustrated American officials had not received permission even to fly supplies to Lublin or "to move anything or anybody anyplace." On 26 February, nine days after formal approval, Deputy Foreign Minister Vyshinskii told Harriman that the trip had been "delayed one or two days [*sic*] for technical reasons." [41] The Soviet definition of a contact team further exasperated U.S. officials. As it turned out Colonel Wilmeth's "team" consisted of himself and Colonel C. B. Kingsbury, a doctor. [42] By the time this first and only American "team" finally left for Lublin at the end of February, General Eisenhower had had forty Soviet repatriation officers at his headquarters for nearly three months. [43]

Dissatisfied with Soviet handling of the POW question, Deane cabled General Marshall in Washington on 2 March, seeking to enlist the help of higher authorities in expediting the repatriation of American servicemen from Eastern Europe. He explained that if repatriation officers were ever to get permission to use American aircraft to deliver supplies and evacuate sick and wounded POWs from Poland, the president would have to appeal to Stalin directly. [44]

The next day Deane seems to have been momentarily reassured. Golubev explained that inadequacies to date could be attributed to "growing pains" within the newly created Soviet repatriation organization and held out the promise of four or five American contact teams in Poland. With uncharacteristic optimism, the ranking U.S. officer in Moscow cabled Washington, "As soon as the plans the Soviets now have which are the same as we have been striving for, are put into effect I think that the situation will clear up and that our ex-prisoners of war will have the best treatment possible under the conditions." But as Deane received more information from the field, his former impatience with Soviet restrictions on him and his staff quickly reappeared. By 7 March he was ready for "a final showdown on the subject." [45]

During the first week of March, while Deane vacillated between praise for and disgust with Soviet repatriation efforts, his cable to Marshall was having considerable impact in a Washington upset generally with Moscow's interpretation of the Polish provisions of the Yalta agreement.

Secretary of War Stimson, sympathizing with Deane's appeal (channeled to him through Marshall), asked Roosevelt to hear him out on the POW question. The president consented and the two men met on 3 March in what Stimson described as a generous seventy-minute session. In two memoranda with eight attachments, the secretary of war laid before Roosevelt U.S. difficulties in retrieving American servicemen from Soviet-occupied territory. The president "read them both through in detail, every paper, something he very rarely does," Stimson noted in his diary. Right away Roosevelt agreed that the situation called for a direct communication at the top level. And when Stimson presented Deane's draft for a message requesting U.S. mercy flights into Poland, the president himself sharpened the cable's tone by appending this question to Stalin: "In view of your disapproval of the plan [for contact teams] we have suggested, what do you suggest for us to do?"[46]

Russia's dictator responded on 5 March, assuring Roosevelt that Soviet officials were doing everything possible to help the liberated POWs. According to his "local representatives in charge of this matter," as of 5 March there was "no accumulation of U.S. prisoners of war on Polish territory" except for isolated hospital cases. Stalin added that 1,200 liberated American servicemen had already arrived in Odessa, with the remainder expected at any time. "Hence, there is no need at the moment for U.S. planes to fly from Poltava to Polish territory."[47]

In his attempts to visit collection centers in Poland, Deane made no progress. He heard on 26 February that the Soviet government had no objections to such a trip if the Polish Provisional Government agreed; Deane easily secured permission from the Lublin Committee that same day.[48] Still, Moscow never granted him final clearance, and he never visited Poland. The Kremlin apparently kept Deane in Moscow in order to avoid another Western observer's unfavorable reflections upon Soviet occupation policy. Also it appears that Moscow hoped to use the issue of contact teams to pressure Washington into extending diplomatic recognition to the pro-Soviet Polish Provisional Government. Moscow's deference to this body, as in the case of Deane's proposed trip, was no genuine reflection of its power and influence, for it had very little of either apart from Red Army backing. Rather the Kremlin hoped such gestures would enhance the Lublin government's standing in Western eyes and eventually lead to *de jure* status for the predominantly Communist provisional government.[49] Because of these two factors—the Kremlin's dislike of foreign observers and its readiness to use the question of contact teams as a lever in its attempts to gain recognition for the Lublin Poles—the repatriation of American POWs became a political issue. Retrieving U.S. servicemen from Eastern Europe, ostensibly an uncomplicated humanitarian project, became inextricably entangled in the question of Poland's political future.

Repatriation teams were not the only American and British parties the Kremlin held at bay. The Allied Polish Commission's (APC) futile attempts to send observers into Poland paralleled the Western Allies' efforts to get contact teams into Eastern Europe. By 25 February APC representatives had sought and secured Moscow's permission for a trip to Poland for the purpose of consolidating Lublin and non-Communist Poles into a single government. Yet in the next two weeks, Soviet authorities withdrew travel authorization for both the APC and Deane. Molotov hinted at such a possibility as early as 1 March, and by the twelfth it was a certainty.[50]

An agitated Harriman immediately answered Molotov's veto with a warning: unless Deane were "permitted to review this situation regarding our ex-prisoners of war in Poland [firsthand], my Government will not be satisfied that it has done everything it should on behalf of its officers and men." Also on the twelfth Harriman cabled Roosevelt, with some feeling, that "after 48 hours of continued pressure on the [Soviet] Foreign Office, I finally received an answer last night disapproving General Deane's trip to Poland on the grounds that there were no longer any American ex-prisoners of war in Poland."[51] The U.S. embassy in Moscow in March 1945 was "full of running feet, voices and phones ringing all night long," but the joy of that spring's military successes was spoiled, the ambassador's daughter contended, not because of the frenzied pace, but because America's "gallant allies" were acting "most bastard-like."[52] Kathleen Harriman's appraisal seemed confirmed by Moscow's decree of 12 March that Colonels Wilmeth and Kingsbury had finished their work and would have to leave Lublin immediately. At that very moment these, the only U.S. repatriation officers in Poland, were sorely taxed to tend to the needs of American servicemen filtering through the city.[53]

Deane knew the two had discovered about one hundred Americans upon arrival in Lublin and, nevertheless, from the outset had faced "constant pressure to leave." Soviet authorities at first had refused them access to the ex-POWs, and when the Russians did relent, Washington's sole repatriation team had to make do with set visiting hours and travel within the city limits. Two seriously wounded Americans close by, but outside, Lublin had to go unattended because Dr. Kingsbury could not secure permission to leave town.[54] The Yalta agreement stipulated U.S. administration of American POW facilities; but the Kremlin claimed no camp existed in Lublin and therefore U.S. overseers were uncalled for. To their great frustration, Wilmeth and Kingsbury had difficulty observing, much less administering, POW camp life and repatriation. Moscow afforded London similar treatment: Soviet officials confined British contact teams in Russian-annexed L'vov and Volkovysk to the hotel and then ordered them out with British POWs still there.[55]

The Yalta repatriation accord called for Allied protection of POW camps from enemy artillery, which gives the strong impression that the signators assumed contact points would be near battle lines. It turned out otherwise: American officials got no closer than 500 miles, at Lublin, and by the time the U.S. took charge of its solitary camp at Odessa, the front was some 1,400 miles to the west.[56] As a result, ex-POWs by the hundreds wandered about eastern Germany, Poland, and Russia unassisted for days, weeks, or months. Posters put up by the Red Army directed them to seven concentration points—"camps" would have required contact teams. But these proved so wretched by American standards that often the servicemen purposefully hid from the Russians to avoid them.[57]

The ex-POWs' aversion to and evasion of their "liberators" also stemmed from the Soviet soldiers' penchant for fleecing friends and foes alike. In particular, lifted timepieces became something of a symbol of the Russian presence in Eastern Europe. Stealing watches, a rather primitive sort of greeting frequently mentioned by American and British repatriates,[58] held true generally for the Red Army's approach to East Europeans. One Soviet defector, who had been stationed in Russian-occupied Hungary after the war, recalled seeing newsreels of the Big Three in a Budapest theatre: "In one of the sequences, Generalissimo Stalin approached Prime Minister Churchill and smilingly laid a Russian hand on the British shoulder. At this point a Hungarian in the audience shouted out the words with which Russia had been tainted throughout the Balkans, 'Give me your watch.' " The show stopped, and the entire crowd was fined "on the theory, probably sound, that all those present had joined in the laughter."[59]

General Deane, however, found nothing humorous about the goings-on in Eastern Europe. On 10 March, two days before the Soviet evacuation order, he sent a message to Colonel Wilmeth indicating his growing frustration: "There is no use of my going over the difficulties I have had in Moscow in attempting to help your situation. Needless to say, our efforts would fill a book, but the results are nil despite the fact that we not only have gone to the Ambassador level but to the Presidential level. . . . I am constantly told that your work is finished which I know is not true."[60]

The Kremlin did not want to advertise that the Polish underground had proven unexpectedly and openly hostile to the Soviet Union and that most of the rest of the population looked upon the Russian presence at the least with misgivings. Two politically naive ex-POWs, Captain Patrick Teel and 1st Lieutenant James Hannon, could not understand

Poland's "ungrateful attitude" toward the Red Army: "At no time, from anyone, did we ever hear one word of praise or thankfulness to the Russians for their liberation." The pair felt they had better warn General Marshall that the Poles might try to jeopardize Soviet-American relations in the interests of "their obscure cause."[61] The reason for wariness of Soviet liberation among independence-minded Poles might be "obscure" to two historically unlettered Americans, but for the better informed it was only logical that the victims of the Nazi-Soviet agreement of 1939, which sanctioned Poland's physical dismemberment, should have reservations about being emancipated by one of the pact's co-signers.

American servicemen consistently reported the Polish peasantry's desire for U.S. and British protection against Soviet domination. The Poles, invariably hospitable toward Western ex-POWs and deeply resentful of Red Army "requisitions," worked hard "to enlist sympathy for their cause in which hatred and apprehension toward Russians was obvious."[62] U.S. repatriates noted "very decided feeling between the Lublin Poles, the London [pro-Western] Poles and the Russians." Liberated American officers ordered their men not to take sides in Polish-Soviet controversies, not out of ingratitude for Polish generosity, but for safety's sake.[63]

The uncomplimentary tales coming from ex-POWs about the heavy-handed Russian occupation of Poland gave the Kremlin ample reason to keep repatriation teams and APC observers away. To be sure, there was wartime confusion and red tape, but "the Soviets were also apprehensive about any stories the ex-prisoners might carry west concerning the behavior of the Red Army in Poland. For all the devastation of the country, resistance to the Soviet-imposed regime was proving harder than the Russians had expected—hence their unwillingness to have Allied observers there or to hold elections, as had been promised at Yalta."[64] It seems Moscow cut short Colonel Wilmeth's stay in Lublin and cancelled the Deane and APC visits because of unanticipated Polish resistance to Russian occupation. "Stalin," Harriman said, "had the idea the Red Army would be accepted as a liberating army. In fact, he told me so. . . . Perhaps the Communist partisans had reported too optimistically to Moscow."[65]

Finally, on 7 March 1945, Golubev proposed to Deane six POW centers: Murmansk, Belgrade, Moscow, Odessa, Poltava, and L'vov. The U.S. rejected Murmansk out of hand as being unsafe and too distant. Belgrade and Moscow, also remote from the points of liberation, never came up again in subsequent conversations. Odessa was already the one and only American repatriation center, and Poltava, site of the Allied shuttle-bombing base east of Kiev, was farther from Poland than Odessa. That left L'vov, a Polish city prior to World War II, which the Soviet Union annexed despite Roosevelt's plea at Yalta that the Poles be permitted to keep it. On 10 March Golubev added Volkovysk and Bronnitz (Bronica) to his list, two more towns of prewar Poland soon to be incorporated into the U.S.S.R. Despite Golubev's denials, Deane knew then, from repatriates' firsthand testimony, that assembly centers existed at Wrzesnia, Lodz, Lublin, Rembertow, Praga, Wegheim, and Brest-Litovsk and that Red Army roadside placards directed liberated POWs to these camps.[66] With Moscow never admitting the existence of facilities for U.S. servicemen in occupied Poland, the need for American contact teams could be dismissed more easily. Simply put, Russia read its obligations under the Yalta repatriation agreement so as not to interfere with the Sovietization of Eastern Europe.

Even those POW assembly centers in former Polish territory, such as L'vov and Volkovysk, were not readily accessible to U.S. officials, much less administered by them as the treaty stipulated. The USMMM learned on 7 March that L'vov and, on 10 March, that Volkovysk were to be contact points, but Soviet officials delayed authorizing repatriation teams to visit these camps until 26 March. And only on 3 April did the teams finally set out by train, after being held up another eight days and after being refused permission to travel by air. With the rail trip consuming five additional days and their passes expiring 15 April, the repatriation officers had only a week to prepare the two locations to receive ex-POWs. As events turned out the two camps never were used, because direct contact between Red Army and SHAEF forces was established on 25 April, making a westward movement of liberated POWs more convenient. Concerning the proposed assembly points, an army study figured it "doubtful that the Soviets ever intended to use them. But by establishing them, they had, in their opinion lived up to the Yalta Agreement." "It seems obvious," Harriman cabled Roosevelt, "that the Soviets have been attempting to stall us off by misinformation from day to day in order to hold up the sending in of more of our contact officers until they get all of our prisoners out of Poland."[67]

Two facts emerge concerning Western personnel in Poland. First, Soviet officials actively worked to keep them out: (1) they cancelled previously approved visits by Deane and the APC; (2) they recalled Colonels Wilmeth and Kingsbury from Lublin; (3) they placed official assembly points in remote locations; and (4) to avoid Yalta provisions requiring U.S. administration of camps holding American citizens, they denied the existence of concentration points within Poland. Second, Soviet devices for isolating Poland from Western observers simultaneously hampered the repatriation of American ex-POWs from Eastern Europe. In particular, Poland's political future and repatriation became inextricably linked—and not always coincidentally.

As suggested earlier, it seems certain the Kremlin sought to link Western personnel in Poland with Western recognition of a heavily Communist Polish government. Shortly after the United States and Britain vetoed Russia's 9 March suggestion that the Lublin rather than the London Poles be invited to the upcoming United Nations' Charter Conference in San Francisco, high-ranking Soviet officials began tying Polish recognition to American repatriation. On 13 March 1945, for instance, when Harriman complained to Molotov about continuing delays in Deane's approved trip to Poland, the Soviet foreign minister replied that he had to consider not only military but Polish objections. Ignoring the Lublin Committee's stated willingness to cooperate in American repatriation, Molotov suggested that the United States "sign some kind of working agreement with the Poles without recognizing the Poles." When Harriman asked if this were a precondition for the entry of American officials into Poland, the answer was no; but when the American ambassador noted the large number of Soviet repatriation officers in France, the canny Molotov replied that the U.S.S.R. had diplomatic relations with France.[68] Presumably, the repatriation of Americans from Poland would be no problem if the United States would only recognize the Lublin Committee.

The next day Harriman cabled Stettinius that Moscow was "trying to use our liberated prisoners of war as a club to induce us to give increased prestige to the Provisional Polish Government." The problem came from the Kremlin, not the Polish embassy, he felt certain, because the latter had been "extremely cooperative." In total agreement, Stettinius passed Harriman's assessment, along with his own, to Joseph Grew and Charles Bohlen in the State Department and to President Roosevelt.[69] On 28 June 1945, the United States did recognize a Polish government with only token non-Communist participation, but concern over stranded American servicemen played no part in the decision. By that date all of them had been repatriated from Soviet-occupied territory.

After the Nazis' defeat the public assumed bringing "our boys" home from Eastern Europe would be a simple matter,[70] but Allied diplomats found the task to be unexpectedly complex, frustrating, and time-consuming. In contrast, *Pravda* correspondents turned up nothing but "the most pleasant memories" of Soviet assistance in their talks with freed Allied personnel: "They are full of thanks to the Red Army which liberated them from Nazi slavery, ecstatically commending . . . all . . . whom they met during their sojourn on Soviet territory."[71]

With first-person testimony from hitchhiking ex-POWs in hand, Harriman knew better. And Roosevelt knew better because Harriman made sure he did. The ambassador relayed details through Stettinius—the basis for Roosevelt's 3 March note to Stalin—and also directly through military channels: "General Deane and I feel strongly that we should make an issue of the matter of having our much needed contact officers in Poland which is clearly within our rights under the prisoner of war agreement signed at Yalta, not only in order to take care of those who are still in Poland but also because of the probability that there will be substantial numbers liberated by the Red Army in the future." This was on 12 March, and by the fourteenth Harriman had decided that if another direct presidential appeal to Stalin failed, Washington should adopt "direct pressure" on behalf of its POWs. The "retaliatory measures" he and Deane had in mind included: (1) restricting Soviet repatriation officers in France to camps as far from the Western front as L'vov and Odessa were from the Eastern front; (2) withholding Lend-Lease commodities not essential to the Russian war effort; and (3) allowing ex-POWs to give newsmen accounts of "the hardships they have been subjected to between point of liberation and arrival at Odessa."[72]

Not only the embassy staff in Moscow but the War Department was "considerably stirred up" over Russian treatment of American POWs. Secretary Stimson told Stettinius he opposed restrictions on Soviet repatriation officers, and he thought the proposal to publicize poor treatment of liberated GIs "very dangerous." But the Lend-Lease measure intrigued him: "It certainly seems silly that we should go on giving them sugar when they are treating us this way."[73] The secretary of state and his department had their doubts on all points, in particular the fear that these proposals, if adopted, might trigger Soviet retaliation against American servicemen still in Eastern Europe. In response to the misgivings Harriman replied forcefully: "At the present time the Soviet authorities could scarcely give our prisoners less considerate treatment than they are receiving. Anything less than this would be deliberate mistreatment, and I do not feel that they would deliberately mistreat our prisoners, especially since we hold ten of theirs to every one that they hold of ours. All of the retaliatory measures suggested are well within our rights, and simply constitute a rigid interpretation of such rights. General Deane concurs."[74]

Harriman sounded convincing, but he probably miscalculated in presuming that Soviet officials would never "deliberately mistreat American POWs." Had Washington purposefully held millions of Soviet citizens hostage, as Harriman hinted, it is possible that thousands of U.S. servicemen could have faced a decade of forced labor in Siberia, as did German POWs—and millions of Russians, for that matter. The American ambassador also probably overestimated the value of Lend-Lease as a bargaining tool. The continuance of the Red Army's destruction of German divisions was in America's interest, unquestionably saving many GIs' lives. "Would we," as Cordell Hull put it, "cut off military aid and thereby hurt ourselves militarily?"[75]

As it turned out the United States adopted no "retaliatory measures."

For one thing, the Civil Affairs Division of SHAEF needed all the help it could get from the Soviet repatriation mission to administer and communicate with the more than 2 million displaced Soviet nationals. Restricting Russian contact teams to remote locations would have delayed repatriation on the Western front—not a happy prospect to commanders interested in dispensing with responsibility for DPs as soon as possible. As for curtailing nonessential Lend-Lease shipments, the president flatly rejected the idea. In addition to Harriman and Deane, the Operations Division of the War Department, General Marshall, and the JCS had all suggested using aid to Russia for greater diplomatic advantage. But Roosevelt, hoping to maintain a cordial, open-handed relationship with the Soviet Union, "consistently blocked all of these attempts to employ lend-lease as a bargaining device."[76] Finally, the idea of publicizing the POWs' predicament was not well received in Washington. General Marshall cautioned Deane directly: "Under no circumstances will press be allowed access to accounts of Russian treatment of liberated personnel which if published might prejudice future Russian handling of liberated prisoners."[77]

Although Roosevelt never agreed to any form of "direct pressure," on 17 March he did send Stalin another complaint about contact team restrictions, this one sharper than the first. In it he disputed the Soviet leaders' assertion that all Americans liberated by the Red Army were in Odessa or soon would be. On the contrary, Roosevelt had information which he considered "positive and reliable that there are still a considerable number of sick and injured Americans in hospitals in Poland and also that there have been certainly up to the last few days and possibly still are, large numbers of other liberated American prisoners either at Soviet assembly points awaiting entrainment to Odessa or wandering about in small groups."[78] Taking to heart Stimson's and Marshall's advice to make this message "red hot,"[79] the president stiffened the tone of the draft prepared for him by Harriman and Deane by inserting a comment that was blunt for a diplomatic note: "Frankly I cannot understand your reluctance to permit American officers and means to assist their own people in this matter. This Government has done everything to meet each of your requests. I now request you to meet mine in this particular matter."[80]

In his 22 March reply Stalin told Roosevelt his information was "inaccurate." The only Americans on Polish soil, apart from a few men on their way to Odessa, were seventeen hospital cases who were to be flown out shortly. Furthermore, the camps used to shelter liberated U.S. servicemen were in good condition. At any rate, they were much better "than those afforded Soviet ex-prisoners . . . where some . . . were subjected to unfair treatment and unlawful persecutions, including beatings." Soviet authorities had been saying much the same thing for some time, but here Stalin elaborated on his reasons for keeping Deane and others out of Poland: "If it concerned me personally I would be ready to give way to the detriment of my own interests. But in the given instance the matter concerns the interests of Soviet armies at the front and of Soviet commanders who do not want to have around odd officers who, while having no relation to the military operations, need looking after, want all kinds of meetings and contacts, [and] protection against possible acts of sabotage by German agents not yet ferreted out."[81] In contrast, Stalin told Harriman past instances of American aircraft "landing in Poland for ulterior purposes in connection with the Polish underground" had caused him to ground U.S. flyers stationed at Soviet bases.[82] That sounded more like the dictator's real concern.

At any rate, in comments to Roosevelt, Harriman took heated exception to every point in the 22 March note: the statement about good conditions in Soviet camps—"far from the truth"; hardships faced by POWs en route to Odessa—"inexcusable"; and Stalin's assertion that the contact teams would be a burden to the Red Army—"preposterous." Although disappointed by the Soviet response, Roosevelt remained calm. Perhaps he sensed this second refusal was final, and, because he hoped to husband what influence he had for the fight over reorganization of the Polish government, he ignored Harriman's renewed call both for retaliatory measures and for another presidential protest to Stalin on the POW issue.[83]

The exchange between heads of state seems to have had no effect, positive or negative, on Soviet repatriation efforts. Through it all, though, Roosevelt may have begun to see that Soviet-American disputes would have to be dealt with adroitly if major discord were to be avoided in the years to come. In the last few weeks before his death on 12 April, he quarreled with Stalin not only about repatriation, but over what constituted a "democratic" Polish government and whether Washington was seeking a separate peace with Hitler, a charge Roosevelt deeply resented.[84]

Soviet officials tended to the repatriation of U.S. POWs liberated by the Red Army without reference to the requests of American authorities or the stipulations of the Yalta agreement. Especially vehement anti-Soviet accounts ascribe delays and unsatisfactory treatment to deliberate neglect: the Russians simply "could not be bothered with the problems of American prisoners or their welfare."[85] More moderate critics argue that lack of Soviet preparations was to blame: Russia's lack of forethought was to be expected, given a tortoise-like bureaucracy and an understandable preoccupation with the Germans. As some evacuated servicemen testified, "Up front lack of organization" and "ignorance, rather than deliberate action," explained much of their difficulty in getting home.[86] Finally, some observers, more lenient toward the Soviet Union, at least on this subject, point to the chaos of war-ravaged districts through which Americans had to travel. "The delays encountered in the repatriation of former American prisoners of war through Odessa," a State Department official argued, "were not out of proportion with the difficulties normally to be expected in traveling through war torn areas."[87]

Without denying the effects of Moscow's seeming indifference, unpreparedness, and inability to make war-ravaged districts function smoothly, the political situation in Poland most decidedly complicated repatriation from the Eastern front. Stalin admitted to Harriman that this was the case. But did the Soviet premier intend all along to make things difficult for Western repatriation officials in Eastern Europe, or did the exigencies of unanticipated Polish resistance force him to cordon the area off, thus unexpectedly snarling the orderly evacuation of American POWs? It is true, as Malcolm Proudfoot has pointed out, that the Yalta agreement made "inadequate provisions for reciprocal concessions."[88] Still, Stalin initially said he was willing to admit contact teams into Poland. Only when Polish opposition proved to be more formidable than expected did he bar all foreigners from the country, in order to prevent Western sympathizers from either aiding the resistance or publicizing its cause through firsthand accounts.

NOTES

1. "History of the United States Military Mission to Moscow," 30 Oct. 1945, NA RG 165, OPD df 336, Case 233, Part 1, 97-98; Harriman and Abel, *Special Envoy*, 419.

2. USMMM memo for Harriman, 23 Mar. 1945, NA RG 334, USMMM-POWs, 13 Mar. 45–26 Mar. 45.

3. Deane, *Strange Alliance*, 183. See also Dennett and Johnson, eds., *Negotiating*, 10; Glenn B. Infield, *The Poltava Affair: A Russian Warning, an American Tragedy* (New York, 1973), 235.

4. SHAEF (Versailles) to WD, 18 Feb. 1945, NA RG 218, JCS Report 1246, 20 Feb. 1945, Enclosure B; *New York Times*, 24 Jan. 1945; Capt. Patrick A. Teel and 1st Lt. James J. Hannon to Gen. George C. Marshall, 31 Mar. 1945, Prisoners of War file, Tab A, p. 2, Marshall Papers, George C. Marshall Research Foundation, Lexington, Va.

5. JCS Report 1168, 14 Nov. 1944, NA RG 218, CCAC file (2-25-44) Sec. 1.

6. Lt. Gen. Lewis H. Brereton, *The Brereton Diaries* (New York, 1946), 290; Perry M. Smith, *The Air Force Plans for Peace, 1943-1945* (Baltimore, 1970), 52; Gaddis, *Origins*, 84. Moscow regarded American pilots interned in the Soviet Union after Japanese bombing raids as a special category. Periodically, the Soviet secret police allowed groups of internees to "escape" across the Russian border

into Iran. Deane, *Strange Alliance*, 60-63; "Hist. of USMMM," 89, NA RG 165, OPD 336, Case 233, Part 1, 30 Oct. 1945; Brig. Gen. Hayes A. Kroner to Brig. Gen. James M. Bevans, 22 May 1943, NAS RG 319.

7. Col. Russell H. Sweet to ACS, 6 Apr. 1945, NA RG 165, Army CS 383.6, Sec. 7, Cases 350. . . 400.

8. Fischer, "New Emigration," 10.

9. Deane to WD, 28 Feb. 1945, NA RG 218, CCAC df 383.6 (2-25-44) Sec. 2, CCS Report 472/8; Deane to AGWAR, 28 Feb. 1945, NA RG 334, USMMM-POWs, Oct. 1943–Oct. 1945. One unpublished military study claims the Yalta accord theoretically provided for these measures. EUCOM, "RAMP's," 46-47.

10. "Statements of Liberated Ps/W Regarding Treatment while in Russian Hands," 9 Apr. 1945, NA RG 165, WDGSS, OPD df 1942-1945, 383.6 Sec. 15, Case 421, compiled by Col. Russell H. Sweet, chief of OPD Captured Personnel and Material Branch. See also the statement by Lt. Col. Harmon S. Kelsey in Sweet to ACS, 6 Apr. 1945, NA RG 165, Army CS df 383.6, Sec. 7, Cases 350 . . . 400.

11. Col. Don Gilmer to Gen. Hull, 24 May 1945, NA RG 165, WDGSS, OPD df 1943-1945, 383.6.

12. Gaddis, *Origins*, 81.

13. Dennett and Johnson, eds., *Negotiating*, 16. For similar British complaints see *New York Times*, 11 June 1945.

14. Angelo Montella to author, 17 Jan. 1979.

15. Sweet to ACS, 6 Apr. 1945, NA RG 165, Army CS df 383.6, Sec. 7, Cases 350. . .400; "Statement of Ps/W Regarding Treatment in Russian Hands," NA RG 165, WDGSS, OPD df 1942-1945, 383.6 Sec. 15, Case 421; Harriman and Abel, *Special Envoy*, 420.

16. Memo for Harriman, 23 Mar. 1945, NA RG 334, USMMM-POWs, 13 Mar. 1945–26 Mar. 1945; Infield, *Poltava*, 235-36; *New York Times*, 21, 23 Feb. 1945; Deane, *Strange Alliance*, 192.

17. Thorwald, *Illusion*, 73.

18. Dennett and Johnson, eds., *Negotiating*, 14-15. See also Deane, *Strange Alliance*, 192-94; and Harriman to Stettinius, 11 June 1945, *FR, 1945*, V: 1097-98.

19. Harriman and Abel, *Special Envoy*, 420; *New York Times*, 12 Mar. 1945; Memo of Deane-Golubev meeting, 26 Mar. 1945, NA RG 334, USMMM-POWs, Oct. 1943–Oct. 1945.

20. Teel and Hannon to Marshall, 31 Mar. 1945, Prisoners of War file, 1, Marshall Papers; Sam Kydd, *for* You *the War is Over* (London, 1973), 300.

21. Teel and Hannon to Marshall, 31 Mar. 1945, Prisoners of War file, 3, Marshall Papers; Sweet to ACS, 6 Apr. 1945, NA RG 165, WDGSS, 383.6, ACS, Sec. 7, Cases 350. . .400; Col. Sweet to OPD (Pentagon), 9 Apr. 1945, NA RG 165, WDGSS, 383.6, OPD df 1942-1945, Sec. 15, Case 2.

22. *New York Times*, 11 July 1945.

23. Juergen Thorwald, *Flight in the Winter* (New York, 1951), 239.

24. Kydd, *Over*, 299; "Hist. of USMMM," 95, NA RG 165, OPD 336, Case 233, Part I, 30 Oct. 1945; Teel and Hannon to Marshall, 31 Mar. 1945, Prisoners of War file, 2,5, Marshall Papers.

25. Sweet to ACS, 6 Apr. 1945, NA RG 165, Army CS df 383.6, Sec. 7, Cases 350. . .400.

26. Kydd, *Over*, 309-10.

27. Deane, *Strange Alliance*, 197.

28. Ibid. Accounts vary somewhat as to the date. Ibid. gives 27 Feb.; *New York Times*, 3 Mar. 1945, says 3 Mar.; EUCOM, "RAMP's," 50, says early March. A translation of the Russian claim, which appeared in *Pravda*, 10 Mar. 1945, can be found in NA RG 334, USMMM-POWs, Oct. 1943–Oct. 1945 (about 10 Mar. 1945).

29. *New York Times*, 11 June 1945. *Pravda*, 11 Mar. 1945, carried an idealized description of the life of an American ex-POW awaiting repatriation in Odessa, summarized in Harriman to Stettinius, 16 Mar. 1945, NA RG 59, 7116.2114A/3-1645). Hall to USMMM, 12 Mar. 1945, NA RG 334, USMMM-POWs, 13 Mar. 1945–26 Mar. 1945.

30. Kydd, *Over*, 310.

31. Deane, *Strange Alliance*, 197; Harriman to Roosevelt, 8 Mar. 1945, NA RG 334, USMMM-POWs, Oct. 1943–Oct. 1945; Sweet to ACS, 6 Apr. 1945, NA RG 165, WDGSS, Army CS, df 383.6, Sec. 7, Cases 350. . .400—Lt. Col. Louis Gershenow; ibid., 10 Apr. 1945, Case 362, "Summary of Seven Statements by Former American POWs."

32. Allied HDQ, Caserta, to Sec. St., 28 Mar. 1945, NA RG 59, 7116.2114A/3-2845.

33. Kydd, *Over*, 310-12.

34. Deane, *Strange Alliance*, 197; EUCOM, "RAMP's," 26; "Hist. of USMMM," 30 Oct. 1945, NA RG 165, WDGSS, OPD df 336, Case 233, Part 1, p. 95; OCMH, "Exchange," 9. By comparison 1,500 Belgian, 4,310 British, and 27,503 French nationals were repatriated through Odessa. EUCOM, "RAMP's," 63-64.

35. In addition to U.S. personnel, Soviet authorities repatriated 25,102 British, 294,699 French, and 794,113 other Allied nationals, including 33,150 Belgian, 32,530 Dutch, and 756 Danish citizens. "Repatriation of Soviet Citizens," *International Labour Review*, 52 (Nov. 1945), 534; *Stars and Stripes* (South Germany ed.), 8 Oct. 1945; Bethell, *Secret*, 65; Molotov, in minutes of second meeting of first plenary conference of Council of Foreign Ministers, 12 Sept. 1945, NA RG 43.

36. Winant to Stettinius, 28 Jan. 1945, and Vyshinskii to Harriman, 18 Feb. 1945, NA RG 334, USMMM-POWs, Oct. 1943–Oct. 1945.

37. Harriman to Molotov, 16 Feb. 1945, NA RG 334, USMMM-POWs, 13 Mar. 1945–26 Mar. 1945.

38. Polish Embassy in Moscow to USMMM, 13 Feb. 1945, ibid.; Dennett and Johnson, eds., *Negotiating*, 14.

39. Memo of Deane-Slavin meeting, 17 Feb. 1945, NA RG 334, USMMM-POWs, Oct. 1943–Oct. 1945.

40. Deane-Golubev meeting, 19 Feb. 1945, NA RG 334, USMMM-POWs, 13 Mar. 1945–26 Mar. 1945; Deane, *Strange Alliance*, 194; Dennett and Johnson, eds., *Negotiating*, 16.

41. Hamptom to Deane, 25 Feb. 1945, NA RG 334, USMMM-POWs, Oct. 1943–Oct. 1945; Vyshinskii to Harriman, 26 Feb. 1945, NA RG 334, USMMM-POWs, 13 Mar. 1945–26 Mar. 1945.

42. Harriman to Roosevelt, 8 Mar. 1945, *FR, 1945*, V: 1075; Dennett and Johnson, eds., *Negotiating*, 16-17.

43. Gromyko to Stettinius, 20 Nov. 1944, and SHAEF to WD (London base), 6 Dec. 1944, NA RG 218, CCS 383.6 (7-4-44) (2) Sec. 2; CS to SHAEF, 28 Nov. 1944, Map Room Files, MR 330 (2) POWs, Refugees, July-Dec. 1944, box 110.

44. Deane to Marshall, 2 Mar. 1945, NA RG 334, USMMM-POWs, 13 Mar. 1945–26 Mar. 1945.

45. Deane-Golubev meeting, 3 Mar. 1945, ibid.; Deane to WD, 3 Mar. 1945, NA RG 218, CCS df 383.6 (7-4-44) (2) Sec. 4; Deane to Hall, 7 Mar. 1945, NA RG 334, USMMM-POWs, Oct. 1943–Oct. 1945.

46. Stimson-Roosevelt conversation, Stimson diary, 3 Mar. 1945, L, 156, 158, Stimson Papers. As finally worded the cable read, "In view of your disapproval of the plan we submitted, what do you suggest instead?" Roosevelt to Stalin, 4 Mar. 1945, Commission for the Publication of Diplomatic Documents, Ministry of Foreign Affairs of the U.S.S.R., *Correspondence between the Chairman of Council of Ministers of the U.S.S.R. and the Presidents of the U.S.A. and the Prime Ministers of Great Britain during the Great Patriotic War of 1941-1945*, II (New York, 1958), 194.

47. Stalin to Roosevelt, 5 Mar. 1945, Commission, *Correspondence*, II: 194; *FR, 1945*, V: 1073; Map Room Files, MR 33 (2) Special Files, "American POWs in Russia and Poland."

48. Vyshinskii to Deane and Polish Embassy in Moscow to Crockett, 26 Feb. 1945, NA RG 334, USMMM-POWs, 13 Mar. 1945–26 Mar. 1945.

49. Durbrow interview, 6 July 1977. See also Dennett and Johnson, eds., *Negotiating*, 17; Harriman to Byrnes, 14 Mar. 1945, *FR, 1945*, V: 1080.

50. Buhite, "Soviet-American Relations," 391-92; Churchill to Roosevelt, 28 Feb. 1945, and Harriman to Roosevelt, 12 Mar. 1945, *FR, 1945*, V: 132, 1077-78; Commission, *Correspondence*, II: 298, note 82. The Commission, established at Yalta, consisted of Molotov and the American and British ambassadors in Moscow: Harriman and A. Clark Kerr, respectively.

51. Harriman to Molotov, 12 Mar. 1945, NA RG 334, USMMM-POWs, Oct. 1943–Oct. 1945; Harriman to Roosevelt, 12 Mar. 1945, *FR, 1945*, V: 1077-78.

52. Harriman and Abel, *Special Envoy*, 419.

53. Harriman to Roosevelt, 12 Mar. 1945, *FR, 1945*, V: 1077-78. For a similar British-Soviet confrontation at Volkovysk, see *New York Times*, 11 June 1945.

54. Dennett and Johnson, eds., *Negotiating*, 16-17.

55. Kirk to Secretary of State, 12 Apr. 1945, NA RG 59, 762.6114/4-1245.

56. Dennett and Johnson, eds., *Negotiating*, 14, 17; "History of USMMM," 95, NA RG 165, OPD 336, Case 233, Part 1, 30 Oct. 1945.

57. Harriman and Abel, *Special Envoy*, 420; Harriman to Byrnes, 2 Apr. 1945, NA RG 59, 711.62114A/4-245; JCS Report 1168, 14 Nov. 1944, NA RG 218, CCAC file (2-25-44) Sec. 1.

58. Bethell, *Secret*, 36; Harold Nicolson, *The War Years, 1939-1945* (New York, 1967), 455; Thorwald, *Flight*, 240.

59. Vasili Kotov, "Stalin Thinks I'm Dead," *Saturday Evening Post*, 220 (17 Jan. 1948), 110.

60. Deane to Wilmeth, 10 Mar. 1945, NA RG 334, USMMM-POWs, Oct. 1943–Oct. 1945.

61. Teel and Hannon to Marshall, 31 Mar. 1945, Prisoners of War file, 1, 3, Marshall Papers.

62. Allied HDQ (Caserta) to Stettinius, NA RG 59, 711.62114A/3-2845.

63. Sweet to ACS, 6 Apr. 1945, NA RG 165, Army CS df 383.6, Sec. 7, Cases 350. . .400 (interviews with Col. G. V. Millett, Jr., and Lt. Col. Harmon S. Kelsey).

64. Ulam, *Expansion and Coexistence*, 380. See also Buhite, "Soviet-

American Relations," 393; "Hist. of USMMM," 97, NA RG 165, OPD df 336, Case 233, Part 1, 30 Oct. 1945; Jefferson, "Bureaucracy," 329; OCMH, "Exchange," 5; Smith, "American Role," 83-84; Winant to Stettinius, 7 Apr. 1945, *FR, 1945*, V: 1090; British Embassy to SD, 27 Apr. 1945, NA RG 59, 740.00114EW/4-2245.

65. W. Averell Harriman, *America and Russia in a Changing World, a Half Century of Personal Observation* (Garden City, N.Y., 1971), 36. See also Deane, *Strange Alliance*, 190; British Ambassador Hallifax to Byrnes, 7 Apr. 1945, *FR, 1945*, V: 1090.

66. Deane-Golubev meeting, 7 and 10 Mar. 1945, NA RG 334, USMMM-POWs, Oct. 1943–Oct. 1945, and 13 Mar. 1945–26 Mar. 1945; "Hist. of USMMM," 283, NA RG 165, OPD df 336, Case 233, Part 2, 30 Oct. 1945; Deane, *Strange Alliance*, 194.

67. "Hist. of USMMM," 283, NA RG 165, OPD df 336, Case 233, Part 2, 30 Oct. 1945; Harriman to Roosevelt, 12 Mar. 1945, NA RG 334, USMMM-POWs, Oct. 1943–Oct. 1945. For similar restrictions on contact teams in Germany, see EUCOM, "RAMP's," 51; and OCMH, "Exchange," 5.

68. Buhite, "Soviet-American Relations," 392; Polish Embassy in Moscow to Crockett, 26 Feb. 1945, and Harriman-Molotov meeting, 13 Mar. 1945, NA RG 334, USMMM-POWs, 13 Mar. 1945–26 Mar. 1945.

69. Harriman to Stettinius, 14 Mar. 1945, NA RG 334, USMMM-POWs, Oct. 1943–Oct. 1945; Harriman to Stettinius, 14 Mar. 1945, *FR, 1945*, V: 1080; Stettinius to Roosevelt, Grew, and Bohlen, 15 Mar. 1945, NA RG 59, 740.00114 EW/3-1545. For secondary accounts linking the recognition and repatriation questions, see Bethell, *Secret*, 368; Bland, "Harriman," 368; Buhite, "Soviet-American Relations," 390, 392, 396; and Smith, "American Role," 81. Apart from this Polish question, there seems to have been no interplay between repatriation discussions and other Allied diplomatic debates of World War II. Conceivably, other American priorities at Yalta may have contributed to Deane's signing a repatriation accord that would come to be regarded as unsatisfactory, but given the extant documentation, that is a surmise at best.

70. Durbrow interview, 6 July 1977.

71. "About to Return to the Home Country," *Pravda* translation, about 10 Mar. 1945, NA RG 334, USMMM-POWs, Oct. 1943–Oct. 1945. For a Soviet photograph of American servicemen at Odessa, see P. M. Pospelov, ed., *Great Patriotic War of the Soviet Union, 1941-1945, a General Outline* (Moscow, 1974), opposite 481.

72. Harriman to Roosevelt, 8 and 12 Mar. 1945, *FR, 1945*, V: 1074-75, 1078; Harriman to Stettinius, 14 Mar. 1945, NA RG 334, USMMM-POWs, Oct. 1943–Oct. 1945.

73. Transcript of phone conversation between Stettinius and Stimson, 16 Mar. 1945, no. 2723, Stettinius Papers.

74. Harriman to Stettinius, 16 Mar. 1945, NA RG 334, USMMM-POWs, Oct. 1943–Oct. 1945.

75. Quoted in Jefferson, "Bureaucracy," 233.

76. Gaddis, *Origins*, 83. See also ibid., 81, 87; Bland, "Harriman," 247, 250; Harriman and Abel, *Special Envoy*, 422; George C. Herring, Jr., *Aid to Russia 1941-1946: Strategy, Diplomacy, the Origins of the Cold War* (New York, 1973), 135-37; Jefferson, "Bureaucracy," 232-33; Gordon Wright, *The Ordeal of Total War, 1939-45* (New York, 1968), 445.

77. Marshall to Deane, 17 Mar. 1945, NA RG 334, USMMM-POWs, Oct. 1943–Oct. 1945.

78. Roosevelt to Stalin, 18 Mar. 1945 [date received], Commission, *Correspondence*, II: 195-96.

79. Stimson diary, 16 Mar. 1945, L, 192, Stimson Papers.

80. Roosevelt to Stalin, 17 Mar. 1945 (date sent), *FR, 1945*, V: 1082. In its final form part of the text was slightly altered: "I cannot, in all frankness, understand your reluctance. . . ." Roosevelt to Stalin, 18 Mar. 1945 (date received), Commission, *Correspondence*, II: 196.

81. Stalin to Roosevelt, 22 Mar. 1945, Commission, *Correspondence*, II: 196-97; Stalin to Roosevelt, 22 Mar. 1945, *FR, 1945*, V: 1082-83. See also Dennett and Johnson, eds., *Negotiating*, 18.

82. Cited in Richard C. Lukas, *Eagles East: The Army Air Forces and the Soviet Union, 1941-1945* (Tallahassee, Fla., 1970), 214.

83. Harriman to Roosevelt, 24 Mar. 1945, *FR, 1945*, V: 1085-86; Roosevelt to Harriman, 26 Mar. 1945, Map Room Files, MR 33 (2) Special Files, "American POWs in Russia and Poland." On 1 April Roosevelt did protest the exclusion of Polish Commission observer teams in a long note dealing with Polish affairs. Roosevelt to Stalin, 1 Apr. 1945, Commission, *Correspondence*, II: 203-4.

84. Commission, *Correspondence*, II: 195-214.

85. Smith, "American Role," 84.

86. Sweet to ACS, 10 Apr. 1945, NA RG 165, WDGSS, Army CS, df 383.6, Sec. 7, Case 362; Conway, "Intellectual Origins," 202.

87. E. Tomlin Bailey to Mrs. Charles Tazewell, 30 June 1945, NA RG 59, 711.62114A/6-645. See also Ulam, *Expansion and Coexistence*, 380; Werth, *Russia at War*, 958.

88. Proudfoot, *European Refugees*, 155. For the unsuccessful efforts of other Allied nations to send repatriation missions to Soviet-occupied territory, see Jefferson Patterson, chargé in Belgium, to Marshall, 26 Feb. 1946, NA RG 59, 800.4016 DP/2-2646; *New York Times*, 10 Feb. 1945; Proudfoot, *European Refugees*, 213.

4

LIVING UP TO YALTA:

"It Just Wasn't Human"

ALTHOUGH MILLIONS MORE SOVIET THAN AMERICAN citizens ended the war as refugees, most Ostarbeiter and ex–Red Army POWs returned home quickly as compared to liberated U.S. servicemen. Soviet nationals found themselves either in Russian occupation zones or in Western camps; in either case the Allies expedited their repatriation. In 1945 American energy and resoluteness in sending these people home was such that only a fraction of the reluctant managed to escape mandatory extradition.

The manner in which the U.S. Army carried out the repatriation agreement clearly demonstrates that the vast majority of Soviet refugees had no option in the matter. By 28 February 1945, two and a half weeks after the close of the Crimean Conference, the various headquarters under SHAEF had received, and passed on to subordinate commanders, the text of the Deane-Gryzlov accord along with instructions concerning its implementation. This action had no immediate practical significance because no overland exchange of West and East European refugees could take place until Allied ground forces linked up, and that was still about two months off. Before that happened SHAEF, which originally had ordered forced repatriation only for POWs who claimed Soviet nationality, received word from Washington that it was to turn all Soviet citizens over to the Red Army, "regardless of their individual wishes."[1] With all possibilities for hesitation thus removed, U.S. commanders set to the task. Unlike the protracted negotiations, the repatriation of most Soviet nationals, once under way, took only a matter of months. Informal exchanges of Russians for West Europeans began immediately after the first contact between SHAEF and Red Army troops on 25 April 1945. At that point the Western Allies held approximately 370,000 Soviet citizens in their custody and were rapidly accumulating even greater numbers.[2]

Even with irregular exchanges on the local level, full implementation of the Yalta accord required an additional agreement detailing logistics. On 30 April 1945, Deputy Foreign Minister A. Y. Vyshinskii proposed to

George Kennan, American chargé in Moscow, that overland exchange points be established for the repatriation of Allied nationals since SHAEF and Red Army forces had, by this time, made contact in Germany. Kennan immediately cautioned Secretary of State Edward Stettinius that "the Russians will do their best to interpret our acceptance in such a way as to oblige us to hand over at once all the Russians we find, regardless of their status, before we have had a chance to do any sifting among those found to have been fighting with the Germans."[3] Neither Stettinius nor the military authorities heeded this warning.

Face-to-face deliberations on this matter began 16 May, the date Lieutenant General K. D. Golubev arrived at Halle, Germany, near Leipzig, heading a Soviet delegation of four major generals, forty additional officers, and a fifty-one-man security detail complete with an armored car. Major General Stanley R. Michelson, chief of DP affairs for General Dwight D. Eisenhower, directed SHAEF's more modest delegation.[4]

Although the war had displaced many more Soviet than American citizens, Stalin's diplomats were no more willing at Halle than at Yalta to compromise in the interest of expediting repatriation. They brought with them an attitude that the American side felt "bordered on arrogance," and a draft agreement from which they could not deviate without time-consuming referrals to Moscow.[5] Apparently expecting unqualified U.S. acceptance of its document, Golubev and party only reluctantly gave up any clause at all, even one entitling Soviet citizens to transport for all their accumulated possessions, including furniture and cattle. The Russian draft also would have bound each side to deliver Allied personnel "without exception," "unswervingly," and "up to the last individual." SHAEF much preferred a less ironclad "technical military plan"; but even without the all-encompassing Soviet phraseology, the Kremlin still got what it wanted by the simple inclusion in the signed document of "all" to make every DP subject to repatriation. Perhaps that was partly the result of the proximity to Halle of U.S. and British ex-POWs under Red Army control; to Robert Murphy, State Department political adviser for Germany, they were "almost . . . hostages." Even avoiding such thorny issues as the definition of "Soviet citizens" or the presence of Russians in German uniform, the negotiations still took eight days.[6]

Signed on 23 May 1945, the Halle or Leipzig agreement designated exchange points, regulated the number of persons to be processed daily, and established a priority for the repatriation of citizens of the Big Three over those of other Allies, neutrals, and ex-enemy nations.[7] The accord called for eleven exchange points in Germany and two in Austria.[8] The agreement stated that the number of Russians and West Europeans to be transferred daily should not exceed 50,000, but in practice the number occasionally did. The average daily total of Russian repatriates from all assembly points for the period May 27–June 5 was 60,000 and for June 9–12, 101,650, with individual exchange points usually handling from 2,000 to 5,000 people.[9]

The heaviest movement occurred between May and September 1945, a period one SHAEF official referred to as the "comparative honeymoon of East-West cooperation."[10] In these five months SHAEF delivered 2,034,000 Soviet citizens, at least 89 percent of all Russians repatriated from Western occupation zones.[11] After September, repatriation slowed to a trickle. From 1 July 1945, when the International Refugee Organization (IRO) took over the work of UNRRA, to 31 December 1951, when the IRO ceased operation, only 1,836 persons returned to the Soviet Union.[12]

Considering the enormous number of displaced Soviet nationals, the U.S. Army carried out most of its obligations in a remarkably short period of time. The transport priority accorded Soviet citizens over all other eastbound DPs helped speed their repatriation. Likewise, the explicit statement in the Leipzig contract that "all former prisoners of war and citizens of the U.S.S.R. . . . will be delivered" accelerated the movement.[13] The West's anxiety over its stranded POWs, which originally prompted the repatriation agreement, also helps explain the energy and speed with which the task was undertaken. Finally, SHAEF realized that all those not repatriated promptly would have to be cared for at the military's expense in the coming winter. General Eisenhower noted, "From our viewpoint repatriation should be expedited as Russians are a considerable charge against Allied resources in this theater." At this juncture moral and humanitarian considerations did not loom as large as one monumental question of logistics: what could the army possibly do with these people if they did not go home?[14]

To repatriate Soviet citizens, Western authorities commandeered every available means of transportation. Prior to the Wehrmacht's defeat, almost all Soviet repatriates had traveled by ship, most to Odessa, a few by way of Murmansk or Vladivostok. After the German capitulation, truck, rail, and air travel quickly supplanted the sea routes. In May and June 1945 a train a day filled with Soviet citizens left France for the Soviet occupation zones. At the same time Western aircraft transported a steady stream of repatriates eastward from France and the Ruhr. General Ernest Harmon, who witnessed C–47 transport planes setting out for Berlin with displaced Soviet nationals, asked one of the pilots how his frightened passengers fared over the long haul. The airman "said they gave no trouble, that he just sloshed down the center of the plane with a bucket of water, and he was ready for another load."[15]

Besides these means, Russian refugees moved eastward by truck, by cart, by ferry, and especially, by foot. This Slavic diaspora included few elderly, many women and children, and young, young soldiers. They rode or marched with suitcases, boxes, crates, canvas sacks, even baby buggies—some filled with babies, some with belongings. The infants cried, but the returners invariably smiled. Were they happy, or did they know they had better be? At the very least the homegoing felicities seemed contrived, better yet, programmed for American cameramen: Red Army repatriates dancing to accordion and drum; trucks bedecked in greenery; and marchers carrying aloft the Red flag, or crudely painted symbols of hammer and sickle, or a poor likeness of Stalin and a worse one of Truman. [16] This was the summer of 1945 when most Soviet citizens went back willingly—or, recognizing they had no choice, knew they had better look willing.

The hard core openly resisting repatriation, approximately 10 percent of the displaced, would give the U.S. Army much trouble in the next two years; going home they would have no smiles for the GIs equipped with billy clubs and tear gas. But those problems were in the future. At the time, the logistics of the summer's refugee transport, which included many millions of Europeans in addition to Russians, seemed challenge enough to the Western allies. SHAEF found the press of humanity so overwhelming that in late May it ordered some bridges in American territory blown up, in order to control the flood of refugees. Civil Affairs Division Director General John Hilldring defined his staggering task as the organization of a "vast mass movement in various directions, with all the uncertainties and difficulties of transportation and arrangements with authorities controlling neighboring countries." [17]

Refugees from Russia, albeit the largest contingent, still constituted but a fraction of the total DPs under SHAEF administration. By 19 November 1945 Western commands had repatriated 2,037,000 Soviet citizens, but many more from other Allied countries: estimates vary from 3.5 to 4.5 million non-Soviet DPs transported by this date. [18] So for SHAEF repatriation officers, displaced Soviet nationals might prove their single most troublesome charges but by no means their only headache. Even if they were perfectly willing to go home, the sheer mass of other refugees made for monumental logistical nightmares.

Part of SHAEF's responsibility involved the administration of numerous camps for DPs, a vexing task for military men who often felt out of their element. To start with, the superior rations that DP camp commanders had to give citizens of the Big Three caused difficulties. The Yalta agreement required that civilian refugees who were nationals of the three major Allies receive the daily calorie allotment issued to army privates (4,000 in the American sectors, 3,600 in the British), rather than the lower figure set for refugees of other friendly powers (2,000). And different ration allowances set for liberated POWs further complicated the matter. U.S. military intelligence discovered that preferential treatment for some resulted in overweight DPs. It also fueled the black market, since the privileged group had surplus goods to sell to the less favored German populace.[19]

The segregation of Soviet nationals from other DPs, as Yalta required, also caused headaches for Western camp commanders. It contributed to the creation of a DP elite who became more and more difficult to control. One official who despaired of gaining the cooperation of Russian refugees by conciliatory means refused to allow his charges to raise the hammer and sickle over the camp until the grounds were cleaned. The incident disturbed General Harmon, who criticized the official for choosing a form of discipline with such obvious political overtones. He told the sergeant he was doing a "grand job," but to avoid "international complications," he had to "contrive some other form of punishment."[20] As a general rule the greater the degree of preferential treatment accorded Soviet nationals, the poorer the management of SHAEF camps. Having them "concentrated in their own camps with a considerable degree of autonomy appears to have contributed to their disorderliness."[21]

The language barrier proved to be another problem. Robert Murphy, the U.S. political adviser in occupied Germany, lamented the "dearth of English-speaking Soviet liaison men and Russian-speaking American officers" available for work among DPs and former POWs. As a result of the scarcity of linguists, repatriation was hampered: many camp officials and camp dwellers could not communicate and the number of screening boards assigned to determine cases of disputed citizenship was inadequate.[22] Still, the military overcame these difficulties and rapidly transferred most Soviet nationals out of Western occupation zones without incident.

Dramatic episodes of forced repatriation usually involved military collaborators who had good reason to fear a vindictive Soviet government. And none had more to fear than General Andrei Vlasov and his Russian Liberation Army. Before its inglorious repatriation the ROA had one fleeting moment of triumph. In an action greatly embarrassing to Moscow, and therefore written out of Russian textbooks, 18,000 anti-Soviet, ex–Red Army soldiers cast off their German connections and helped Czech partisans liberate Prague. By 5:30 P.M. on 6 May Vlasov's First Division had disarmed 10,000 Germans at a cost of 300 casualties. An American reconnaissance patrol entered the capital the same night. With unconscious but "staggering artlessness" a blissfully ignorant U.S. officer advised the Russians to remain in the Czech capital and preserve order until Soviet forces arrived. Aghast at the suggestion, the First Division considered it an invitation "to walk open-eyed into certain death."[23]

At this moment the Czechs were as uncomfortable as the Americans were confused. With the Red Army on its way, Prague's provisional government quickly sought to put distance between itself and its awkward anti-Stalinist "allies." On 6 May, the same day the ROA rendered thousands of Wehrmacht troops harmless, Czech insurgents broadcast to the population: "We don't want help from traitors. . . .We have only scorn for their offer. Do not stain the clean shield of anti-German resistance by allying yourselves with the Vlasov traitors."[24] Less because of Czech ingratitude than the approach of Soviet forces under Marshal I. S. Konev, ROA division commander Sergei Buniachenko ordered his troops to evacuate Prague and head westward for American lines, some fifty miles away. In addition to forestalling any possible military move by the United States, Moscow was anxious to extinguish all traces of an anti-Soviet Russian army and to foster the Red Army's designation as sole liberator of Eastern Europe. The Red Army entered the Czech capital on 9 May and has considered itself the city's savior ever since. Even General Konev says his troops liberated Prague.[25]

Hoping for political asylum, the remnants of Vlasov's army struggled to reach Western lines. The bulk of Buniachenko's First Division, some 15,000 soldiers, surrendered to the U.S. Third Army on 10 May. At the same time the incomplete Second Division, which never saw action, disbanded and scattered throughout Bavaria and Austria. A handful escaped, but in the next few weeks SHAEF rounded up the majority of the Second's 18,000 men, most of them recent transfers from prison camps. Third Army Generals George Patton and Alexander Patch felt sympathy for the plight of these prisoners, but the War Department and General Eisenhower made it clear that all collaborator units had to be turned over to Soviet officials. And so most were by the simple expedient of a mid-May shift in the Soviet-American demarcation line out of Czechoslovakia, which placed the ill-fated ROA in the hands of the Red Army. In this instance mass extradition proved comparatively painless for SHAEF.[26]

The exact timing for the repatriation of General Vlasov himself may have been accidental—he was not returned so much as commandeered by a special Soviet unit while in American custody—but no matter: he would have been turned over in any event. On the afternoon of 12 May 1945, a small American convoy including two tanks set out with Vlasov for U.S. regimental headquarters at Pilsen. The column had no more than left Vlasov's last residence, a picture postcard castle near Schlusselburg, Czechoslovakia, when it ran into a Red Army roadblock. Immediately, a

Soviet officer made directly for Vlasov's car and removed him at the point of a machine gun. The Americans, with superior numbers and weapons, made no attempt to hold on to their high-ranking prisoner, leaving questions to this very day about the U.S. role in Vlasov's repatriation. "Unspeakably weary" and letting events carry him as they would, he is said to have opened his coat yelling, "Fire," at Captain M. I. Yakushev, his third captor in a war not kind to its prisoners. But the Red Army officer did not harm Vlasov, since, as General Georgii Zhukov recalled, it had been "decided to capture him alive to make him pay in full for his treachery."[27]

At the end of the month and on into June, America's British ally repatriated tens of thousands of Osttruppen at Lienz and Judenburg, Austria. Nikolai Krasnov, Jr., a Yugoslav citizen forcibly turned over with Soviet nationals at Lienz, was allowed to leave Russia in 1955 after ten years' imprisonment. His memoirs corroborate other sources that charge the British with wholesale forced repatriation not only of Soviet citizens, but of pre–World War II émigrés. At Lienz alone, this amounted to several dozen white Russian generals and hundreds of lesser officers.[28] With some passion, Solzhenitsyn labels this "an act of double-dealing consistent with the spirit of traditional English diplomacy."[29] In contrast to Britain, the United States explicitly exempted pre-1939 émigrés as early as March 1945, one small source of consolation to opponents of indiscriminate repatriation.[30]

In the summer of 1945 the extradition of a relative handful of Osttruppen from New Jersey proved much more taxing to U.S. officials than the entire ROA operation of May. Now the military had to contend with adverse stateside publicity, which more easily found its way into the newspapers; with a cabinet-level controversy in Washington over implementation of the Yalta accord; and with embarrassing and dangerous confrontations with emotionally distraught prisoners. After the German surrender, Acting Secretary of State Joseph Grew saw no need to postpone further the repatriation of "claimants" of POW status of Soviet origin on the grounds of possible Nazi retaliation against American prisoners. Consequently on 12 May 1945 he advised the military to reevaluate the classification of ex–Red Army men captured in Wehrmacht ranks— 118 moved from Camp Rupert to Camp Ruston, Louisiana, and any others discovered in stateside German POW camps.[31] Despite the longstanding objections of Secretary of War Henry Stimson and Attorney General Francis Biddle (see ch. 2), SWNCC voted on 18 May to repatriate the remaining Osttruppen on U.S. territory. Apparently as a sop to their opponents and as a means of circumventing the lack of an extradition treaty with the U.S.S.R., SWNCC specified Germany rather than the United States as the site for the turnover. By mid-June the U.S. Army had moved the 118 men from Camp Ruston to Fort Dix, New Jersey, along with thirty-six other Soviet citizens captured in Wehrmacht uniform, the last to be screened out of the more than 600 German POW camps across the country.[32]

Nerves by now were on edge—those of the jailed and those of the jailers. Most of the POWs at Fort Dix had been moved from Europe to England, then to camps all over the United States, then to Idaho, Louisiana, and finally New Jersey. Kept in perpetual turmoil by transcontinental shuffling, many disconcerting screenings, and more rumors, the mood of these prisoners could turn nasty and dangerous at the slightest provocation. Tensions at Fort Dix continued to mount as passing time fueled growing dread among the unhappy inmates. But the waiting continued because of ongoing controversy in Washington over their impending repatriation. The Provost Marshal General's Office (PMGO), in charge of all stateside POWs, thus had to contend not only with fire below, but fire above.

The first episode of the summer, mid- to late June, involved State Department personnel. R. W. Flournoy, the department's legal adviser, strongly objected to forced repatriation from Fort Dix. He took particular exception to use of the Geneva Convention in support of this action. Article 75's requirement that "repatriation of prisoners shall be effected with the least possible delay" did not pertain to this case, Flournoy maintained, because the treaty applied "as between allied belligerents. . . . it can hardly be said that it can properly be invoked as between the United States and the Soviet Union." But more than this technical point, he argued that the Geneva accord's "true spirit and intent" was being violated: "From beginning to end, the Convention contains provisions for the welfare of prisoners of war, based upon the dictates of humanity and decency. I find nothing in the Convention which either requires or justifies this Government in sending the unfortunate Soviet nationals in question to Russia, where they will almost certainly be liquidated."[33]

Nevertheless, other State Department officials worked out a plan for simultaneous, technical compliance with the Geneva and Yalta accords—treaties whose aims were hardly compatible. On 23 June, E. A. Plitt of the Special War Problems Division spelled out the procedure and the rationale: "The obligation under the Geneva Prisoners of War Convention to repatriate prisoners of war provides a way out via repatriation to Germany where our military authorities [to satisfy Yalta] will be able to turn them over to the Soviet authorities." Flournoy had nothing but contempt for this solution, which he perceived as jesuitic: "The object of the treaty is to protect the rights of prisoners of war . . . whereas the object of this proposed measure is to return the persons in question to Russia. Apparently it is proposed to send them via Germany merely in order to bring their return within the letter of the Geneva Convention."[34]

With Flournoy overruled, the matter seemed settled. At 9:00 A.M. on 29 June 1945 guards at Fort Dix began preparations for transferring their 154 prisoners to New York for passage to Germany. A full-fledged riot ensued. The crazed inmates tried unsuccessfully to provoke U.S. soldiers into firing on them. When that failed, they barricaded themselves in their quarters and tried to set fire to the building. Next camp officials ordered tear gas, which brought a charge out a rear door. POWs armed with mess kit knives wounded three GIs, then rushed another group of guards who opened fire, wounding seven prisoners. The disarming of this group finally ended the turmoil, which had lasted about thirty minutes. Upon entering the smoking barracks to put out the fire, camp guards discovered three cases of suicide by hanging. Fifteen other ropes were strung up, suggesting that fatalities might have been much higher but for the timely use of tear gas.[35]

The day after the violent demonstration at Fort Dix, military officials moved this last remaining group of Vlasovites in the United States to Camp Shanks, New York, en route to the ship that was to return them to Europe. Anxious to avoid further trouble, army officials ordered that the convoy carry one guard with each driver. Three hundred spectators and eighty military police armed with submachine guns were waiting when the unusual procession, which included eight ambulances, arrived at Pier 51 on the North River. With the timing of a movie scenario, the War Department countermanded the deportation order just as the POWs were about to be transferred to the waiting ship. Secretary Stimson ordered the group returned to Fort Dix, pending a complete examination of the entire affair. The Inspector General's Department conducted an investigation and concluded that fear of repatriation caused the riot, not the use of force to prevent their return, as Soviet General K. D. Golubev alleged.[36]

A final decision on the fate of the Vlasovites came on 11 July 1945. That day, at a State Department meeting with Grew presiding, it was decided that, given the Yalta repatriation accord, the United States had no choice but to turn the Vlasovites over to Soviet authorities and had to use force, if necessary. Grew informed Stimson of this decision the next day. From the twelfth to the twenty-first, representatives of the State Department and PMGO conducted further interviews with the remaining Vlasovites, now numbering 153. Seven proved to be mistakenly classified as Soviet citizens. Still not satisfied that all were properly identified, Grew and Robert Patterson, who later succeeded the ailing Stimson as secretary of war, ordered yet another investigation on 23 July 1945.[37] After this screening of all 153 men, the investigators compiled a thirty-nine-page paper that elaborated on but did not alter the conclusion reached earlier by the Inspector General's Department. The report related the obvious: the Fort Dix POWs did not want to go home.[38] "Only two prisoners, one officer and one enlisted man, expressed either a desire or willingness to return to Soviet Russia."[39]

Because of the story's dramatic character, because repatriation from Fort Dix was a protracted affair, and because the episode took place on home soil, the American press covered the story in considerable detail. No doubt the continuing publicity helps explain the unusually close attention Washington paid to this relative handful of reluctant repatriates. Also, Acting Secretary of State Grew may have been using the final investigation to delay a decision until the new secretary, James F. Byrnes, returned from the Potsdam Conference.[40]

As prudent as the repeated screenings may have been, they made things difficult for PMGO, especially the camp commander at Fort Dix, Brigadier General Madison Pearson. He had to contend not only with the volatile POWs but also with worrisome Russian officials. A Colonel Malkov asked General Pearson to single out the more cooperative POWs for talks with Soviet representatives. Such interviews had been common in the past, but in this instance Pearson refused, tensions being what they were. As one of the general's officers put it, "Since the incident [of June 29], the POWs have been held closely and let alone because nobody has said what was to be done. We have been sitting on a powder keg for two weeks."[41]

Even without visits from hostile Soviet officials, guards reported that the prisoners remained "somewhat ugly and morose." The multiple screenings had not helped matters: "those who were interviewed did not sleep well if at all during the night immediately after the last interview." Pearson could not undo the past interrogations that had so frightened his charges, but he could order a regimen that would minimize the possibility of suicide. He put the Vlasovites in three barracks under twenty-four-hour surveillance and stationed enough guards carrying machine guns to cover every floor, stairwell, entrance, and latrine. The men ate from paper plates and cups without use of knives or forks. GIs collected their metal spoons after every meal. The POWs lost their shoe laces, belts, and suspenders, everything that conceivably could be fashioned into a noose. Mattresses, yes, but no bunks, since parts of bedsteads "could be used as weapons or implements of self-destruction."[42]

As tough as this policing was on all concerned, it at least held out the possibility of reprieve should Byrnes, upon his return from Potsdam, set in motion a fundamental reevaluation of America's policy of forced repatriation. The secretary of state, however, simply allowed the transfer to proceed. After the extraordinary preliminaries the oft-postponed repatriation finally took place without incident—at least on the U.S. side of the line. As SWNCC had proposed, for legal convenience, the transfer took place in Germany, at Hof, a point on the Nuremburg-Leipzig autobahn. Soviet repatriation officers finally took custody of Fort Dix's 146 confirmed Vlasovites on 31 August 1945, two months and two days after the New Jersey riot that delayed but did not change their fate.[43]

Suicide saved three of the Fort Dix prisoners from extradition. Instead of north to New York harbor and east to Germany, then Russia, the bodies of one ex–Red Army private and two second lieutenants were moved south to Finns Point National Cemetery, near Fort Mott State Park, New Jersey. Three tombstones there, on the left bank of the Delaware River, constitute the sum total of physical evidence that the United States forcibly repatriated at least 4,000 Soviet citizens from American soil.

By August the British in Austria were old hands at this unseemly business, but American occupation forces in Europe were just learning that violent opposition could accompany the transfer of Soviet citizens eastward. A disturbance that month at Camp Kempten in extreme southwestern Bavaria opened the eyes of privates and generals alike to the unpleasantness that accompanied forced repatriation. U.S. participants came away perplexed, shocked, disgusted, or all three. Obliged by Soviet officers to check DP rosters, American officials at Kempten found 410 persons, including some women and children, who were subject to removal eastward, regardless of their individual wishes. U.S. interrogators, who discovered quite a few members of Von Pannwitz's First Cossack Division and some ROA men, at least took care to screen out old émigrés. Still, the prospects for handling these people without incident appeared remote, what with the entire camp population nervous and edgy, especially after 16 July when a survivor of British repatriation in Austria turned up at Kempten with many horror stories. Finally, on 11 August camp officials announced that those subject to repatriation would leave for the Soviet zone the next day.

Panic seized the camp. That night those with some presence of mind, maybe half of the 410, slipped away past a light security detail. The rest took refuge in Kempten's makeshift church along with many old émigré sympathizers. Early on the twelfth U.S. troops entered the building calling out the names of proven Soviet citizens. None stepped forward. Believing orders were orders, the GIs set about prying their victims out of the mass huddled against one wall of the church. The altar and icons fell; fists and rifle butts flew; shots rang out. The soldiers dragged every last person from the building, some by their arms or legs, some by their hair.

An unsubstantiated émigré account exaggerates in claiming thirty-five dead.[44] But at the very least some of the numerous injured were seriously hurt, including an Orthodox priest hospitalized with head wounds. Oleg Lutkov, a survivor of Kempten, relates: "People cut their throats and slashed their wrists, jumped out of upper-story windows, and used any means they could think of to kill themselves to keep from falling into Soviet hands."[45]

With the church cleared, camp officials again sorted out old émigrés from those bound for repatriation. Minus the injured and the absent, American troops had only ninety persons left to truck to a waiting train. Before its departure the next morning no more than fifty remained, the rest having evaded their none-too-strict guards.[46]

About the same time as the Kempten trouble, an eighteen-year-old private from Pennsylvania found himself in the midst of a similar operation. The First Division, Third Army, of which he was a part, was transferring hundreds of Vlasovites captured in Italy from Bavaria to Soviet-occupied Czechoslovakia. This ex-GI, willing to tell his tale if his name was not used, knew at the time precious little of what his orders entailed. It seems U.S. officers had learned by experience that only reluctantly would their men use force to return unwilling subjects to Soviet control; thus, American commanders kept participating troops in the dark as to their assignment, as much as they could, as long as they could. The Pennsylvania ex-private recalled his company and others being pulled for a rare, full-scale inspection. No one passed—no one was supposed to. The result was assignment to an unknown but very special detail: "Nobody knew a damn thing; they tricked us." Only when the GIs arrived at a rail line did they learn they had drawn guard duty on a POW train bound for Czechoslovakia. Why their Russian charges, merely going home, had to be strictly supervised perplexed American soldiers until, finally, they learned their prisoners had fought for the Germans. These men were "no young kids," but rather high-ranking officers, all the more reason for their reluctance to go home.

U.S. authorities took elaborate precautions to prevent suicides. The POWs had been issued blue shirts and a pair of pants, but no shoes and no belts. Each boxcar held thirty inmates and four guards, but no fixtures save a makeshift toilet—an empty three-foot tall carbide can with blunted edges. A U.S.–inspired rumor that the prisoners were to be freed had no effect. Instead, despair reigned. Some sobbed to themselves; some tried to set fire to their boxcars; some bared their chests pleading with GIs to shoot them. One POW somehow cut his throat; others tried to escape. "One, we were told, jumped out a boxcar window and died. Anyway, the train stopped [to pick him up]."

Three or four young looking Soviet guards who got on each car at the border "chewed out" the ex–Red Army men unmercifully, all the while pointing submachine guns at them in a knowing way. Over and over the ex-GI recalled, "They was giving them heck." Sending back those Russians "dead or alive" was "an awful sight"; but what was a private supposed to do? "If you didn't it'd be your hide I suppose." The U.S. guards had rumors about Stalin and Roosevelt agreeing to repatriation, ready or not; they had their weapons; and they had their orders. One Pennsylvania summer night in 1977 a veteran of World War II answered a host of hard questions about repatriation—but he also asked the hardest one: "Who's going to have to answer for all this suffering?"[47]

Americans found it not only shocking but incomprehensible when Soviet refugees targeted for extradition "bit each others' jugular veins . . . rather than submit to repatriation."[48] Appalled by the consequences of the Yalta exchange accord, which he originally had supported, General Eisenhower, on 4 September, ordered a ban on the use of force, at least until Washington had time to reconsider its position.[49] But with rumors rife and falsehoods nearly as common, DPs did not always believe the welcome news that, for now anyway, no one would be made to go home. On 6 September, U.S. authorities attempted to move 600 Ukrainian and ninety-six Armenian men, women, and children from Mannheim to a Stuttgart DP center. Camp wags had it that the real destination would be the Soviet Union, whereupon rumor quickly gave way to riot. A subsequent War Department investigation, prompted by stateside émigré protests, revealed that "a huge, powerful individual, attempting to incite the crowd to riot, refused to obey orders and was subdued forcibly. . . . the crowd surged toward the American soldier guard. One shot was fired in the air, and the crowd became quiet." The melee led either to the resistance leader's injury (official account) or death (émigré account). At any rate, U.S. guards did not forcibly load their trucks that day, and as a result, no DPs left Mannheim for Stuttgart. Although this incident may have resulted from innocent misunderstanding, news of it, on top of knowledge of the use of force all summer, prompted Congresswoman Clare Booth Luce to query the War and State departments about "the apparent conflict which exists between unpublished paragraphs of the Yalta Agreement and our common understanding here of the kind of freedom for which our soldiers fought."[50]

On 20 December SWNCC revised its "unpublished paragraphs" by exempting Soviet civilians from mandatory repatriation. (For details, see ch. 5.) While former Ostarbeiter could now rest easier, the SWNCC decree had the effect of lifting General Eisenhower's ban on the use of force in repatriating military collaborators and ex-POWs. On 16 January 1946

Eisenhower, in an address before the U.S. Congress, emphasized the army's role in repatriating millions of DPs with, as he said, "sympathy and high regard for the humanitarian nature of the problem."[51] Yet those sentiments hardly squared with the U.S. military's part in returning Soviet citizens in Germany, some of whose departure commenced the day after the general's speech.

Dachau, the Nazis' first concentration camp, also served up America's first forced repatriates under the new SWNCC guidelines. Violence erupted on 17 January 1946, when camp guards failed in an attempt to load 399 Russians onto a train bound for the Soviet zone. On their second try, two days later, U.S. authorities took elaborate precautions to keep casualties to a minimum. Five hundred American and Polish guards carrying night sticks surrounded the two barracks housing Soviet collaborators. The POWs left the first building without incident, but inmates of the second barricaded themselves in; tried but failed to set the building on fire; tore off their clothes; and linked arms in a vain attempt to stay put. Finally, using tear gas to subdue the resisters, troops wearing gas masks stormed the barracks.

The scene inside was one of human carnage. The crazed men were attempting to take their own lives by any means. Guards cut down some trying to hang themselves from the rafters; two others disemboweled themselves; another man forced his head through a window and ran his throat over the glass fragments; others begged to be shot. In a moving dispatch to Washington Robert Murphy reported that "tear gas forced them out of the building into the snow where those who had cut and stabbed themselves fell exhausted and bleeding in the snow." Thirty-one men tried to take their own lives. Eleven succeeded: nine by hanging and two from knife wounds. Camp authorities managed to entrain the remaining 368. Despite the presence of American guards and a Soviet liaison officer, six of these escaped en route to the Soviet occupation zone. More and more the repatriation of unwilling persons was coming to disturb battle-hardened troops. A GI who had had Russians at Dachau beg him to shoot them and who had cut others down from their makeshift gallows detested the job. Thoroughly unnerved by the business, he concluded, "It just wasn't human."[52]

Once the Dachau wounded were well enough to travel, American troops escorted them to Plattling, Bavaria, ninety miles to the northeast, where U.S. authorities were now concentrating the several thousand remaining Vlasovites in Germany. Elements of the ROA's Second Division had been there since September 1945 and were joined by even more men from Buniachenko's First Division, including remnants of the notorious Kaminskii Brigade.[53]

William Sloane Coffin, Jr., served in 1946 as the chief U.S. interpreter at Plattling. Although he came to regret his part in repatriation, the job of translating for three screening boards of three full colonels each involved him intimately in the process of sorting out eligible and exempt Russians. Officially, only the brigadier general in charge, the screening boards, and Coffin knew the purpose of the "Top Secret" interrogations, but the tales of Dachau survivors left little to the prisoners' imagination. Besides, they wanted to believe the U.S. promises that no one would be forced to go home.[54]

Although at first hostile toward these military collaborators, Plattling's chief interpreter came to abhor the prospects of repatriation nearly as much as the prisoners:

> When the screening began, I had little sympathy for these Russians in their battered German uniforms. I couldn't see how any decent Russian could have volunteered to fight for so arch a villain as Hitler, who had invaded and pillaged their country, had incarcerated their compatriots in labor camps and put six million Jews to death in gas chambers. But as the colonels, eager to establish their cover and satisfy their curiosity, encouraged the Russians to tell their personal histories, I began to understand the dilemma the men had faced. They spoke not only of the cruelties of collectivization in the thirties but of arrests, shootings and wholesale deportations of families. Many of the men themselves had spent time in Soviet jails. . . . Soon my own interest was so aroused that I began to spend evenings in the camp hearing more and more tales of arrest and torture. . . . Hearing . . . the personal histories of those who had joined Vlasov's army made me increasingly uncomfortable with the words "traitor" and "deserter," as applied to these men. Maybe Stalin's regime was worthy of desertion and betrayal?[55]

As daily the screening boards heard multiple renditions of human agony, the colonels' discomfort compounded as well. They found their work at Plattling less and less to their liking, but "they had their orders." The unseemly side of the operation simply increased their desire to be done with it. The very night before their surprise repatriation the Russians staged a major production with the screening board colonels as guests of honor. The officers, however, declined, instead spending that last night drinking. They ordered their chief interpreter to fill in for them. Although incensed at the colonels' desertion, Coffin did as he was told. Knowing what the morrow would bring, he spent what ordinarily would have been a delightful evening in misery. Escorted to front row center, Coffin found himself immersed in the performers' bittersweet nostalgia: Lermontov's patriotic verse lauding Russia's stand against Napoleon, haunting choruses and balalaikas, and folk dances. That night homesick children celebrated a motherland they greatly loved—and feared.

For a while I thought I was going to be physically ill. Several times I turned to the commandant sitting next to me. It would have been easy to tip him off. There was still time. The camp was minimally guarded. Once outside the men could tear up their identity cards, get other clothes. It was doubtful that the Americans would try hard to round them up. Yet I couldn't bring myself to do it. It was not that I was afraid of being courtmartialed; the commandant probably wouldn't give me away. But I too had my orders. . . . The closest I came was at the door when the commandant said good night. . . . I almost blurted out . . . "Get out and quick." But I didn't. Instead I drove off cursing the commandant for being so trusting.[56]

U.S. officials set 24 February as the date for the Plattling operation, again taking great precautions to deliver their charges to Soviet authorities intact. In the predawn hours troops—and tanks, if numerous reports are to be believed—surrounded barracks containing nearly 1,600 men. Truck headlights and camp searchlights shone on GIs as they went about loading the last sizeable remnant of the abortive Russian Liberation Army onto waiting lorries. Again the barricades went up and came down; again men hung themselves and were cut down; again heads smashed windows and necks voluntarily met glass fragments still fixed in their frames; again chests and wrists bled from razor blades and homemade knives. It was a wonder only five died. Trucks accompanied by armored cars delivered 1,590 men to the Plattling railway station. GIs made a second, careful body search and double-checked the POW roster, then loaded their charges onto boxcars for the trip to Schoenberg in the Soviet zone.

As dramatic as the scene was, very little had occurred so far to distinguish Plattling from Camp Rupert or Lienz or Fort Dix or Kempten or Dachau. That changed when some officer somewhere ordered the pathetic scene filmed. The record is extraordinary. From it one learns the day opened bleak and bitter cold—GIs wore heavy down jackets. Army Signal Corpsmen captured the Russian POWs in barbed wire stockades; in lorries; in boxcars; enduring the frigid temperatures, the close searches, and the eyes of a Soviet observer. But the most telling footage of all shows two guards pulling one particular prisoner aside; in the cold he is made to bare his chest, criss-crossed with more than a dozen self-inflicted wounds—all for the Army Signal Corps. No longer with his injuries solely his own, Konstantin G. faces the camera with icy breath, frightful expression, and heavy sobs. A week and a half after his repatriation to, at best, a decade of forced labor, the army's *Stars and Stripes* volunteered a picture of the man, wounds and all. SHAEF censors, supremely embarrassed by the military's role in repatriation, have spared the average Library of Congress researcher this gruesome scene, for almost all library copies of the 6 March 1946 edition carry a blank page instead.[57]

On 13 May Plattling dispatched an additional aftershock of 222 Vlasovites and one suicide, but the February spectacle proved to be the last instance of large-scale forced repatriation of Soviet nationals. The business did not end there, but did taper off—the army unintentionally but appropriately codenamed the Plattling transfer "Operation Taper."[58]

What the Western public has learned of forced repatriation has pertained for the most part to episodes involving Western complicity. But more Soviet nationals uprooted by the war returned to Russia from Eastern than Western Europe: approximately 3.2 million from the East versus some 2 million from the West. But as long as the Russian flag bears a hammer and sickle, little of the painful saga of those millions recovered directly by the Red Army is ever likely to be known.

Western and Russian tallies for the total number of Soviet repatriates are amazingly close, all falling between 5,115,709 and 5,326,445. Colonel General Filip Golikov, head of the Soviet Repatriation Commission, placed the number at 5.2 million, a figure certainly compatible with other estimates.[59]

Although documentation is limited, the approximate composition of Soviet repatriates in terms of sex, military status, age, and nationality can be determined. The 5,236,130 returners included 3,104,284 men; 1,498,153 women; and 633,693 youth under sixteen years of age.[60] Roughly 3 million were surviving POWs and military collaborators (out of about 5.75 million originally in Nazi captivity). Civilian repatriates numbered at least 2 million.[61]

The size of the last-minute voluntary fugitive contingent that fled westward before advancing Soviet troops, as opposed to Ostarbeiter, POWs, and Osttruppen, remains a mystery. Two émigré sources estimate 1 million, but these are simply guesses, and probably inflated ones, given the low priority afforded Slavs in the chaotic German retreat.[62] One characteristic seems more certain: Army Signal Corps film shows that liberated Soviet troops going home were very, very young, especially in comparison to adult DPs. They look even younger than their twenties, which Solzhenitsyn gives as the average age.[63]

In terms of nationality Soviet citizens abroad bound for repatriation included disproportionately large numbers of non-Russians. Several factors accounted for this. First, Moscow discriminated against minorities. In the purges for instance, they suffered more on the average than Russians, and this made them more willing to cooperate with Germany, militarily and economically. Second, Wehrmacht Army Group North, in direct control of the German's one major region of Great Russian population, vigorously resisted deportations to the Reich. But in the South the army had less control over occupation policy, and consequently Nazi manhunts netted hundreds of thousands of Ukrainians. Finally, and perhaps decisively, the areas of German occupation and exploitation, western and southern European Russia, held many of the largest Soviet minorities. [64] (For more on the nationality composition of Soviet citizens abroad, see ch. 7.)

In summary, repatriates were most likely to be male, in their early twenties, and members of Soviet minorities, with Ukrainians forming the largest contingent. Most of them had *not* collaborated with the Germans. The Vlasovites, the most talked-about of Soviet citizens abroad, and the most violent in their resistance to return, provided the substance for the majority of contemporary newspaper articles about repatriation. But Red Army men captured in Wehrmacht ranks accounted for only some 17 percent (about 900,000 of 5,236,130) of Soviet citizens going home after World War II. Even among military repatriates, collaborators constituted less than one-third (29 percent, or 900,000 of 3,100,000) of the total. Perhaps the most intriguing speculation about the Soviet diaspora concerns the extent of voluntary versus involuntary return. The question does not lend itself to empirical evaluation, but the matter is so central to the World War II saga of Soviet citizens abroad that a best guess will be hazarded—but only after an examination of Washington's struggle over an ending to the policy of forced repatriation.

NOTES

1. Proudfoot, *European Refugees*, 461. The entire memo appears on pp. 445-69. See also OCMH, "Exchange," 3; EUCOM, "RAMP's," 47.

2. Proudfoot, *European Refugees*, 207; Donnison, *North-West Europe*, 350; Stimson to Secretary of State, 17 May 1945, NA RG 165, WDGSS OPD df 383.6 Sec. XV Case 413.

3. Kennan to Secretary of State, 30 Apr. 1945, NA RG 334, USMMM-POWs, 25 Apr. 1945–15 June 1945.

4. Col. Don Gilmer (general staff) to Gen. Hull, 24 May 1945, NA RG 165, WDGSS OPD df 1942-1945; Deane to WD (London base), 12 May 1945, NA RG 218, CCS 383.6 (7-4-44) (2) Sec. 5; Donald R. Heath, deputy U. S. political adviser, to Secretary of State, 1 June 1945, NA RG 59, 740.00114 EW/6-145; *New York Times*, 25 May 1945.

5. Proudfoot, *European Refugees*, 207; Murphy to Secretary of State, 24 May 1945, NA RG 59, 740.00114 EW/5-2445.

6. Murphy to Secretary of State, 24 May 1945, NA RG 59, 740.00114 EW/5-2445; Heath to Secretary of State, 1 June 1945, NA RG 59, 740.00114 EW/6-145.

7. For the complete text see Proudfoot, *European Refugees*, 208-10. Reitlinger (*House Built on Sand*, 392) incorrectly states that the Allies reached no formal agreement on repatriation until 23 May, thus ignoring the Yalta accord.

8. OCMH, "Displaced Persons, Refugees, and Recovered Allied Military," General Board Report No. 35, p. 22. After an adjustment in the zonal boundaries on 4 July 1945, the Allies closed some of these sites and opened new ones: EUCOM, "Displaced Persons," 60; Donnison, *North-West Europe*, 350.

9. Donnison, *North-West Europe*, 350; Malcolm J. Proudfoot, "Anglo-American Displaced Persons Program for Germany and Austria," *American Journal of Economics and Sociology*, 6 (Oct. 1946), 45-46; Proudfoot, *European Refugees*, 208-11; U.S. Congress, House Committee on Military Affairs, *Investigations of the National War Effort*, H. R. 2740, 79th Cong., 2d sess., 1947, 2.

10. Proudfoot, *European Refugees*, 229.

11. Ibid., 211, 218; U.S. Forces European Theater, Military Government, *Weekly Field Report*, 14 (Oct. 1945), 27. In the midst of the movement, the *New York Times* (26 June 1945) carried an article claiming that three-fourths of all Soviet repatriates came from U.S. zones of occupation.

12. Louise W. Holborn, *The International Refugee Organization, a Specialized Agency of the United Nations: Its History and Work, 1946-1952* (London, 1956), 361; International Refugee Organization, *Statistical Report with 51 Months Summary* (Geneva, 1951), 20.

13. John Balfour to Grew, 4 Aug. 1945, *FR, 1945*, II: 1181; Proudfoot, *European Refugees*, 208; George Woodbridge, *UNRRA: The History of the United Nations Relief and Rehabilitation Administration*, II (New York, 1950), 515. In contrast to 1945, the 1.5 million Russian POWs in Germany at the end of World War I received no priority in repatriation. Margaret R. Gottlieb, "Repatriation in Theory and in Practice throughout the First World War" (M.A. thesis, Bryn Mawr College, 1945), 276; Willis, *Hoover and Russian Prisoners, 6*, 16.

14. SHAEF (Eisenhower) to WD, 8 Dec. 1944, NA RG 218, CCS 383.6 (7-4-44) (2) Sec. 2; Murphy to Byrnes, 24 July 1945, *FR, 1945*, II: 1178.

15. CCS Report 657/9, 13 Apr. 1945, NA RG 218, CCS 383.6 (7-4-44) (2) Sec. 5; Proudfoot, "Displaced Persons Program," 45; EUCOM, "Displaced Persons," 59; "Notes on Russian Relations," 5, 7, Ernest N. Harmon Papers, Military History Research Collection, Box 3, part d.

16. Army Signal Corps film nos. 4105, 4500, 4536, 4745, 4864, NA RG 111.

17. Bethell, *Secret*, 65; Hilldring to Chief, Legislative and Liaison Division, 22 Dec. 1945, NA RG 165, CAD WDSCA 383.7 Poland 6 Nov. 45–10 June 46.

18. NA RG 165, WDGSS CAD, Executive Office, Administrative Section, 383.7 Section I, WDSCA Russia (25 Aug. 1945–10 June 1946); IRO, *The Facts about Refugees* (n.p., 1948), 4; Sister M. Madeline Lorimer, "America's Response to Europe's Displaced Persons, 1945-1952: A Preliminary Report" (Ph.D. diss., St. Louis University, 1964), 27; Woodbridge, *UNRRA*, II: 515.

19. EUCOM, "RAMP's," 55; "Repatriation of Displaced Persons from Germany and Austria," 1 Mar. 1946, NAS RG 165, WDGSS, Military Intelligence Service Project File, Project 2897.

20. "Notes on Russian Relations," 6, Box 3, part d, Harmon Papers.

21. OCMH, "Exchange," 6. See also EUCOM, "Displaced Persons," 15; EUCOM, "RAMP's," 45.

22. Murphy to SD, 2 June 1945, NA RG 59, enclosure to dispatch no. 451 (no decimal number on document); EUCOM, "RAMP's," 69.

23. Thorwald, *Flight*, 291; Ewald Osers, "The Liberation of Prague: Fact and Fiction," *Survey*, no. 76 (Summer 1970), 102; Romanov, *Nights*, 150.

24. Osers, "Prague," 102.

25. Ibid.; Seweryn Bialer, "Biographical Index," in his edited *Stalin and His Generals; Soviet Military Memoirs of World War II* (New York, 1969), 624; Michael Schatoff's introduction to Osokin, *Vlasov*, 9; Solzhenitsyn, *Gulag*, I: 259; Zhukov, *Memoirs*, 640. As a rule, Soviet accounts have ignored the embarrassing part played by anti-Soviet Russians in the liberation of Prague: for example S. S. Lototskii, ed., *Armiia sovetskaia* (Moscow, 1969), 355-57; and V. G. Kulikov, "Internatsional'naia pomoshch' sovetskikh vooruzhennykh sil narodam Evropy," *Novaia i noveishaia istoriia*, no. 1 (Jan.-Feb. 1974), 45-46. (Inexplicably, an American study on *The United States in Prague, 1945-1948* by Walter Ullmann [Boulder, Colo., 1978] manages a chapter on the city's liberation without reference to Vlasov or the ROA.) But Solzhenitsyn's *Gulag*, with passages on Vlasov that Moscow claimed advocated treason, prompted a Soviet response that included a gross distortion of the ROA's part in expelling the Germans from Prague. See Vaclav David, "The Truth about Who Saved Prague in May 1945," 117-20, and Taratuta, "Tell Me Who Your Friend Is," 115-16, both in *The Last Circle*.

26. Huxley-Blythe, *East*, 176; George Patton, *War as I Knew It* (Boston, 1947), 310; Reitlinger, *House Built on Sand*, 386; Strik-Strikfeldt, *Against Stalin and Hitler*, 233-34; Thorwald, *Illusion*, 256, 300.

27. Zhukov, *Memoirs*, 641. See also Huxley-Blythe, *East*, 177-78; Gen. S. M. Shtemenko, *The Last Six Months: Russia's Final Battles with Hitler's Armies in World War II* (Garden City, N.Y., 1977), 417-19; Thorwald, *Illusion*, 298-99; Tolstoy, *Secret*, 300-1. Vlasov's German widow claimed he escaped the roadblock on an American tank, but the story is no more than a curiosity. U.S. Political Adviser for Germany to SD, 6 Jan. 1948, NA RG 59, 740.00114 EW/1-648.

28. Nikolai N. Krasnov, Jr., *The Hidden Russia: My Ten Years as a Slave Laborer* (New York, 1960), 27-28, 332. The author, although born in Russia, was not legally a Soviet citizen, having been raised in Yugoslavia. As a result, after his release from a forced labor camp in 1955, he was able to leave the Soviet Union. For British repatriation of old émigrés, see also Bethell, *Secret*, chs. 4-6; "The Cossack Corp," NA RG 338, Foreign Military Studies, Historical Division, HDQ, USFET, P-064; Gehlen, *Memoirs*, 92; Huxley-Blythe, *East*, 100-1, 159, 168; Rudolf Karmann, "Die Tragödie der Kosaken," *Neues Abendland*, 9 (1954), 664; Naumenko, *Velikoe predatel'stvo*, I and II; Steenberg, *Vlasov*, 215-17; Tolstoy, *Secret*, chs. 7-10.

29. Solzhenitsyn, *Gulag*, I: 259. See also Yaroslav J. Chyz, "Russians in America" (1951), 46, American Council for Nationalities Service files, Immigration History Research Center.

30. SWNCC to Byrnes, 9 Mar. 1945, *FR, 1945*, V: 1076-77; EUCOM, "RAMP's," 53.

31. Plitt to Byrnes, 10 Aug. 1945, NA RG 59, 711.62114/8-1045; Henry to Deputy CS, 2 Jan. 1945, NA RG 165, Army CS 383.6 Sec. 5, Cases 200 . . . 270; Col. R. Ammi Cuttur to CS, 29 Dec. 1944, NAS RG 165, WDGSS ACS 383.6 (8 May 42) Sec. 6, Part 1; Grew to Stimson, 12 May 1945, NA RG 165 OPD df 1942-45 383.6, Box 1303.

32. Plitt to Byrnes, 10 Aug. 1945, NA RG 59, 711.62114/8-1045; Minutes of 18th SWNCC meeting, 18 May 1945, NA RG 218, CCS 334 SANACC (12-19-44) (1) Sec. 1; Stettinius Briefing Papers, 3-4; Edward John Pluth, "The Administration and Operation of German Prisoner of War Camps in the United States during World War II" (Ph.D. diss., Ball State University, 1970), introduction.

33. Flournoy (Le) to Herrick (SWP) and Elbridge Durbrow (EE), 22 June 1945, pp. 3-4, NA RG 59, FW 740.00114 EW/6-1145.

34. Plitt to Durbrow, 23 June 1945, and Flournoy to Matthews and Durbrow, 25 June 1945, NA RG 59, 740.00114 EW/6-1145.

35. Grew to Kennan, 27 July 1945, *FR, 1945*, V: 1100-1; *New York Times*, 30 June 1945.

36. Grew to Kennan, 27 July 1945, *FR, 1945*, V: 1101; Plitt to Byrnes, 10 Aug. 1945, NA RG 59, 711.62114/8-1045; *New York Times*, 1 July 1945; *Washington Star*, 1 July 1945; Tolstoy, *Secret*, 326-27. One source inaccurately reports that the delay in repatriating the Fort Dix Vlasovites was caused by the POWs sabotaging the engines of the ship about to carry them to Europe: deWeerd, "Operation Keelhaul," 30.

37. Plitt to Byrnes, 10 Aug. 1945, NA RG 59, 711.62114/8-1045; Lt. Col. Yudelson to ACS, 14 July 1945, NA RG 165, ACS df 383.6 Sec. 8, Cases 400 . . . 450; Henry to WD Deputy CS, 12 July 1945, NAS RG 165, G1, 383.6 (8 May 42) Sec. 6, Part 2.

38. "Report on Inquiry Made by Officers of War and State Departments into Citizenship Status of German Prisoners of War Believed to be Soviet Citizens at Fort Dix, New Jersey," about 6 Aug. 1945, NAS RG 165, G1 383.6 (8 May 42) Sec. 6, Part 1.

39. Brig. Gen. R. W. Berry to Deputy CS, 6 Aug. 1945, NA RG 165, Army CS df 383.6 Sec. VIII Cases 400 . . . 450.

40. Ibid.

41. Report on Fort Dix Conference, 19 July 1945, NA RG 59, 711.62114/7-1945.

42. Pearson to PMGO, 20 July 1945, NAS RG 165, G1 383.6 (8 May 1942).

43. SD to Soviet Chargé, 20 Aug. 1945, NA RG 59, 711.62114/7-2045; Gen. B. M. Bryan, Asst. to PMG, to G1, 6 Sept. 1945, NAS RG 165, G1 383.6 (8 May 42) Sec. 6 Part 2.

44. Testimony of Mgr. Perridon and Father Poperechig, 26 Sept. 1945, United Ukrainian American Relief Committee (UUARC) papers, Box 192, Immigration History Research Center.

45. Louis Fischer, ed., *Thirteen Who Fled* (New York, 1949), 238.

46. For the Kempten incident, besides Fischer and the UUARC account, see: Bethell, *Secret*, 171-74; "Forcible Repatriation of the Soviet Citizens," *Lithuanian Bulletin*, 5 (Jan.-Feb. 1945), 8-9; Huxley-Blythe, *East*, 185-86; Lyons, *Secret*, 264; B. M. Kuznetsov, comp., *V Ugodu Stalinu*, 1 (New York, 1958), unnumbered page after title page; Naumenko, *Velikoe predatel'stvo*, II: 378; T. L. Smith, "Refugee Orthodox Congregations in Western Europe, 1945-1948," *Church History*, 38 (Sept. 1969), 326; Tolstoy, *Secret*, 337-38.

47. Confidential interview, 8 Aug. 1977.

48. Paul Titman to author, 14 Apr. 1979.

49. Eisenhower to SD, 4 Sept. 1945, *FR, 1945*, V: 1106.

50. All of these sources can be found at the Immigration History Research Center. *Amerika*, 27 Oct. 1945; Gallan to Acting Secretary of War Kenneth C. Royall, 17 Jan. 1946, folder 7, Panchuk Papers; Diehl to Chancellor of the Ukrainian Greek Catholic Diocese of the U.S.A., 11 Sept. 1945, and "Plight of Ukrainian DPs" and "Pogroms of Refugees in U.S. Occupied Zone," *Lithuanian Daily News*, 20 Sept. 1945, both in box 192, and Luce to Gallan, 17 Oct. 1945, box 193, UUARC.

51. Quoted in Lorimer, *Population*, 43.

52. *Stars and Stripes* (Germany ed.), 23 Jan. 1946; Huxley-Blythe, *East*, 188; Murphy to Byrnes, 14 Feb. 1946, *FR, 1946*, V: 141-42; *New York Times*, 20 Jan. 1946; Tolstoy, *Secret*, 355. Bethell's figure of 135 Dachau repatriates is too low: *Secret*, 191.

53. Bethell, *Secret*, 191; Coffin, *Once*, 75-76; Dallin, "Kaminsky," 277; Thorwald, *Illusion*, 313; Tolstoy, *Secret*, 356.

54. Coffin, *Once*, 73; EUCOM, "RAMP's," 69; Thorwald, *Illusion*, 313; Tolstoy, *Secret*, 356.

55. Coffin, *Once*, 73-76. See Bethell, *Secret*, 38-40, for the similar agonies of a British interpreter.

56. Coffin, *Once*, 76.

57. Bethell, *Secret*, 191-93; Coffin, *Once*, 76; "Death to the Tune of Fox-Trots," *Rossiya*, 20 June 1946, NA RG 59, FW800.4016; OCMH, "Exchange," 14; *Stars and Stripes* (Germany ed.), 6 Mar. 1946; Thorwald, *Illusion*, 314; Tolstoy, *Secret*, 356-57. Army Signal Corps film no. 5824, NA RG 111, stored at To-byhanna, Pa., but available at the National Archives upon request, is apparently the only extant film footage of forced repatriation. Tolstoy mistakenly writes that the Plattling film is not available to researchers: *Secret*, 357-58, 470. Film no. 1357 is another instance in which Army Signal Corps cameramen seem to have been intent upon documenting what they regarded as curiosities: in this case, the facial features of ten Soviet "Turkmen" captured in Wehrmacht ranks.

58. Bethell, *Secret*, 193; OCMH, "Exchange," 14. The temptation of research-ers always is to validate the importance of the topic they have chosen; in this case the normal tendency is to maximize the suffering of repatriates, thereby confirming the writer in his choice of subject. The possibility is acknowledged here consciously as a check against exaggeration. The Swedish novelist, Per Olov Enquist, rummaged his own soul on this account in writing *The Legionnaires* (New York, 1973). Speaking of himself in third person (p. 477), he recalled the opening stages of his investigation of forced repatriation from Sweden and "his delight at the suicides he came across, his disappointment that there were not more of them."

59. Michael K. Roof and Frederick A. Leedy, "Population Redistribution in the Soviet Union, 1939-1956," *Geographical Review*, 49 (Apr. 1959), 211, cite "five million plus"; George Ginsburgs, "Soviet Union and the Problem of Refu-gees and Displaced Persons, 1917-1956," *American Journal of International Law*, 51 (Apr. 1957), 348, says 5,115,709; Semiriaga, *Sovetskie liudi*, 327, quoting Gen. Golikov, *Pravda*, 4 Oct. 1945, says 5,200,000; Proudfoot, *European Refugees*, 212, cites 5,213,000; Eugene Kulischer, *Europe on the Move: War and Population Changes, 1917-47* (New York, 1948), 308, cites 5,236,000; "Repatriation," 533, records 5,236,130; Fischer, *Soviet Opposition*, 111, says 5,326,445.

60. "Repatriation," 533.

61. Dallin, *German Rule*, 427; A. Nemirov, *Dorogi i vstrechi* (Munich, 1947), 39.

62. Petrov, *Retreat*, 274-75; Solzhenitsyn, *Gulag*, I: 85.

63. Compare Army Signal Corps film no. 4454 with no. 4517, NA RG 111; Solzhenitsyn, *Gulag*, I: 238.

64. Panchuk to Gallan, 10 June 1945, folder 5, Panchuk Papers; Anismov, *German Occupation*, 29-30.

5

FORCED REPATRIATION AND GROWING RESERVATIONS:

"The Cries of These Men . . .
Still Plague My Memory"

AT FIRST AMERICAN ARMED FORCES STRICTLY adhered to the Yalta repatriation agreement. But General Eisenhower recalled, "We quickly saw that . . . rigid application would often violate the fundamental humanitarian principles we espoused. Thereafter we gave any individual who objected to return the benefit of the doubt."[1] Actually, the accord was eleven months old before the United States officially provided that benefit even to Soviet civilians, much less military personnel, and then only after a protracted struggle within the government.

After the Crimean Conference American repatriation policy drifted toward ever more restricted application of the use of force, although at a very leisurely pace. Unfortunately for the great majority of reluctant returners, the snail-like evolution of the American position away from coercion proved to be a case of too little, too late. Nevertheless, some refugees did escape an undesired homecoming through a gradually growing number of safe categories.

The United States began to put certain limitations upon involuntary repatriation even before the Yalta Conference. Just as the use of force antedated the Crimean accord, so did exemptions to it. On 6 January 1945, the State Department ruled that individuals from areas annexed by the Soviet Union during the course of the war did not have to go home if they feared doing so.[2] Most of these stateless refugees had been prewar residents of eastern Poland or the Baltic states of Estonia, Latvia, and Lithuania; others came from partitioned portions of Rumania, Czechoslovakia, East Prussia, and Finland.

The question of DPs from annexed territories surfaced again as the United States considered the first Soviet draft for a repatriation agreement. On 24 January General Joseph T. McNarney of Eisenhower's staff also advised that care be taken to exclude these refugees from mandatory return. Thus, SWNCC's counterproposal to the Soviet and British drafts specified repatriation only for "claimants to U.S.S.R. or U.S. citizenship." Undersecretary of State Joseph Grew was so confident that the Yalta delegates would not obligate the United States to return refugees from annexed areas that prior to the signing of an agreement he cabled the American ambassador to France stating that the accord would pertain only to those persons "domiciled within the 1938 (repeat 1938) Soviet frontiers."[3]

As previously noted, U.S. negotiators at Yalta failed to follow SWNCC's advice. Instead, the treaty signed on 11 February 1945 closely followed the British and Soviet drafts and failed to define "Soviet citizens."[4] The State Department, Eisenhower's staff, and SWNCC as a whole felt the repatriation of refugees from annexed areas should be a voluntary matter, but the accord did not specify that, leaving Washington's future attitude toward this group uncertain. Because of the agreement's ambiguity SHAEF at first could not pass down the chain of command any clear-cut directives.

Hoping to clear up the confusion, SACMED (Supreme Allied Command Mediterranean Theater) queried JCS on 17 February about the interpretation of the Yalta agreement, "particularly" as it related to Baltic nationals and eastern Poles. Washington settled the issue for good on 9 March with a firm refusal to require the return of refugees from annexed territories. SWNCC even advocated pressing the Soviet Union for the return of persons in this category inadvertently repatriated by Western authorities.[5] In the months ahead, Moscow monotonously reiterated its opposition to the American position on the annexed territories. With the same regularity, the United States reiterated its intention to withhold recognition of Soviet territorial expansion and to consider refugees from newly occupied areas as stateless. As it turned out, this one exemption accounted for 42 percent of all nonreturners.[6]

A number of other breaches in the policy of indiscriminate repatriation developed in the spring of 1945. Civilian defectors within U.S. territory, such as ex-Soviet Purchasing Commission employee Viktor Kravchenko, remained outside Moscow's grasp because Attorney General Francis Biddle and Federal Bureau of Investigation Chief J. Edgar Hoover would not deport them in the absence of an extradition treaty with the U.S.S.R.[7] A similar but inexplicable loophole, adopted by the JCS on 4 April 1945, concerned the exemption of "liberated Soviet Civilians who were physically within the territorial limits of the United States."[8] To whom this could have been applied is a mystery. It did not deal with Soviet citizens captured in German ranks and then interned in the United States, for these individuals consisted entirely of military personnel. In any case, their forcible repatriation is well documented. Nor did it fit such celebrated defectors as Kravchenko, since he and his kind were not liberated from Nazi captivity. Whoever they were, JCS afforded them special treatment. Because the United States did not consider the treaty retroactive, Washington also exempted approximately 40,000 Soviet civilians liberated prior to the signing of the Crimean accord who were cared for by French and Belgian officials.[9]

Besides persons from annexed territories, Soviet civilians in the United States, and those civilians liberated prior to the Yalta agreement, several other categories qualified for freedom of choice by August 1945. For instance, the U.S. military determined that Soviet women married to citizens of other Allied powers were exempt from forced repatriation–but not wives of ex-enemy nationals nor Soviet males married to citizens of other Allied or ex-Axis countries. Washington also officially excluded "old émigrés," persons who had left Russia prior to the beginning of World War II.[10] The United States sometimes mistakenly, and the British, quite a number of times deliberately, forced the homegoing of those who had fled the Russian Revolution of 1917. Nikolai Krasnov, Jr., for example, had been born in Russia and was the son and grandson of famous White generals who had fought in the Russian Civil War. Although he had not been in Russia since the year of his birth and he possessed Yugoslav citizenship, the British repatriated him from Lienz, Austria, with a host of other old émigrés who had joined the ranks of the Vlasovites.[11]

Some Soviet refugees who did not meet the criteria for one of the approved exemptions still evaded repatriation through the good offices of soldiers intent upon sparing them the ordeal. Those who bent the rules or simply disobeyed orders did so because they found forced repatriation repugnant and "un-American." Brigadier General Frank L. Howley recalled the involuntary return of Vlasovites in terms akin to a nightmare: "The cries of these men, their attempts to escape, even to kill themselves rather than be returned to the Soviet Union against which they had fought still plague my memory."[12] As not only generals but guards and interpreters and drivers came to learn firsthand the predicament of Soviet citizens abroad, hardened hearts began to soften. At Plattling, for example, William Sloane Coffin moved from "little sympathy" for Vlasovites to speculating whether the label traitor should apply. On hindsight he regretted not having had "the courage to fight for the lives of these men." After thirty years he still found the memory so painful he could hardly write about it; but he did, both to confess and to accuse: "My part in the Plattling operation left me a burden of guilt I am sure to carry the rest of my life. Certainly it influenced my decision in 1950 to spend three years in the CIA opposing Stalin's regime. And it made it easier for me in 1967 to commit civil disobedience in opposition to the war in Vietnam. . . . repatriation . . . showed me that in matters of life and death the responsibility of those who take orders is as great as those who give them."[13]

Men who had seen war firsthand still recalled repatriation with the greatest difficulty. A British colonel could rank the horror of it with that of Belsen exterminiation camp; a battle-hardened American general could rate his part in the affair, as a DP commandant, as "the most trying" of his "entire military career."[14] After describing the brutality and carnage that accompanied one incident of forced repatriation, another participating soldier admitted that "nothing has ever affected me like that scene."[15] It was no wonder that military authorities came to view each impending refugee movement "with considerable foreboding."[16] For the soldiers involved, the bad taste in the mouth did not always go away. For some, like Coffin, ugly memories and guilt lingered on; for others, recurring nightmares sometimes led to nervous breakdowns. An ex-sergeant in Patton's Third Army wrote in late 1977, "Forced repatriation . . . was very difficult and bitterly opposed by the rank-and-file. We felt then, and still do, that they surrendered to us, were our Prisoners-of-War, should have been processed by us and that those who chose to return to Russia should have been returned, and that those *not* wishing to return should not have been forced to."[17] In *Before Winter Comes*, a film with a picturesque Alpine setting and an ugly plot, camp commandant Burnside declares, just after having tricked his interpreter into repatriation, "When it gets down to dirty politics soldiers are just paid to obey, that's all." With more than a little irony he swears, "O God, to get back to clean fighting instead of this trading in flesh."

In 1945 U.S. military men generally accepted the assumption that obeying orders and soldiering went hand in hand. Germans at the Nuremberg trials might be expected to have disobeyed inhumane commands, but GIs on repatriation details were, as usual, to put discipline before conscience, or else. Nevertheless, at least some men did not accept their orders as unalterable, especially as time passed. A few commanders faced near mutiny and at least one uncooperative British officer found himself courtmartialed. But more often, those in opposition to forced repatriation preferred circumvention to confrontation. Officials might connive at falsifying documents. A frightened Soviet citizen, for instance, might knowingly be classified as a Pole. Such a deception, admitted one UNRRA worker, allowed reluctant returners to be "safely sequestered in our statistics." Another subterfuge involved sick-call. On one occasion 21 of 25 GIs assigned to repatriation work in Germany reported ill to avoid the unseemly business.[18]

The army's distaste for the task thus led to breaches in the policy of mandatory repatriation never spelled out in official directives. A good deal of leeway developed between the letter of the law and its interpretation in the field. As one SHAEF civil affairs officer put it, "Complicated, conflicting, or inconvenient instructions were often ignored in practice. Undoubtedly, the ruthless attitude of the Soviet Repatriation Officers, conducting the equivalent of manhunts for their nationals, was met with stubborn resistance in very many instances." This "rough and ready interpretation" saved many nonreturners from repatriation.[19]

If individual Americans had an inkling of the fate of returners and had the opportunity, they often gave their Soviet charges an oportunity to escape. Coffin, for example, relates his handling of Red Army deserters: "Wherever they were captured in the American occupied zone, they were brought by military police to corps headquarters. From there a member of our liaison team accompanied them to the border. The first deserter I accompanied was taken by a drunken captain into a field to one side of the guard house and shot. Thereafter I dismissed the MPs and drove the deserter by myself into a forest where I could slow down until he understood that he was to jump out." With the exception of stateside extradition, large-scale escapes could easily accompany U.S. repatriation operations. At Kempten in August 1945, for example, a sizeable group of fleeing Russians avoided the transfer because their guards, when not closely supervised, looked the other way.[20]

A particularly poignant illustration of the U.S. Army's permissiveness occurred at Cina Citta, a camp near Rome where forty-seven Soviet nationals captured in German ranks made a spectacular getaway. In November 1944 the Russian Military Mission in Italy had demanded that U.S. guards forcibly turn over these miscreants. AFHQ asked for this in writing, but the Soviet Mission refused—no doubt fearing to sign a document that could damage Moscow's fiction that all Soviet citizens went home willingly. On 11 November the forty-seven, by some means, "absented themselves from the camp." They returned that night for their belongings, stole a seven-ton lorry, and broke out for good by smashing through the locked camp gate.[21]

General George Patton, always closer to insubordination than servility in his relation to authority, did not bother with appearances. He simply released 5,000 Russian POWs in mid-June 1945, orders notwithstanding. In not as blatant a fashion but with an identical outcome, at least a portion of U.S. commanders came to handle repatriation orders on the basis of what one Eisenhower staffer called a loose "field policy." This euphemism covered an unwritten rule of thumb whereby U.S. officers, so inclined, allowed DPs, POWs, even ex-Vlasovites to disappear, and resorted to force only under pressure. Instances of this sort of well-intentioned insubordination proliferated in the summer of 1945, but naturally did not receive the publicity of a Fort Dix or a Camp Kempten.[22]

In mid-March 1945 SACMED became the first theater to question openly the general policy of forced repatriation. Admiral Ellery W. Stone, chief of the Civil Affairs Division in Italy, suggested to his superiors that "the sole test . . . be whether a person claims Russian citizenship and that if he or she does not do so, her or she be treated as stateless." SWNCC, with JCS concurrence, responded unequivocally that the inclinations of individual Soviet citizens did not matter. The orders stood to repatriate all Red Army soldiers liberated from German POW camps, all Soviet civilians except those physically in the United States, and all Vlasovites except those claiming German POW status under the Geneva Convention.[23]

Mandatory repatriation also distressed Alexander C. Kirk, former consul general in the U.S. embassy in Moscow and ambassador to Italy from December 1944. On several occasions he questioned Washington, hoping to precipitate a reappraisal of the policy. On 7 August 1945, for example, Kirk queried Secretary of State James F. Byrnes: "What is policy concerning Soviet civilians who will not admit Soviet citizenship but yet cannot claim other nationality?" Seeking a more humane approach, he added, "Are they to be treated as 'stateless' and placed in category of displaced persons, or are they to be screened by Soviets and returned if demand is made?" Byrnes replied that forced repatriation would be continued.[24]

Before the month was over, support for a reexamination of the policy had grown to such mammoth proportions that Washington could no longer flatly reject all objections. On 25 August, aiming at a review of standing orders, General Alexander Patch, commander of the U.S. Seventh Army, requested SHAEF to spell out American policy "on the use of troops to turn over unwilling repatriates to the Soviet authorities." In the meantime he would suspend the use of force.[25] Two days later, Robert Murphy, a State Department political adviser attached to SACMED, described to Byrnes his own feelings of revulsion at the events that had taken place at Camp Kempten two weeks before: "In applying the policy of forcible repatriation there has been a number of unpleasant incidents involving violence such as the forcible seizure by our troops of one hundred Russians at a church service resulting in serious injuries on both sides." He went on to admit he was at a loss to explain the military's use of force, since "in the [Yalta] protocol which I have seen informally I find no reference to this subject." In answering for Byrnes, H. Freeman Matthews could not refer to the need to protect American POWs in Eastern Europe from reprisals since most were home by late August. Still

Matthews, in a limp if novel approach, conjured up a largely nonexistent category that conceivably could require protection from Soviet reprisal. He told Murphy, "For your confidential information, Department has been anxious in handling these cases to avoid giving Soviet authorities any pretext for delaying return of American POWs of Japanese now in Soviet occupied zone, particularly in Manchuria."[26]

On 29 August, Eisenhower's month-old Combined Displaced Persons Executive (CDPX) cabled the Adjutant General and JCS putting in a "request that subject be reviewed in its entirety." CDPX cited a number of reasons, including the frequency of suicides among those subject to forced repatriation, fear of injury or loss of life to "both sides," and "the failure of Russian authorities to admit U.S. repatriation representatives' entry into U.S.S.R. zones as agreed in the Yalta agreement." Brigadier General C. L. Adcock, assistant chief of staff of SHAEF's Civil Affairs Division (G-5), requested the chief of staff to urge a policy review upon JCS "because of the serious repercussions which may result in public opinion in the U.S. if U.S. troops were killed or injured in attempting to force repatriation of unwilling Soviet citizens."[27]

Finally, General Eisenhower himself had a change of heart during the summer of 1945. Mindful of the staggering logistical problems in caring for masses of refugees, he initially had written JCS in early June strongly requesting the authority to turn over all Vlasovites who, as Wehrmacht POWs, had claimed the protection of the Geneva Convention. Treating an international covenant rather flippantly, the SHAEF commander had noted: "Danger no longer exists that German government may make reprisals on our prisoners in case we turn these prisoners over to Soviet authorities." But on 4 September, Eisenhower responded to the summerlong groundswell of military opposition by requesting the State Department to reexamine repatriation policy. In the meantime troops were not to use force. Besides the rumble of protest from below, the general also may have been motivated by the dictates of his own conscience, quickened and sensitized since early June by the frightful violence of the Fort Dix riot of 29 June and the Camp Kempten incident of 12 August.[28]

SWNCC, which had objected to indiscriminate repatriation of Soviet nationals all along, appointed a subcommittee to work out alternatives to the existing policy. On 25 September 1945, this body suggested that the United States "facilitate" the return of Soviet nationals "based on the interpretation that the [Yalta] Agreement does not require forcible repatriation of Soviet citizens who do not wish to return." Here was a thinly veiled call for an end to the use of force. And the sooner, the better: "Instructions are immediately required as to the steps to be taken to prevent injury to our troops and action of a type inconsistent with American traditions and interests." But whatever was decided, the subcommittee felt the question "of such gravity and urgency as to require determination by the SWNCC at the highest level."[29]

Opposition to existing repatriation policy was also growing within the State Department. On 29 September 1945, Undersecretary of State Dean Acheson, who had always opposed the wholesale use of force, raised the subject in a cable to Byrnes, then attending a Council of Foreign Ministers meeting in London. The undersecretary noted Eisenhower's request for a policy review, the similar communication from Kirk, and the growing distaste of American troops for sending Soviet nationals home against their will. Acheson summarized the four-day old SWNCC paper, which argued that the Yalta agreement obligated signatory powers to "facilitate" but not to force repatriation. He concluded by urging the adoption of this interpretation, although he admitted that it had "no specific justification in the text of the agreement."[30]

By the end of his conference, Byrnes, too, was inclined to favor a more lenient reading of the Yalta repatriation accord. But to start with, British Foreign Secretary Ernest Bevin's references to the West's traditional role as a haven for political exiles, including Marx and Lenin, had moved neither Soviet Foreign Minister V. M. Molotov nor Byrnes. For instance, on 12 September at the first plenary session the American secretary of state assured his Soviet counterpart that he would talk to U.S. military authorities again "to see that every Soviet citizen whose nationality was not in doubt was sent back." And on the twenty-seventh, when Molotov insisted upon the repatriation of 500 Vlasovites in Italy, Byrnes volunteered that "if any were in U.S. possession no sympathy would be given them."[31]

The next day, however, he balked when he heard from Bevin that repatriation would require the use of force. Byrnes's repeated frustrations at the London meeting also may have been a factor. By 28 September the conference had reached an angry impasse, and he was in no mood to make any further accommodation with Molotov. Byrnes postponed a decision by insisting that he first needed a ruling from the Combined Chiefs of Staff (CCS) in Washington. That same day, while instructing Grew to obtain a CCS opinion specifically on these 500 Vlasovites, Byrnes communicated a heretofore unexpressed hesitation "about the use of force." Byrnes well knew that the American interpretation of its Yalta repatriation obligations had long since included coercion, especially with Soviet citizens captured in German uniform, but he no longer felt as certain as he had before about this policy's correctness. And Acheson's 29 September note strongly favoring revision of the American position helped to strengthen the secretary's new found reservations. By the end of the month, Byrnes had joined the ranks of second echelon officials, such as Kirk and the undersecretary, who for some time had been seeking a more lenient reading of the Yalta accord; he further suggested that the United States reconsider the use of force in repatriating Soviet citizens captured in Wehrmacht ranks, a group that even Acheson felt "should be returned to their native land as traitors."[32]

Bevin wrote Byrnes at the beginning of October, trying to keep American policy in line with British insistence on the use of force. After reminding the secretary that he had told Molotov the U.S. would show Vlasovites "no sympathy," the foreign secretary argued, "It is most important to get rid of these people as soon as possible . . . using such force as may be necessary." Bevin could be as tough-minded as he liked; American policy still was drifting slowly in the opposite direction. On 4 October, for instance, General Eisenhower confounded the British by making public his previous 4 September suspension of forced repatriation pending a policy review. Apparently he advertised his objections as a means of increasing the pressure upon Washington to reverse its policy. At any rate that was the effect. On 5 October the *New York Times* reported that Eisenhower had ordered "American troops [to] discontinue forcing Russian nationals to return home unless the United States Government rules otherwise." The publicity contributed to a reevaluation of the policy, but was far from a full disclosure of what had been going on. At the press conference of 5 October, in response to a query about the element of coercion, a spokesman for the general answered with more care than candor: "Possibly for a time some of them were being pushed onto trains without our asking many questions but that's all stopped now."[33] More than some had been pushed, and pushing was nearly two years from being over.

SWNCC debated the obligations of the United States under the repatriation agreement throughout the fall of 1945. On 21 November its Subcommittee for Europe completed a report similar to the 25 September proposal, which Acheson had found so convincing. With some exceptions Yalta again was interpreted as facilitating rather than forcing the repatriation of Soviet nationals abroad. SWNCC as a whole agreed to this explanation on 28 November, and the JCS concurred shortly after. As a result, this significant modification of American repatriation policy officially went into effect 20 December 1945.[34] In an effort to minimize Soviet objections, the new orders stated that U.S. officials were to make every effort to encourage voluntary repatriation; the Kremlin's representatives would continue to have free access to DP camps in order to persuade the reluctant to return; and the United States promised to put a stop to organized resistance movements within the camps and to "continue vigorous efforts to prevent dissemination of propaganda . . . against repatriation."[35]

The McNarney-Clark directive (named after the U.S. generals in Germany and Austria who received it) not only adopted the principle of voluntary return for Soviet civilians but spelled out in great detail those instances in which coercion still applied. No Soviet national would be given a choice who: (1) had been captured in German uniform, (2) had been in the Red Army on or after 22 June 1941, and who subsequently had not been discharged, or (3) had "voluntarily rendered aid and comfort to the enemy." On the last point the new directive carefully placed the burden of proof on the Soviet government, which was to provide "in each case, with reasonable particularity, the time, place and nature of the offenses and the perpetrators thereof." The document specified that resistance to repatriation or an individual's wartime employment in German industry or agriculture did not constitute sufficient evidence to warrant the conclusion that that person had voluntarily aided the enemy.[36]

No future directive officially expanded the exemptions beyond those granted in the policy revision of 20 December. As a result, this document, which spared the remaining Soviet civilians in the West from forced repatriation, proved to be the most important single written decision dealing with the subject other than the Yalta accord itself. But in practice neither document substantially altered the status quo nor significantly changed the course of events. Both forced repatriation and certain specific exemptions to it predated the Yalta Conference. The agreement signed there relating to liberated DPs and POWs merely put the seal on established American policy. Similarly, exemption of civilians from forced repatriation made little difference, for with more than 2 million Soviet citizens returned by 21 December 1945, a scant 20,000 remained for SHAEF's consideration.[37] Since most displaced Soviet nationals had already been removed from Western occupation zones, the directive had little practical effect.

Some of the factors contributing to the modifications of the policy have been explored already; others have not. As noted, the widespread disapproval of the policy within the army can be regarded as one of the major stimuli behind the 20 December civilian exemption. Slowly building from grass-roots opposition among the rank and file, objections to the use of coercion gradually worked their way up the chain of command until even generals expressed misgivings. Commanders of this rank including Alexander Patch, George Patton, Mark Clark, Joseph McNarney, and Dwight Eisenhower came to view the use of force as both unjust and unsavory.

Eisenhower's promotion to Army Chief of Staff in November 1945 also may have hastened the modification of American repatriation policy.[38] By the fall of 1945 the general's views on the use of force had softened considerably. In contrast, the man he was succeeding, General George C. Marshall, had carried out forced repatriation without flinching. It may not have been a total coincidence that one month after Eisenhower joined the JCS, that body decided to exempt the remaining displaced Soviet civilians from forced repatriation.

Also, SWNCC never had favored indiscriminate repatriation and voiced its disapproval on a number of occasions. Its authority, however, was too limited to effect a change in policy without the support of other, more powerful groups. This included the army to be sure, but it also consisted of high echelon State Department officials whose protests, taken collectively, could not be ignored forever. R. W. Flournoy, Dean Acheson, Joseph Grew, Averell Harriman, George Kennan, Alexander Kirk, and Robert Murphy all questioned the advisability of unconditional repatriation.

Acheson's reservations especially counted for something as he more and more gained the trust of Harry Truman. The new president, undeniably a novice in foreign affairs, needed much more advice than the secretary of state could give him, since Byrnes had pitifully little diplomatic expertise himself. Besides, the secretary was away from Washington on State Department business for 350 of his 562 days in office. Powers thus falling to Byrnes's first deputy were unusually great. "Never in American history," writes Charles Jefferson, "had the second-ranking officer of the Department of State exerted as much influence on foreign policy as did Undersecretary of State Acheson from August 1945 through June 1947." Even though Truman read all of the Washington-Moscow telegrams within a week of taking office, and therefore knew of the repatriation issue from the start, he apparently had no hand in the McNarney-Clark directive. The most that can be said for Truman's role is that his closeness to Acheson, who opposed indiscriminate repatriation, lent the undersecretary additional leverage and perhaps in this indirect way contributed to the exemption of civilians from forced repatriation.[39]

At the very least Eisenhower's promotion to the JCS, Byrnes's change of heart in London, and Acheson's rising star demonstrated that the groundswell of military opposition to forced repatriation and the long-standing reservations of State Department rank and file had percolated to the top by the late fall of 1945. SWNCC finally had the crucial support to permit a reading of Yalta as facilitating rather than forcing the repatriation of Soviet civilians.

Cabinet-level officials such as Attorney General Biddle and Secretary of War Henry L. Stimson had opposed indiscriminate repatriation before to no effect, but by the time of the civilian exemption of December 1945 all American POWs liberated by the Red Army were home. Given the grave concern for U.S. servicemen in Soviet custody, which a multitude of officials repeatedly expressed, it is unlikely that Washington would have dared tamper with repatriation policy until the Soviet Union had returned its GIs stranded in East Europe. The homecoming of U.S. servicemen from Soviet-occupied territory did not automatically bring about an end to the use of force in the repatriation of Soviet citizens abroad, but it was, no doubt, a prerequisite for an American change of position.

The general deterioration in Soviet-American relations in the early postwar period also probably contributed to the late 1945 decision to ban the forced return of civilians. Between the formalization of American repatriation policy in February 1945 and its modification in December, the Allies defeated Germany and Japan, thereby severing the bond that held them together. East-West disagreements seemed to intensify in direct proportion to the diminution of the military threat. Previously nonexistent problems, including Moscow's uneasiness over American possession of the atomic bomb, the abrupt cancellation by the United States of Lend-Lease to Russia, Washington's failure to approve a postwar loan to the Soviet Union, disagreement over German reparations, and Soviet control of Eastern Europe, swelled to dangerous proportions.

To expect that the United States and Russia would comply with each other's demands on repatriation indefinitely amidst the ruins of the wartime coalition would be to assume that the issue could be divorced from its diplomatic context. On the contrary, the bitter climate engendered by various East-West disagreements probably hastened the revision of the American interpretation of the Yalta accord. The interrelationship of the Polish political question and the repatriation of American POWs in Poland provides the most convincing proof of this assertion (see ch. 3). In more general terms, each side's disapproval of the other's handling of its obligations under the Yalta exchange agreement contributed to the atmosphere of suspicion and mistrust that had so much to do with the onset of the Cold War.

The British, who had rigidly adhered to a forced repatriation policy throughout 1945, found the 20 December revision of American policy quite disturbing. London urged Washington to reconsider its new interpretation of the Yalta accord, but to no avail. The British need not have worried that the United States would renounce coercion categorically, because the specifics of the policy revision clearly indicated that certain groups were still subject to forced return. The eastward movement did continue, but the volume rapidly declined since civilians were now exempt and most Soviet DPs already had been sent back. Even the eligible remnant stayed put until spring for want of heated transport.[40]

The exemption of Soviet civilians from mandatory return to Russia did not satisfy the U.S. military, which still held ex-POWs and Vlasovites keenly opposed to repatriation. On 9 January 1946, army intelligence sought State Department approval to hold back for questioning eighteen well-informed Soviet collaborators. Undersecretary of State Acheson, whose sympathy inexplicably seemed not to extend beyond Soviet civilians, refused, as did SHAEF.[41]

A more formidable attempt at curtailing the use of force came from General Joseph McNarney, commanding general of U.S. forces in Germany. On 19 April 1946, his headquarters took steps that would have ended coerced repatriation had they not been overruled. McNarney informed the War Department that screening boards under his command had ruled against the forced return of several hundred Soviet nationals on the grounds that their citizenship could not be positively confirmed. The boards could not agree on the legal status of persons denied one of several inalienable rights of a citizen, such as the right to bear arms, to vote in elections, or to hold public office. Clearly uncomfortable with the Yalta exchange accord, the general urgently requested a "legal opinion as to whether such loss [of rights] . . . is considered deprivation of citizenship, thus rendering the individual non-repatriable by force."[42] Both the State Department and the JCS found McNarney's imaginative arguments unacceptable. On 7 June 1946, the JCS tersely advised him, "What right a Soviet citizen has are matters which concern the Soviet Government solely."[43]

Since no sizeable transfers occurred in Germany after Plattling (13 May 1946), McNarney's discomfort in June could not compare with that of AFHQ, which had to face much more of the unpleasantness. Even with the British repatriating 42,000 Soviet citizens from Italy by that date, thousands more remained to be screened and "processed." Much of the repatriation backlog in this theater can be traced to one individual extremely adverse to the whole business: Field Marshal Sir Harold Alexander, supreme Allied commander in Italy and a veteran of anti-Bolshevik fighting in the Russian Civil War. Historian Hugh Trevor-Roper bluntly but correctly wrote, "He positively evaded the explicit orders of his government."[44] Alexander himself admitted as much in mid-June 1945: "So far I have refused to use force to repatriate Soviet citizens, although I suppose I am not strictly entitled to adopt this attitude." Writing the War Office in London in late August he explained, "To compel . . . repatriation would certainly either involve the use of force or drive them into committing suicide. . . . Such treatment, coupled with the knowledge that these unfortunate individuals are being sent to an almost certain death, is quite out of keeping with the traditions of democracy and justice, as we know them."[45]

Up to his transfer to Canada in December 1945 Alexander evaded the use of force in processing displaced Soviet nationals in Italy by repeatedly calling for reviews in London with coercion proscribed in the meantime. More than once he managed to circumvent his orders with impunity because his was a joint British-American command and Washington's approach suited him better than London's, especially after 6 September, when Eisenhower instituted his own suspension of the use of force pending policy review. In Italy, Lord Bethell writes, "The British government was . . . in the strange position of needing American approval before it could issue an order to one of its generals."[46] Even after Alexander's departure, the awkward necessity for joint control and coordinated policy in this theater frustrated advocates of forced repatriation. Until Washington and London could agree on their interpretation of the Yalta accord, AFHQ forbade the use of force except in extraditing proven war criminals.[47]

Finally, on 6 June 1946, the British cabinet approved Foreign Secretary Bevin's recommendation that it adopt the U.S. exemption of Soviet civilians from forced repatriation, as detailed in the McNarney-Clark directive of 20 December 1945.[48] Paradoxically, this British expansion of categories excluded from mandatory return precipitated the last instances of the widespread use of force, for now Washington and London were in definite agreement that military personnel, especially collaborators, were bound to be turned over to Soviet authorities.

By June 1946 the overwhelming majority of Soviet nationals uncovered in the West had been repatriated. Most of the remainder had either disguised their identity or now came under the exempt civilian category. But in Italy, owing to Alexander's opposition and the general complications of joint command, the Allies still held over 1,000 ex-Osttruppen and related women and children, concentrated at Aversa and Bagnoli, near Naples. AFHQ decided to move all of them further north for more careful screening, a necessary step before their "final disposal." Consequently, on 14–15 August 1946 Allied troops moved 432 ex-Vlasovites and 128 women and children, mostly Azerbaidzhani and Crimean Tatars, from Aversa to an American camp at Pisa and 498 ex-Vlasovites and 105 dependents, mostly Russians, Ukrainians, and Don and Kuban Cossacks, from Bagnoli to Riccioni, a large multinational British camp just south of Rimini on the Adriatic. In both cases the move also involved transfer from civilian (UNRRA) to military (AFHQ) jurisdiction.[49]

At a joint U.S.–British staff conference the previous July a Royal Artil-

lery colonel-turned-DP-commandant "raised the point as to the advisability of using guile rather than force to accomplish the removal of alleged
Soviet citizens."[50] In the end AFHQ resorted to both, but in this specific
operation in August 1946, apparently more craftiness than coercion.
Word went out at the end of July that the upcoming "phase one" transfer
to Pisa and Riccioni would be a "routine un-escorted move." AFHQ, according to its own records, maintained the appearance of unexceptional
DP-business-as-usual by dispatching this last remnant of the phantom
"Russian Liberation Army" on "ordinary trains, without any escort or
supervision." Since records show that only eleven persons turned up
missing of hundreds disembarked at Riccioni, the guise of voluntary
transfer seems to have worked well in preventing incidents.[51]

It did not prevent anxiety, however. The mid-August operation proved
extremely disconcerting to people who received no explanations for the
move and who now found themselves deposited in locked and guarded
compounds. AFHQ records have preserved one petition from the American facility at Pisa, which speaks ungrammatically but eloquently of camp
members' deep anxieties:

> 10 days ago, have I put to your kindly attention, a request concerning our, why
> we are locked in this compound. Not having received any answer until to day,
> we take the liberty to ask ones more for it. . . . we have been erected in two
> groups. The group, who was transferred to REGIA FILLIA is also living free. It is
> only our group with 445 [*sic*] people just the group combined of 50 children and
> many women and old men, who has been locked here. It is about 20 days we are
> asking the reason of this, but nobody can tell us the reasons. Criminal have also
> the right to know why they are imprisoned, while therefore we, who are just
> guilty not to be home, we that the terror of the war spared us nothing, can not
> know why we are locked here. Many of us on war reason having lost family,
> relation and every possession, and as last salvation; . . . are now living one
> and a half years in American English compounds, knowing the American and
> English people as their protectors, are now astonished to all at ones, without
> any reason locked in this enclosure. We are people, who have the right to live
> like every being.[52]

Granted, most of those held at Pisa were guilty of having fought in
Wehrmacht ranks; granted, many were guilty of having aided the German war economy; and granted, a fraction may have been guilty of participating in Nazi atrocities—AFHQ claimed some were "of war crime interest."[53] Still, the vast majority of these, the hard-core collaborators,
had lent Germany a hand unwillingly and simply to stave off starvation or
the blows and bullets of their captors. Whatever their culpability—and all
military collaborators combined represented but a fraction of those repatriated against their will—they, along with ex-Ostarbeiter and liberated

POWs, were but pawns of the war: passive, battle-weary players shunted about Europe's gameboard at the whim of the chessmasters of Moscow, Berlin, Washington, and London.

Some intelligence officer with a penchant for lively code names designated the mid-August transfer Operation Keelhaul. (AFHQ toyed with "Enchain" and "Denude" as well.)[54] Normally the labels and the undertakings had nothing in common, but in this case they did. Keelhauling meant punishing a sailor by dragging him under the rough, barnacled hull of a ship, which might or might not prove fatal. Likewise, repatriation, which for some would follow Operation Keelhaul, entailed punishment that the returners might or might not survive. Whether the association was intentional remains a matter of speculation, but this much can be documented definitively: the code name applied exclusively to the mid-August transfer within Italy and not to mass forced repatriation, as Julius Epstein and others mistakenly assert.[55] Ironically, Operation Keelhaul, which did include final processing at Pisa and Riccioni, did not entail the turnover of a single person to Soviet authorities, forcibly or otherwise.[56] That phase of the "final disposal" of ex-Osttruppen in Italy had its own designation: Operation Eastwind.

Fully aware of the unpleasantness before it, the joint Anglo-American command sought to minimize its difficulties by establishing elaborate procedures to screen out any Soviet citizens not subject to involuntary extradition. This, plus careful preparations for a repatriation free from violence or suicide, and one fully coordinated between Washington and London, consumed almost nine months time, from mid-August 1946 to early May 1947. Most of the work of the Western Allies in the processing stage of Operation Keelhaul involved screening. Before it was over the ex-Osttruppen at the American camp at Pisa underwent five separate interrogations, not to mention sessions prior to mid-August.

First, UNRRA officials questioned them; but an Albanian member of this team repeatedly antagonized his subjects and put down as facts things that camp members later would heatedly deny. AFHQ regarded a second screening unreliable because ex-enemy personnel had assisted Allied enlisted men in the work. Nor did the third attempt to classify camp members, this one by UNRRA, prove productive: resentment ran so high against the Albanian interrogator that he had to be protected by military police. Finally, a military board consisting of a captain, two lieutenants, and three enlisted men obtained a credible evaluation. But even this did not satisfy AFHQ, which was determined to give Soviet repatriation officers no legitimate cause for complaint. The fifth and definitive screening board, which included three senior officers under Colonel Virgil N. Cordero, took great pains to identify precisely the war record of each of the 432 men. (The women and children were automatically exempt from forced repatriation due to the December 1945 civilian exemption.) By the end of February 1947 it had ruled 190 definitely were not Soviet citizens, mostly nationals of southeastern Europe or the Middle East, especially Turkey. The board also ruled 191 definitely were Soviet citizens, and of these, seventy-seven had to be repatriated as ex-military personnel. Enough doubts lingered about the remaining fifty-one to place them in the exempt category.[57]

Even though some AFHQ officers unsympathetically categorized the Pisa detainees as "congenital liars" whose "whole cloth" falsehoods were "stupid and without reason," a majority of the fifth screening board generously exempted many Soviet citizens from the upcoming Operation Eastwind. The final American interrogators, for example, passed over an ex-Ostarbeiter who, in an earlier screening, had admitted previous Red Army duty. He conceded birth in Russia and residence there on 1 September 1939, but somewhat unconvincingly claimed Turkish citizenship. The board gave him the benefit of the doubt, ruling it "did not find evidence of membership in the Red Army." In a similar case a twenty-three-year-old lad claimed to be from Turkey but spoke a Crimean dialect of Turkish. Some of his answers led the board to suspect he had seen Red Army service, but lacking hard proof, he was "found not subject to forcible repatriation but possible Russian citizen."[58]

The fifth screening board headed by Colonel Cordero completed its work by the end of February 1947. Repatriation under Operation Eastwind likely would have followed in March had it not been for Colonel Pavel Iakovlev, a Soviet liaison officer in Italy. At the last minute he submitted "wanted" lists with 487 names, which forced a delay. AFHQ did not want to risk the possibility of an additional operation after working through Iakovlev's roster. In this instance the Western Allies placed the burden of proof on Moscow. If the boards had not judged those on Iakovlev's list subject to forced repatriation already, Soviet authorities had to document each individual's military status to secure their involuntary return. This did not lead to the extradition of a single additional person above those already screened, but Iakovlev's "wanted" list did push Operation Eastwind into May 1947.[59]

Meanwhile, American officials took extreme pains to see that the upcoming repatriation from Pisa would be free of incidents. Émigré groups in the West knew something was in the offing, which was all the more reason to proceed with caution.[60] From experience U.S. and British authorities in Italy considered reluctant returners to be explosive commodities: "All are deathly afraid of being returned to Russia or any country under U.S.S.R. control. Many will choose suicide rather than return to

U.S.S.R. control." One American colonel advised Allied Forces Head-quarters: "These Soviets . . . are likely to go to any extreme to resist their removal. To insure the success of this operation it is imperative that the strictest security measures are observed before D-Day and that during the operation a high standard of co-ordination is maintained. . . . The execution of the operation will be the responsibility of the respective escort commanders and it will be for them to judge the extent of military action to be taken."[61]

To prevent escapes, injuries, or suicides, Operation Eastwind guards had the authority to use handcuffs, straightjackets, billy clubs, tear gas, and firearms. The first draft of plans for Eastwind also included a refer-ence to the repatriation of Soviet military personnel, "dead or alive." By May 1947 the Hollywood-like phrase had been struck from operational orders, but not the policy of mandatory extradition. AFHQ anxiously sought Soviet assurances that, in the event the operation led to fatalities, corpses would be accepted; Moscow agreed.[62]

Britain and the United States carried out Operation Eastwind on 8–10 May 1947, moving 256 persons from Riccioni and Pisa to San Valentino, Austria, an exchange point on the border of Soviet-occupied territory southeast of Linz. The British repatriated 171 prisoners on 8–9 May and a final nine married men on 9–10 May. (The latter were given twenty-four hours to decide with their wives whether to proceed together; no wives chose to go.) American forces turned over seventy-six prisoners on 9–10 May.[63] They averaged thirty years of age; all definitely had served in the Red Army and, subsequent to capture, in Wehrmacht ranks; and all, for-tunate to have survived German captivity while millions had not, now un-derwent a long-delayed but no less dreaded rendezvous with an unforgiv-ing homeland. Some unknown fan of code names dubbed various segments of Operation Eastwind "Intrusion" and "Enchain": melodra-matic perhaps, but apt.[64]

In a few cases screening board records have left faint glimpses of the personal dimension of this last sizeable coerced extradition. On 13 De-cember 1946, one of the last interrogations determined that a certain doc-tor who was both a citizen and resident of the U.S.S.R. on 1 September 1939 nevertheless did not have to go back. Although he had worked for the Germans, his interrogators judged him a "doubtful subject for forced repatriation" because he possessed a medical certificate exempting him from Soviet military service and since December 1945 civilians in U.S. custody were free to remain abroad. But on 27 February 1947, the fifth screening board reversed the decision, placing the now-distraught physi-cian on the repatriation roster. Had he forged his medical certificate? Was he found to be an ex-POW or a war criminal? AFHQ records pro-

vide no explanation for this reclassification. The doctor's wife could accompany him back to Russia but, as a civilian, she was not bound to. The
couple parted. One can only imagine the agony entailed by the last entry
in the records for this "Female Age 31": "24 May 1947–Not interviewed
by Russian Mission as she had previously elected in writing not to accompany her husband on this forcible repatriation, and pursuant to policy,
was not required to do so."[65]

After the completion of operations Keelhaul and Eastwind, Italian
authorities turned over to AFHQ ten Soviet Georgians, all unmarried
and all bound to be sent home as military collaborators. One escaped; a
second suffering from a "leaking liver" and a third with active tuberculo-
sis were not expected to live; officials declared a fourth "demented." On
6 June Allied Forces Headquarters had the remaining six shipped out of
Rimini bound for turnover, this time at Semmering, south of Vienna.
About 4:00 P.M. on 8 June 1947, Russian officials took custody of the half-
dozen Georgians, placing them in a railroad prison van bound for
Vienna. From the military viewpoint, no "incidents" occured on this, the
last documented instance of forced repatriation.[66]

To hear many U.S. officials talk, one would think involuntary repatriation had never occurred. Five days after Eastwind, Major General Daniel
Noce in the War Department's Civil Affairs Division assured New York's
Council for Democracy that "the United States Government has taken a
firm stand against any forced repatriation and will continue to maintain
this position. At the same time, the United States Government is ready to
assist those people who wish to return voluntarily to their country of origin. . . . There is no intention that any refugee be returned home against
his will." On 13 June, five days after the last Georgians went home, Colonel R. H. Chard, also of the Civil Affairs Division, answered a Russian
émigré's inquiry in a more discriminating, but still grossly mistaken, manner. After enumerating the three categories still subject to forced
turnover to Soviet authorities (ex-Osttruppen, ex-POWs, and proven civilian collaborators), this official allowed that "it is not and has not been
[*sic*] the policy of the U.S. and British Government involuntarily to repatriate any Russian not falling into one of the above three groups." That
same week Major General John H. Hilldring, director of SHAEF's Civil
Affairs Division, publicly claimed DPs could either stay in the West or go
home as they wished: "We steadfastly refuse to force them back."[67]

In July 1947 Lieutenant Colonel Jerry M. Sage, attached to European
Command Headquarters and directly involved with DP camp administration, somehow testified to a Congressional committee that "it has not
been [*sic*] and is not the policy of the United States government to force
displaced persons to return to the area from which they came." The sum-

mer of 1945 also saw Secretary of State George C. Marshall emphatically maintain that opposition to forced repatriation was "fixed policy" with the United States; that "no instances of coercion have been brought to our attention"; and that "it is against American tradition for us to compel these persons, who are now under our authority, to return against their will." Yet as U.S. Army chief of staff until November 1945, Marshall himself had been directly involved with JCS in orders effecting indiscriminate mass transfers of Soviet citizens.[68]

In 1949, General Lucius Clay, postwar commander of occupied Germany, likewise asserted proudly—and inaccurately—"The United States has consistently refused . . . to accept the Russian thesis that citizens of the Soviet Union should be forced to return." No less mistaken was General Walter Bedell Smith in praising U.S. fidelity to "the traditional American attitude toward giving sanctuary to political refugees." The onetime ambassador to Moscow even maintained that, except for "actual war criminals," those crowded into the camp church at Kempten were *not* repatriated. No conclusion can be drawn but that an array of high-level spokesmen, including majors, colonels, generals, even one cabinet-level secretary, knowingly misled the nation in their public statements on American repatriation policy.[69]

The Keelhaul-Eastwind affair appears to have been a concluding sacrifice of a relative handful of ex-collaborator soldiers in an unspoken tradeoff with Moscow, since it coincided with the AFHQ declaration that several thousand Soviet DPs in Italy were finally eligible for resettlement abroad. This Italian operation does seem to have been a last "sop" to Soviet Russia, to use Lord Bethell's blunt characterization, when one considers that of 509 persons held at Pisa only seventy-six were repatriated forcibly. American review boards ruled 286 camp members to be non-Soviet and 110 Soviet but nonrepatriable; thirty-four escaped, and three died. The vast majority at Pisa, spared the ordeal of Eastwind, "were outshipped [to ordinary DP camps] from PWE 339 at Pisa on 23 June 1947, concluding MTOUSA [Mediterranean Theater of Operations, United States Army] responsibility in this Allied Project."[70]

While the use of force in repatriation ended with the northern Italian episodes of May and June 1947, uncertainty remains concerning any formal abrogation of the policy. Throughout 1947 and on into 1948 General Smith, American ambassador to Moscow, dealt with the issue of claimants to U.S. citizenship among East Europeans deported to Soviet prison camps.[71] Soviet officials repeatedly refused American embassy personnel permission to contact these persons. By 31 July 1947 the lack of Soviet cooperation had prompted the State Department to consider barring Russian liaison officers from Western DP camps or declaring "that the

Yalta Agreement is no longer in effect."[72] All through the fall and on into
January 1948 various American military commands responded, almost
always in favor of some countermeasure against the Russians.[73] No more
came of the July 1947 proposals than of Ambassador Harriman's calls for
quid pro quo handling of Moscow back in 1944. The State Department
assumed that SWNCC would rule on its recommendations, but apparently the coordinating committee never did.[74] The last Soviet repatriation team did not leave the West until March 1949.[75] And Washington
never issued a statement declaring the completion of U.S. obligations under the Yalta exchange agreement.[76]

Involuntary repatriation ended with no momentous U.S. policy rever-
sal finally and totally proscribing the use of force.[77] Rather, the number of
persons subject to removal to Russia simply dwindled until none were left
to coerce.[78] With the realization that Washington continued to require
formally the repatriation of at least some Soviet citizens through 1946 and
1947, the true significance of the 20 December 1945 ruling becomes apparent. As it turned out this was the last modification of U.S. policy: civilians were no longer required to return, unless proven to have been collaborators, while military personnel still had to go home. The eastward flow
of these pawns of war slowed of its own accord after the flood of refugee
movement in the summer of 1945; the stream was further reduced by
loose interpretation in the field, by Eisenhower's temporary suspension
of the use of force in September, and by the civilian exemption of December 1945. But in the last analysis, the trickle of Soviet nationals to the east
in 1946 and 1947 dried up not because of any Western change of heart
reflected in concrete policy revision, but because the military finally ran
out of eligible candidates to return.

The answer to the troubling question of how many persons returned to
Russia unwillingly and how many willingly is elusive. To start with, the
roughly 500,000 nonreturners clearly did not desire to go home, Soviet
charges of Western brainwashing notwithstanding (see ch. 7). Second, all
repatriates were not apoplectic or suicidal in the face of repatriation, contrary to émigré and like-minded accounts, just as all repatriates were not
ecstatic about their reunion with the motherland, contrary to Soviet apol-
ogetics. Thus, while it is a certainty that some returners went home unwillingly and others willingly, it is a mystery what percentage desired and
what percentage dreaded repatriation. The best that can be managed are
random samples of DP sentiment. Naturally, those who had served in
German ranks were the most likely of all Soviet citizens abroad to object
to repatriation, though surprisingly, not all did.[79] Those civilians who had
collaborated openly with the Germans or curried their favor also had reason for anxiety about going home. Even ordinary POWs might oppose

their repatriation if they dwelled long on Moscow's automatic designation of surviving POWs as traitors. Those with the least visible cause for alarm were the Ostarbeiter deported to Germany as forced laborers—yet numbers of them also left the West against their will.

As always in the study of Soviet history the tendentiousness or the silence of the sources requires that judgments be made with circumspection. So it is in attempting to quantify the personal inclinations of repatriates. Firsthand reports can play havoc even with the above estimates of categories of people more or less likely to object. In one instance, for example, older civilian deportees vociferously objected to being sent home, defying the logic that they had the least to fear from repatriation. "We had to go round the farms," a British lieutenant working in the Ruhr related, "to collect the Russians who had been working as labourers on the farms—mostly old men and women, and were amazed and somewhat perplexed to have people who had literally been slaves on German farms, falling on their knees in front of you and begging to be allowed to stay, and crying bitterly—not with joy—when they were told they were being sent back to Russia."[80]

In the same vein a former U.S. Army sergeant recalled over thirty years later, "From my own observations and numerous conversations with Military Police of 11th armored Division and of 12th Corps, some of whom I had known for quite a few years, it is painfully clear that many Soviet nationals did not *want* to return to Russia."[81] Without a doubt force played a role at Camp Rupert in 1944, at Fort Dix and Camp Kempten in 1945, at Dachau and Plattling in 1946, and at Pisa in 1947. Uncontestably, then, there were Soviet citizens opposed to going home.

And just as surely as there were reluctant repatriates, there were those resigned to or even eager about returning to Russia. First, there were those naive enough to think that Russia's dictator harbored no reservations about POWs and forced laborers exposed to Nazism and capitalism. Soviet literature, distributed in DP camps by cooperative Western officials, emphasized—it would be more accurate to say manufactured—this positive side to repatriation, thus contributing to the delusion of the more gullible.[82] In wartime Russia the sentiment was widely held that victory would be followed by liberalization at home.[83] Such credulity extended to at least a portion of Soviet citizens abroad and inclined some to accept repatriation passively, especially as no other option seemed open anyway. Thus, the less politically articulate, including a portion of the POWs, frequently went home willingly, even if uneasy and apprehensive about their reception.[84]

Having endured unspeakable hardships and dangers for years, a large number of Soviet citizens abroad were not prepared for liberation or decision-making of any kind. Physically and emotionally spent, a certain percentage, including even some Vlasovites, faced freedom from Nazi captivity in a daze and repatriation with indifference. These people who had followed orders all their lives (some, the tsar's; and all, Lenin's and Stalin's, then Hitler's) did not possess any reservoir of initiative necessary to check the momentum of mass repatriation, particularly in the frenzied, chaotic refugee movements of the summer of 1945. It is safe to say that a majority of returners were of humble peasant or worker origin. And many of these folk went home without a fuss because they had wearied of trying to cope with foreign ways; or were overwhelmed with homesickness and nostalgia; or simply possessed a primitive, inchoate craving for the familiar. The desire to be reunited with loved ones, for instance, was a natural enough motivation and a powerful one, even if unrealistic, given the harsh reception awaiting repatriates.[85]

While some refugees absolutely opposed their transfer to Soviet custody, and some faced the prospect with ambivalence or resignation, still others looked homeward with genuine anticipation. A Red Army defector, almost incapable of a generous remark about Soviet Russia, nevertheless admitted that he had seen DPs in 1945 clearly willing to return home of their own accord: "They told us about their lives in small German towns since their liberation from concentration camps. They had waited and waited for Soviet authorities to appear, but their patience gave out and they started to walk home. They wanted to be back in Russia."[86] An American colonel witnessed a nearly identical demonstration of patriotic fealty. About the first week of May 1945, near Augsburg, Germany, this officer's unit came across twenty Russian ex-POWs heading home: "They had walked out of the POW camp where they had been incarcerated after the guards had fled. . . . This group was hiking east with the hopes of reaching the Russian army."[87]

In reckoning the proportion of voluntary and involuntary repatriates, perhaps the greatest difficulty lies in distinguishing between genuine and feigned expressions of loyalty to the Soviet Union. How much credibility can be afforded the holiday trappings commonplace at exchange points: garlands, streamers, pictures of Stalin, smiles, laughter and singing, mandolins, accordions, even orchestras? Or how can one know the degree of sincerity behind the banners carried by marching columns or the slogans chalked on wagons and boxcars: "Long live the First of May," or "Long live our Motherland," or "Glory to the Father of our Victories, the Great Stalin"?[88]

The air of lightheartedness and exuberance among some repatriating ex-Ostarbeiter and ex-POWs, which the Army Signal Corps captured on film, and to which numerous sources attest, may have been the attempts of anxious folk to put the best face on events they felt powerless to control. Germany's defeat notwithstanding, they were still the pawns of war. The coming interrogations could only go worse for them if they did not appear eager from the start to get home. Thus it was "in their interest to pretend to be delighted at the prospect of repatriation."[89]

Disguising resignation to the inevitability of return as joyful anticipation was the work not only of the displaced themselves but of Moscow's repatriation commission as well. U.S. and British acquiescence in Soviet internal administration of Western DP camps made it extremely dangerous for any refugee to voice reservations about going home. The extraterritoriality of the compounds holding ex-Ostarbeiter and ex–Red Army men, conceded by the West at Yalta, not only aided the political reconditioning of displaced Soviet citizens even before they left the West, but it absolutely decreased the size of the nonreturning faction.[90] In the absence of a firm figure for the number of Soviet citizens desiring to remain abroad, the only sure conclusion is this: many more would have stayed in the West had they been given the opportunity.

In summary, the United States along with Britain gave millions of anxious Soviet citizens no choice other than repatriation. This nightmarish game of chess, which the German invasion had set in motion, ended as it had begun, with soldiers making sure the unwilling pawns of war moved as directed. Many in the U.S. military, though, came to object strongly to orders involving them in so sordid a task. And the objections, from privates and generals alike, multiplied until the makers of policy belatedly responded to the growing reservations of its implementers. American repatriation policy, then, did evolve toward a humanitarian consideration for the welfare of Soviet war refugees, but not fast enough to make much difference. The December 1945 decision to exempt Soviet civilians from forced returned to Russia proved to be limited and late. It did not cover those persons most desiring to remain abroad, and it took effect after the vast majority of Soviet nationals already had been repatriated.

The most convincing explanation for American insensitivity toward displaced Soviet citizens is to be found in Washington's frantic preoccupation with ways and means—any means—of retrieving United States POWs from Eastern Europe. But that does not explain the continuation of the use of force well into 1947, until all subject to return had been repatriated. The mounting opposition to coerced extradition, the expansion of exempt categories, the military's often lax field policy, and the collapse of the East-West alliance: all of these postwar developments together still did not bring a complete halt to the involuntary homegoing of reluctant Soviet citizens. Repatriation seemed to take on a momentum and an existence apart from the forces that had called it into being in the first place.

Events outstripped the ponderous evolution of U.S. policy toward a more flexible approach to Soviet nationals afraid to go home. Those were the days when orders were orders; in the case of orders based on the Yalta repatriation accord, reinterpretations of any use to reluctant returners most frequently came after the fact.

NOTES

1. Eisenhower, *Crusade*, 439.
2. Special War Problems Division memorandum by Bernard Gufler, 6 Jan. 1945, NA RG 59, 762.61114.
3. McNarney to AGWAR, 24 Jan. 1945, NA RG 334, USMMM-POWs, Oct. 1943–Oct. 1945; Draft counterproposals and JLC Corrigendum to JLC 203/10, 29 Jan. 1945, NA RG 218, CCS 383.6 (7-4-44) (2) Sec. 2; Grew to Ambassador Reber, 3 Feb. 1945, NA RG 59, 800.4016DP/1-1945.
4. Buhite, "Soviet-American Relations," 394.
5. EUCOM, "RAMP's," 53; SWNCC to Byrnes, 9 Mar. 1945, *FR, 1945*, V: 1076-77. SHAEF concurred in a 16 April revision of its Memorandum 39. Proudfoot, *European Refugees*, 463-64.
6. Briefing book, 2 July 1945, *FR, Potsdam*, I: 794; Grew to Murphy, 11 July 1945, *FR, 1945*, V: 1098; USFET, Military Government, "Soviet Repatriation," *Weekly Information Bulletin*, 19 (1 Dec. 1945), 27; *New York Times*, 30 May 1945. The 42 percent figure comes from Kulischer to Feldmesser, 13 Aug. 1953, Harvard Project on the Soviet Social System, Russian Research Center, Cambridge, Mass.
7. Viktor Kravchenko, *I Chose Freedom* (New York, 1946); Grew to Stettinius, 8 Feb. 1945, *FR, Yalta*, 697; Appendix B of JLC report 1266/3 to JCS, 2 Mar. 1945, NA RG 218, CCAC file, 383.6 (2-25-44) Sec. 2; Stettinius Briefing Papers, 1-3.
8. OCMH, "Exchange," 7; EUCOM, "RAMP's," 53.
9. SHAEF to WD, 10 Mar. 1945, NA RG 218, CCS 383.6 (7-4-44) (2) Sec. 5. See also CCS Memorandum, "Implementation and Interpretation of . . . Agreement on Liberated Prisoners of War and Civilians," 11 May 1945, NAS RG 165, WDGSS G1 383.6 (8 May 42) Sec. 6, Part 2. Estimates of their number range from 30,000 to 46,065. The latter figure is probably more accurate, since it includes those turned over to the Belgians. The first figure refers only to those in French custody. An enclosure in Stimson to Secretary of State, 17 May 1945, NA RG 165, WDGSS OPD df 383.6, Sec. 15, Case 413, gives 30,000. OCMH, "Exchange," 4, and EUCOM, "RAMP's," 48, both say 46,065.
10. CDPX to AGWAR for JCS, 29 Aug. 1945, NA RG 331, USFET.
11. Krasnov, *Hidden Russia*. The details of this British operation have been amply covered by Bethell, *Secret*; Tolstoy, *Secret*; Naumenko, *Velikoe predatel'stvo*, I and II.
12. From Frank L. Howley's introduction to Krasnov, *Hidden Russia*, x. For similar responses by a British general see Kirk to Secretary of State, 11 Sept. and 6 Dec. 1945, NA RG 59, 800.4016 DP/ 9-1145, and 800.4016 DP/ 12-645, respectively.

13. Coffin, *Once*, 72, 77-78.

14. Ernest Harmon, *Combat Commander: Autobiography of a Soldier* (Englewood Cliffs, N.J., 1970), 256.

15. Anthony Hlynka, "On Behalf of Ukrainian Displaced Persons," *Ukrainian Review*, 2 (Winter 1946), 171.

16. Murphy to Secretary of State, 22 Feb. 1946, NA RG 59, 800.4016DP/2-2246. See also Eugene Lyons, "Orphans of Tyranny," *Plain Talk*, 2 (Mar. 1948), 44; Proudfoot, *European Refugees*, 214-15.

17. BBC, *Orders from Above*; Coffin, *Once*, 72, 77-78; Tolstoy, *Secret*, 366, 369; confidential letter to author, 28 Dec. 1977.

18. Bethell, *Secret*, 179-80, 208; Kathryn C. Hulme, *The Wild Place* (Boston, 1953), 49-51; Lyons, *Secret*, 263-64.

19. Proudfoot, *European Refugees*, 217. See also Gaddis, *Origins*, 81; OCMH, "Exchange," 13. Some British officers used the same stratagem: Cook, "Revealing," 86; Tolstoy, *Secret*, 344.

20. Coffin, *Once*, 65; Bethell, *Secret*, 174.

21. Lt. Gen. J. A. H. Gammell to British Resident Minister, 25 Nov. 1944, NAS RG 331, AFHQ.

22. Demitrii Shimkin to author, 17 Aug. 1976.

23. Harry L. Coles and Albert K. Weinberg, *Civil Affairs: Soldiers Become Governors* (Washington, D.C., 1964), 582; SWNCC (with JCS concurrence) to SACMED, 31 Mar. 1945, NA RG 59, 740.99114 EW/3-345; AGWAR (for JCS) to SHAEF (Eisenhower), 5 Apr. 1945, NA RG 331, USFET.

24. Kirk to Byrnes, 7 Aug. 1945, *FR, 1945*, V: 1103; Byrnes to Kirk, 9 Aug. 1945, ibid., 1104; Thomas M. Ruddy, "Charles E. Bohlen and the Soviet Union, 1929-1969" (Ph.D. diss., Kent State University, 1973), 59.

25. Kuznetsov, *V ugodu Stalinu*, II: 114; Office of the Chief Historian, European Command, *Survey of Soviet Aims, Policies and Tactics* (Frankfurt, 1948), 264; OCMH, "Exchange," 10.

26. Murphy to Byrnes and Byrnes [H. Freeman Matthews] to Murphy, 27 Aug. 1945, NA RG 59, 740.62114/8-2745.

27. CDPX to AGWAR (for JCS), 29 Aug. 1945, and Adcock (with approval of Lt. Gen. Walter B. Smith) to CS, 31 Aug. 1945, NA RG 331, USFET, G5 Division, 383.7.

28. SHAEF (Eisenhower) to JCS, 5 June 1945, NA RG 218, CCAC file 383.6 (2-25-44) Sec. 2, Enclosure A of JCS 1324/3; Eisenhower to SD, 4 Sept. 1945, *FR, 1945*, V: 1106. A member of Eisenhower's staff, now a professor of geography at the University of Illinois, wrote me, identifying himself as the drafter of the 4 September memo. Shimkin to author, 17 Aug. 1976.

29. SWNCC Memorandum, "Use of United States Troops in Repatriating Soviet Citizens," 25 Sept. 1945, NAS RG 165, WDGSS, ACS 383.6 (8 May 42) Sec. 6, Part 1.

30. Acheson to Byrnes, 29 Sept. 1945, *FR, 1945*, V: 1106-8. In a 17 Aug. 1976 letter to the author Shimkin, formerly of Eisenhower's staff, wrote, "The Acheson position was always one of favoring repatriation on legalistic grounds." Furthermore, the undersecretary was a "philistine" and "sycophant of the first order," who played a "disgraceful role" in the forced return of Soviet citizens. The available evidence does not support this harsh a view of Acheson's part in repatriation.

31. Bethell, *Secret*, 181; Byrnes to Molotov, 12 Sept. 1945, Council of Foreign

Ministers, NA RG 43; Byrnes to Kirk, 27 Sept. 1945, NA RG 59, 740.62114/9-2745.

32. Byrnes to Grew, 28 Sept. 1945, and Acheson to Byrnes, 29 Sept. 1945, *FR, 1945*, V: 1106-8. For a blisteringly hostile biography of Byrnes see Messer, "The Making of a Cold Warrior." Byrnes's move at the London meeting of the Council of Foreign Ministers away from the original interpretation of the Yalta repatriation accord parallels Messer's thesis that the secretary of state rode the Cold War tide by disassociating himself as much as possible from FDR and Yalta. See also Athan Theoharis, "James F. Byrnes: Unwitting Yalta Myth Maker," *Political Science Quarterly*, 81 (Dec. 1966): 581-92.

33. Bethell, *Secret*, 181-82; *New York Times*, 5 Oct. 1945. See also Hlynka, "Displaced Persons," 173.

34. One unpublished source mistakenly contends that 20 Dec. was the date the JCS "announced categorically" that forced repatriation was United States policy: EUCOM, "RAMP's" 65. Published accounts repeating the error include: "Document Tells Allied Part in Deaths of Thousands," *Sunday Oklahoman*, 21 Jan. 1973; Epstein, "American Forced Repatriation," 359; Steenberg, *Vlasov*, 221.

35. SWNCC to Byrnes, 21 Dec. 1945, *FR, 1945*, V: 1109. The editors provided a great deal more information about this document than most, suggesting that they recognized its unique significance. SWNCC 46/8, 21 Nov. 1945, NA RG 353, SWNCC, 46 Series, 383.6 POW, Russia. On the difficulties and delays in effecting any policy changes through SWNCC, see Zink, "American Civil-Military Relations," 227-28.

36. SWNCC to Byrnes, 21 Dec. 1945, *FR, 1945*, V: 1109. See also JCS to McNarney and Gen. Clark, 20 Dec. 1945, NA RG 218, CCS 383.6 (7-4-44) (2) Sec. 7; Tolstoy, *Secret*, 353.

37. SWNCC to Byrnes, 27 Aug. 1945, *FR, 1945*, V: 1108.

38. Epstein, "Forced Repatriation," 210.

39. Jefferson, "Bureaucracy," 101; Gaddis, *Origin*, 218; Harriman, *America and Russia*, 40. Truman also learned of the problem from Earl G. Harrison, dean of the University of Pennsylvania Law School, whom he sent on tour of European DP camps and who advised him in August 1945 that forced repatriation was not the answer to the refugee problem. *Amerika*, 13 Oct. 1945. Finally, Clark Clifford's 100,000-word Soviet affairs report of 24 Sept. 1946 misinformed Truman that "the United States has not met many Soviet demands for repatriation of unwilling U.S.S.R. citizens not clearly shown to be war criminals." Gaddis, *Origins*, 321-22. See also Arthur Krock, *Memoirs: Sixty Years on the Firing Line* (New York, 1968), 223, 419-62 (for the full report); Russia folder, box 15, Clark Clifford Papers, Harry S. Truman Library, Independence, Mo. Apparently the only instance of Truman's direct involvement with the Soviet DP question came with his personal approval of a strongly worded State Department press release of 30 Apr. 1945, rebutting charges made by Golikov in *Pravda* that Washington was not living up to the Yalta repatriation accord. Secretary of State to Grew, 30 Apr. 1945, NA RG 59, 740.00114EW/4-3045.

40. Roger Makins to Matthews, 6 Oct. 1945, *FR, 1945*, II: 1193; memorandum of conversation by Elbridge Durbrow, 27 Dec. 1945, *FR, 1945*, V: 1110. For a later repetition of British objections, see Byrnes to Kirk, 14 Mar. 1946, *FR, 1946*, V: 152. On transport delays, see "Repatriation Progress Virtually Stalled," 14 Feb. 1946, NAS RG 165, WDGSS, Intelligence Review, no. 1, p. 53.

41. Memorandum by Matthews, 9 Jan. 1946, NA RG 59, 762.6114/1-946.

42. McNarney to WD, 19 Apr. 1946, *FR, 1946*, V: 154. See also McNarney to WD, 27 Apr. 1946, ibid., 155; EUCOM, "RAMP's," 69; OCMH, "Exchange," 12.

43. JCS to McNarney, 7 June 1946, *FR, 1946*, V: 170; memorandum by SD member of SWNCC attached to "Use of United States Troops in Repatriating Soviet Citizens," 1 May 1946, NA RG 218, CCS 383.6 (7-4-44) (2) Sec. 8.

44. Bethell, *Secret*, xiii. See also ibid., 176; Tolstoy, *Secret*, 157; Cook, "Revealing," 83.

45. Bethell, *Secret*, 178; Alexander to War Office, 23 Aug. 1945, NAS RG 331, Roll 228-B, AFHQ, Forced Repatriation, W0204/Item 359. Initially, U.S. forces in Italy transferred all Soviet citizens to British control: Col. E. E. Hyde, GSC exec., to Sec. Gen. Staff, 7 Dec. 1944, NAS RG 331, AFHQ. For accounts of the early British operations, which involved large numbers of Soviet Asiatics, including remnants of the Wehrmacht's 162nd Turkic Division, see Thorwald, *Illusion*, 311-12; Tolstoy, *Secret*, 304-6, 360-62.

46. Bethell, *Secret*, 181. See also ibid., 177-79, 184; Tolstoy, *Secret*, 273-345.

47. Minutes of AFHQ meeting, 7 Feb. 1946, NAS RG 331, Roll 228-B, AFHQ, Forced Repatriation, W0204/Item 359; Troopers to GHQCMF, 11 Feb. 1946, Roll 312, W0204/Items 661-66, ibid.; Kirk to Secretary of State, 6 Feb. 1946, *FR, 1946*, V: 133-34.

48. Tolstoy, *Secret*, 360.

49. Maj. Gen. T. S. Airey, CS, to AFHQ, 27 July 1946, NAS RG 331, AFHQ, Roll 41-J; Naumenko, *Velikoe predatel'stvo*, II: 209. The same operation entailed the transfer of 200 Croats (Ustashi) from Fermo to Afragola.

50. "Forcible Repatriation of Displaced Soviet Citizens—Operation Keelhaul," Vol. I, 161, NAS RG 331, AFHQ, G-5 file 383.7-14.1, Reel 17-L (hereafter cited as "Keelhaul").

51. Airey to AFHQ, 27 July 1946, NAS RG 331, AFHQ, Roll 41-J. Tolstoy, using an émigré source, attributes the lack of incidents to the Allies' "elaborate precautions against suicides," including guards provisioned with "small-arms, handcuffs and tear-gas grenades." Tolstoy, *Secret*, 361, citing Naumenko, *Velikoe predatel'stvo*, II: 192-93, 211. The irreconcilable discrepancy of no guards versus heavily armed guards on the 14-15 Aug. transfer is not crucial in the light of the subsequent, well-documented forcible repatriation of these same ex-Osttruppen from Pisa and Riccioni to the Soviet zone of Austria.

52. "Keelhaul," I: 79-80.

53. Ibid., 8.

54. Airey, CS, to AFHQ, 27 July 1946, NAS RG 331, AFHQ, Roll 41-J.

55. Tolstoy, *Secret*, 361, 371; Epstein, *Operation Keelhaul*; Huxley-Blythe, *East*, 216. Epstein, an émigré journalist, published many articles and the first book-length documented secondary account specifically on Soviet repatriation (reviewed by Ralph T. Fisher, Jr., in *Slavic Review*, 34 [Dec. 1975], 823-25; Elliott in *Canadian American Slavic Studies*, 9 [Spring 1975], 125-26). Epstein equated Operation Keelhaul with the involuntary return of millions from all over Europe rather than the hundreds in Italy to which it actually pertained. The confusion arose in part from the title of the three-volume dossier of AFHQ documents, "Forcible Repatriation of Soviet Citizens. Operation Keelhaul" (NAS RG 331, AFHQ), unavailable to scholars until Mar.-Apr. 1978. Epstein assumed these records covered much more than Italy and saw their continued classification as a cover-up. The State Department's readily available *Foreign Relations* series,

which Epstein failed to use in his book, documents forced repatriation at great length. American archivists are almost certainly correct in arguing that delays in releasing "Operation Keelhaul" stemmed from Britain's longstanding veto over the declassification of these joint-command records.

56. "Keelhaul," I: 70.

57. Ibid., 6-7, II: 2, 65, 107, 156, 247.

58. Ibid., II: 155, 157, 31, 40. See Tolstoy, *Secret*, 363, for similar, though rarer, instances of liberal rulings by the British at Riccioni.

59. "Keelhaul," II: 104-6.

60. SD to American Consular Officer, Winnipeg, Canada, 12 Mar. 1947, NA RG 59, 740.62111/2-1947.

61. "Keelhaul," II: 157; Col. Perry McC. Smith, GSC, Actg. ACS, to AFHQ and MTOUSA, 18 July 1946, NAS RG 331, AFHQ, Roll 41-J.

62. "Keelhaul," II: 76, 98, 113; Bethell, *Secret*, 196.

63. AFHQ, Rome, to AGWAR for CCS, 20 May 1947, NA RG 165, CAS Exec. Office Admin. Sect. One POW subject to forced repatriation escaped the night of 18 Feb., possibly before the tally of seventy-seven mentioned earlier; and another POW bound for extradition died of a heart condition 23 Feb., thus bringing the total transferred from Pisa down to seventy-six. "Keelhaul," II: 51. Accounts that allege "numerous suicides" and "savage violence employed by troops" (Tolstoy, *Secret*, 368) or 100 prisoner fatalities and thirty to forty AFHQ dead and wounded (Naumenko, *Velikoe predatel'stvo*, II: 210) greatly exaggerate this episode. R. R. Stokes, M.P., repeated these exact figures in his 1947 parliamentary protest of forced repatriation, which, in turn, found its way into the Keelhaul file. In the spring of 1978, journalists, rapidly scanning the newly declassified documents, mistakenly took these figures as accurate, even though adjoining correspondence cast grave doubt on their validity. For example, see Mike Feinsilber, UPI dispatch, 17 Apr. 1978. An abridged version appeared in *Ann Arbor News*, 23 Apr. 1978, under the title, "Post-War Forced Repatriations to Soviets Reported." "Keelhaul," III: 59-60. For the 8-10 May British episode see Epstein, *Operation Keelhaul*, 82-86; Bethell, *Secret*, 194-203; Tolstoy, *Secret*, 364-70.

64. "Keelhaul," II: 60-61; Col. Smith, GSC, Actg. ACS, to AFHQ and MTOUSA, 18 July 1946, NAS RG 331, AFHQ, Roll 41-J.

65. "Keelhaul," II: 37.

66. Ibid., 1A, 5, 9, 13, 18.

67. Maj. Gen. Daniel Noce, GSC Chief, CAD, to James E. Greer, Council for Democracy, 15 May 1947, NA RG 165, CAD WDSCA 383.7, 1-30 Apr. 1947, Sec. XVI; Col. R. H. Chard, GSC Exec., to Nicholas Rybakoff, 13 June 1947, NA RG 165, CAD, WDSCA, 383.7, 1 July 47 to Sec. XIX; Hilldring, "Position on Resettlement," 1165. See also George L. Warren, SD adviser on Refugees and DPs, to Rybakoff, 27 June 1947, NA RG 59, FW 800.4016 DP/6-2747.

68. Jerry M. Sage, "The Future of DP's in Europe," *Department of State Bulletin*, 17 (13 July 1947), 87; George C. Marshall, "Policy of Repatriation of Displaced Persons," ibid., 16 (1 June 1947), 1085; Marshall, "Concern Expressed on Resettlement of Displaced Persons," ibid., 17 (27 July 1947), 195. See also Epstein, "Forced Repatriation," 210; Marshall to Acting Secretary of State, 17 Apr. 1947, *FR, 1947*, II: 352. JCS interpreted the Yalta repatriation treaty as requiring force and, though not the instigator of the policy, played a major role in its enforcement. CCAC Report for JCS, 8 July 1945, *FR, Potsdam*, I: 798; and Kirk to

Stettinius, 7 Aug. 1945, *FR, 1945,* V: 1103.

69. *New York Times,* 17 Feb. 1949; Walter Bedell Smith, *My Three Years in Moscow* (Philadelphia, 1950), 25. Other sources that evade the fact or flatly deny that the United States once subjected ordinary Soviet citizens to forced repatriation include: Mark Clark, *Calculated Risk* (New York, 1950), 476; Coles and Weinberg, *Soldiers Become Governors,* 582; Robert Divine, *American Immigration Policy, 1924-1952* (New Haven, Conn., 1957), 111; Eubank, *Russians,* 76-77; Friedrich, *Military Government,* 181; U.S. Department of State, *Occupation of Germany, Policy and Progress, 1945-46* (Washington, D.C., 1947), 26.

70. Bethell, *Secret,* 203; "Keelhaul," II: 66.

71. Smith to SD, 16 Jan. 1947, NA RG 59, 740.162114/1-1647; Smith to SD, 5 Feb. 1947, *FR, 1947,* IV: 720; SD to Soviet embassy, 28 May 1947, ibid., 728-29.

72. H. A. Fierst to CAD Exec. Officer, NA RG 165, CAD WDSCA 383.7, 1 July 47 to Sec. XIX.

73. COMGENUSFA Vienna to CAD Washington, 26 Sept. 1947, and HQ EUCOM Frankfurt to Dept. of the Army, 1 Nov. 1947, NA RG 165, CAD WDSCA, 383.7 Sec. XXI; Fierst to Exec. Officer, CAD, 5 Dec. 1947 and Asst. Sec. of State Charles E. Saltzman to Undersecretary of the Army William H. Draper, Jr., 8 Jan. 1948, NA RG 165, CAD WDSCA 383.7, 1 July 1947 to Sec. XIX.

74. Fierst to Exec. Officer, CAD, 31 July 1947, NA RG 165, CAD WDSCA 383.7, 1 July 47 to Sec. XIX. This researcher could find no record of a decision on the State Department's 31 July proposals.

75. Walter M. Kotsching, "Problems of the Resettlement Program," *Department of State Bulletin,* 20 (13 Mar. 1949), 307-8; OMGUS to CS of CAD, 22 Mar. 1949, NA RG 165, WDGSS, "IRO Feeding of Soviet Mission"; "U.S. Requests Withdrawal of Soviet Repatriation Mission from American Zone in Germany," *Department of State Bulletin,* 20 (13 Mar. 1949), 320-22.

76. Inexplicably, Bohlen telegrammed Ambassador Smith at the end of July 1948, demonstrating that he at least believed U.S. policy no longer permitted the return of any Soviet nationals against their wills: "It is believed that the *forced* repatriation of any category of displaced person would be an undesirable departure from the present repatriation policy of this Government." Bohlen, for Secretary of State, to Smith, 30 July 1948, *FR, 1948,* IV: 906. How Bohlen arrived at his understanding remains a mystery. American repatriation of postwar Red Army defectors up to the start of the Soviet blockade of Berlin in July 1948 further confuses the matter. Fischer, *Soviet Opposition,* 115.

77. In contrast, the BBC documentary, *Orders from Above,* states that June 1947 saw not only denunciations of forced repatriation by Parliament but an end to British adherence to the policy.

78. All indications in the documentary record are that the United States never formally rescinded the order requiring the use of force in repatriating Soviet World War II military personnel. Yet numerous commentators, including some with highly respectable credentials, mistakenly have stated that 1946 or 1947 saw Washington consciously put a stop to coerced returns: Bohlen, *Witness,* 199; Burton, "Vlasov," 123; Alice H. Bauer, "A Guide for Interviewing Soviet Escapees," Harvard Project on the Soviet Social System, 30; Dvinov, *Politics,* 6; Merle Fainsod, "Controls and Tensions in the Soviet System," *American Political Science Review,* 44 (June 1950), 268; Fischer, " 'Non-Returners,' " 13; Harriman and Abel, *Special Envoy,* 416; Krasnov, *Hidden Russia,* 326; Lyons, *Secret,*

258, 265; M. I. Mandryka, *Ukrainian Refugees* (Winnipeg, 1946), 7; Martin, "Not 'Displaced Persons,' " 112; Donald Treadgold, *Twentieth Century Russia*, 3rd ed. (Chicago, 1972), 440; Wyle, "Memorandum," 11.

79. Tolstoy, *Secret*, 392; memo of telephone conversation, Col. Rogers to E. Tomlin Bailey, Special War Problems Division, *FR, 1944*, IV: 1272-73.

80. Tolstoy, *Secret*, 313; see also ibid., 314-16.

81. Confidential letter to author, 28 Dec. 1977.

82. *Otvety na volnuiushchie voprosy sovetskikh grazhdan nakhodiashchikhsia za granitsei na polozhenii peremeshchennykh lits* (Moscow, 1949).

83. Werth, *Russia at War*, 852-53.

84. Bethell, *Secret*, 67.

85. Fischer, *Thirteen*, 130; Romanov, *Nights*, 169; Thorwald, *Illusion*, 301; Tolstoy, *Secret*, 299-300, 309, 314, 392. Col. Vernon E. McGuckin, 94th U.S. Infantry Division, had responsibility for 55,000 Soviet DPs after VE-Day. Most left for the Soviet occupation zone willingly, particularly those transferred in May and June. Tolstoy, *Secret*, 312, citing letter to the editor, *Sunday Oklahoman*, 22 Oct. 1972.

86. Koriakov, *I'll Never Go Back*, 231.

87. Col. D. C. Howell to author, 2 Jan. 1978. See also OSS, "Reichswehr," 20.

88. Army Signal Corps film no. 4308, NA RG 111; Bethell, *Secret*, 65; Tolstoy, *Secret*, 313.

89. Bethell, *Secret*, 67. See also ibid., 16, 18; Tolstoy, *Secret*, 85, 113. Since Soviet nationals in Liechtenstein had a choice, Tolstoy takes the high volume of return from there, about two-thirds, as an indication of their genuine willingness. But since Tolstoy himself points out some "feared they might eventually in any case be delivered by force," one has to question how accurate this episode is in reflecting the overall sentiments of repatriates. Tolstoy, *Secret*, 392.

90. Army Signal Corps film no. 4572 (NA RG 111) shows young men in a Soviet-run DP camp being taught a Red Army version of the goose step.

General Andrei Vlasov, the Red Army officer who collaborated with Germany after his capture in 1942.

Patch worn by members of the Russian Liberation Army, the German collaborator unit headed by General Vlasov.

General Filip I. Golikov, head of the Soviet Repatriation Commission.

Stalag 326, Reitberg, Germany, contained 10,000 Soviet POWs when the Second Armored Division, U.S. Ninth Army, liberated it in April 1945.

This German camp for Soviet POWs near Fischbach, Germany, was liberated by the 45th Division, U.S. Seventh Army; many of the men had typhus.

Olaf Jordan's *Russian Prisoner of the Germans.*

V. V. Medvedev's stylized representation of a Soviet POW in German captivity.

IUrii E. Piliar, *Liudi ostaiusia liud'mi* (Moscow, 1966)

Soviet citizens found in German ranks on their arrival in England after their capture on the Western front; March 24, 1945.

Displaced Soviet nationals bound for repatriation from a U.S. Ninth Air Force field in Ger:•any.

A DP camp in Luxemburg for former Soviet forced laborers.

An Army Signal Corpsman films this Russian POW, who was forced to bare his chest to reveal his self-inflicted wounds; Plattling, Germany, 1946.

Nonreturners (adults and children) aboard a boxcar. The group came from pre-war Polish territory that the Soviet Union annexed at the end of the war.

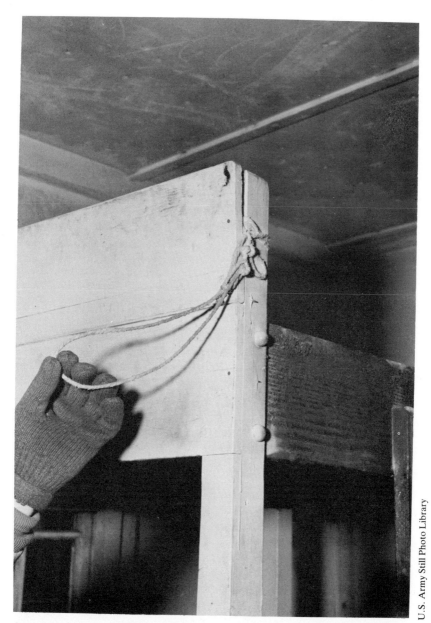

At a former concentration camp at Dachau, Germany, eleven opponents of forced repatriation committed suicide on 17 January 1946; nine men hanged themselves, some with this noose that was attached to a bunkbed.

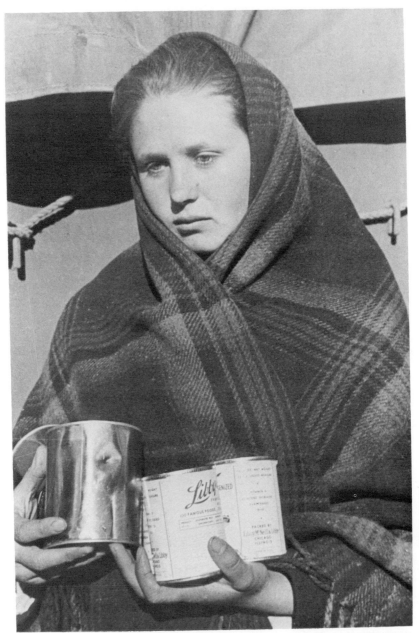

A nonreturner from prewar Polish territory that the Soviet Union annexed after World War II.

6

THE SOVIET REPATRIATION CAMPAIGN:

"Many Times . . . Comrade Stalin Called to Mind You Who Languished in Fascist Camps"

THE SOVIET UNION'S CALCULATED AND ADAMANT demands for the return of all its citizens, which helped retard the liberalization of American repatriation policy, stemmed from a variety of motives—some vindictive, others psychological, economic, demographic, propagandistic, and strategic. Soviet statutes defined treason broadly enough to include not only military collaborators but also POWs and, in numerous instances, forced laborers. A deeply rooted desire for vengeance, a longing "to punish the guilty," which had been enflamed by innumerable Nazi atrocities on Russian soil, meant that repatriation spelled retaliation.[1] Those associated with the Germans, rightly or wrongly, would be severely handled (see ch. 8).

Psychologically, too, Moscow felt it deserved to have its own way on the DP question due to the disproportionate cost of the war to Russia. The Soviet Union faced the postwar era painfully conscious of its huge losses, proud of its herculean success in battle, and in no disposition to brook opposition on repatriation from Allies it did not consider its equals in victory. Soviet fatalities in World War II ran to 20 million, compared to 300,000 for the United States and 330,000 for Britain, which Soviet authorities and ordinary citizens both resented.[2] The 130,000 American fatalities from three and a half years of war in Europe "did not even equal the average number of civilian casualties Russian suffered each fortnight before 1943." For the war the Soviet Union inflicted and suffered 90 percent of the total casualties in the European theater.[3] Besides the human losses, 60 percent of transportation facilities and 70 percent of industrial capacity in the invaded portions of Russia had been destroyed. The government wrote off 1,700 cities and towns and 70,000 villages as total losses.[4] The passage of time has not erased in the least Soviet consciousness of the heavier price paid in the East for Hitler's defeat.[5]

The repeated postponements in launching the second front probably contributed to Soviet bitterness. From the Russian perspective, Lend-Lease shipments simply could not compensate for the delays in the cross-channel invasion of occupied France. Soviet leaders likely would have been suspicious of the Allies' ultimate intentions no matter where or when large-scale Western military actions on the continent commenced. As events unfolded, the Kremlin, bound to think the worst of its partners no matter what, seems to have interpreted Roosevelt's ill-advised promise to Molotov of a second front in Europe in 1942, and its delay until 1944, as evidence that the West was content to see the Wehrmacht bleed Russia white. For example, Ivan Maiskii, wartime Soviet ambassador to London, saw the postponement of Operation Overlord as a deliberate, "ruthless calculation" to let Russia bear the brunt of the fighting.[6]

Paradoxically, American technical and material assistance to the Russian war effort may have heightened suspicion of U.S. motives. Moscow could wonder if the aid were not payment for services rendered, much as England had bankrolled continental armies in centuries past. Whatever the intention, it is easy to see why Russians concluded that that was the effect. Obviously circumstances beyond the control of either the United States or the Soviet Union played an independent role in determining who would sacrifice what in the defeat of Hitler. Nevertheless, the contribution of the United States to victory is best calculated in organizational, technological, and economic terms; Russia's, in casualties. As compensation for its great sufferings and in recognition of its equally great military accomplishments, the Soviet Union seemed to expect its Western Allies to bend over backward to accommodate it in all outstanding disputes. "Convinced that they had won the war," John Gaddis writes, "the Russians showed little inclination to compromise."[7] On repatriation the Kremlin proved to be as insistent and inflexible as on any other issue.

Besides Moscow's vindictive spirit and its psychological predilection to expect full Western cooperation, economic factors contributed to demands for wholesale repatriation. At the end of World War II, within the Soviet age groups that bore arms, only 31 million men survived compared to 52 million women, even counting those displaced by the war, who included more males than females.[8] Reconstruction required the services of every able-bodied Soviet citizen, including the millions abroad in the West at the end of the war. European Russia had been devastated by the fighting, and restoration of the region's productive capacity would require huge outlays of scarce capital and labor. (To be sure, the squandering of millions of repatriates' talents in Soviet labor camps was not an efficient use of people, but it did ease to some degree the postwar labor deficit.)[9]

Similarly, Moscow's long-standing demographic policy influenced its stance on repatriation. Soviet theoreticians believed, and still believe, state encouragement of population growth to be to the country's benefit. Total repatriation then would be a natural corollary. Modern totalitarian states generally have favored the return of national diasporas, and all save the People's Republic of China have favored the sustained growth of human resources. Mussolini, Hitler, and Stalin all implemented pronatalist and anti-emigration demographic policies. Each halted all but political emigration, Mussolini even doing so despite Italian overpopulation; each encouraged women to have large families; and each frowned on foreign travel, not to mention resettlement abroad. Soviet insistence upon repatriation neatly fit the pattern.[10]

The view that totalitarian governments hold of the proper relationship between the state and the individual helps explain their jealous husbanding of population assets. The individual's existence is justified by service to the state, not vice versa. The democratic model of the government existing at the discretion of the people by means of a social contract is reversed. Alfred Sauvy notes, "The feeling that men belong to the community" is "naturally stronger in dictatorial countries. . . . Thus, the Soviet Union tries, sometimes violently to reunite all its nationals inside its borders, even claiming refugees from other countries."[11]

The Soviet Union also demanded total repatriation because nonreturners posed a threat to the credibility of propaganda stressing the unqualified wartime devotion of all Soviet citizens. Upholding the international image of the world's first Marxist state necessitated the rapid, forcible return of all displaced nationals before dramatic instances of resistance could damage its reputation abroad. From Moscow, George Kennan cabled Washington that Soviet leaders feared their standing in the world community would suffer "if it becomes generally known that some Soviet citizens are not accepting with enthusiasm offers of repatriation." Similarly, Robert S. McCollum, a State Department specialist on refugee problems, observed, "Each refugee from the Soviet orbit represents a failure of the Communist system" and thereby "constitutes a challenge to the fundamental concepts of that system."[12]

Leonid Brezhnev has contended that "the Great Patriotic War showed very well that any attempt 'to blast the Soviet Union from within' was bound to be thwarted by the monolithic solidarity of the Party and the people, the Soviet people's loyalty to socialist ideals, and the solid national unity of the USSR's nations, who stood firm in the face of the hard trials."[13] World War II showed no such thing, but it would have been far more difficult for Moscow to have perpetuated this ideological fairy tale had 5.5 million instead of 500,000 of its charges remained abroad. A vote of no confidence of that proportion would have underscored widespread disaffection and grievously compromised the Soviet myth of an unwavering patriotic response to German aggression from all the peoples of Russia. [14]

The prospect of a concentration of anti-Communist political expatriates in the West also unnerved Soviet authorities. Ambassador Averell Harriman noted "extreme touchiness" whenever the subject of reluctant repatriates came up. [15] Without forced repatriation, the millions of disenchanted Soviet DPs remaining abroad might have posed a threat to Russia's national security. Soviet authorities, it seems, were frightened by the spectre of an anti-Stalinist movement in the West coordinated by the remnants of Vlasov's Russian Liberation Army and other collaborator units.

Moscow took the impotent Vlasovites much more seriously than did the Germans or the Western Allies. The story told by captured Soviet agents parachuted behind Wehrmacht lines convinced General Reinhard Gehlen that this was the case. German interrogation of these infiltrators revealed that many had been given "explicit orders to infiltrate . . . [the ROA] army at all costs and to bring Vlasov back dead or alive into Communist hands." Gehlen subsequently advocated that more effective use be made of the anti-Stalinist inclinations of many Soviet POWs. The racial bigotry of party zealots, however, prevented any higher officials from acting upon such advice. And as long as Red Army captives were treated as *untermenschen*, massive support for an anti-Soviet movement was out of the question. [16]

The Nazis' failure to capitalize upon Soviet disaffection no doubt relieved the Kremlin. But Russia's leaders, fearing that the Western powers might succeed where Germany had failed, could not relax until repatriation was complete. Evidencing that concern, Soviet Deputy Commissar of Foreign Affairs Andrei Vyshinskii told the United Nations General Assembly in early November 1946 that "it is no secret that refugee camps, situated in the western zones of Germany, Austria and certain other countries of Western Europe, are springboards and centers for the formation of military reserves of hirelings, which constitute an organized military force in the hands of this or that foreign power." Soviet sensitivity on this issue seemed to fulfill the prediction of U.S. military intelligence that "since the majority of displaced persons and refugees are anti-Communist, the U.S.S.R. undoubtedly will view with suspicion Allied action to allow them to remain abroad free of supervision." It may be, as the *New York Times* contended, that the Kremlin feared postwar political expatriates had "the same potential for causing trouble for Russia as did the White Russians in western Europe after the first World War." [17]

In the early years of the Cold War no one in the West attempted to exploit the anti-Soviet attitudes of nonreturners or even recognized these people as potential partners in the struggle against world Communism. But by the early 1950s East-West hostility had gained a great deal of momentum, and this notion finally did surface. A 1953 call to arms by Eugene Lyons bemoaned the past neglect of *Our Secret Allies, the Peoples of Russia*. To the author of this aggressively anti-Communist piece, the Vlasov movement was a lost opportunity, and the forced repatriation of disaffected Soviet nationals was a "Betrayal of Natural Allies." A Cold War polemic by Boris Shub, a Western journalist, went even further: to free themselves from Red slavery all the Soviet people needed, it was alleged, was a little help from their friends. That being so, "how shall we launch our offer to the Russians of an immediate fighting alliance against our common enemy, the enemy of peace and freedom?" Shub answered his own question by proposing that "the first step should be a solemn proclamation by the President . . . announcing that the United States will throw its full support behind all groups [Vlasovites included] . . . who will act to replace the present Politburo leadership with an interim government pledged to the reestablishment of legitimate and representative government in Russia."[18]

After World War II the U.S. government did not contemplate overthrowing the Soviet regime by force. Nor did it use, or even consider using, disaffected Soviet émigrés as the nucleus for an army bent upon eradicating Communism in Russia. The powerless émigrés did not jeopardize U.S.S.R. national security. Nevertheless, given the Kremlin's innate suspiciousness of the West, it is not surprising that the Soviet Union might have been anxious about this possibility.[19]

Soviet leaders thus had ample cause, from their point of view, to demand that the United States and Britain repatriate all Allied nationals. Proper handling of the matter necessitated a campaign to gain full Western cooperation and total refugee participation. To regain control over all Soviet citizens abroad, the Kremlin relied upon three devices: (1) repatriation agreements (used to pressure the West into returning all DPs by means of accusations of noncompliance); (2) aggressive utilization of Soviet repatriation missions in the West; and (3) direct appeals to persuade the hesitant to return home.

Moscow's program for obtaining the West's unreserved assistance in repatriation relied heavily upon the American and British exchange accords signed at Yalta and similar instruments negotiated with France, Belgium, Switzerland, Norway, and the East European countries occupied by the Red Army.[20] If interpreted to the Kremlin's liking, these documents would have settled the question by requiring the return of all Soviet nationals abroad, regardless of their individual wishes. Since Soviet authorities could not consider Western concurrence a foregone conclusion, they coupled demands for adherence to repatriation agreements with accusations of Allied mistreatment of Russian refugees. These complaints served not only to bolster Soviet repatriation efforts, but also to counteract Western dissatisfaction with Red Army handling of POWs on the Eastern front. As one Western repatriation official noted, "It was soon apparent that these complaints were intended to serve Soviet purposes by silencing potential counter-claims concerning Soviet noncompliance with the Yalta Agreement pertaining to British and United States prisoners of war."[21]

One complaint of this type came from Colonel General Filip Golikov, head of the Soviet Repatriation Commission, who in late April 1945 accused the United States and Britain of not living up to the Yalta agreement. Displaced Soviet nationals were being mistreated, he claimed, and the Western powers were deliberately slowing down the pace of repatriation. This public criticism surprised SHAEF officials in London, who had previously been accustomed not to complaints but to a show of appreciation from resident Soviet officers and DPs. George Kennan, United States chargé in Moscow, reacted more sharply, dismissing Golikov's accusations as "shameless distortions."[22]

By early May disagreements over repatriation led to what historian William Hardy McNeill has called "a public exchange of incivilities." The charges and countercharges dragged on month after month and year after year. As late as 1949 Moscow alleged that the United States and Britain were detaining 247,000 Soviet citizens in Germany and Austria. Acrimony over repatriation led to an increase in mutual suspicion and mistrust, which certainly contributed to the postwar deterioration in East-West relations.[23]

The Kremlin also depended upon the resourcefulness of its repatriation missions in Europe to secure the return of those hesitant about going home. These bodies, self-consciously although not officially autonomous, served a variety of functions: covertly, as intelligence outposts in the West and as agents of coerced return; and overtly, as legitimate expediters of repatriation and as conduits for positive appeals to reluctant returners.

The Soviet government, in October 1944, established the Main Administration for Repatriation of Soviet Citizens, better known as the Soviet Repatriation Commission. Serving as the nominal head of the organization was General Golikov, a party member since 1918, a veteran of the civil war, and a combat commander in the Moscow, Stalingrad, and Voronezh campaigns.[24] He had a reputation as a "spit-and-polish professional officer," a hardened soldier, and a man headed upward in the military hierarchy. (By 1957 he would be chief of the Main Political Administration of the Red Army and eighth in standing among top Soviet generals.) His wartime transfer from a fighting command to repatriation work, however, may have been a demotion—Nikita Khrushchev so charged and claimed it stemmed from cowardice at Stalingrad.[25] Be that as it may, Golikov perfectly served Stalin's purpose as a repatriation figurehead, unrelated to the Soviet security organs yet with extensive experience in military intelligence as former chief of the Main Intelligence Administration (GRU) of the General Staff.

As head of the Soviet Repatriation Commission he lacked real authority, the responsibility being concentrated, in reality, in the hands of the secret police: the NKGB (the People's Commissariat for State Security) within the U.S.S.R. or Soviet-occupied territory, and SMERSH ("Death to Spies") abroad. The Soviet Repatriation Commission, working primarily in the West, received its directions and portions of its personnel from the Main Administration of Counterintelligence (GUKR) of SMERSH.[26]

After the war Soviet authorities had little trouble maintaining an extensive intelligence apparatus in the West because of the vast network of Soviet refugee compounds all over the continent, literally from Norway to Greece. Besides providing the rationale for the existence of the Soviet repatriation missions, with their extracurricular activities, the camps themselves contained Soviet agents recruited and stationed there in a variety of ways. Some purposefully fell into Nazi hands with the aim of offering their services to collaborator groups, such as the Committee for the Liberation of the Peoples of Russia (KONR). A number of these agents simply maintained their cover after the German defeat, and for purposes of later reckoning, continued keeping their tallies of the behavior of Soviet citizens abroad.[27]

SMERSH, the branch of Soviet security operating abroad, also secured help from some DPs by means of bribery, blackmail, and threats. A defector, formerly employed by SMERSH in repatriation work, recited typical tactics: "Some agents were bought for money, others paid in service to us for their own ill-calculated drunkenness and moral depravity. We used special female personnel for this. . . .[Others] might be promised complete forgiveness for all past sins and an honourable homecoming to their Motherland. They might also be threatened with reprisals and of course threats would be made against their families, if they happened to be in Soviet hands." The task of tracking down relatives and even close friends of potential agents in the West proved to be "vast" and "laborious"—but rewarding from the Kremlin's perspective.[28]

As mentioned, Soviet repatriation operations served double duty: returning the maximum number of DPs to Russia and providing cover for

Moscow's espionage activities in the West. The inextricable nature of the
two assignments is symbolized in the biography of a minor character in
Solzhenitsyn's *First Circle*: before making life difficult for the inmates of
Mavrino Institute, Major Shikin, a long-time employee of the Soviet security services, had been detailed to repatriation work. A Red Army
general as much as told Isaiah Berlin in the British embassy in Moscow
that the postwar homecoming of Soviet citizens was the responsibility of
the secret police. One former SMERSH officer emphasized in his postde-
fection memoir that Soviet repatriation personnel "travelled freely about
the western zones, at one time without even being accompanied by allied
representatives, and collected a mass of useful information about the lo-
cation and strength of allied troops, etc., in addition to doing their basic
job of rooting out former Soviet citizens."[29]

   None of the handicaps imposed by the Yalta settlement upon U.S. and
British DP camp administrators proved as troublesome as the well-nigh
impossible task of satisfying and keeping track of the sizeable Soviet repa-
triaton mission. By the end of June 1945 its staff numbered 153 in Germany alone, and SHAEF refused a Soviet request to more than double
it.[30] Difficulties arose at an early stage with these liaison officers over the
limits of their authority, a problem that persisted throughout their stay in
the West.

   Incidents involving Soviet repatriation officers occurred in widely scattered locations. On 31 July 1945 General Sir Andrew Thorne, commander of Allied forces in Norway, asked General Ratov, head of the
Red Army's military mission in that country, to reduce drastically his staff
of 170 men. SHAEF objected to the dragnet-like activities of Ratov's
men; and besides, all but a few of the 80,000 Soviet citizens found there
had been repatriated. The Soviet general objected, claiming that at least
1,000 of 4,000 "disputed persons" had to be returned to Russia. SHAEF
personnel came to detest Ratov, describing him variously as "uncooperative, rude, contentious, antagonistic, not to mention stupid." The State
Department's Robert Murphy characterized him similarly as "quar-
relsome, uncouth, contrary *and* stupid." Ratov even got in an unprecedented public fight with his own superior by claiming jurisdiction over the
U.S.S.R.'s DPs not only in Norway but in Britain, Holland, and Denmark as well. In one of the few instances of open quarreling among Soviet
authorities, General V. N. Dragun in Paris made an apparently legitimate counterclaim that he, not Ratov, was charged with the task of repatriating Soviet nationals in these countries. SHAEF finally declared Ratov *persona non grata*. Possibly piqued by the unseemly, open-air
squabbling, Moscow, in August 1945, also replaced General Dragun with

Major General Alexander N. Davidov, who became the chief Soviet repatriation official in Europe.[31]

Repatriation did not hold as high a priority in Allied negotiations as the East European settlement, German reparations, zonal boundaries, access to Berlin, or the like, but it could never be ignored either, partly because the problem was not localized but continent-wide. Top officials had to attend to the question because Moscow would not let them forget it, to be sure, but also because of the conspicuous presence of innumerable DPs all across liberated Europe. Members of Soviet repatriation teams in a score of countries continually clashed with SHAEF civil affairs officers and regular army commanders who in turn passed the problem up the chain of command. Whereas a problem such as reparations had little effect upon field commanders, the disposition of Soviet citizens demanded immediate attention. Whether the machinery of a half-bombed-out factory ultimately went for Russian reparations was not a pressing question for the lower levels in the command structure; repatriation, however, was another matter. Subordinate officers bombarded their superiors with requests for instructions on how to handle displaced Soviet citizens. They wanted to know how to treat nationals of an Allied power and simultaneously how to control the meddling members of the Kremlin's repatriation missions.

The answer that AFHQ gave to the second question was to "take such steps as you may consider necessary" to keep Russians out of prohibited zones. This British Foreign Office response went to General Harold Alexander, commander of Anglo-American forces in Italy. By September 1945 he had had his fill of troubles with the Soviet repatriation mission, including two Red Army lieutenants who were arrested twice without identification in the compound of General Anders's Polish Corps and a General Basilov who had commandeered 300 DPs traveling by rail to a screening center and demanded their immediate repatriation. Alexander called these actions "gross interference" with his command and determined to tolerate them no longer.[32] The Soviet mission in Italy, which at one point numbered 101, lost its right to virtually unrestricted movement in Italy in September 1945 and could no longer "break all travel regulations and get away with it."[33]

From the very start SHAEF commanders north of the Alps had their suspicions about the role of Soviet repatriation officials. General Mark Clark, commander of U.S. forces in Austria, took great pains to keep under surveillance Moscow's representatives in his occupation zone. He had circumstantial evidence that certain members of the repatriation mission had engaged in espionage, and he made known his objections to General

I. S. Konev, military governor of the Soviet zone of Austria. The latter offered to recall the offending parties and replace them with new representatives who would be placed on a thirty-day trial. Clark agreed, but before the plan could be implemented he learned that the team leaving the American zone planned to kidnap a U.S. counterespionage agent in conjunction with its departure. The general, hoping to obtain proof to verify his long-standing suspicions, set a trap. On 23 January 1946, when several members of the Russian mission arrived at the intended victim's house and threatened him at gunpoint, concealed lights came on to prevent the kidnappers' escape, and Clark's men quickly arrested the entire group. One Soviet repatriation officer had on the complete uniform of a U.S. military policeman. Two others had on civilian coats over Red Army uniforms. All were armed. Enraged by their clandestine activities, Clark informed Konev that the offenders "would be shoved over the line into the Russian zone" that next day.[34]

This incident did not end the general's troubles with the Soviet mission because he could not act according to his own inclinations but had to accede to the War Department's orders. Despite Clark's contention on 25 January "that all members of this mission have been involved in intelligence activities since they have been in our Zone," Washington required him to admit a new Soviet repatriation team. The outspoken general, hoping that eventually his objections would be taken to heart, continued his complaints. In mid-March 1946 he advised the War Department that Moscow was trying to extend the life of the mission indefinitely for intelligence reasons. Clark also let it be known that the British and French representatives in Vienna "are as anxious as I to get rid of these missions, feeling that their most important work is espionage." Again in late June 1946, after the departure of one Soviet team, Clark cabled Washington reiterating his conviction that "the main object behind Soviet insistence in establishing another mission in the United States zone is for intelligence purposes."[35]

General Walter Bedell Smith, prior to his appointment as ambassador to Moscow in January 1946, had similar troubles with Soviet repatriation officers in Germany. Requiring the members of one especially meddlesome Soviet team to eat at a central facility, in order to keep close check on their number, proved ineffective, for as General Smith discovered, several Red Army officers often used the same meal ticket. This deception was part of a larger scheme designed to move unauthorized "transient Russians" about the Western zones undetected.[36] A new rationing system put a stop to the underground railroad, but conflicts continued as long as Soviet repatriation teams operated in the West.

Evidence of illegal seizures of DPs by Soviet officials applied to Germany as well as Austria. At Bad Kreuznach an American officer of Ukrainian descent saved thirty members of his own nationality from unauthorized repatriation. Members of the Soviet mission had loaded the group onto trucks bound for the eastern zone of Germany and might have succeeded in their abduction but for this Ukrainian-speaking American officer who understood the refugees' pleas for help and stopped the transfer. The saga of high-handedness on the part of Moscow's repatriation officials was the same all over Europe. In Brussels Soviet representatives, searching for reluctant returners, broke into private homes without warrants. In Greece Moscow's repatriation mission managed to spirit Bulgarian Communists out of the country "unscathed" by the Greek police.[37]

In France the Soviet Union had perhaps its most pliant Western government. Here Moscow's prerogatives clearly included flagrant examples of disregard for the assigned tasks of repatriation representatives. A large, effectively autonomous compound at Camp Beauregard, outside Paris, served as the major processing point for persons returning to Russia. The provisions of the Yalta repatriation accords, and the French one, which permitted Soviet internal administration of refugee centers, greatly facilitated clandestine activities. In effect, Moscow was able to establish extraterritorial islands throughout Europe.[38] Yet Camp Beauregard, with its obligatory, large-scale likeness of Stalin over the entrance, represented but a fraction of Soviet repatriation activities in France: witnesses even attested to abductions undertaken without interference from the French police. The meddlesomeness of the Kremlin's officials on French soil became so commonplace that Parisian wags declared that German occupation had been replaced by Russian. Nevertheless, the Red Army's repeated delays in repatriating hundreds of thousands of French POWs in the East most decidedly helped to insure that General DeGaulle would tolerate the excesses of the Soviet repatriation mission.[39]

From the evidence available for Norway, Italy, Austria, Germany, France, and elsewhere, Soviet repatriation missions regularly engaged in a variety of intrigues. Still, their selective participation in strictly illegal repatriation, that is, in genuine kidnapping, had less effect than two other approaches: (1) Moscow's aforementioned emphasis upon Western compliance with its interpretation of the Yalta exchange accords; and (2) an extensive effort to woo Soviet citizens back into the fold by means of an enormous barrage of verbal and printed appeals.

After the transfer to Russia of the majority of clearly identified Soviet nationals, SHAEF officials still permitted the Kremlin's representatives access to DP camps. In particular, "stateless" refugees, those from East European countries or provinces annexed by the Soviet Union, could be addressed by Moscow's repatriation workers. Far from convincing their captive audiences to return home, Moscow's speechmakers more commonly provoked agitation and, on occasion, violence. By every means possible they told the story of the happy life that awaited the refugees back home: by speeches and personal interviews, and by films, pamphlets, and newspapers. But promises of improved living conditions, the right to return to their old homes and jobs, and pardon for delayed repatriation rarely moved skeptical DPs. One refugee mentioned receiving a letter from his father stating that there was nothing to fear in returning home. The Soviet repatriation representative beamed at such a positive response—until the same DP added that his father had been dead for ten years.[40]

An ex-Vlasovite held at Fort Dix, New Jersey, reminded a certain Colonel Malkov that the Soviet government considered surrender to the enemy a treasonable offense. The Soviet repatriation officer replied that the law had been changed; those returning were "freely settling" and "nobody has said a word to them." When Malkov added that no one would be held responsible for what the Germans had made him do, the hapless POW was openly skeptical. Another prisoner asked this same officer for something more concrete than his own oral assurances or Soviet statements to the press, but Malkov had nothing else to offer.[41] The United States did repatriate the Wehrmacht's ex–Red Army men held at Fort Dix, but certainly not of their own free will and not because they found the appeals and assurances of the Soviet mission convincing.

More than once the commotion provoked by Soviet visits to DP camps took a sinister turn. At a Leipzig refugee center, an émigré source related, a call for return to the homeland ended abruptly when "an old man with an ax in his hand mounted the speaker's platform and extending to the Soviet officer the ax, said: 'Here is my ax, and here is my head. Chop it off, but I won't go back.' An American officer witnessed this scene, and upon learning what the old man had said, promptly ordered the Soviet officials to leave."[42]

In July 1945 a disorder in one British camp resulted in a Russian officer shooting a DP. The foolhardy assailant, an eyewitness recalled, "was subsequently lynched by an infuriated mob." Because of repeated physical assaults upon Soviet officials, the United States ruled in May 1946 that the Kremlin's repatriation personnel had to be accompanied by American guards when entering multinational compounds.[43]

Because of DP camp incidents, AFHQ informed the Soviet mission in Italy that it would do its best to "assure the bodily safety of . . . authorized visitors" but that it could not "assume responsibility for any untoward incident." Things got so bad that one Red Army general toured a refugee camp with an escort of two armored cars.[44]

In one instance of candor a Soviet representative admitted to a United Nations refugee worker that the chances of persuading the so-called "hard core" DPs to leave the West were negligible. But to their own superiors repatriation teams from the U.S.S.R. had to present a picture of energetic, ceaseless activity that, of course, was on the very brink of productivity. One intercepted Russian communication between repatriation officers and their headquarters provides a rare glimpse at the curious combination of obsequiousness and braggadocio seemingly endemic to the Soviet chain of command: "We are about to carry on to incredible measures the pilferage in the so-called 'Ukrainian UNRRA camps.' . . . We are able to bring about a mass dissatisfaction, but we did not quite achieve total despondency."[45] Whether or not they convinced many wary DPs, Soviet officials had to appear successful to their superiors out of fear for their own safety in Stalin's purge-prone empire.

After the repatriation of the great majority of displaced nationals in the summer of 1945 and the exclusion of civilians from forced repatriation in December of that year, American military officials sought to limit the size and activity of the Soviet repatriation missions in Western zones of occupation. Efforts to curtail and finally terminate them only began with Generals Thorne, Alexander, and Clark. Conflict over this Russian presence in the West provided a protracted test of wills that coincided with other superpower controversies that spelled the onset of the Cold War in the late 1940s.

On 5 August 1947 General Lucius Clay ordered a reduction in the Soviet repatriation mission in Germany from thirty-four to four. The number crept back up, however, so that by late March 1948 Moscow still had seventeen men at least officially charged with DP work. On 17 February 1949, during the Soviet blockade of Berlin and the Western airlift of supplies to the beleaguered city, Clay further aggravated Moscow by finally ordering the remaining Soviet repatriation personnel to leave the Western occupation zones. The commander of U.S. forces in Germany stated, "It is apparent that sufficient time has elapsed . . . for voluntary repatriation to be completed."[46] This incensed the Kremlin, which argued that the United States was not only detaining 247,000 Soviet citizens in violation of the Yalta accord, but was now adding to its misdeeds by forcing the termination of the repatriation mission's work. The Soviet Union considered this a flagrant "unilateral abrogation" of a signed agreement. Washington replied to the Russian charges by stating that the United States was not preventing anyone from repatriating; most remaining DPs simply did not want to return home. Besides, the majority of the nearly 250,000 refugees referred to were not citizens of the U.S.S.R. but were former inhabitants of Russian-annexed territories. Finally, the United States did not consider the closing of the repatriation mission a violation of the Yalta agreement since the Soviet attaché could easily handle the small number of persons desiring to return to the Soviet Union.[47]

Unmoved by these explanations, Moscow ordered the Soviet Repatriation Mission in Frankfurt to stay put. When General Clay's deadline of 1 March had passed without compliance, Western occupation officials cut off the group's utilities, including gas, water, electricity, and telephone service. A departing German cook warned that the Russians had enough food to last for some time. It appeared momentarily that if the United States was to be rid of the repatriation mission, it would have to resort to physical eviction. On 4 May, just as the crisis seemed to be reaching a climax, Moscow capitulated: the mission was ordered home. General Clay had electricity restored long enough for the eight officers and their families to pack; the Red flag came down; and the Soviet party finally took leave of Frankfurt. The *New York Times* reported that one Soviet soldier, especially angered by the eviction, spat on an American girl standing in a crowd of onlookers. At a higher level Marshal V. D. Sokolovsky, Soviet military governor in Germany, renewed the charge that the action of the United States was a violation of an international agreement. Moscow retaliated by ordering a British-American graves registration team to leave the Soviet zone of Germany.[48]

Besides the POW and refugee exchange agreements and Soviet missions in the West, Moscow's campaign for total repatriation employed a massive propaganda blitz designed to reassure the reluctant of a cordial homecoming. Soviet spokesmen presented DPs with an elaborate variety of misleading or demonstrably false information about the prospects for repatriates. (See ch. 8 for their actual reception.)

Normally appeals directed toward Soviet citizens abroad or persons from annexed territories did not risk a negative approach. One 1947 communication that did came from the government of the Soviet Latvian republic. Nonreturners could hardly find comfort in the veiled censure of "You . . . are more than two years serving strange masters in a foreign country, eating strange masters' bread" or "Every honest Latvian has to come home."[49]

But ordinarily Moscow's propagandists avoided pronouncements so chillingly devoid of consolation. Rather they offered an array of positive psychological and material inducements. Playing the chord of the motherland's long-suffering proved a popular theme among the Kremlin's phrasemakers. In 1945 the Soviet Repatriation Commission's

Domoi, na rodinu! [Home to the Motherland!] returned again and again to this theme in the course of thirty pages: "The mother country remembers its children. Not for a minute did the Soviet people, our government, or the party of Lenin and Stalin forget about the fate of Soviet citizens who temporarily found themselves under the yoke of fascist oppressors. . . . Many times throughout the war Comrade Stalin called to mind you who languished in fascist camps and said that the freeing of Soviet people from the German yoke was an important objective of the Soviet people and the Red Army."[50] In a similar vein Robert Murphy learned from a Red Army colonel that "these poor unfortunates who were deported to Germany are looked upon at home as martyrs and will be received with open arms by the entire Russian people." Feigned compassion figured as the common denominator in many appeals. *Vot kak eto bylo* [That's How It Was], Aleksei Briukhanov's memoir of repatriation work, illustrated this approach in its description of the ex-DP–staffed Committee for Return to the Homeland: "Like a beacon, the Committee pointed out to the displaced the path to their native shores."[51]

A closely related approach involved heart-tugging sentimentality. *Vstrecha o rodinoi* [Encounter with the Homeland], a Soviet film designed specifically for Armenian émigrés, cultivated homesickness as a means of encouraging return to the motherland. This relatively sophisticated soft-sell contained no direct appeal for repatriation. Still that message resounded as the narrator proclaimed, "Soviet Armenia is the last harbor for all our wandering ships." Particularly in appeals designed to lure old émigrés this inclination towards sentimentality figured prominently. The Soviet government issued a number of edicts concerning the "Restitution of Nationality to Former Subjects" specifically for them. By means of these proclamations pre–World War II expatriates could reacquire citizenship. For many refugees of 1917–21 the second German invasion of their homeland in their lifetime reawakened dormant patriotic feelings that in some cases were translated into postwar repatriation.[52]

Another of Moscow's psychological approaches to DPs consisted of reassurances of forgiveness for past sins, including capture alive by the enemy, delay in returning home, even collaboration with the Germans. The success or failure of noncoercive attempts to retrieve displaced nationals depended upon this more than anything else. That the Kremlin's promises left the vast majority of hard-core DPs cold was not for want of trying. One Red Army colonel in Germany told Murphy that military personnel taken prisoner by the Germans had no cause for uneasiness. "We understand perfectly well that under modern conditions of warfare, large bodies of troops may be cut off and forced to surrender. There is no more stigma connected with capture in the eyes of the Soviet Government than there is in the American Army."[53] This charitable sentiment contrasted sharply with Decree Number 270 of 1942, which declared surrendered Red Army men *ipso facto* traitors. Sources as diverse as the wartime edition of *Bol'shaia sovetskaia entsiklopediia*, the Soviet Constitution, the criminal codes of the constituent republics, the Red Army field manual, the leading Soviet scholar on military criminal law, and Stalin himself confirmed the point.[54]

Moscow also tried to convince its refugees abroad that no stigma was attached to delayed repatriation. A 1949 catechism for DPs asked the question, "Are Soviet citizens held to account for not returning home at once after the war was over?" The answer was no: "their long sojourn in a foreign land will not be considered their fault" but rather the responsibility of "reactionary elements" in the West.[55] Actually, the Soviet Union did and still does consider its citizens' refusal to return home from abroad as treason.[56]

Convincing ex–Red Army soldiers who had served in the Wehrmacht that repatriation entailed no dangers taxed the ingenuity of Soviet propagandists as few assignments could. The standard line ran that no retribution awaited collaborators, "provided they honestly fulfill their duties on their return," an innocent-sounding reservation that, nevertheless, could not have helped but raise the suspicions of wary refugees.[57] A section entitled "How Freed People Are Received in the Homeland" appeared in the same tract that carried Stalin's alleged, pained remembrance of those torn from the motherland. Here, author Brychev shouts in bold-faced type, "All freed Soviet people are received in their homeland not with contempt or distrust but with consideration, warm encouragement, and affectionate sympathy." A Soviet notice in the British army paper, *Union Jack*, emphasized to DP readers that this applied even to "Soviet citizens, who, under German opposition and terror, had acted contrarily to the interests of the Soviet Union."[58]

Like all the other pleas to Soviet nationals who had served in Wehrmacht ranks, those of Alexander Bogomolov, Moscow's ambassador to France, lacked any trustworthy safeguards: "Some of these are heroes, some of them have been less strong-minded. No nation consists exclusively of heroes. But the Motherland would not be a mother if she did not love all her family, even the black sheep. . . . Every man will be given a chance to redeem himself at home—if he is of military age, in the army; otherwise, in a factory. We take into full account the special circumstances under which each man has lived, the mass psychology of camps and pressure by the Germans."[59] The American embassy staff in Moscow noted that even the regular Soviet press, prepared for domestic consumption, occasionally reflected this solicitous, forgive-and-forget attitude.

But these same officials, who caught glimpses of Soviet repatriation first-hand, knew that the reception afforded returners in all categories was anything but cordial.[60]

Besides appeals constructed to work on the emotional level, Moscow's campaign to retrieve all of its nationals abroad included a variety of material incentives. In addition to promises of free transportation home, job security, work in one's native region, and even residence in one's former dwelling, Soviet literature offered repatriates agricultural and building loans, educational opportunities, the right to vote, and for ex-POWs, veterans benefits. Also, those coming home were told they could count on social services such as pensions for the elderly, workmen's compensation, and convalescent homes for the disabled. The detailed specification of advantages to be afforded repatriates' physical security and well-being, no matter how remote from the true circumstances of their reception, were intended to allay their apprehension and to convince them that back home they would be "treated with the maximum of care and attention."[61]

At first glance the crowded schedule of inducements might seem to have appeared enticing. But to be convinced of Stalin's goodwill, the Soviet diaspora, raised on a diet of Orwellian doublethink, required more than unverifiable pledges of a warm welcome home. In the U.S.S.R.'s campaign for total repatriation, results based on the Soviet missions in the West were modest, but results based on Moscow's litany of promises and direct appeals fell between negligible and nonexistent.

Its monumental dimensions notwithstanding, the Soviet campaign for total repatriation failed. The U.S.S.R. retrieved 3 million of its nationals from Eastern Europe and 2 million from Western occupation zones. Even so, the Kremlin faced with trepidation the prospect of a residue of 500,000 permanent nonreturners. For a host of reasons—vindictive, psychological, economic, demographic, propagandistic, and strategic—Russia wanted them all back and, as described, went to great lengths to effect their return. Yet the Soviet Union had no way to acquire control of all nonreturners, despite all of its efforts. With the United States exempting some and others living under assumed nationalities, it became obvious that a diaspora of no mean proportion would remain abroad. Adverse publicity concerning repatriation could not be avoided completely, so the Kremlin adopted strenuous countermeasures to put the best face on events. The regime entrusted to its generals, to its missions abroad, and to its propaganda apparatus this herculean responsibility, which proved every bit as formidable as convincing wary DPs to come home. The trick was to explain to the West and to the nation how it happened that some persons with firsthand experience with life under socialism had taken up arms against their homeland and why, not only among collaborators but also among ordinary POWs and forced laborers, there were those who chose to remain abroad.

At first Moscow stubbornly denied the possibility of disloyalty among Soviet citizens abroad. Prior to the Normandy invasion, when members of SHAEF's planning staff informed Moscow of intelligence reports of ex–Red Army men in Wehrmacht ranks, Soviet officials challenged their accuracy. But once Allied troops started pouring into France, thousands of Soviet citizens turned up among captured German troops. If, after D-Day, the Kremlin could no longer ignore the facts, it still could distort them. On 13 July 1944, five weeks after the Normandy landing, a Soviet representative protested to Secretary of State Cordell Hull that the Western Allies were slandering Red Army POWs who had been in German custody. At a 9 July press conference in London a member of General Eisenhower's staff allegedly made "an extremely ambiguous statement regarding Soviet prisoners of war in the German Army [which] . . . contained a number of improbable and evidently fictitious data . . . drawn, apparently, from German sources." The government of the U.S.S.R. wanted the United States to understand clearly that it considered "inadmissible" such declarations "defaming Soviet people . . . who found themselves in German captivity." Soviet charges relating to the press conference were themselves ambiguous. Moscow evidently could not yet bring itself unequivocally to admit the active participation of Soviet citizens in the German army.[62]

By the early fall of 1944 Soviet representatives had backed down somewhat, at least to the degree that they would acknowledge some ex–Red Army men had served in Wehrmacht ranks. Ambassador Andrei Gromyko did not deny the presence of Russians in German uniform in a 12 September conversation with Undersecretary of State Edward Stettinius. But he adamantly maintained that they had not served in front-line fighting units. Instead, Gromyko argued that these men had been deployed in such support roles as drivers or medics. Later that month, as noted earlier, the Soviet ambassador spelled out to Hull in great detail what Moscow expected of the United States: displaced Soviet nationals liberated by SHAEF forces were to be treated as citizens of an Allied power, not as POWs.[63]

As late as April 1945 Gromyko denied that Russians captured in Wehrmacht units had been fighting alongside German troops. His explanation continued to be that these people had been forced to "work in the immediate rear of the German army, in connection with which the Soviet citizens mentioned are occasionally outfitted . . . in German military uniforms." In trying to convince Secretary of State James F. Byrnes he argued that they "cannot be counted as military personnel of the German army." Late that same spring the *New York Times* carried General Filip Golikov's complaint that not all liberated Soviet personnel were being treated as allies, a circuitous criticism of Western handling of collaborators.[64]

Thus, from June 1944 to May 1945 the U.S.S.R gradually but grudgingly accommodated itself to the inescapable fact that SHAEF forces were capturing thousands of Soviet citizens in German uniform. At the same time spokesmen for the Kremlin refused to concede the presence of Russians in German fighting formations. As explanations for the collaboration of some Soviet citizens they stressed extenuating circumstances such as starvation or brutal treatment by the Germans. While it is unquestionably true that many former Soviet soldiers filled combat roles, it is also a fact, as Moscow claimed, that many Red Army POWs in German ranks served solely to stay alive and occupied support roles. Soviet authorities seldom permitted Russian publications to comment on Russians abroad who rendered aid to the Germans, no matter what the circumstances. On those rare occasions when *Pravda* or other newspapers did treat the subject, they placed emphasis upon the force Germans employed to effect the enlistment of Red Army POWs in the Wehrmacht.[65]

Besides neutralizing the adverse publicity of outright collaborators, the U.S.S.R. had to contend with the unflattering implications of ordinary Soviet citizens abroad unwilling to return home.[66] As a means of saving face, Moscow tendered numerous explanations. Publicly the Soviet Union did not stress its insistence upon forced repatriation; that was saved for the relative privacy of diplomatic exchanges. For popular consumption the Kremlin disseminated the argument that the use of force did not concern the vast majority of repatriates, since Soviet citizens abroad wanted to return home. Those who ostensibly refused to do so were, in reality, barred by various forms of Western trickery or coercion.

General Georgii Zhukov and other Soviet commentators charged the Western powers were recruiting spies from among the ranks of nonreturners.[67] A more plausible and more easily documented allegation focused on economic opportunities abroad, which made nonreturners of some Soviet refugees. As the relations of the former Allies continued to deteriorate, Soviet spokesmen began characterizing Western economic policy as Fascist. Like the Nazis before them, the United States and Britain relished the prospect of "a ready supply of cheap, virtually indentured, labour."[68] Even the French, who accommodated Moscow on the repatriation issue more than any other Western power, were criticized for being DP "slave merchants."[69]

With some success Zhukov and other Soviet authorities pressured the United States to put a stop to the "well paid jobs" and the "easy life" of refugee camps. On 5 December 1945 American occupation headquarters in Germany issued a comprehensive order excluding Soviet nationals from assistance or employment. "It is hereby announced," the command read, "that . . . all food, shelter, etc., for those displaced persons who . . . are Soviet citizens are to cease forthwith. . . . All local burgomasters [sic] have been informed that Soviet citizens are not to be employed and the German population must refuse them food."[70]

Moscow could still protest the employment in Belgian coal mines of 35,000 Baltic DPs, whom it claimed as Soviet citizens. But in April 1947 Undersecretary of State Dean Acheson and President Truman refused to ban their employment since they were not subject to mandatory repatriation. To Soviet Deputy Foreign Minister Andrei Vyshinski actions like this illustrated the fragility of a tottering capitalist system in the throes of crippling labor shortages.[71]

The economic rationale for the continued presence of Soviet nationals in the West waned in the 1950s as Kremlin apologists no longer would admit that living standards in a non-Communist society had ever tempted refugees to remain abroad. A 1958 Soviet publication rejected the idea as slanderous fabrication: "Why has the hallowed natural desire of Soviet people to return home so frightened the American press that it talks about the political defeat of the U.S.A.? Because this voluntary repatriation signifies a crack in the anti-Soviet myth which bourgeois propaganda has regaled the society of their countries in for many years—the myth that thousands of people supposedly fled their socialist countries preferring life in the conditions of capitalism."[72]

Moscow also accused the United States and other Western nations of brainwashing DPs to prevent their repatriation. Zhukov charged that "the Americans and British were indoctrinating the Soviet citizens and war prisoners to get them to defect. . . . In this process lies, slander of the Soviet Union, and intimidation were brought into play, especially with regard to those who had served under the traitor Vlasov, or who had been in the service of the Germans as policemen." All this the Red Army general emphatically categorized as a "dirty anti-Soviet campaign."[73]

In a similar vein General Golikov took Western authorities to task for trying to "poison the minds" of Soviet refugees. The idea spread abroad that the Soviet Union might deal harshly with repatriates Moscow labeled "fairy stories," "a monstrous lie," and "nonsense."[74] The U.S.S.R. became so sensitive about hostile propaganda appearing in Western DP compounds that it introduced a resolution in the United Nations General Assembly to ban any camp publication critical of any member of that organization.[75] The Russian proposal failed to carry, but that did not diminish the Kremlin's campaign to saddle American and British propaganda with responsibility for the continued presence of Soviet nationals abroad.

Western toleration of Fascist influences in refugee centers, an allegation closely related to the charge of brainwashing, also surfaced among Soviet explanations for the nonreturner phenomenon. According to the Kremlin, DP camps served as "nests for Fascists" who were "fleeing from just punishment as war criminals."[76] Moscow also assumed all anti-Soviet literature to be Nazi-inspired, and anti-Communism among Russian refugees to be *prima facie* evidence of collaboration with the enemy.[77] After hearing Soviet complaints at the Potsdam Conference about alleged Nazi activity in Western occupation zones, Admiral William Leahy concluded that "the Russian definition of 'Fascist' was elastic and could include anyone who did not support Communism."[78]

One line of reasoning employed by Moscow to explain the hesitation of refugees to return to Russia contradicted other declarations claiming the unbreakable solidarity of the Soviet peoples. Going beyond the assertion of Fascist influences in DP camps, the Kremlin equated POW or nonreturner status with treason. According to the official government newspaper *Izvestiia*, "The only persons who do not wish to return to their country are traitors. . . . All honest people taken from their homes by the Germans wish to return."[79] Zhukov similarly maintained that persons refusing to repatriate "were those who had committed grave crimes against their country and had really become enemies." And a Soviet tract on the subject of collaborators hiding in the West spoke of the need to "rip the mask off 'political refugees' " and thereby expose their wartime roles as "quislings and accessories to murder."[80]

An émigré account claimed that during the war the Soviet Air Force deliberately bombed German camps containing Red Army POWs. Leaflets dropped on the compound read: "So will it be with all those who betray the cause of Lenin and Stalin." A popular saying in Russia, earthy but accurate, illustrates the lack of room for extenuating circumstances in the country's posture toward service in the war: "Either your chest in medals or your head rolling in the bushes."[81]

A less embarrassing Soviet explanation for nonreturners centered on charges of Western obstructionism, including harassment and outright physical detention. According to a Russian memoir excerpt published in *Istoriia SSSR*, American troops, upon liberating Mauthausen concentration camp, disarmed resistance fighters. Next, they confined Soviet citizens to barracks partitioned off from the rest of the camp. (But the Yalta agreement required this.) "Only after a few days in Mauthausen when a representative of the Soviet command arrived did the return of Soviet citizens to their homeland finally commence." The repatriates' recollection made it appear that U.S. troops, besides being unfriendly and inconsiderate, did not do all in their power to expedite the repatriation of Soviet nationals.[82]

Besides accounting for nonreturners, accusations of ill treatment could be employed to explain the large number of DP deaths by poisoning—400 by 14 May 1945. Soviet refugees had such an affinity for spirits that they consumed even the most lethal grades of alcohol. One whimsical British memoirist, amazed at Russian drivers' emptying their fuel tanks into their own bodies, called it "Down the hatch with Shellski!" But with fatalities the end result, and accumulating Soviet accusations of physical abuse, the situation lacked humor to Western occupation officials.[83]

Charges of intimidation, abuse, and coercion flew at Western officials regularly for years, and in quantity: Soviet citizens, victims of "abduction," were being "forcibly transported to the U.S.A., Canada, Australia, and other countries"; or were being "detained" and "restrained" in "concentration camps"; were denied their "legal rights"; and were "given no opportunity to return home."[84] Inverting the facts at Fort Dix in the summer of 1945, the Kremlin maintained that asphyxiation and physical injury to POWs resulted from attempts by American troops to *prevent* repatriation.[85]

According to the memoirs of a Soviet repatriation officer, the blame lay with the "dark powers of international reaction which hold to their terror, provocations, and anti-Soviet slander." N. A. Bulganin, titular prime minister of the Soviet Union, presented that same argument in West Germany on a 1955 state visit. He complained, "Many cases are known to us of displaced Soviet citizens who do not accept their lot of being gaoled on the territory of the German Federal Republic. Certain organizations hostile to the Soviet Union, supported by the relevant authorities, are waging spiteful propaganda and impeding the repatriation of these persons, frightening and terrorizing those who wish to return home."[86]

These Soviet complaints usually employed only vague references to force—but not always. In July 1945 one Russian diplomat in Washington informed the State Department that Russians favoring repatriation were being "badly treated and were even beaten up." More fantastic, Major General A. Vasiliev, an ill-tempered member of the Allied Advisory Council for Italy, accused AFHQ forces of killing a Soviet citizen "for insisting on his repatriation." Furthermore, "Russians are undergoing inhuman tortures in damp prison[s], built underground, where they are bound in chains and continually beaten with rubber sticks and iron gloves." In part these unfounded allegations stemmed from mean-spirited, ideologically hostile Soviet officials, but also from a desire to neutralize the complaints of American POWs repatriated through Russian territory.[87]

The most far-fetched accusation advanced by Kremlin propagandists had the Western powers drafting Soviet nationals into foreign military formations. Again, the element of intimidation formed an integral part of the charge. *Pravda* alleged: "This recruiting is carried out under a condition of terror directed against the Soviet citizens who refuse to join up with the Foreign Legion." Secretary of State Hull vehemently voiced his denials, but without effect on Soviet officialdom.[88]

The Soviet Union also frequently asserted that its Western Allies violated the Yalta repatriation agreement and the tenets of international law. "Instead of aiding our countrymen," one Soviet repatriation official argued, "the U.S.A. and England, in violation of their own international commitments, detained them in 'displaced persons' camps. . . . If the British-American powers had endeavored to aid us in this period—no obstacles or barriers could have stopped the flow of people back to Russia."[89] This line of reasoning closely paralleled Soviet accusations relating to the Fort Dix incident: the Western powers were to blame for incomplete repatriation because of their failure to comply with the stipulations of the Yalta accord. Refusing to own up to its aggressive but unsuccessful campaign for total repatriation, Moscow instead argued that it had "simply demanded . . . the fulfillment of the appropriate international agreement." One complaint of noncompliance with the Yalta accord, made in April 1945, concerned DP camp arrangements of the summer and fall of 1944, months before the Crimean conclave.[90]

The Kremlin, employing its own interpretation of interstate jurisprudence, dismissed the "so-called principle" of voluntary repatriation as a "flagrant breach of all written authority and of the general principles of international law." "After the cessation of hostilities," the standard Soviet encyclopedia declared, "belligerent governments are obliged to carry out the unconditional [*bezuslovnuiu*] repatriation of prisoners of war. . . . in accordance with the universally recognized norms of international law."[91]

Forced repatriation never has been an established tenet of international jurisprudence. The first instance in modern times of involuntary repatriation formally sanctioned by a bilateral treaty occurred less than a quarter century before the signing of the Yalta accord—the 1923 Treaty of Lausanne providing for a compulsory Greco-Turkish population exchange.[92] Prior to World War II even the Kremlin had frowned upon such legalized coercion of DPs and POWs. As previously noted, the Soviet state, in the first years of its existence, had explicitly agreed to the principle of voluntary return in numerous POW treaties.[93] In the years of debate over repatriation no one seems to have embarrassed Moscow by pointing out this inconsistency.

On occasion the United States and other Western nations unwittingly aided the Soviet effort to minimize bad publicity stemming from Soviet collaborators and nonreturners. It did not occur to most postwar planners in the West to consider repatriation other than as a problem of logistics, that is, a matter of finding sufficient transportation to carry it out rapidly. European population experts readily conceded that DPs would require immediate attention at the end of the war, but they overlooked possible complications resulting from shifting political allegiances among the estimated 30 million displaced Europeans. "Foreign laborers in Germany," a League of Nations study mistakenly assumed, "will certainly wish to return to their native lands following the war." The State Department also anticipated their "great impatience to return."[94] This misjudgment resulted in part because the ideological barriers that separated Russia and its Western Allies tended to blur before the more immediate threat of Hitler. With the euphoria of a successful East-West military alliance went the unfounded assumption that under a peacetime coalition freedom of choice for DPs would override more mundane political considerations.

Sparse coverage of forced repatriation by the American and British news media also aided Soviet ends. For the most part the West overlooked or misinterpreted the dilemma facing politically disillusioned Soviet citizens abroad. Ignorance of DP disaffection or equating it with Fascist leanings reinforced the Soviet propaganda line.

Certain Western officials charged with refugee responsibilities also contributed directly to Soviet objectives by their consciously aggressive repatriation tactics against those not subject to forced return. UNRRA, established under Allied auspices in November 1943, leaned heavily toward repatriation as a solution to the refugee problem. While charges of being Communist-infiltrated are probably overstated, it is true that UNRRA had high officials who looked favorably upon the Soviet economic system and felt there was no valid reason for East European DPs to refuse to go home.[95] UNRRA leadership translated this point of view into its directives, of both the carrot and stick variety. Illustrating the former, one program implemented to increase repatriation went by the name "Operation Carrot": those agreeing to go home received a free two-month supply of canned goods.[96]

The same organization's Administrative Order 199, a document infamous in émigré circles, provided not only for Soviet camp visits and Russian newspaper and film distribution but urged the use of "emotional devices" at "the propitious time" to effect refugees' return home: "The skillful Repatriation Officer will change the present drift of camp population thinking in terms of fear of returning home and nebulous dreaming of emigration, to one of calm consideration of alternatives and acceptance of repatriation." UNRRA's in-house *Repatriation News* carried a myriad of tactics to be employed on DPs. In June 1947 Area Team 1041 received "Repatriation Orchids" for its effective work that included: "posters dwelling on homeland appeals"; small group meetings with Soviet liaison officers; song groups "to arouse national pride and longing for homeland"; permanent and mobile displays with the same purpose; and farewell parties and church services for returners. The same issue of this newsletter carried suggestions for repatriation poster contests; ways to enliven repatriation reading rooms; and the success story of Lucille Pillow, a worker in Frankfurt who, with the aid of a Soviet sports film, convinced a Baltic boxer to go home. The moral to other staff members: "Maybe you've got some ex-athletes who could be impressed!"[97]

UNRRA speeches made up in bravado what they lacked in accuracy. In May 1947 one by a high ranking figure in the organization urged: "Go home this spring, those of you who can. Go home to help your countrymen rebuild—and to share the fruit of that rebuilding. . . . They are working at a great task, the task of reconstruction, and they call upon you to join them. There is work for all. There is livelihood for all. There is dignity for all. . . . Seize this opportunity—now. Your relatives, your friends, your country wait for you." As for the stick, UNRRA came to favor occasional ration cutting and camp closings to speed the processing. No wonder some Baltic refugees concluded: "We have been persecuted one year by the Soviet[s], three years by the Germans and two years by UNRRA."[98]

The Preparatory Commission of the International Refugee Organization (PCIRO) and IRO itself succeeded UNRRA in July 1947 and August 1948, respectively—but had no better reputation among DPs. The IRO constitution specifically acknowledged repatriation rather than resettlement to be its primary function. Furthermore, no aid could go to refugees who "had become leaders of movements hostile to the government of their country of origin being a Member of the United Nations, or sponsors of movements encouraging refugees not to return to their country of origin."[99] Incredibly, an IRO leaflet claimed the organization took "no part in any effort to influence the decision of the refugees." U.S. authorities arrested one DP for publishing a serial unequivocally titled *Anticommunist*. At the trial his embarrassed American judge felt bound to fine the refugee but gave the DP the money for it out of his own pocket. In the words of a Mannheim DP camp director, American aid to the Soviet campaign for total repatriation had as its objective "to be rid of all . . . guests" as quickly as possible.[100] But even with the aid of some prorepatriation persuaders in the West, Moscow retrieved few of its citizens other than by force.

In summary, the Kremlin's various efforts to retrieve all Soviet nationals abroad did not succeed. Nor did Moscow's explanations for the refusal of some Soviet citizens to repatriate prove irresistible. The Soviet government distrusted persons captured alive by the enemy and declared them traitors, prepared a hostile reception for collaborators, and construed a refusal or even reluctance to return home as most unpatriotic. Refugees with time to ponder sensed these attitudes through the veil of promises and solicitous concern, even without proof that repatriation boded ill for them. Although concern for effect more than accuracy determined what went into Soviet appeals to refugees abroad, few returned home on account of Kremlin propaganda. In the final analysis the Soviet Union's campaign to regain custody of every one of its displaced citizens failed because refugees with a choice detected the insincerity of Moscow's appeals. Halfhearted promises of a happy homecoming did not successfully disguise the regime's vindictive spirit.

NOTES

1. Col. T. R. Henn, Act. ACS, G5 to Dep. CS, AFHQ, 5 Jan. 1945, NAS RG 331, AFHQ, Roll 227-B, Sacs 400-7, Russian Matters.

2. Gaddis, *Origins*, 80; Lorimer, *Population*, 181; Werth, *Russia at War*, 707; Wright, *Ordeal*, 263; Zhukov, *Memoirs*, 643.

3. Levering, *American Opinion*, 96, 77.

4. Wright, *Ordeal*, 264.

5. John Erickson, "The Soviet Union at War (1941-1945): An Essay on Sources and Studies," *Soviet Studies*, 14 (Jan. 1963), 268; "Hist. of USMMM," 30 Oct. 1945, NA RG 165, WDGSS OPD 336, Case 233, Part II; N. Lebedev, "The Truth about the Second World War," *International Affairs*, no. 1 (Jan. 1974), 101-2; V. A. Val'kov, *SSSR i SSha. Ikh politicheskie i ekonomicheskie otnosheniia* (Moscow, 1965), 340; P. A. Zhilin, "O problemakh istorii vtoroi mirovoi voiny," *Novaia i noveishaia istoriia*, no. 2 (Mar.-Apr. 1973), 12.

6. Ivan Maisky, *Memoirs of a Soviet Ambassador. The War: 1939-43* (New York, 1967), 277. See also Gaddis, *Origins*, 80; Keith M. Heim, "Hope without Power: Truman and the Russians, 1945" (Ph.D. diss., University of North Carolina, 1973), 42; Zhilin, "O problemakh," 12.

7. Gaddis, *Origins*, 80.

8. Alexander Werth, *Russia: The Post-War Years* (New York, 1971), 24.

9. A desire for more "working hands" also contributed to the Soviet drive for the repatriation of its Armenian diaspora. Reuben Darbinian, "The Proposed Second Repatriation by the Government of Soviet Armenia: What Does Moscow Want from Its Armenian Collaborators of the Armenian Diaspora?" *Armenian Review*, 15 (Apr. 1962), 6.

10. Zhukov, *Memoirs*, 676-77.

▼

11. Alfred Sauvy, "Psycho-Social Aspects of Migration," in *Economics of International Migration*, ed. by Brinley Thomas (London, 1958), 299.

12. Kennan to Hull, 10 Nov. 1944, *FR, 1944*, IV: 1264. McCollum was quoted in Anthony J. Bouscaren, *International Migrations since 1945* (New York, 1963), 15-16.

13. Leonid I. Brezhnev, *The Great Victory of the Soviet People* (Moscow, 1965), 29. See also Alexander Borisov, "Recent Anglo–U.S. Bourgeois Historiography of the Soviet Union's Great Patriotic War," in *Soviet Studies on the Second World War*, ed. by M. Goncharuk (Moscow, 1976), 233.

14. Romanov, *Nights*, 170; Pfc. Dmytro Staroschak to *Narodna Volya* (weekly of the Ukrainian Workingmen's Association), Box 192, UUARC; Shub, *Choice*, 51.

15. Harriman to Stettinius, 10 Jan. 1945, *FR, Yalta*, 455. See also Dallin and Mavrogordato, "Soviet Reaction," 322.

16. Gehlen, *Service*, 90. See also Erickson, *Stalingrad*, 353.

17. Andrei Y. Vyshinski, *Speech Delivered by A. Y. Vyshinski . . . in the General Assembly—November 6, 1946* (Washington, D.C., 1946), 12; "EP's Problem in Europe," 2 Apr. 1946, NAS RG 165, WDGSS Military Intelligence Service Project File, no. 2996; *New York Times*, 19 Oct. 1945.

18. Lyons, *Secret*, 271; Shub, *Choice*, 201-2. See also John Scott, "Interview with a Russian DP," *Fortune*, 39 (Apr. 1949), 81.

19. Speaking specifically of the Soviet campaign for the repatriation of Armenians abroad, Darbinian suggests that one of Moscow's goals was the destruction of the émigré Armenian Revolutionary Federation. "Second Repatriation," 7.

20. George Ginsburgs, "Displaced Persons," in *Encyclopedia of Soviet Law*, I, ed. by F. J. M. Feldbrugge (Leiden, 1973), 231-32.

21. Proudfoot, *European Refugees*, 213.

22. *New York Times*, 1 May 1945; Lt. Col. Zapozin and Maj. Berizoeski to Eisenhower, 9 Apr. 1945, in Chandler, ed., *The War Years*, IV: 2603; Kennan to Stettinius, 30 Apr. 1945, NA RG 334, USMMM-POWs, 25 Apr. 1945–15 June 1945.

23. McNeill, *America, Britain, and Russia*, 580; Ginsburgs, "Problem of Refugees," 352.

24. Briukhanov, *Vot kak eto bylo*, 38; F. I. Golikov, *V Moskovskoi bitve, zapiski komandarma* (Moscow, 1967), 5; Nemirov, *Dorogi i vstrechi*, 38; Romanov, *Nights*, 170; Seaton, *Russo-German War*, 15; Semiriaga, *Sovetskie liudi*, 326; Solzhenitsyn, *Gulag*, I: 240, 624; Tolstoy, *Secret*, 399-400; Zhukov, *Memoirs*, 216. By one of history's curious quirks the future head of the Russian Liberation Army (Vlasov) and the future head of the Soviet Repatriation Commission both participated in the successful defense of Moscow.

25. Raymond L. Garthoff, "The Marshals and the Party: Soviet Civil-Military Relations in the Postwar Period," in *Total War and Cold War: Problems in Civilian Control of the Military*, ed. by Harry L. Coles (Columbus, Ohio, 1962), 259-61; "Biographical Index," in *Stalin and His Generals*, ed. by Bialer, 630. For additional biographical data see Edward L. Crowley *et al.*, *Prominent Personalities in the USSR, a Biographic Directory Containing 6,015 Biographies of Prominent Personalities in the Soviet Union* (Metuchen, N. J., 1968), 184; and Borys Levytsky, *The Soviet Political Elite* (Munich, 1969), 156. For the allegation of cowardice see Khrushchev's *Khrushchev Remembers* (Boston, 1970), 194-95.

26. Harriman and Abel, *Special Envoy*, 416; Romanov, *Nights*, 170, 172; Tolstoy, *Secret*, 400.

27. Romanov, *Nights*, 124, 127; Thorwald, *Illusion*, 254; Tolstoy, *Secret*, 401-2; Vought, "Inquiry," 177.

28. Romanov, *Nights*, 127.

29. Solzhenitsyn, *First Circle*, xiii, 509. The Red Army general's admission is related in Tolstoy, *Secret*, 427-28; the account of the ex-SMERSH officer is in Romanov, *Nights*, 171.

30. Murphy to SD, 22 June 1945, NA RG 59, 800.4016 DP/6-2245; Deane, *Strange Alliance*, 201; OCH, EUCOM, *Survey*, 276; OCMH, "Exchange," 10.

31. M. Iskrin, "V bor'be protiv gitlerovskikh okkupantov Norvegii," *Novaia i noveishaia istoriia*, no. 6 (Nov.-Dec. 1962), 127; Lithgow Osborne to Secretary of State, 21 Aug. 1945, NA RG 59, 762.61114/8-2145; SHAEF to WD, 22 Apr. 1945, NA RG 218, CCS 383.6 (7-4-44) (2) Sec. 5; Murphy to SD, 28 Apr. 1945, NA RG 59, 740.00114 EW/4-2845, enclosure, p. 2; EUCOM, "RAMP's," 66.

32. Brig. Gen. H. Floyd, 8th Army, to AFHQ, 7 Nov. 1944; Maj. Gen. F. G. Beaumont-Nesbitt to CS, AFHQ, 9 Jan. 1945; Lt. Gen. R. L. McBreery, 8th Army, to 15th Army Group, 30 Mar. 1945, NAS RG 331, AFHQ, Roll 227-B, SACS 400-7, "Russian Matters"; Gen. Alexander to Troopers, London, 12 Sept. 1945, NAS RG 331, AFHQ, 383.7-14.4, Reel 17-L, G-5, DP Div., "Travel of Russian Repatriation Representatives."

33. ACC Bulgaria (British delegation) to AFHQ, 7 Apr. 1945, NAS RG 331, AFHQ 383.7-14.4, Reel 17-L, G-5, DP Div., "Travel of Russian Repatriation Representatives"; Kirk to Secretary of State, 14 Sept. and 8 Oct. 1945, NA RG 59, 740.62114/8-2745 and 10-845.

34. Clark, *Calculated Risk*, 476-77.

35. CG (Clark), USAFE (Vienna), to WD, 25 Jan., 13 Mar., and 29 June 1946, NA RG 218, CCS 383.6 (7-4-44) (2) Sec. 7 and 8. See also U.S. Political Adviser for Austria (Erhardt) to Byrnes, 26 Dec. 1946, *FR, 1946*, V: 197-98.

36. Smith, *Three Years*, 256.

37. "Plight of Ukrainian DPs," reprint from the Ukrainian newspaper, *Amerika*, no date, Box 192, UUARC; Jefferson Patterson, Chargé d'Affaires, to Secretary of State, 8 Mar. 1946, NA RG 59, 840.4016/3-846; SACMED (Greece) to CIGS, 2 Sept. 1945, NAS RG 331, AFHQ, Roll 228-B, SACS 400-7, "Russian Matters."

38. OCMH, EUCOM, *Survey*, 216.

39. "Plight of Ukrainian DPs," *Amerika*, and cablegram received by UUARC, 8 Oct. 1945, p. 6, and letter by a former Ukrainian member of the pre-war Polish Parliament, 16 July 1945, pp. 7-8, box 192, UUARC; *I'll Never Go Back*, 226-27; Kotov, "Stalin," 57; Lyons, *Secret*, 268; Tolstoy, *Secret*, 373, 377. See also First Plenary Conference, 12 Sept. 1945, NA RG 43, Council of Foreign Ministers, Second Meeting, London.

40. Alec Dickson, "Displaced Persons," *National Review*, 129 (Dec. 1947), 490-91; Jaroslaw Tomasziwskyj, " 'Vozrozhdenie': A Russian Periodical Abroad and Its Contributors" (Ph.D. diss., Vanderbilt University, 1974), 18. For the text of a Soviet Camp appeal, remarkable in its psychological ineptness, see: minutes of meeting with Soviet Liaison Officer, Mittenwald Camp, 28 Aug. 1947, enclosure to dispatch 409, 14 Oct. 1947, NA RG 59, 800.4016 DP/10-1447.

41. Fort Dix Report, 19 July 1945, NA RG 59, 711.62114/7-1945.

42. "Plight of Ukrainian DPs," *Amerika*, 9, box 192, UUARC.

43. Donnison, *North-West Europe*, 357; Murphy to Byrnes, 16 May 1946, *FR, 1946*, V: 163-64.

44. ACC to Col. P. G. Jakovlev, U.S.S.R. repatriation delegate in Rome, 13 Jan. 1947, NAS RG 331, AFHQ 383.7-14.4, Reel 17-L, G-5, DP Div., "Travel of Russian Repatriation Representatives"; Holborn, *International*, 351.

45. Samuel Snipes, UNRRA Team 1062, to Dorothy Thompson, Refugee Defense Committee, 3 June 1947, folder 38, Panchuk Papers; OCMH, EUCOM, *Survey*, 279. See also Maj. Gen. F. G. Beaumont-Nesbitt to AFHQ, 5 Dec. 1944, NAS RG 331, AFHQ.

46. OCMH, EUCOM, *Survey*, 227; *New York Times*, 17 Feb. 1949. Ginsburgs ("Displaced Persons," 232) mistakenly states that 1948 saw an end to the Soviet Repatriation Mission in the West.

47. U.S. Department of State, *Germany, 1947-1949; the Story in Documents* (Washington, D.C., 1950), 123, 125-26. See also Ginsburgs, "Refugees," 352; Triska and Slusser, *Soviet Treaties*, 174.

48. 3-5 Mar. 1949. See also Walter M. Kotschnig, "Problems of the Resettlement Program," *Department of State Bulletin*, 20 (13 Mar. 1949), 307-8; OMGUS to CS of CAD, 22 Mar. 1949, NA RG 165, WDGSS "IRO Feeding of Soviet Mission"; "U.S. Requests Withdrawal," 320-22. According to Holborn (*International*, 344), the British were not rid of all their Soviet repatriation personnel until 1950.

49. *Repatriation News*, 14 (14 June 1947), 3, folder 9, Panchuk Papers.

50. Nikolai F. Brychev, *Domoi, na rodinu!* 2nd ed. (Moscow, 1945), 4, 6.

51. Lt. Col. Gorbatov, quoted in Murphy to SD, 2 June 1945, NA RG 59, no decimal number, enclosure to Dispatch 451; Briukhanov, *Vot kak eto bylo*, 203.

52. *Vstrecha o rodinoi* [Encounter with the Homeland], Soviet Embassy, Washington, D.C.; Vladimir Gsovski, *Soviet Civil Law; Private Rights and Their Background under the Soviet Regime*, 2 (Ann Arbor, Mich., 1949), 305-6.

53. Lt. Col. Gorbatov, quoted in Murphy to SD, 2 June 1945, NA RG 59, no decimal number, enclosure to Dispatch 451. See also A. P. Ivushkina, *Rodina zovet! Sbornik. Po materialam gazety "Za vozvrashchenie na rodinu"* (Berlin, 1955), 95.

54. David Dallin and Boris Nikolaevskii, *Forced Labor in Soviet Russia* (New Haven, Conn., 1947), 282-83; Brig. Gen. R. W. Berry, GSC, Dep. ACS, G1, to Dep. CS, 6 Aug. 1945, NA RG 165, ACS 383.6 Sec. 8, Cases 400 . . . 450. See also ch. 7.

55. *Otvety*, 4.

56. *Osnovy sovetskogo voyennogo zakonodatel'stva* (Moscow, 1966), 271 (Soviet Military Translations, No. 286. JPRS 36,420).

57. "Repatriation of DPs from Germany and Austria," NAS RG 165, WDGSS, Military Intelligence Service Project File, no. 2897, 1 Mar. 1946. See also *Otvety*, 25.

58. Brychev, *Domoi, na rodinu!*, 10; Kirk to Stettinius quoting the *Union Jack*, 2 Mar. 1945, NA RG 59, 800.4016DP/3-245. See also Ivushkina, *Rodina*, 34, 52.

59. Memorandum by Donald Lowrie, 20 Oct. 1944, NA RG 59, 762.61114/14-344.

60. Harriman to Stettinius, 10 Jan. 1945, *FR, Yalta*, 455; Kennan to SD, 15 Nov. 1944, NA RG 59, 762.61114-1544; Solzhenitsyn, *First Circle*, 463.

61. Walter Dushnyck and William J. Gibbons, *Refugees Are People: The Plight of Europe's Displaced Persons* (New York, 1947), 89; *Otvety*, 5, 20, 30, 39, 40-42; Kirk to Stettinius quoting the *Union Jack*, 2 Mar. 1945, NA RG 59, 800.4016 DP/3-245.

62. Deane, *Strange Alliance*, 186-87. Donnison, *Central Organization and Planning*, 198; Proudfoot, *European Refugees*, 152; A. Kapustin to Hull, 13 July 1944, NA RG 165, WDGSS OPD 383.6 Sec. 9, Case 290.

63. Stettinius memorandum of conversation with Gromyko, 12 Sept. 1944, and Gromyko to Hull, 23 Sept. 1944, *FR, 1944*, IV: 1247, 1252-53.

64. Gromyko to Byrnes, 10 Apr. 1945, *FR, 1945*, V: 1090; *New York Times*, 1 May 1945.

65. Statement by General F. I. Golikov in *Pravda*, 9 Nov. 1944, cited in Deane, *Strange Alliance*, 187-88. There is no way to determine accurately what percentage were or were not combatants. However, it is probably safe to say that Solzhenitsyn's claim that most Soviet military collaborators were noncombatants overstates the case. Blake, "Solzhenitsyn," 39.

66. The best single treatment of this topic in short compass is Ginsburgs, "Displaced Persons," 232.

67. J. Silabriedis and B. Arklans, *"Political Refugees" Unmasked* (Riga, 1965), 4; Zhukov, *Memoirs*, 666.

68. Ginsburgs, "Displaced Persons," 232. See also Grzybowski, *Soviet Public International Law*, 243; EUCOM, "Displaced Persons," 69.

69. G. Mikhailov, "Rescue Soviet People From Foreign Bondage!" *Trud*, 20 Dec. 1950, translated in Raymond, "Juridicial Status," 374.

70. Zhukov, *Memoirs*, 666. The American order is quoted in Hlynka, "On Behalf," 174. See also U.S. Military Government, *Weekly Information Bulletin*, 19 (1 Dec. 1945), 27.

71. Acheson to Truman, 2 Apr. 1947, NA RG 59, FW800.4016 DP/4-247. For Vyshinskii's attitude see Ginsburgs, "Problems of Refugees," 352.

72. Briukhanov, *Vot kak eto bylo*, 204.

73. Zhukov, *Memoirs*, 666. See also Donald R. Taft and Richard Robbins, *International Migrations, the Immigrant in the Modern World* (New York, 1955), 239.

74. *New York Times*, 12 Nov. 1944; "Refugees and Displaced Persons," *Great Soviet Encyclopedia*, 3rd ed. (1970), 3: 749; minutes of meeting with Soviet Liaison Officer, Mittenwald Camp, 28 Aug. 1947, enclosure to dispatch 409, 14 Oct. 1947, NA RG 59, 800.4016 DP/10-1447.

75. Briukhanov, *Vot kak eto bylo*, 41.

76. John Mair, *Austria*, in *Four-Power Control in Germany and Austria, 1945-1946* (London, 1956), 360; *New York Times*, 21 Nov. 1945.

77. "Acceleration of the Repatriation of Soviet Citizens," memorandum of the Soviet delegation at the Council of Foreign Ministers meeting, 13 Sept. 1945, *FR, 1945*, II: 153; Dvinov, *Politics*, 4; Smith, "American Role," 136; Wyle, "Memorandum," 11. For an impassioned rebuttal see Manning, "Significance," 21.

78. Leahy, *I Was There*, 425. See also Bethell, *Secret*, 180.

79. Quoted in *New York Times*, 1 Aug. 1945. See also Clark to Marshall, 5 Feb. 1947, *FR, 1947*, II: 126.

80. Zhukov, *Memoirs*, 666; Silabriedis and Arklans, *"Political Refugees" Unmasked*, 5.

81. Burton, "Vlasov," 9, quoting *Vozrozhdenie* (Sept.-Oct. 1949), 4. Bernard Guilbert Guerney, ed., "A Quota of Soviet Saws and Sayings," in *An Anthology of Russian Literature in the Soviet Period from Gorki to Pasternak* (New York, 1960), 440. See also Tolstoy, *Secret*, 398.

82. N. F. Kiung and U. R. Talmant, "Iz istorii dvizheniia soprotivleniia sov-

etskikh liudei v lageriakh gitlerovskoi Germanii (1941-1945gg.)," *Istoriia SSSR*, no. 5 (Sept.-Oct. 1959), 54-55.

83. *New York Times*, 14 May 1945; Kydd, *Over*, 298.

84. Nemirov, *Dorogi i vstrechi*, 5; "Refugees and Displaced Persons," *Great Soviet Encyclopedia*, 3rd ed. (1970), 3: 749; Keesing's Research Report, *Germany and Eastern Europe since 1945: From the Potsdam Agreement to Chancellor Brandt's "Ostpolitik"* (New York, 1973), 128; Briukhanov, *Vot kak eto bylo*, 203; *Otvety*, 4; Mikhailov, "Rescue," in Raymond, "Juridical Status," 373, 379; Ginsburgs, "Problems of Refugees," 352.

85. Annex to memorandum by Soviet delegation at meeting of Council of Foreign Ministers, contained in Grew to Kennan, 27 July 1945, *FR, 1945*, V: 1100-1. Moscow reiterated the charge at two subsequent CFM meetings: 12 Sept. 1945, NA RG 43, First Plenary Session, London; 19 Dec. 1945, *FR, 1945*, II: 704.

86. Briukhanov, *Vot kak eto bylo*, 207. For Bulganin's speech see Keesing's, *Germany*, 120. See also deWeerd, "Operation Keelhaul," 36; Nemirov, *Dorogi i vstrechi*, 48.

87. K. Novikov to Asst. Secretary of State James C. Dunn, 23 July 1945, *FR, Berlin*, II: 1163; Vasiliev to Alexander, SACMED, 29 Sept. 1945, NAS RG 331, AFHQ, Roll 227-B, SACS 400-7, Russian Matters; "History of USMMM," 30 Oct. 1945, NA RG 165, WDGSS, OPD 336, Case 233, Part II, 286.

88. The *Pravda* translation is in Deane to Walter B. Smith, 11 Sept. 1944, NA RG 334, USMMM-POWs, Oct. 1943–Oct. 1945. Hull's reaction is in a Memorandum of Conversation with Gromyko, 24 Sept. 1944, *FR, 1944*, IV: 1251. For similar complaints raised in Italy and the French zone of Germany see: Col. Iakovlev to Lt. Gen. J. A. H. Gammell, 23 Nov. 1944, NAS RG 331, AFHQ; Mikhailov, "Rescue," in Raymond, "Juridical Status," 378.

89. Briukhanov, *Vot kak eto bylo*, 2, 39. See also Sh. P. Sanakoev and B. L. Tsibulevskii, *Tegeran. Ialta. Potsdam. Sbornik dokumentov* (Moscow, 1970), 199.

90. Nemirov, *Dorogi i vstrechi*, 48; Murphy to SD, 28 Apr. 1945, NA RG 59, 740.00114 EW/4-2845, enclosure, p. 2.

91. Gutteridge, "Repatriation," 208; "Repatriatsiia," *Bol'shaia sovetskaia entsiklopediia*, 2nd ed. (1955), 36: 394. The seriously ill and those indicted for or serving a sentence for a crime were quantitatively inconsequential exceptions. See also "Bezhentsy i peremeshchenny litsa," *Bol'shaia sovetskaia entsiklopediia*, 3rd ed. (1970), vol. 3; "Repatriatsiia," *Diplomaticheskii slovar'*, 3 (Moscow, 1964), 53.

92. Mark Elliott, "The Greco-Turkish Compulsory Exchange of Populations of 1923" (unpublished study in author's possession, 1970), 1; Stephen P. Ladas, *The Exchange of Minorities: Bulgaria, Greece and Turkey* (New York, 1932), 1.

93. Gutteridge, "Repatriation," 209; Grzybowski, *Soviet Public International Law*, 238-39, 276-77; "Soviet Citizenship Law," 361-70; Triska and Slusser, *Soviet Treaties*, 201.

94. Frank Notestein *et al.*, *The Future Population of Europe and the Soviet Union, Population Projections, 1940-1970* (Geneva, 1944), 89; Harley Notter, ed., *Postwar Foreign Policy Preparation, 1939-1945* (Washington, D.C., 1949), 642. See also John E. Fried, *Exploitation of Foreign Labour in Germany* (Montreal, 1945), i; Hilldring, "Position on Resettlement," 1163; Bertram Pickard, *Europe's Uprooted People: The Relocation of Displaced Population* (Washington, D.C., 1944), 8.

95. Atle Grahl-Madsen, *The Status of Refugees in International Law*. Vol. I: *Refugee Character* (Leyden, 1966), 18; Huxley-Blythe, *East*, 187; Lorimer, "America's Response," 48; Lyons, *Secret*, 261; Samuel Snipes, UNRRA Team 1062, to Dorothy Thompson, Refugee Defense Committee, 3 June 1947, folder 38, Panchuk Papers.

96. Dushnyck and Gibbons, *Refugees*, 54; Lorimer, "America's Response," 48.

97. Dushnyck and Gibbons, *Refugees*, 55; *Repatriation News*, 14 (14 June 1947), 1, 4-6, folder 9, Panchuk Papers. See also Dushnyck and Gibbons, *Refugees*, 87-88.

98. "UNRRA's Chief of Displaced Persons Operations Urges Repatriation," Annex No. 2, 4 May 1947, folder 9, Panchuk Papers; "Nobody Cares About DP's Anymore," *Washington Daily News*, 14 May 1947, folder 37, Panchuk Papers; author's confidential interview with former State Department official, 29 July 1977.

99. Grahl-Madsen, *Status of Refugees*, 18, 137. See also IRO, *Facts*, 7, 12; Lorimer, "America's Response," 48; Lyons, *Secret*, 262; Sergej Utechin, "Refugees," *Everyman's Concise Encyclopedia of Russia* (New York, 1961), 452. The Soviet Union sent delegates to help draft the document but refused to join or contribute to it financially: Ginsburgs, "Displaced Persons," 232.

100. IRO, *Facts*, 12; Scott, "Interview," 84; Col. Chauncey G. Parker, Jr., to McCloy, 7 Nov. 1945, NA RG 165, CAD WDSCA 383.7 Germany, Aug. 45–30 Mar. 46, Sec. I.

7

THE NONRETURNERS:

Betrayers or Betrayed?

As a result of the Soviet Union's failure to effect unconditional repatriation, the Western powers had to contend with a new category of refugee: the "stateless." These DPs, who disclaimed all ties to
their country of origin, included the surviving remnants of European Jewry but consisted primarily of East European nationals unwilling to go
back to Soviet-controlled homelands. A substantial portion of the "stateless" held Soviet citizenship or came from districts annexed by Russia at
the end of the war. Neither *exile* nor *émigré* serves as a completely satisfactory label for these refugees, unmoved by the prospect of going home,
because none had been planted abroad with their government's consent,
and few with their own. [1] In the Soviet Union this peculiar variety of diaspora is called the *nevozvrashchentsy*, or the nonreturners, a designation
that serves as well as any.

Given the opportunity, East European DPs found numerous reasons
for not going home. A few had started second families abroad and hesi-
tated to repatriate out of fear of the wrath of two spouses. [2] The higher
standard of living outside Russia impressed others, who also contemplated the inevitable sacrifices and hardships of reconstruction back
home. Not just Germany and Austria but even "backward" Poland
amazed displaced Soviet nationals used to bare subsistence: "all of us,
officers and men, saw the riches and prosperity of a capitalist country and
couldn't believe our eyes. We had never believed there could be such an
abundance of goods." [3] Only in contrast to even more desperate Russian
conditions could war-ravaged Europe impress Soviet refugees.

Apart from the West's economic allurements, negative appraisals of
the Soviet system figured in all refugee reasons for hesitating to go home.
DPs often feared repatriation because of past ill-treatment at the hands of
Soviet officials. Among various motives for their opposition to Stalin's
regime, the Fort Dix POWs most frequently cited the exile, imprisonment, or execution of a parent or close relative. A defecting NKVD
officer claims over 50 percent of all Soviet families of the 1940s had had a

close relation whom the secret police had investigated, arrested, or convicted.[4]

Many sought to remain in the West because they represented one of several oppressed classes within the Soviet Union. A "wrong" social origin could be anything from kulak (well-to-do peasant opposed to collectivization) to bourgeois, aristocrat, or intelligentsia—or descendants of any of the above.[5] According to Soviet data, for example, kulaks constituted a maximum of 10 percent of the farm population prior to collectivization. In contrast, 75 percent of the peasants refusing repatriation, as surveyed by the Air Force–sponsored Harvard Project, came from "dekulakized" families.[6]

Other categories of Soviet citizens with ample reason to dread homegoing were the religious, the national minorities, and persons with arrest records. "What struck me in my numerous contacts with the Displaced Persons," Alexandra Tolstoy observed, "is that notwithstanding the atheistic propaganda of the communists, the majority of the former Soviet citizens are very religious." A representative of the Refugee Commission of the World Council of Churches estimated that émigré Russian Orthodox congregations numbered 133 by the fall of 1947 and noted that "even in the smaller camps of the French Occupation Zone of Germany which often contained as few as fifty Russian displaced persons . . . lay people organized and maintained Orthodox worship at great personal sacrifice using for the purpose a part of the building assigned to them for a dwelling." The number of Catholic, Orthodox, and Protestant clergy ministering to former Soviet subjects ran to 508 and another 339 for Baltic nonreturners.[7] Church life flourished in DP camps partly because freedom of worship was a novelty to many refugees; partly because the camp dwellers had an abundance of time on their hands; and partly because their desperate plight stimulated a search for divine strength and consolation. But the post–World War II Soviet diaspora also underwent a spiritual renaissance because believers persecuted by Lenin and Stalin had an additional incentive to avoid repatriation and consequently worked harder than average to become part of the "stateless" population.

Also a higher ratio of minority nationalities existed among nonreturners than in the Soviet population as a whole. Ukrainians, for example, accounted for 52.6 percent of all nonreturners who had held Soviet citizenship prior to World War II, but they constituted only 16.5 percent of the Soviet population in 1939. In comparison, Great Russians amounted to 14 percent of the postwar emigration yet 58.1 percent of the total Soviet population in 1939. Great Russians sometimes, but Ukrainians regularly, suffered heavy losses under charges of bourgeois nationalism, especially in Stalin's purges of the 1930s.[8] It is also true that the Germans occupied the entire Ukraine for a time, whereas only a portion of the Great Russian population had to endure German occupation. Thus, because of accessibility the Nazis deported more Ukrainians than Great Russians, and more of the former were in a position to choose between Russia and the West at the end of the war. Nevertheless, the Ukrainian percentage is so high that one cannot help but conclude that Moscow's rough handling of subject nationalities at least contributed to the disproportionate number of non-Russian Soviet citizens avoiding repatriation.

Trouble with the police emerged as the most predictable feature of nonreturners' negative appraisal of the Soviet system. The arrest rate among adult Soviet refugees surveyed by the Harvard Project came to 25 percent. And 80 percent of the respondents had either been arrested or had had some family member arrested.[9] Unquestionably, World War II émigrés had run afoul of the law with regularity, even more so than the Soviet population as a whole.

Motives for disaffection and refusal to repatriate often intermingled. Julius Braun, for example, found himself at odds with the regime at every turn. His father, considered a rich kulak, had been shot. As a descendant of German and Lowland Mennonites brought to the Ukraine by Catherine the Great, Julius faced persecution on account of both his nationality and his religious convictions, especially his refusal to bear arms. The Braun household, predictably, had had more than its share of encounters with the police. Not only had Julius's father been jailed and shot, but nine uncles had been arrested. Five had died in Siberia, and four he assumed were still in prison.[10]

Some nonreturners had received no special mistreatment but simply opposed the oppression and restrictions of a totalitarian political system. This applied particularly to DPs from recently annexed territories. A high ranking U.S. refugee official told a Congressional Subcommittee on Immigration that he had repeatedly asked refugees,

> "Why don't you go home—to the piece of ground you know, the members of your family and old friends, to the place where you can use your native tongue?"
>
> These are the answers I receive, and I receive them every day from people of nearly every walk of life. The Baltic Peoples—the Lithuanians, Latvians and Estonians—have said to me, "I would rather die than return to my home—it is no longer mine."[11]

Past Soviet treatment certainly made DPs wary about going home, but not as much as fear of reprisals should they ever again fall into Russian hands: Vlasovites and Osttruppen because of outright collaboration;

POWs because they knew Moscow equated surrender with treason; and Ostarbeiter simply because exposure to the West rendered them suspect and tainted. Obviously, Red Army POWs who ended the war in Wehrmacht ranks had reason to fear repatriation. German propagandists warned them what defeat would entail and, in this instance, the Nazis deserved to be believed. As Solzhenitsyn records, fear of recapture by Soviet forces sometimes led collaborator units to unusually desperate fighting.[12]

Moscow's concept of proper battlefield deportment, considering capture tantamount to treason, played an important part in the decision of many POWs to seek refuge in the West. The U.S.S.R. consistently took a dim view of surrender. In World War I the ratio of captives to fatalities among German combatants was 11 to 17, but for the tsar's troops, 25 to 17. This tendency to surrender rather than fight to the death, which Lenin dubbed the "save-the-skin mentality," disturbed the new Soviet leaders so much that they decided not to adhere to international agreements safeguarding the treatment of POWs: the Hague Convention of 1907, and later, the Geneva Convention of 1929. They reasoned that troops guaranteed nothing in captivity would give stiffer resistance. Moscow's stratagem backfired. While surrender did thus appear less attractive to Red Army troops in World War II, the lack of international protection for POWs also motivated the German opposition to avoid capture. Writes one observer, "This has had the inevitable effect on Russia's enemies, as well as the Russian soldiers themselves, of raising the determination to fight to the bitter end."[13] Here in part is an explanation for the extraordinary barbarity of the struggle on the Eastern front.

Stalin's measures went well beyond Lenin's rejection of POW conventions to include widely publicized and stringent warnings to Red Army troops. The wartime edition of the standard Soviet encyclopedia explained that "the penalty for premeditated surrender into captivity not necessitated by combat conditions is death by shooting." Decree Number 270 of 1942 spelled out explicitly that "a prisoner captured alive by the enemy [is] *ipso facto* a traitor."[14] The Soviet constitution stated that any infringement of the military code (which included surrender to the enemy) was an act of treason. Article 193, paragraph 22, of the Criminal Code of the Russian Soviet Federated Socialist Republic declared "a serviceman's unauthorized abandonment of the battlefield, surrender not called for by military operations," to be "punishable by death by shooting." And the criminal codes of the other constitutent republics had equivalent clauses. In the same vein, the Red Army field manual allowed for retreat only when ordered by a high superior. "Good troops have no rear," the manual proclaimed, "for they have a front everywhere."[15] It is no wonder then that Soviet POWs liberated in the West told American intelligence that they feared repatriation. Their orders had been "to commit suicide rather than allow themselves to be taken prisoner." A loyal soldier was either fighting or dead.[16]

Viktor Chkhikvadze, legal scholar and head of the Military Judicial Academy, reiterated these harsh strictures in a 1948 textbook on military criminal law: "Surrender of military forces to the enemy is not permitted under any circumstance. . . . Even being lightly wounded, losing the use of one's weapon, or the lack of ammunition, does not justify a serviceman's abandonment of the battlefield or surrender to the enemy." Considering the universal Soviet condemnation of soldiers not fighting to the death, it is not surprising that Red Army officers at the U.S. shuttle-bombing base at Poltava found the American attitude toward POWs perplexing. George Fischer, stationed there for part of the war, recalled that Soviet military personnel "could not understand and bitterly objected to our welcome of liberated American POWs as loyal and devoted combat men."[17]

During World War II Moscow considered those who fell into enemy hands beyond the pale. In late November 1941 Foreign Minister V. M. Molotov did protest German atrocities against Soviet POWs; the next April he stated that the Soviet Union would abide by the Hague Convention; and in May 1942 he hinted that Moscow looked to all international conventions for the protection of its citizens under German control.[18] But other than to publicize Nazi war crimes, the Kremlin took no practical steps to alleviate the horrible conditions facing captured Red Army men. As previously noted, at a White House meeting in May 1942 Molotov emphatically rejected President Roosevelt's suggestion that the Russians negotiate with the Germans on POW matters. Similarly, Soviet Ambassador Ivan Maiskii in London treated with contempt a German feeler, channeled through a neutral party, seeking clarification on Moscow's attitude toward the Hague Convention. The ambassador replied that the Soviet Union had no interest in the fate of its POWs: "If they had fulfilled their duty as soldiers to fight to the last they would not have been taken prisoner."[19]

True to form, Moscow denied repeated requests by the International Red Cross for an exchange of lists of captured troops. Furthermore, the U.S.S.R. never bothered to make formal complaints about German treatment of Russian POWs directly or indirectly through neutral channels. Svetlana Alliluyeva, Stalin's daughter, succinctly laid out the captive soldier's predicament: "Everyone who was taken prisoner, even if they'd been wounded . . . was considered to have 'surrendered voluntarily to the enemy.' The government thereby washed its hands of millions of its own officers and men during the war and refused to have anything to do with them. Is it any wonder that when the war ended many of them didn't want to come home?"[20]

The Kremlin's vindictiveness hardly knew limits, as seen by the punishment visited even upon the relatives of those unpatriotic enough to have been captured alive by the Germans. The criminal codes of the various Soviet republics and military orders 356 (1940) and 274 (1941) condemned adult members of traitors' families to exile or imprisonment for up to five years.[21] Because Stalin's son, Jacob Dzugashvili, fell into German hands, his wife spent two years in prison. The Soviet dictator allowed this to happen to his daughter-in-law, even though he knew it meant the separation of his own grandchild, Gulia, from her mother.[22]

The fate of Stalin's oldest son illustrates the oft-repeated tragedy of a prisoner forsaken by his native land. Jacob was the Soviet ruler's son by his first wife, a simple, devout, Georgian peasant woman. After her death the child's maternal grandparents had cared for him. The boy had seen little of his father until 1923, twelve years after Stalin had left his native Georgia. In that year the future dictator had sent for Jacob and installed him in his Kremlin apartment. Not much is known of their subsequent relationship except that it was not a close one. On 16 July 1941 German forces wounded and captured a Major Jacob Dzugashvili near Vitebsk in one of the many large encirclements of the first months of fighting on the Eastern front. After Hitler's propagandists discovered this POW's identity, they momentarily toyed with the idea of making a Quisling leader out of their prize catch. But Jacob, although not overly fond of his father, would have no part of such a scheme. According to one of his German interrogators, Stalin's son behaved like a model Soviet patriot: belligerent, anti-Fascist, ever hopeful of his homeland's ultimate triumph.[23]

Unfortunately for Jacob his faith in his country was not matched by his country's or his father's faith in him. Svetlana, his half-sister, recalls that "to my father the fact that Jacob had become a prisoner of war was nothing but a 'disgrace' before the whole world. In the U.S.S.R. the news was kept under cover both during the war and after, although the press in the rest of the world was writing about it." When a foreign war correspondent dared broach the subject with Stalin, he coldly replied, "I have no son called Jacob."[24]

According to an eyewitness, Stalin's words, carried into German POW camps by radio broadcasts, crushed young Major Dzugashvili, who straightaway "went in search of death, and perished by throwing himself on electrified barbed wire."[25] It is no wonder that dissident Soviet historian Roy Medvedev calls Stalin's attitude toward POWs "one of the grimmest pages in his record." The hapless captives did not betray their coun-

try, Solzehnitsyn argues. Rather, "their calculating Motherland . . .
betrayed them" because it wrote off millions of Jacobs dying slow deaths
in Nazi camps.[26]

Soviet handling of prisoners repatriated after the Winter War with
Finland confirmed the misgivings Red Army POWs had about the reception awaiting them. Apparently few, if any, of those returned from
Finland made it home: a certain percentage were shot and the rest dispatched to labor camps in the far north or Siberia.[27] Even a POW, who
returned from the Winter War on crutches because of a double amputa-
tion, came home not to a hero's welcome but to imprisonment.[28] With
these and similar stories freely circulating in Western camps, Red Army
men captured by the Germans had ample justification for staying put.

Fear of reprisal provided the paramount motivation for remaining
abroad not simply for collaborators and POWs but for the entire Soviet
émigré population. Whether they aided the Germans or not, Soviet DPs
easily could imagine their actions being interpreted as such.[29] Nor did
they have to depend solely upon their imagination to envisage a rough
reception from Soviet officials. Stories filtered back to the Western occupation zones in a number of ways. A few refugees went through some or
all of repatriation processing and then escaped to the West. Others witnessed Soviet authorities physically abusing repatriates as they were being turned over by American or British officials. These frightening tales
naturally spread quickly in the DP compounds.[30]

The Harvard studies of nonreturners yield convincing evidence that
fear of ill-treatment discouraged repatriation more than anything else.
George Fischer, one of the project's scholar-researchers, determined
that "many Soviet émigrés will admit that it is definitely this fear of automatic exile upon return to the U.S.S.R. that led to the decision to stay
away, rather than any ideological or materialistic considerations. . . . It
appears to me that in most cases the other factors, i.e., basic anti-Soviet
sentiments and admiration for the Western 'way of life' became crystal-
lized and decisive only later."[31] Harvard Project analysts estimated that
two-thirds to three-fourths of all displaced citizens interviewed would
have returned home but for fear of the reception they expected.[32] In summary, refugees from the U.S.S.R. had ample reasons for dreading repatriation: Western allurements; a history of mistreatment at Soviet hands;
possession of suspect social origins; but especially, the expectation of reprisal for collaboration, surrender to the enemy, or simply exposure to
the West.

Motivation, however, meant nothing without opportunity, and that
proved scarce. No matter what Soviet citizens abroad might prefer, their
ultimate disposition usually depended upon the interplay of forces be-

yond their control. Just as they had no control over the German attack, which ultimately planted them on foreign soil, so they were powerless, in most instances, to determine for themselves whether repatriation would be their lot. These vagaries included: (1) the degree of German neglect and malevolence; (2) the inclination of Western officials on the local level to practice discretion and compassion toward reluctant repatriates; (3) the speed of the Russian advance; and (4) the placement of the boundary dividing Soviet and Western occupation zones. Many never lived to be repatriated, much less choose between East and West. More than half of the survivors found themselves in Soviet-occupied territory at the end of the war. And most of the rest quickly landed in DP camps set aside for those subject to repatriation under the Yalta agreement. Only about 375,000 of some 8,346,000 Soviet citizens captured by the Germans or forced to work in the Nazi empire—fewer than one in twenty-seven— ever succeeded in exercising an option to remain abroad.[33]

Many of the relative handful who escaped forced repatriation did so by disguising their identity. Since the United States and Britain refused to use force to return persons to territories seized by Russia, Soviet nationals particularly favored forged documents disguising themselves as Polish-Ukrainians. The U.S.S.R. annexed 44 percent of prewar Poland, thereby making the claim of Polish-Ukrainian extraction a large and believable loophole, especially since more Ukrainians than Poles had lived in the eastern provinces before the war.[34] UNRRA statistics document a jump in the number of Ukrainians claiming Polish citizenship, from 9,190 in December 1945 to 106,549 in June 1947, demonstrating the popularity of this exemption.[35]

Some 10,000 of General Pavlo Shandruk's Ukrainian division escaped extradition as collaborators on the grounds that they hailed from Galicia, part of prewar eastern Poland. In actuality, 20 to 50 percent or better came from undisputed Soviet territory. But in this instance at least, the British, as well as the Americans, screened the interned soldiers in such a casual fashion that every last soldier could opt for resettlement in Britain.[36] Other potential repatriates claimed membership in a wide assortment of exempt categories: Baltic, Hungarian, Yugoslavian, Rumanian, Bulgarian, "stateless," or old émigré. These transformations, one refugee worker told Alexandra Tolstoy, could take place "overnight."[37]

Time also came to the aid of nonreturners once the sweeping round-ups and transfers of the spring and summer of 1945 had passed. As General Mark Clark noted in January 1947, "Persons desiring to conceal their past have had eighteen months to build up documentary support of their story." General Joseph McNarney, as well, became skeptical of the ability of screening boards to determine the nationality of people who had "lived by their wits for a long period." Understandably, facts such as these led a skeptical George Fischer to refer to a very modest IRO figure for Soviet nationals abroad as a "pigmy number."[38]

Next to posing as non-Soviet Europeans, nothing proved more helpful in circumventing repatriation than the avoidance of refugee centers altogether. In this instance the successful nonreturner either never entered a DP camp or took pains to exit at the first opportunity. In Bruce Marshall's novel, *Vespers in Vienna*, a character relates that there were "all sorts of nefarious dodges." An aide to General Eisenhower said a host of Vlasovites in Western zones "simply vanished into the countryside."[39] In widely scattered locations all across Europe Soviet nationals with intuition and initiative, who could no longer accept their lot as pawns of war, steered clear of DP sorting centers or, to use Alexandra Tolstoy's apt phrase, "leaked out."[40] Those who actively struggled against repatriation, especially young men free of family ties, took "to the hills" of Crete or Austria or wherever, lest the Soviet dragnet sweep them back into the arms of a suspicious and unforgiving motherland.[41] "Bright and active" Soviet refugees, wary of repatriation, quickly realized that safety lay either in a healthy distance between themselves and DP camps or in securely obscured identities.[42]

Finally, some DPs, utterly desperate in their aversion to going home, chose suicide—or dangerous escape attempts tantamount to suicide. By every conceivable means, using every conceivable instrument, in locations as scattered as Seattle, Washington, Fort Dix, New Jersey, and Dachau, Germany, those violently opposed to repatriation took or tried to take their own lives. For this tragic group practically no estimates exist, reliable or otherwise. Possibly as many as several thousand Soviet nationals committed suicide rather than go back to the U.S.S.R.[43]

Needless to say, unknown numbers of DPs in disguise, in flight, or in a suicidal frame of mind play havoc with Soviet refugee computations. Frederick Wyle, in the most intelligent quantitative analysis of the nonreturner phenomenon, frankly conceded that published estimates amounted to, at best, "well informed guesses." His own work, he candidly admitted, attempted "to answer questions which remain . . . unanswerable." Eugene Kulischer, the eminent demographer, put the case even more bluntly. In a letter to the Harvard Project staff, after three and a half pages of detailed calculations of refugee numbers, he conceded, "Up to this point, I think, only God knows."[44]

Displaced persons from Russia, with motives for remaining abroad and means to act upon their reservations, did not represent a cross-section of the Soviet population, partly because of their unique wartime experiences and partly because those evading repatriation naturally saw the

Soviet system in a different light than did willing returners or those never exposed to the West. [45] In nationality, religion, occupation, age, sex, and Communist party affiliation, the composition of the nonreturner community differed from the Soviet population as a whole. As noted earlier, variations in ethnic structure set the two groups apart as sharply as any one characteristic. Great Russians, not as directly in the wake of the German attack as some of the minorities, and less disaffected generally under Stalin's chauvinistic yoke, constituted 54.6 percent of the Soviet population in the first published postwar census, but less than 10 percent of the nonreturners from both prewar Russia and annexed territories. In contrast, Ukrainians, accounting for 17.8 percent of the postwar Soviet population, amounted conservatively to 28 percent of those refusing to repatriate. [46] And most dramatically, Estonians, Latvians, and Lithuanians made up approximately 50 percent of the refugee community refusing to return to Soviet-controlled territory, but only 2.3 percent of Russia's postwar population. [47]

Wyle conceded in a Harvard Project paper that any attempt to classify nonreturners by nationality was "doomed to frustration." But project staffer Robert Feldmesser asked prominent European demographer Eugene Kulischer for one anyway, assuming an educated guess superior to none at all. His effort survives as the only known professional breakdown ever attempted (Table 3). [48]

Table 3. Nationalities of Nonreturners, Based on an Estimate Compiled by Eugene Kulischer

Nationality		Number
Great Russians		40,000
Ukrainians ⎫	Some from	150,000
Belorussians ⎭	annexed territories	15,000
Ingermanlanders (Finnish extraction)		18,000
Swedes		6,000
Other "Soviet citizens"		80,000
Subtotal		309,000
Latvians ⎫	All from	100,000
Estonians ⎬	annexed	55,000
Lithuanians ⎭	territories	65,000
Total		529,000

Source: See note 48.

The devout also, as discussed earlier, had greater than average incentive to escape from the grasp of a Soviet homeland openly hostile toward religion. Affiliations varied from Catholic—among Lithuanians, Latvians, Belorussians, and some Ukrainians; to Orthodox or Uniate—among Great Russians, Belorussians and Ukrainians; to Protestant—among Estonians and Latvians; to Jewish—particularly from European Russia and newly annexed regions.[49] Persuasions then did vary, but a disproportionately high interest in religion among DPs, in comparison with the total Soviet population, remained a constant.

As with nationality and religion the occupational differentiation of nonreturners varied appreciably from that of the Soviet labor force as a whole. For example, in 1940 agricultural workers constituted 61 percent of adult employees in the U.S.S.R. But a much smaller proportion of nonreturners listed farming as their vocation: for instance, 36 to 55 percent of Ukrainian DPs and only 12.3 percent of Latvian DPs.[50] In contrast skilled workers, but especially representatives of professional classes and the intelligentsia, probably made up a greater proportion of nonreturners than held true for the Soviet population at large. V. M. Molotov claimed 9.5 million members for the Soviet intelligentsia in 1939, or 12.2 percent of the working age population. Yet only 10 percent of postwar Soviet refugees *reported* themselves to be intelligentsia or skilled workers.[51] However, these statistics do not afford a true comparison for two reasons. First, Molotov greatly exaggerated by including among the intelligentsia not only doctors but midwives, not only factory directors but managers of shoe-repair shops, etc.

Second, well-educated Soviet DPs frequently falsified their documents, claiming a lesser status in order to circumvent the occupation quotas of resettlement countries. (Intellectuals and professionals had more trouble emigrating because receiving countries preferred refugees with easily adaptable manual skills.)[52] Thus, in spite of the above figures, the Soviet diaspora very likely contained a higher proportion of intellectuals and skilled workers than the Soviet population as a whole.

In a short but informative essay on "The New Soviet Emigration," George Fischer, one of the most reliable authorities on the subject, discussed means by which members of the Soviet intelligentsia reached the West. Many technical and administrative experts with commissions as officers in the Red Army found themselves abroad as POWs. Those civilians who ended the war outside Russia did so via the German occupation. After the invasion, Moscow hurriedly ordered the evacuation of academic and research institutes to the East. The staffs of several dozen made for the Caucasus, but as was the case for millions of Soviet citizens of all classes, the Wehrmacht still overran them. Intellectuals and professionals in German hands, especially the contingent in enemy service, had the opportunity and ample reason to flee before the Red Army. The Soviet government had placed a premium on the highly skilled and highly educated and had afforded them priority in evacuation. Consequently, their capture automatically cast suspicion upon them from Moscow's point of view. And the likely prospect of retaliation for collaborators goes without saying. An unpublished Harvard Project study noted that during the German retreat "older, nonmanual city dwellers," who would include intellectuals and professionals, left Russia voluntarily more than any other category of persons in occupied territory.[53]

One nonreturner, twelve years old at the end of World War II, related that his father, a scientist of Ukrainian nationality, had become disenchanted with the Soviet regime and had purposefully evaded evacuation to the east. While in German hands he had done research in Kiev on the development of synthetic rubber. This "nonmanual city dweller" and his family knew that charges of collaboration would jeopardize their safety should Soviet authorities ever overtake them. Consequently, when the Wehrmacht pulled out, they joined the stream of Soviet citizens attempting to flee their homeland. This Ukrainian scientist and his family successfully outdistanced the Red Army's advance—but barely. When the Allies divided Germany into occupation zones, they were a mere ten miles west of Soviet lines.[54]

No comprehensive figures for the sex ratio of nonreturners exist, but statistics available for some Soviet DP nationalities indicate that the new emigration likely contained more men than women, possibly 51 to 60 percent of the total, unlike the postwar Soviet population which was only 45 percent male.[55] This substantial difference in the sex ratios of the postwar diaspora and the Soviet population at large is easily accounted for since the vast majority of POWs and more than half the Ostarbeiter were male. Similarly, Germany's prisoners and forced laborers from the Soviet Union—and consequently nonreturners—were, on the average, younger than the population of the U.S.S.R. as a whole. In the case of POWs, the age specifications of military service, and in the case of Ostarbeiter, the Third Reich's preference for youthful, able-bodied workers, accounted for the difference. Some 58 percent of the Harvard Project's refugee respondents "were born or came to maturity after the Bolshevik Revolution," that is, were twenty-eight to forty-nine years old in 1945.[56] This age group, which constituted more than half of all Soviet nationals remaining abroad, accounted for only one-third of Russia's 1939 population.[57]

Soviet nationals abroad who both survived German captivity and escaped Allied repatriation not only were younger, on average, than the total population of the U.S.S.R. but generally possessed more vigor and staying power than the population back home. Simply being younger and having endured the Nazis' terribly rigorous and inhumane process of "unnatural selection" helps to explain why survivors commanded extraordinary powers of endurance. Clearly, millions of Soviet citizens did not survive German captivity or deportation. But, in the words of Lieutenant Colonel Jerry Sage, an American POW turned refugee official, those who did possessed "great moral and physical stamina." And many refugees barely alive at the war's end quickly revived on DP rations, which were nearly always better and more plentiful than those afforded the German population. In fact, Sage testified before a Congressional Subcommittee on Immigration that the diet, heavy in starches, proved to be more than "sustaining": by July 1947, the average DP in the U.S. zone of Germany weighed 2 percent more than the army considered healthy.[58]

Besides nonreturners being younger and healthier than average, Harvard Project data suggest they also had been surprisingly successful members of Soviet society. Even more unexpected, they frequently had ties with or descended from Russia's prerevolutionary elite. These ambitious individuals achieved rank and standing after 1917 in spite of "explicit policies designed to make it difficult for persons of such backgrounds to attain positions of status and responsibility."[59] Evidently the same initiative, drive, and savvy that allowed some refugees to survive German captivity and evade Allied repatriation also had helped them succeed under both tsarist and Soviet regimes.

Nonreturners deserved their virulently anti-Communist reputation but, paradoxically, they had belonged to the Komsomol (Communist youth organization) and the Communist party in greater percentages than the Soviet population as a whole.[60] The strong correlation that always has existed in the U.S.S.R between Communist affiliation and career success helps to explain this anomaly. Since a disproportionate number of nonreturners had done well under the Soviet regime, it follows therefore that a higher rate of Communist party membership would have obtained also. The contradiction comes unraveled best when it is realized that pragmatic individuals with political presence of mind and a knack for survival would have sought party membership under Communism and would have sought nonreturner status abroad.

The incongruity of anti-Communist refugees with past Communist party affiliation points up but one of a number of instances of political ambivalence on the part of nonreturners. The new emigration, for instance, registered markedly bitter feelings against the Soviet regime, but still felt pride in Russia's industrial achievement and dramatic improvement in literacy since 1917. A third admitted having once favored the rule of Lenin and Stalin.[61] Also, American intelligence found that military collaborators, who naturally abhorred the thought of repatriation, nevertheless "took pride in the accomplishments of the Red Army." A Harvard Project study labeled nonreturners "anti-Soviet and anti-Communist" but "simultaneously anti-capitalist and pro-welfare state." Despite the universality of hostile feelings toward the Communist system, "almost all of them bear, to some extent the stamp of the regime."[62]

While a comparison of nonreturners with the total Soviet population in rate of party membership is possible (as with nationality, occupation, sex, age, and health), there is little empirical basis for judging variations in the two groups' political views. Other features of Soviet DP life warrant characterization but, again, do not lend themselves readily to comparisons with the homebound population. In particular, the intellectual and cultural predilections of Soviet refugees and their psychological disposition merit consideration.

Given the difficult conditions of refugee life, the postwar Soviet diaspora supported a remarkably vigorous and diverse intellectual and cultural life. In addition to the lively church renewal already discussed, nonreturners devoted a great deal of attention to education. The refugee school system developed into a respectable, comprehensive network, at one point including a university, two seminaries, a technical college, an economic institute, 40 technical schools, 54 high schools, 147 elementary schools, and 86 kindergartens. The technical schools enrolled 1,713 students and had a teaching staff of 189. High school students numbered 5,406 with 688 teachers. Pupils and faculty at the primary level totaled 8,161 and 634, respectively, and in kindergartens, 4,415 students under 189 instructors. If schools for Baltic refugees were added, totals in all categories would rise sharply, in some cases more than doubling. One remarkable Ukrainian refugee center near Munich established an education system running from the elementary through the university level.[63] (Bavaria served as the unofficial headquarters for displaced Ukrainians, the largest and most active element among nonreturners. This region formed part of the U.S. zone of occupation, which harbored the largest contingents of DPs and had a reputation for the most benevolent camp administrations.)[64]

The cultural life of the new Soviet emigration also encompassed seminars and addresses by DP scholars, English language courses, choirs, theater troops, boy scouts, girl scouts, athletic clubs, and an émigré press that was both prolific and profoundly factious.[65] By one count refugees from the U.S.S.R. published five Russian, fifteen Ukrainian, six Belorussian, and two Cossack papers, not including the press of other East European, especially Baltic, nationalities. Citing "the wide differences in political orientation and preference" as a partial explanation, an émigré encyclopedia estimated that as many as 250 different Ukrainian press organs raised their mastheads in Germany and Austria between 1945 and 1950. [66]

In the 1950s the East European Fund, the handiwork of George F. Kennan, Philip Mosely, and the Ford Foundation, underwrote the publication of numerous literary and academic projects of the post–World War II Soviet emigration. Through the Fund's subsidiaries, the Research Program on the U.S.S.R. and Chekhov Publishing House, hundreds of émigré poems, novels, articles, and monographs appeared, which again dramatically demonstrated the intellectual vitality of the Soviet diaspora. [67]

The image built up of DPs as being relatively youthful and healthy and possessing initiative and the instincts for survival contrasts, admittedly, with evidence of the debilitating psychological toll of their wartime trials and refugee status. Not all but many sources document substantial emotional damage. Years of separation from loved ones and captivity in a strange land with its attendant malnutrition, phyisical exhaustion, and abuse spelled, at the least, disorientation for the liberated. German illtreatment and torture of Soviet *untermenschen* not only threatened the emotional stability of the survivors, but it also prompted some refugees to anarchic escapades through the German countryside or, on occasion, to violent acts of revenge against former tormentors. General Ernest Harmon recalled an incident at a Soviet DP camp near Aachen, which held 14,000:

> One night all hell broke out . . . as they had managed to make some whiskey out of potatoes and put a [sic] orgy of drunkeness [sic]. When the smoke cleared some 4000 had broken down the enclosure and were loose on the countryside. . . . believe it or not, we got them all back without any bloodshed, although we had to use force on a certain small isolated group who hid in the woods and refused to come back. Most of the Russians came on back down the road laughing, singing and cracking jokes with our soldiers like children caught in some mischief and thoroughly enjoyed it. [68]

One study of the "Social and Psychological Aspects of Displacement and Repatriation" determined "disrespect for law and convention" to be a predictable end product. Outside the camps Soviet DPs expressed this tendency in pillaging, brigandage, and random attacks on Germans. Inside refugee compounds authorities had to deal with disorderliness, squabbling among various ethnic groups, and a thriving black market— known to flourish in DP camps as nowhere else. [69] The regular occurrence of at least some degree of regressive, asocial behavior among those released from German camps led one writer to dub the phenomenon the "Liberation Complex." [70] Thus Western officials described some liberated Soviet personnel as "arrogant, belligerent, and noncooperative"; others, especially those among them who had been concentration camp victims, exhibited an "almost hysterical fear of any show of authority." Desire for revenge motivated a goodly share of the trouble: one U.S. Army study argued that the pervasiveness of this passion among Soviet nationals made them the most difficult group of DPs to control.[71]

The Western Allies did restore order, and rather quickly, but the curtailment of violence and near anarchy hardly meant a return to normality. For years after the end of open aggressiveness, exhausted DPs continued to suffer from a host of quiet mental agonies. Even voluntary migration can disorient ordinarily stable folk. But under the extreme duress of Hitler's forced movements, the surviving pawns of the Russo-German war had to cope not only with unfamiliar surroundings but with the memories of appalling living conditions and outrageous mistreatment and a whole catalog of attending psychological maladies. Helping keep refugees off balance were: the strain of unemployment and idle hours; feelings of isolation, helplessness, and depression; and anxiety about the future. (Would the Soviet Union move from Cold War to an invasion of Western Europe? Could they remain in an unfriendly Germany? Would they be forcibly repatriated? And would America or some other country take them in?)[72]

Moscow's repatriation teams played on these weaknesses. One maudlin Soviet DP camp speech, for instance, struck a biblical tone in an adaptation of the story of the Prodigal Son: "You shall be the long lost children of a loving mother who will hold out her arms to her erring children, scold them when it is necessary and when it is necessary stroke their hand in contentment." Despite the speech's syrupy and suspect attempt at reassurance, it played on genuine uncertainties in reminding the displaced that "the situation in which you find yourself at the present cannot go on forever and, what is more, for long. The decisive moment is not far away when you will have to make a last choice for your life. Everyone must think for himself. Emigration on a large scale is very problematical. Conditions in Germany are not the best."[73]

The possibility of repatriation struck fear into nonreturners more than did any other factor. It so dismantled and unnerved some DPs that refugee camp life seemed hardly distinguishable from Nazi captivity. Boris Dvinov's very able study puts it this way:

> As a general rule these people might be described as stunned and lost. Their political education was limited; first, to Stalin's Russia, and then to Hitler's Germany. Even after the end of the war, their first contact with the democratic world was such that they could discern no great difference between past and present. The barbed-wire camps, the deprivation of rights, the forced camouflage of their origins and the peculiarly extralegal situation engendered by extraditions and threats of extradition—all these things aroused feelings of skepticism about democracy.[74]

The years of physical and psychological torments proved too much for some of the displaced. Naturally, for a short while right after the fighting stopped, GIs would witness "long (in fact endless) columns of refugees walking haphasardly [*sic*] along the roads," literally dazed by their ordeal. The Nazis had thought their captives uncivilized and made them so, turning them into "people who pushed, screamed, clawed for food, smelled bad, who couldn't and didn't want to obey orders," who could greet friendly troops only with "dull faces and vacant and staring eyes."[75] But some *never* recovered mentally and emotionally. A study of 572 Danes, who had averaged less than eighteen months in Nazi camps and under much more tolerable circumstances than Soviet nationals, found over 20 percent still "suffering from severe symptoms two years after repatriation, the majority of these symptoms being mental ones."[76] Refugees refusing to return to the U.S.S.R. no doubt experienced a higher rate of disturbance, not only because of the more brutal treatment afforded non-Germanic prisoners and workers, but because, in contrast to Danes and other West Europeans, the very thought of going home was, for Soviet nonreturners, a nightmare.

Many ultimately succeeded in resettling in the United States, Canada, Australia, or Latin America; but some simply despaired of life. One eyewitness of particularly troubled DPs recalled those who "because of caution, age, or trauma, or simply because the doors of circumstances had closed upon them, could hope only for the impossible, for the past to become the future and their old homes free again." William Sloane Coffin described the wartime exiles from Russia as "full of memories but essentially without hope." For instance, there was Vanya, a nonreturner in Paris terrified by the periodic Soviet raids and dragnets through refugee quarters. This distraught DP, whom Coffin had once saved merely by his presence during one such sweep of suburban Drancy, was driven to drinking by bitter recollections and uncontrollable fear of the future. "At three o'clock one morning he made his way to the subway station that had recently been renamed 'Stalingrad.' There, with his one necktie, he hanged himself."[77]

It would seem from the evidence presented above that those commentators describing postwar Soviet émigrés as unstable have had their case proven for them. But this would be a mistaken conclusion, for the documentation in its entirety points in two directions. Granted, it does demonstrate that many, maybe most, refugees experienced some degree of psychological and emotional difficulty upon liberation and that a fraction of unknown size may never have recouped their mental equilibrium. But credible sources also exist that indicate that most nonreturners eventually recovered from their psychological wounds and hardly deserved characterization as "a collection of misfits or historical 'leftovers.'"[78]

To start with, the strikingly diverse and comprehensive array of cultural and intellectual activities within DP camps testifies to humankind's remarkable recuperative powers. Colonel Sage made a point of this in his remarks before the Congressional Subcommittee on Immigration: "I must say that I have been continually surprised by the resiliency of the vast majority of these displaced persons. I have seen, in my present tour of duty, the same prisoners and forced laborers of the Nazis who had been with me in Germany in '43 and '44 still residing in the depressing atmosphere of the abnormal camp-type life . . . and have been amazed at their ability to make the best of their situations by studying, working, and striving to improve themselves." Sage also considered "exaggerated" the publicity about refugee misbehavior. As a civil affairs official, he personally had helped arrest and prosecute DP offenders; but their crime rate, he noted, did not exceed that for the German population, and in some cases, fell below it. Edward Homze, in his important study of *Foreign Labor in Nazi Germany*, found evidence of "widespread random looting and some individual murders," but for the most part, surprising restraint among those fresh out of German captivity.[79]

Further indication of the postwar Soviet diaspora's overall stability comes from the psychological testing program of the Harvard Project. From the Rorschach test, analysts concluded that while recent defectors reflected "grave indications of disturbance," former citizens of the U.S.S.R. displaced by World War II presented "on the whole, a rather normal group personality picture."[80] Given the multiplicity of shocks endured by these refugees since 1941, such a finding again demonstrates the human race's extraordinary ability not only to survive but to prevail.

The nature of the evidence makes it impossible to present unqualified generalizations about the mental condition of displaced Soviet citizens. But many of the discrepancies can at least be reconciled by comparing the origins in time of various primary sources. The overall psychological normality and stability of nonreturners, determined by interviews and tests conducted in 1950–51, logically would contrast with data collected right after the war that demonstrated abnormality and instability. Thus, negative and positive observations occupy opposite ends of a spectrum bridged by the healing powers of time and the refugees' gradual adjustment to new environments.[81]

The existence of a nonreturner community in the West demonstrates that the collective will does not always override the will of determined individuals. Some Soviet citizens abroad successfully defied an international contract that took no account of their wishes. By disguising their identity or by avoiding DP camps altogether, one-third to one-half million Soviet citizens personally took exception to the rule of forced repatriation. This diaspora did not form a homogenous group; nationality, occupation, sex, age, and politics divided it. But two emotional forces bound nonreturners together spiritually as nothing else could: an abiding fear of Soviet reprisals and a strong desire to be the masters of their own fate.

NOTES

1. Raymond A. Bauer, "Some Trends in Sources of Alienation from the Soviet System," *Public Opinion Quarterly*, 19 (Fall 1955), 283; Lyons, *Secret*, 254.

2. POW interrogation, Frankfurt-am-Main, 14 Apr. 1945, NA RG 226, SHAEF, Psychological Warfare Division, OSS no. 126291. Three studies attempt a comprehensive discussion of nonreturners' motives: Fainsod, "Controls and Tensions," 266-82, especially 269; Alex Inkeles, Eugenia Hanfmann, and Helen Beier, "Modal Personality and Adjustment to the Soviet Sociopolitical System" in *Social Change in Soviet Russia*, ed. Alex Inkeles (Cambridge, Mass., 1968), 11; and Lyons, "Orphans," 41-46.

3. Fischer, ed., *Thirteen*, 36. See also ibid., 13, 129; P. J. Juris, president of American Friends of Lithuania, to Gen. John H. Hilldring, 3 Aug. 1947, NA RG 165, WDSCA, 383.7 CAD, Sec. 20, WDGSS, p. 4.

4. 10 Aug. 1945, NA RG 59, 711.62114/8-1045; Peter Deriabin and Frank Gibney, *The Secret World* (Garden City, N. Y., 1959), 98.

5. Eugenia Hanfmann and Jacob W. Getzels, "Inter-personal Attitudes of Former Soviet Citizens as Studied by a Semi-Projective Method," *Psychological Monographs*, 69 (no. 4, 1955), 2. See also Dvinov, *Politics*, 7.

6. Raymond A. Bauer, Alex Inkeles, and Clyde Kluckhohn, *How the Soviet System Works: Cultural, Psychological and Social Themes* (Cambridge, Mass., 1956), 14; Alex Inkeles and Raymond A. Bauer, "Patterns of Life Experience and Attitudes under the Soviet System (Composite Survey)," 46, Harvard Project on the Soviet Social System.

7. Alexandra Tolstoy, "The Russian DPs," *Russian Review*, 9 (Jan. 1950), 57; Smith, "Refugee Orthodox Congregations," 317, 320; Il'nytz'kyi, *Free Press*, 40.

8. The percentages are based on the following calculations: 150,000 Ukrainians and 40,000 Great Russians among 285,000 nonreturners from pre-1939 Soviet territories. This excludes an estimated 220,000 refugees from the annexed Baltic states. Warren W. Eason, "Demography," in *Handbook of Soviet Social Science Data*, ed. Ellen Mickiewicz (New York, 1973), 58; Alex Inkeles and Raymond A. Bauer, *The Soviet Citizen* (Cambridge, Mass., 1959), 39; Eugene Kulischer to Robert Feldmesser, 13 Aug. 1953, "Estimated Ethnic Composition of USSR Migratory Gains and Losses 1939-1951," Harvard Project on the Soviet Social System. On the disproportionate abuse of national minorities, see Walter Kolarz, *Russia and Her Colonies* (New York, 1952), 11; and Ivan Bahryany, "Why I Do Not Want to Go 'Home,' " *Ukrainian Quarterly*, 2 (Winter 1946), 236.

9. Inkeles and Bauer, "Patterns," 48-50; Inkeles and Bauer, *Soviet Citizen*, 36; U.S. Department of State, Intelligence Research Office, *The Soviet Union as Reported by Former Soviet Citizens; Interview Report* (Washington, D.C., 1952), 2.

10. David Pablo Boder, *I Did Not Interview the Dead* (Urbana, Ill., 1949), 161-63. See also Bauer, "Trends"; Brig. Gen. R. W. Berry, GSC, Dep. Asst. CS, G1 to Dep. CS, 6 Aug. 1945, NA RG 165, Army CS, 383.6, Sec. VIII Cases 400 . . . 450.

11. Sage to Congressional Subcommittee on Immigration, 2 July 1947, "Repatriation," 3, Panchuk Papers.

12. OSS, "Reichswehr," 22-23; Solzhenitsyn, *Gulag*, I: 254.

13. Vagts, "Combatant Casualties," 433. See also Albrecht, "German Camps"; Dallin and Nikolaevskii, *Forced Labor*, 282.

14. Quoted by Dallin and Nikolaevskii, *Forced Labor*, 282-83. The Germans learned of this pronouncement from a captured member of the Red Army general staff. Strik-Strikfeldt, *Against Stalin and Hitler*, 34. Another source contends the decree was dated September 1941 and numbered 260: Burton, "The Vlasov Movement," 7.

15. Harold J. Berman and Miroslav Kerner, *Soviet Military Law and Administration* (Cambridge, Mass., 1955), 73; Berman and Kerner, "Soviet Military Crimes," *Military Review*, 32 (July 1952), 14-15; "Field Service Regulations for the Red Army," 1943 ed., NAS RG 165, WDGSS, Military Intelligence Service I D file, no. 924348.

16. OSS, "Reichswehr," 20. See also Artiemev, "Crime and Punishment," 69; Ginsburgs, "Refugees," 360; Gordon, "Partisan Warfare," 31; Lyons, "Orphans," 44; "Minutes of Meeting with Soviet Liaison Officer," Mittenwald Camp, 28 Aug. 1947, NA RG 59, 800.4016 DP/10-1447, p. 4; OSS no. 126291, "Two Russian Ps/W in Frankfurt-am-Main," 15 Apr. 1945, NA RG 226, SHAEF Psychological Warfare Division, Intelligence Section, p. 4.

17. Viktor M. Chkhikvadze, *Sovetskoe voenno-ugolovnoe pravo* (Moscow, 1948), 422, 427. (A more recent edition of the Soviet military code still comes close to equating surrender with treason: *Osnovy*, 313-15.) Fischer, "New Emigration," 10.

18. John N. Hazard, *Law and Social Change in the U.S.S.R.* (Toronto, 1953), 289; F. Solasko, ed., *War behind Barbed Wire; Reminiscences of Buchenwald Ex-Prisoners of War* (Moscow, 1959), 5; Urlanis, *Wars and Population*, 174; U.S.S.R. Commissar of Foreign Affairs, *Note Submitted by V. Molotov, People's Commissar of Foreign Affairs of the U.S.S.R., Concerning the Wholesale Forcible Transportation of Soviet Civilians to German Fascist Slavery and the Responsibility Borne for This Crime by the German Authorities and by Private Persons Who Exploit the Forced Labor of Soviet Citizens in Germany* (Moscow, 1943); Jessica Smith, ed., *The Molotov Note on the Abduction of Soviet Citizens into German Slavery. Hitler's Slave Markets* (New York, 1943), 6; Trainin, *Hitlerite Responsibility*, 61-62. A wartime volume of *Bol'shaia sovetskaia entsiklopediia* belied the assertions of the three Molotov notes by stating that "in regard to the rules concerning prisoners of war the Government of the USSR does not consider itself bound by any international agreements whatsoever." Dallin and Nikolaevskii, *Forced Labor*, 282.

19. Albrecht, "German Camps," 57.

20. Dallin, *German Rule*, 420; Albrecht, "German Camps," 58; Svetlana Alliluyeva, *Twenty Letters to a Friend* (New York, 1967), 185.

21. Berman and Kerner, "Soviet Military Crimes," 5-6; J. N. Kaasik, "The Legal Status of Baltic Refugees," *Baltic Review*, 1 (Dec. 1945), 21; Alfred Toppe, "Russian Methods of Interrogating War Prisoners," 14, NA RG 338, Foreign

Military Studies, P-018b; Seaton, *Russo-German War*, 90. For evidence of apprehension this caused Red Army soldiers in German hands see Bauer, "Guide," vii; Boder, *Interview*, 189; and Alexander Dallin, "From the Gallery of Wartime Disaffection," *Russian Review*, 21 (Jan. 1962), 76-77.

22. Alliluyeva, *Twenty Letters*, 185. Thorwald, *Illusion*, 222, claims Stalin had close relatives of some high-ranking collaborators executed.

23. Dallin, *German Rule*, 509, 528; Bertram D. Wolfe, *Three Who Made a Revolution*, rev. ed. (New York, 1964), 450-52; Strik-Strikfeldt, *Against Stalin and Hitler*, 32-33. A surviving POW corroborates this German evaluation in Svetlana Alliluyeva, *Only One Year* (New York, 1969), 370.

24. Alliluyeva, *Only One Year*, 370.

25. Testimony of Thomas Cushing, ibid. Roy Medvedev's version says the Nazis shot Jacob after Stalin refused a German offer to exchange him for Field Marshal Friedrich Paulus, while a February 1980 UPI dispatch quotes recently released British documents to the effect that an argument with British prisoners led Jacob to attempt suicide on an electrified fence. According to this account, death finally came from a German bullet for which Stalin's son himself pleaded. Medvedev, *Let History Judge*, 468; Lexington (Ky.) *Leader*, 25 Feb. 1980. According to Tolstoy, *Secret*, 397, Hitler once proposed an exchange of Jacob for his nephew, Leo Raubal, captured at Stalingrad. See also Dallin, *German Rule*, 528.

26. Medvedev, *Let History Judge*, 467; Solzhenitsyn, *Gulag*, I: 240.

27. Solzhenitsyn, *Gulag*, I: 77; Fischer, ed., *Thirteen*, 12; Fort Dix Report, 10 Aug. 1945, NA RG 59, 711.62114/7-1945 and 711.62114/8-1045; Koriakov, *I'll Never Go Back*, 129-30; " 'Liberation'—and Life Thereafter . . .," *Lithuanian Bulletin*, 5 (May-June 1947), 8; Tolstoy, *Secret*, 396.

28. Solzhenitsyn, *Gulag*, I: 243.

29. Ibid., II: 371; Amalrik, "Victims," 94; Helen Beier and Eugenia Hanfmann, "Emotional Attitudes of Former Soviet Citizens as Studied by the Technique of Projective Questions," *Journal of Abnormal and Social Psychology*, 53 (Sept. 1956), 143; Alexander Dallin and Sylvia Gilliam, "Aspects of the German Occupation of the Soviet Union," 81, Harvard Project on the Soviet Social System; Inkeles, Hanfmann, and Beier, "Modal Personality," 131; Inkeles and Bauer, *Soviet Citizen*, 32-33; Major F. N. Leonard to Col. Ilia M. Sarayev, Acting Military Attaché, Soviet Embassy, 8 May 1943, NAS RG 319; Murphy to SD, 2 June 1945, NA RG 59, no decimal number, enclosure to dispatch no. 451.

30. Fischer, "New Emigration," 10; Inkeles and Bauer, "Patterns," 41; "Nobody Cares About DP's Anymore," *Washington Daily News*, 14 May 1947, folder 37, Panchuk Papers; Smith, "American Role," 98.

31. Fischer, "New Emigration," 10. See also Eugenia Hanfmann and Helen Beier, *Six Russian Men: Lives in Turmoil* (North Quincy, Mass., 1976), 41, 59, 63.

32. Bauer, Inkeles, and Kluckhohn, *Soviet System*, 12.

33. Mark Elliott, "The Repatriation Issue," 10-21. Estimates for nonreturners range wildly from 200,000 to 1,000,000; see Fischer, "New Emigration," 8, "Soviet Non-Returners," 13, and *Thirteen*, 15; Lyons, "Orphans," 41, and *Secret*, 244. Still, most authorities put the figure between 250,000 and 500,000, the Soviet figure of 400,000 being quite compatible with those of Western sources. Fainsod, "Controls and Tensions," 266, cites 250,000, as do Fischer, *Soviet Opposition*, 111-12, and Proudfoot, *European Refugees*, 214. Tolstoy, "DPs," 53, reports 300,000 to 400,000. Soviet sources quoted by both Fischer, *Soviet Opposition*,

111-12, and Wyle, "Memorandum," 11, give 400,000. Isaac Deutscher, "Strange World of Russian 'Non-Returners,' " *New York Times Magazine*, 24 July 1949, 9, gives 500,000, as do Epstein, "American Forced Repatriation," 356, and Kulischer to Feldmesser, 13 Aug. 1953, Harvard Project on the Soviet Social System. Wyle, "Memorandum," 12, reports "half million, with a reserved margin of error of several hundreds of thousands."

34. Charles F. Delzell, "Russian Power in Central-Eastern Europe," in *The Meaning of Yalta: Big Three Diplomacy and the New Balance of Power*, ed. John L. Snell (Baton Rouge, La., 1956), 77; Dvinov, *Politics*, 5; Smith, "American Role," 110; Roman Umiastowski, *Poland, Russia, and Great Britain, 1941-1945: A Study of the Evidence* (London, 1946), 478; Notter, "Poland: Ethnic Composition of the Population East of the Soviet-German Demarcation Line of September 28, 1939," in his *Postwar Foreign Policy*, 492; Tadeusz Grygier, *Oppression; a Study in Social and Criminal Psychology* (Westport, Conn., 1950), 106.

35. Woodbridge, UNRRA, 423.

36. Kubijovych, *Ukraine*, II: 1094; Reitlinger, *House Built on Sand*, 394; Smith, "American Role," 96-97; Thorwald, *Illusion*, 312-13; Tolstoy, *Secret*, 256-59; Jacques Vernant, *The Refugee in the Post-war World* (New Haven, Conn., 1953), 87. One nonreturner interviewed by the author alleged that London exempted Shandruk's troops because of the large number of young, eligible males who might immigrate to Britain and marry English girls.

37. Fischer, "New Emigration," 8; Posdnjakoff, "German Counter-intelligence," 114; Tolstoy, *Secret*, 371-72; Utechin, "Refugees," 452; Tolstoy, "DP's," 53.

38. U.S. Forces Abroad (Vienna) to WD, 3 Jan. 1947, NA RG 218, 383.6 (10-16-43), Sec. 3; "Repatriation of DPs from Germany and Austria," 1 Mar. 1946, NAS RG 165, WDGSS, Military Intelligence Service Project File, no. 2897; Fischer, "New Emigration," 9. See also Wyle, "Memorandum," 12-13.

39. Bruce Marshall, *Vespers in Vienna* (Boston, 1947), 57; Shimkin interview. See also "Personal and Confidential Note," 30 Jan. 1946, Box 192, no folder number, p. 2, UUARC.

40. Tolstoy, "DP's," 55. See also ibid., 53; Krasnov, *Hidden Russia*, 12-13, 331; *New York Times*, 4 May 1945, 3; Smith, "American Role,"138.

41. NAS RG 331, AFHQ, Roll 228-B, Sacs 400-7, "Russian Matters"; Bethell, *Secret*, 107, 151, 154.

42. Smith, "Refugee Orthodox Congregations," 323.

43. Bethell, *Secret*, 35; Lyons, *Secret*, 269. Epstein put the number of suicides at "many thousands." This calculation, however, should be viewed with caution due to his inclination to overestimate. For example, in Epstein's recounting of the Fort Dix episode, the three verified suicides also became "many." Epstein, "American Forced Repatriation," 360-61.

44. Wyle, "Memorandum," i; Kulischer to Feldmesser, 13 Aug. 1953, Harvard Project on the Soviet Social System. See also Dvinov, *Politics*, 5.

45. Nonreturners' unrepresentativeness greatly complicated the work of Harvard Project analysts, who sought to use this unscientific sample to determine general characteristics of Soviet society. Bauer, Inkeles, and Kluckhohn, *Soviet System*, 3-15. For Soviet criticism of studies based on refugee interviews, see I. Zenushkina, *Soviet Nationalities Policy and Bourgeois Historians* (Moscow, 1975), 11.

46. Eason, "Demography," 58; Ginsburgs, "Refugees," 356; Kulischer to

Feldmesser, 13 Aug. 1953, Harvard Project on the Soviet Social System. Other estimates of Ukrainian nonreturners dwarf Kulischer's figure of 150,000. A "Personal and Confidential Note," 1-2, dated 30 Jan. 1946, Box 192, UUARC, says 350,000 to 400,000. Dushnyck and Gibbons, *Refugees*, 27, report 342,861, and the U.S. Strategic Bombing Survey random sample of May-June 1945 as reported in Ansbacher, "Attitude Survey Data," 127, gives the number as 43 percent of all nonreturners from pre-1939 Soviet territory.

47. Eason, "Demography," 58; *FR, Potsdam*, I: 795; J. N. Kaasik, "The Baltic Refugee in Sweden: A Successful Experiment," *Baltic Review*, 2 (Dec. 1947), 56.

48. Wyle, "Memorandum," 13; Kulischer to Feldmesser, 13 Aug. 1953, Harvard Project on the Soviet Social System. An émigré estimate (Dushnyck and Gibbons, *Refugees*, 16, 19, 23, 27) figured 342,861 Ukrainian nonreturners; 153,300 Latvian; 58,683 Estonian; and 78,775 Lithuanian. The USSBS random sample (Ansbacher, "Attitude Survey Data," 127) calculated percentages of nonreturners strictly from prewar Soviet territory: 43 percent Ukrainian; 28 percent Great Russian; 9 percent Belorussian; 8 percent South Russian Tartar; 7 percent Siberian and Tartar; and 5 percent miscellaneous (Georgian, Armenian, Turk, and Dagistani).

49. Yaroslav J. Chyz, "Statistical Data on the Number of Persons in the U.S. Born in the U.S.S.R. or Pre-War Russia and Their Descendants," 1951, Shipment 4, Box 5, p. 6, American Council for Nationalities Service files, Immigration History Research Center.

50. Eason, "Demography," 55; Dushnyck and Gibbons, *Refugees*, 20; Il'nytz'kyi, *Free Press*, 42-43; Mandryka, *Ukrainian Refugees*, 25. In IRO camps, 25 percent of the refugees of all nationalities had been agricultural workers: IRO, *Facts*.

51. Bauer, Inkeles, and Kluckhohn, *Soviet System*, 174; Dushnyck and Gibbons, *Refugees*, 20; Warren W. Eason, "Population and Labor Force" in *Soviet Economic Growth, Conditions and Perspectives*, ed. by Abram Bergson (Evanston, Ill., 1953), 108; Fischer, "New Emigration," 9; IRO, *Facts*, 19.

52. Fischer, "New Emigration," 9; Il'nytz'kyi, *Free Press*, 43.

53. Fischer, "New Emigration," 9; Dallin and Gilliam, "Aspects of the German Occupation," 76.

54. Interview with scientist's son, spring 1971, name withheld on request. For an enumeration of literary figures among the post–World War II Soviet emigration, see Gleb Struve, *Russian Literature under Lenin and Stalin 1917-1953* (Norman, Okla., 1971), 334; Tomasziwskyj, "Vozrozhdenie," 55-64, 76-81. Fischer ("'Non-returners,'" 14) provides information on other prominent nonreturners, particularly scientists.

55. For Soviet population figures see Eason, "Demography," 53. Several sources estimate the percentage of male DPs by nationality: 51.3 percent of Latvians (Dushnyck and Gibbons, *Refugees*, 20); 54 percent of Lithuanians (Juozas Pašlaitis, *Hearken Then Judge, Sidelights on Lithuanian DPs* [Tubingen, 1950], 24); about 60 percent Ukrainians (Kubijovych, *Ukraine*, I: 912). Women outnumbered men among Soviet Mennonite DPs, but large numbers of adult males had been deported to Siberia in Stalin's purges of the 1930s. Boder, *Interview*, 165.

56. Bauer, Inkeles, and Kluckhohn, *Soviet System*, 12. This calculation figures 21 as maturity and assumes the sample to be representative of nonreturners gen-

erally. The percentage would presumably be higher if children of respondents were included.

57. Those born or maturing after 1917 would have been between twenty-two and forty-three at the time of the 1939 census when that age bracket represented about 33.7 percent of the total population of the U.S.S.R. Eason, "Demography," 52. See also Dvinov, *Politics*, 10; IRO, *Facts*, 19; Lyons, *Secret*, 259; Pašlaitis, *Hearken*, 24-25; Sage to Congressional Subcommittee on Immigration, 2 July 1947, "Resettlement," 6, Panchuk Papers.

58. Sage to Congressional Subcommittee on Immigration, 2 July 1947, "Resettlement," 10, Panchuk Papers; Woodbridge, *UNRRA*, II: 503.

59. Inkeles and Bauer, "Patterns," 2.

60. Bauer, Inkeles, and Kluckhohn, *Soviet System*, 12-13.

61. Ibid., 13; Deutscher, "Strange World," 19.

62. OSS, "Reichswehr," 20; Bauer, "Guide," 3. See also Hanfmann and Beier, *Six*, 94.

63. Il'nytz'kyi, *Free Press*, 24-25; Kubijovych, *Ukraine*, I: 913, II: 387; Clarence A. Manning, *Twentieth Century Ukraine* (New York, 1951), 163-164; Smith, "Refugee Orthodox Congregations," 320.

64. Dushnyck and Gibbons, *Refugees*, 16, 19, 23, 27; Fischer, "New Emigration," 7; Interview with Mgr. Perridon, Paris, 26 Sept. 1945, Box 192, UUARC; Kubijovych, *Ukraine*, I: 912-13, II: 1216; Pašlaitis, *Hearken*, 24.

65. Social Service Bureau of the Lithuanian American Council, "Situation of Displaced Lithuanians in Western Germany Up to the Middle of October 1945," NA RG 165, CAD, WDSCA, 383.7, Lithuania, 17 Nov. 45–10 June 46, 12 Nov. 1945, p. 4; Oleksii I. Voropai, *V dorozi na zakhid: shchodennik utikacha* (London, 1970), 277.

66. Il'nytz'kyi, *Free Press*, 84-87; Dvinov, *Politics*, 12; Kubijovych, *Ukraine*, I: 914.

67. East European Fund, *Second Annual Report, 1952-1953*, Box 20, and "Books in Russian," Chekhov Publishing Company files, Box 23, Philip Mosely Papers, University of Illinois Archives, Urbana.

68. "Notes on Russian Relations," 5-6, Box 3, part d, Harmon Papers. Similar episodes of violent forays through the countryside by Soviet refugees and the resulting consternation among the local populace are reported by Donnison, *North-West Europe*, 347; Mair, *Austria*, 360.

69. Edward A. Shils, "Social and Psychological Aspects of Displacement and Repatriation," *Journal of Social Issues*, 2 (Aug. 1946), 14; Donnison, *North-West Europe*, 358; EUCOM, "RAMP's," 53; Homze, *Foreign Labor*, 295, 297-98; interview with Mgr. Perridon, Paris, 26 Sept. 1945, Box 192, UUARC; B. Panchuk to Walter Gallan, president, Ukrainian American Relief Committee, 10 June 1945, folder 5, Panchuk Papers; Tolstoy, *Secret*, 309.

70. Coles and Weinberg, *Civil Affairs*, 858.

71. Col. E. E. Hyde, GSC Exec. to Sec. Gen. Staff, 7 Dec. 1944, NAS RG 331, AFHQ; Lorimer, "America's Response," 27; EUCOM, "RAMP's," 52.

72. Beier and Hanfmann, "Emotional Attitudes," 144-45; 148; *In the Name of the Lithuanian People* (Wolfberg, Germany, 1945), 29; Sage to Congressional Subcommittee on Immigration, 2 July 1947, under "Shall We Close the Camps?," 4, Panchuk Papers. Those with the greatest uncertainty about the future were the two extremes of ex-Communist and ex-Vlasovite, both practically

banned from resettlement in the United States. Hanfmann and Beier, *Six*, 85, 117.

73. "Minutes of Meeting with Soviet Liaison Officer," Mittenwald Camp, 28 Aug. 1947, NA RG 59, 800.4016 DP/10-1447, p. 5.

74. Dvinov, *Politics*, 10. See also Bethell, *Secret*, 38; Coffin, *Once*, 57; Donnison, *North-West Europe*, 358; Dushnyck and Gibbons, *Refugees*, 85; Fischer, "New Emigration," 7; Capt. Walter I. Rand to HDQ—PCIRO, Rome, 6 Aug. 1947, "Keelhaul," III; Sage to Congressional Subcommittee on Immigration, 2 July 1947, 3, Panchuk Papers.

75. Panchuk to Gallan, 10 June 1945, 1, folder 5, Panchuk Papers; Lorimer, "America's Response," 26, quoting *Army Talk*, 151 (Washington), 30 Nov. 1946.

76. Eduard Bakis, " 'D.P. Apathy,' " in *Flight and Resettlement*, ed. by Henry B. M. Murphy (Paris, 1955), 12.

77. Smith, "Refugee Orthodox Congregations," 323; Coffin, *Once*, 59-60.

78. Cited in Inkeles, Hanfmann, and Beier, "Modal Personality," 131. See also Bauer, Inkeles, and Kluckhohn, *Soviet System*, 11-14; Inkeles and Bauer, "Patterns," 40-41; Inkeles and Bauer, *Soviet Citizen*, 28, 34.

79. Sage to Congressional Subcommittee on Immigration, 2 July 1947, "Resettlement," 6-7, Panchuk Papers; Homze, *Foreign Labor*, 297-98.

80. Helen Beier, "Responses to the Rorschach Test of Former Soviet Citizens," 1, Harvard Project on the Soviet Social System.

81. Four films that address the psychological problems of displaced persons are: *Before Winter Comes*, 1969, Windward Productions; *Landscape after the Battle*, 1970, Andrzej Wajda, director; *Report on the Refugee Situation*, 1950, British Information Services; and *The Search*, 1948, MGM. For descriptions see Manvell, *Films*, 244-46, 343, 361-62; and *New York Times Film Reviews*, 3 (24 Mar. 1948), 2242-43.

8

THE REPATRIATES' RECEPTION:

"In Hitler's Camps There Are . . . Only Russian Traitors"

THE WEST HAS PAID SLIGHT ATTENTION to the fate of repatriates, especially when compared with the exhaustive work of the Harvard Project on nonreturners. The inaccessibility of those Moscow retrieved from abroad has meant that the plight of several hundred thousand prewar émigrés is better known than the unquestionably more difficult trials of over 5 million who returned to an unsympathetic and unforgiving homeland. But that is changing. Alexander Solzhenitsyn, for one, has brought the subject up time and time again in his work: in "An Incident at Krechetovka Station," in *One Day in the Life of Ivan Denisovich*, in *The First Circle*, and most recently in *From under the Rubble*, *The Gulag Archipelago*, and the prose poem, *Prussian Nights*.[1] The opening volume of his "literary investigation" of Soviet prison camps volunteers first hand evidence: "Back when the Red Army had cut through East Prussia, I had seen downcast columns of returning war prisoners—the only people around who were grieving instead of celebrating. Even then their gloom had shocked me, though I didn't yet grasp the reason for it."[2]

Through years of imprisonment the ex–Red Army captain had kept in his head a poem that was flush with the revelry of the last heady months of the German campaign—but also burdened with remorse and matters of conscience. Among the most discordant notes in *Prussian Nights* is a brief but poignant reflection on those Russians not invited to the victor's feast:

> See in formation—with a guilty look,—
> March Russians. Prisoners. Endless. On each back
> Brand of a flame that no atonement quenches.
> They tramp the hard path under hanging branches.
> And always "Why?" their thought runs on and on.
> They've not been summoned to the celebration,
> And to our feasts they've had no invitation.
> So they, alone in all the world unwanted,

Move forward, their necks bowed as though to bend
Under the harsh stroke of a clumsy ax blade
Toward the distant parts of a cruel land.[3]

The pattern of unvarying distrust of every Soviet citizen returning from abroad surfaced early on. As already noted, Red Army repatriates from the 1939–40 Winter War in Finland fared very poorly: for their capture alive, they paid with death or imprisonment. After the German attack even temporary separation from direct Soviet supervision, as so frequently happened in the massive Wehrmacht encirclements of 1941–42, provided sufficient cause for stringent interrogations and penalties. On 20 July 1941, with the war in the East barely begun, a wary Stalin ordered that "men coming out of German encirclement should be rigorously investigated by the NKVD 'Special Sections' [*Osobyi Otdel*:00] to root out 'German spies.' "[4]

Solzhenitsyn has designated those flowing into Soviet labor camps in the summer and fall of 1941 "the wave of *the encircled*":

These were the defenders of their native land, the very same warriors whom the cities had seen off to the front with bouquets and bands a few months before, who had then sustained the heaviest tank assaults of the Germans, and in the general chaos, and through no fault of their own, had spent a certain time as isolated units not in enemy imprisonment, not at all, but in temporary encirclement, and later had broken out. And instead of being given a brotherly embrace on their return, such as every other army in the world would have given them, instead of being given the chance to rest up, to visit their families, and then return to their units—they were held on suspicion, disarmed, deprived of all rights, and taken away in groups to identification points and screening centers where officers of the Special Branches started interrogating them, distrusting not only their every word but their very identity.[5]

For Solzhenitsyn it is no incidental theme. The first volume of the *Gulag* devotes a full chapter to "That Spring" of 1945, which saw cruel judgments passed on millions of returning Soviet citizens. And Ivan Denisovich Shukhov, the hero of his 1962 novella, was a Red Army soldier who had escaped from momentary German captivity only to be arrested as a German spy with ten years in Siberia the reward for his patriotism.[6]

A hostile, menacing reception also confronted those who escaped from German POW camps, even the wounded who trekked miles to regain their own lines. Whatever their heroics, the Soviet secret police still greeted them with: "Tell us, how long have you been collaborating?"; or "tell us for what purpose the Gestapo sent you here!"; or "you rat, what *assignment* did they give you?" Petr Vershigora, partisan and part-time interrogator, exalted his responsibility with the declaration, "To cleanse the land of filth is never easy."[7]

Some American officers got wind of this mean-spiritedness before the German surrender. On one occasion late in the war Soviet inspectors touring DP camps for their countrymen in Italy declared that conditions were "too good."[8] In contrast, recovered American POWs in Eastern Europe processed through the shuttle-bombing base at Poltava received royal treatment from their countrymen—new clothes, the best food, and plenty of rest before their trip home to America. This approach proved profoundly unsettling to Soviet officials who strongly questioned the wisdom of magnanimity towards those captured by the Germans: "How can you know why these men were taken prisoner; maybe they gave themselves up out of sympathy for Germany or because they didn't want to fight. Maybe the Nazis propagandized them in the prison camps and converted them to fascism. These ex-prisoners should not stay here at all, but be rushed instead, via Odessa, to an American screening point for interrogation."[9] The Soviet Union assumed the worst of its POWs and failed to comprehend why the United States did not.

The Soviet regime's distrust of its own people ran so deep that it deemed all foreign influences unpatriotic and Fascist or capitalist inspired. Not just the repatriates, but the entire population had to contend with the mind-shackling nativism of the postwar period, called the *Zhdanovshchina*, after Stalin's de facto cultural inquisitor, Andrei Zhdanov. The government's apprehension over the recent exposure of the masses to alien ideas and capitalism's material wealth seemed to be the root cause of this Soviet version of McCarthyism. "Dangerous thoughts from the West," an American literary critic suggests, "may have entered the heads of Soviet citizens during the period of collaboration, and the regime was concerned over the admiration for Western achievements and Western culture which it had itself encouraged during the war."[10]

While the fighting raged, Stalin told a foreign reporter, "In Hitler's camps there are no Russian prisoners of war, only Russian traitors, and we shall do away with them when the war is over." Yet at the close of hostilities two unavoidable realities restrained his vindictiveness toward repatriates, at least to the extent of sparing many immediate executions: the enormous requirements of reconstruction in a country thoroughly devastated by war; and, as a result of the multiple catastrophes of modern Russia, the critical shortage of manpower. (Andrei Amalrik suggests his homeland has suffered 60 million unnatural deaths in this century.)[11]

Stalin's security forces did execute a sizeable contingent of flagrant collaborators, in what an ex-secret policeman characterized as prophylaxis;[12] unknown numbers fell victim to front-line revenge. But for the majority of displaced Soviet nationals, including even most Vlasovites, repatriation meant rough handling, but abuse short of capital punishment. General V. N. Merkulov, second in rank to Lavrentii Beriia in the secret police, explained at the time, "We've got to build. . . . And where will we get the labour? There's no great profit in the gallows. Times have changed. Death by shooting—that's used only in rare instances. We need hands to do work, hands we don't have to pay for."[13] Healthy repatriates, then, even those who had aided the enemy, could go a long way toward minimizing the shortage of workers. "Those who have worked actively against the interests of the USSR can expect to be executed," American intelligence accurately predicted, but because of "the present shortage of manpower in the USSR, it seems unlikely that the Soviet authorities would shoot so many able-bodied men. Many of the men from the Eastern Troops may, however, face imprisonment and forced labor for some time after their return to the USSR."[14]

For political as well as economic reasons the Soviet Union inflicted forced labor upon the masses returning from abroad. To serve as a warning to the general population and to indulge its desire for vengeance, the Kremlin used the Gulag to punish millions who had collaborated—or who might have. Also, the prison camp archipelago guaranteed repatriates' isolation from the country at large and thus quarantined dangerous ideals and outlooks that Ostarbeiter and POWs were bound to have picked up abroad.

Those who had been outside Soviet-controlled territory knew that life abroad bore little resemblance to the Communist party's portrayal of it and therefore presented a threat to thought control. Had the captives voluntarily surrendered to the Germans? Had they aided the enemy willingly or joined collaborator units? Had the forced laborers and POWs succumbed to Nazi or capitalist propaganda? And had they drawn unfavorable comparisons between socialist and nonsocialist standards of living? The Kremlin assumed the answer to each of these questions was yes, unless confronted with overwhelming evidence to the contrary. Soviet leadership had always constrained its subjects' political and material aspirations by isolating Russia, by prohibiting any honest basis of comparison between Communist and non-Communist systems, and by manufacturing contrasts carefully skewed in Moscow's favor. Solzhenitsyn has effectively capsulized the Soviet philosophy of population management: "What the eye doesn't see, the heart doesn't grieve for."[15]

Continuing in this repressive manner after the relative ideological laxity of World War II required rigorous controls including segregation of returners from the Soviet masses. The secret police isolated refugees from Hitler's Europe in barbed-wire compounds during processing and forbade their communicating even with relatives. In mid-June 1945 U.S.

Ambassador Averell Harriman noted, "Trainloads of repatriates are passing through Moscow . . . incommunicado."[16]

Besides isolating persons returning from abroad, Soviet authorities sought to neutralize any alien influences by means of intensive reindoctrination. The repatriation commissions set out to purge returnees of ideas inappropriate for patriotic Soviet citizens, a job one author characterized as "political laundering of gigantic scope."[17] Processing, which began as soon as the repatriates reached assembly points in Soviet zones of occupation and extended throughout their journey home, included refresher courses in Marxist ideology and on the evils of Fascism and capitalism. According to Soviet statistics, officials working with repatriates delivered 78,000 political lectures and distributed 1,615,000 books, pamphlets, and newspapers in 1945.[18]

In the World War II saga of Soviet refugees no greater contrast can be drawn than that between the appearance and the reality of Moscow's reception of repatriates. John F. Melby, a member of the American diplomatic staff in Moscow, traveled to Murmansk in mid-November 1944 to witness the arrival of the "first batch" of displaced Soviet citizens returning by way of the difficult Arctic route. To Melby the scene had its incongruities: repatriates "were first welcomed at the dock with a brass band and then marched off under heavy armed guard to an unknown destination."[19] His recollection symbolically represents the contrast between Soviet assurances and performance. The brass band sounded the last note of the Kremlin's campaign to woo Soviet nationals back with promises of compassionate treatment. The forced march under armed guard to points unknown gave repatriates the first hint of worse things to come: a homecoming that would make lies of all the Kremlin's public declarations of goodwill toward those returning from abroad.

The same contrasts jolted returners at countless points of exchange all across liberated Europe. "Repatriate trains were hung with 'welcome home' signs when they left the west for eastern Germany," recounted an eyewitness who later defected, "but once over the line, the placards were ripped down and passengers were given to understand that they were prisoners."[20] At an Elbe River crossing the Soviet side of a pontoon bridge sported red flags and welcoming banners full of good tidings. Sometimes bands, sometimes recorded music greeted the trekkers. The U.S. Army Signal Corps filmed the scene, which included a crude portrait of Stalin taking it all in. But once out of view of Western observers the reception turned a great deal cruder. Kisses and hugs gave way to abusive language, harsh confinement, and worse.[21]

Stalin gave explicit orders not to kill Vlasovites outright, but to save them for systematic processing.[22] However, not only the secret police but

ordinary Red Army units indulged themselves in summary executions of
suspect returners, especially in the bedlam of Nazism's final collapse.
The hanging or shooting of military collaborators prior to any formal investigation or sentencing followed one of two patterns: random, spontaneous attacks, or premeditated, organized killings in apparent contradiction of Stalin's wishes. One eyewitness, a Red Army officer who later
defected, recounted the spontaneous and heartfelt character of aggression directed against collaborators, in this instance not fatal, but often so:

> We had moved into a village in the former "Polish Corridor" that had just been
> cleared of the Germans. They brought in a Vlasovite prisoner. Around him
> crowded our soldiers, who looked him over as if he were some strange beast.
> All of a sudden, one very young soldier came up to the prisoner, punched him
> in the face with all his strength, and then ran away. . . . I am in a position to
> attest that, irrespective of official propaganda, the Vlasovites entered the con-
> sciousness of our soldiers as traitors to the national cause.[23]

Usually, however, front-line capital punishment evidenced signs of being premeditated, systematic slaughter, tolerated if not initiated by senior officers. A former German prisoner of the Russians reported having
seen the bodies of Vlasovites who had been mown down along the roadside by Red Army fire. On another occasion this same witness passed "a
column of prisoners, two to three hundred Russians in German uniforms
surrounded by Red Army men with whips; the prisoners, already
stripped of their clothing and freezing to death, were waiting to be shot."
As an artillery captain, Solzhenitsyn also saw his share of doomed collaborators: "When we captured them, we shot them as soon as the first intel-
ligible Russian word came from their mouths."[24]

Arbitrary beatings and unsanctioned executions then did occur, carried out either on impulse or with deliberate forethought. But Stalin's
directive forbidding on-the-spot retribution, while not always obeyed,
did postpone momentarily the day of reckoning for the majority of repatriates. Most returners survived to face a rigorous and elaborate screening process. Immediately upon arrival in Soviet-held territory, they had
all their personal possessions confiscated, in some cases even including an
exchange of passable DP camp clothing for ragged, moldy garb taken off
dead German soldiers. Also Soviet guards segregated repatriates by sex,
a move that inevitably meant the enforced separation of families for
years, in some cases forever. Moscow prescribed separate quarters not
only for women but for children under fifteen; for ex-officers; for ordinary POWs; for collaborators; and for forced laborers.[25]

The work of interrogation, of "sifting sheep from goats," as Averell
Harriman put it, fell to the NKGB's Vetting and Screening Commissions
(PFKs).[26] To start with, Soviet inquisitors devised massive question-

naires, which took hours to complete. It took one returner who admitted German espionage training ten days to document everything the NKGB required.[27]

One did not have to have experience as a secret agent, however, to sign spy-thriller confessions. One true-to-life vignette in Solzhenitsyn's *First Circle* has returning POW Andrei Potapov admitting to the sabotage of the Dnieper Hydroelectric Power Station, which he himself had helped construct. The NKGB's sole shred of proof was this terror-struck engineer's admission that he had sketched a plan of the facility for his German captors—no matter that the dam by that point had been blown to pieces or that far more detailed instructions of the facility had been published in Russia before the war.[28]

Soviet interrogators approached each case not just with suspicion but with a routine assumption of treason. For Western audiences, or to lure the reluctant home, Soviet officials could speak of sympathy for Ostarbeiter forced to work for the Germans to survive, or even of understanding for those who donned Wehrmacht uniforms: "It was comprehensible in a way that people had worked for the oppressor, as one had to live"; then, too, hunger served as "the most important factor" in military collaboration, POWs having been reduced to eating the flesh of dead comrades (which incidentally was true). Abroad, Moscow somehow managed to excuse ROA troops by claiming they had "preserved untouched their moral principles and political views."[29] But once the same came home a deep-seated, venomous, often lethal animosity immediately overwhelmed all pretenses of solicitude. One repatriate who later escaped to the West well remembered his shocking reception:

> We reached the Soviet zone. A few minutes after the departure of the American vehicles we were ordered to line up in formation. I was unpleasantly surprised by the number of armed soldiers surrounding us on all sides. We were kept waiting for over an hour, without being allowed to sit down and talk. Finally an officer appeared and, without returning our salute, ordered us to remove our shoulder straps in language that was not entirely appropriate in the presence of the women and children. Then, speaking to all of us, he said we had deliberately surrendered, betrayed our country, gone voluntarily to work in Germany, and that the women had served a special purpose, namely to satisfy the low instincts of the enemy.[30]

The sorting and sifting of returning Soviet citizens, Solzhenitsyn emphasized, "began with the hypothesis that you were obviously guilty." In *The First Circle* he has Soviet prison inmates, including those guilty of nothing more than time spent abroad, acting out a mock trial of tenth-century Prince Igor, who "was recruited by Polovtsian intelligence and sent back to assist in the disintegration of the Kievan State," a bittersweet spoof on the manufactured cases against World War II repatriates.[31]

Even when addressing the West on the criteria used in judging returners, Soviet officials sometimes peppered their explanations with dark
hints and discomforting innuendos. At Mittenwald, Germany, a Russian
liaison officer allowed,

> In such a war which went on in the beginning with the tempo it did, many peo-
> ple did not have the presence of mind to escape captivity. These cannot be con-
> sidered as criminals, but the Government looks on them as weaklings, not ma-
> ture enough to fight against disaster. The Government understands this and
> considers these weak characters should be reeducated. . . . War criminals,
> however, have a reason to fear return. Those people who have committed
> crimes against their nation and want to return had better think about the pun-
> ishment that may await them.[32]

Delivered in the presence of apprehensive refugees from the East as well
as U.S. officials, the speech proved revealing and incredibly inept.

Elsewhere in Germany a Soviet DP camp commandant sought to put a
more reasonable face on the sorting operations with these words:

> Prisoners who were taken in large enveloping actions certainly have nothing to
> fear. As far as soldiers captured individually are concerned, it will be the task
> of appropriate Soviet organs to check the circumstances of capture and thus
> identify deserters. If a man has a clear conscience and has never traded his So-
> viet uniform for that of a WEHRMACHT, he need not worry. As for civilians who
> worked in Germany, it will be easy enough to check with their neighbors at
> home and thus separate those who volunteered to work in Germany from the
> majority who were deported as slave labour.[33]

It still appeared as a terrifying ordeal for repatriates. And as the statement vaguely suggested, vetting and screening entailed not only the un-
raveling of each subject's crimes, guilt being assumed from the outset, but
also extracting the maximum amount of incriminating evidence against
other repatriates. Those with special knowledge were given paper and
pencil and told to name all their compatriots who evaded or tried to evade
repatriation and those who had served with Vlasov or other collaborators.

Interrogators made use not only of evidence supplied by other repatriates but, in the case of forced laborers, the testimony of persons from
their home districts and, in the case of ex-POWs, captured Nazi archives.
The Soviet examiners' responsibility "to check the circumstances of capture" often meant a search through German records, which frequently
revealed precisely who had resisted and who had collaborated.[34]

With a case by case search not for the truth but for a crime, any crime,
whether committed or conjured up, the inquisitions could take years.[35] In
one instance even heroic resistance fighters, Soviet Georgians on the
Dutch island of Texel who had revolted against the Germans and had

engaged them in pitched battles spent at least four and a half months in postrepatriation "processing."[36] But the time involved cost Stalin nothing, for his secret police made sure to locate screening compounds next to factories, mines, or construction sites. No matter what, the work went on—as grueling for the innocent as for the guilty. And the form of existence in these way station netherworlds differed in no appreciable respect from thousands of other points in the Gulag: starvation rations; omnipresent guards; hardly habitable barracks; beatings; suicides.[37] The shock of it all weighed heavily on those unprepared for this sort of homecoming: "We sat down on the floor. No one expected quite this reception, and we were all disheartened. . . . I tried to believe it was all a mistake that would be corrected before the day was over, and that I'd be reassigned to the army. I tried to reassure the others, arguing that the presence of guards at the windows and door did not mean we were already condemned."[38]

No outcome offered repatriates much consolation. Once within Soviet-controlled territory escape rarely presented much hope of success, the attempt itself being tantamount to suicide. An unknown number of returners took their own lives; but many of these, the most desperate, acted solely to cut short the agony of awaiting a predictable and literal dead end. In existential terms returners thus had "no exit." Apart from the few who escaped and the suicides, who in effect can be counted with those given the death penalty, every repatriate faced one of four fates: execution; forced labor; induction or reinduction into the Red Army; or return to civilian life under strict surveillance.

Without a doubt large numbers of ex–Red Army officers did not survive the screening and vetting. Nikolai Tolstoy's examination of British archives and memoir literature and his personal interviews with eyewitnesses led him to conclude that "it was normal practice for the officers in returning batches of prisoners to be shot."[39] Most commonly Soviet firing squads aimed their barrels at those captured in German uniforms; but for Red Army officers, having been captured alive by the enemy without having joined an active resistance movement could suffice to send them before the same rifles. One repatriate who lived to tell of the screenings, the camps, and his eventual escape to the West recalled the high mortality rate in NKGB processing of soldiers of rank. After one night's interrogation his contingent of ex-POW officers had suffered substantial casualties:

> Two of our comrades were called out, taken away somewhere. . . . One of them soon came back but would not tell us where he had been and what he had been asked. The other did not return. . . . When I asked . . . [my examiner] to what unit I would be assigned he smiled, remarking that I would have to expi-

ate my guilt and purify my contaminated ideology. . . . I said I would complain to Marshal Zhukov and demand a thorough inquiry. The interrogator replied I was lucky not to be buried in a hole in the ground. . . . By the following morning our barrack had thinned out. Twelve of the occupants, nearly half, did not return after being interrogated. They were shot after questioning in a garage requisitioned for this purpose. Of our entire group, about sixty were liquidated.[40]

Rarely did the Soviet Union admit publicly this ultimate form of retribution. Even in reporting the execution of a few choice culprits—Andrei Vlasov, his immediate entourage, and a handful of other military collaborators—Stalin's preference kept the announcements low profile and brief. On 2 August 1946 *Pravda* noted that the Military Collegium of the Soviet Supreme Court had tried Vlasov and ten others and had convicted them of treason, espionage, and sabotage. The court required death by hanging for the eleven, which, the account stated, had been carried out. *Pravda* relegated this short piece of less than 150 words to the lower left-hand corner of the back page of the paper. The Kremlin staged a number of public trials of persons who committed treasonous acts in occupied territory. But it decided the fate of Vlasovites in private in order to avoid publicizing the existence of an organized anti-Stalinist movement during the war, a movement that constituted the most serious native-Russian threat to the regime since the Civil War.[41]

Beyond the sketchy 2 August declaration neither the West nor the Soviet populace knew anything of Vlasov's trial. Twenty-eight years later, however, a Soviet legal journal carried a surprisingly detailed account of it. (Solzhenitsyn's sympathetic comments toward the general and his movement in *The Gulag Archipelago* probably prompted this new tack.) According to A. V. Tishkov, writing in *Sovetskoe gosudarstvo i pravo* [The Soviet State and the Law], the Military Collegium of the U.S.S.R.'s Supreme Court began hearing the trial of Vlasov and ten other defendants on 30 July 1946. By then the former hero of the Battle of Moscow and commander of the makeshift Russian Liberation Army had been in Soviet custody over fourteen months. The delay, no doubt calculated, afforded military prosecutors ample time to prepare an elaborate, painstakingly detailed criminal case.[42]

After SMERSH's seizure of its prize catch on 12 May 1945, the doomed general had been transported from Czechoslovakia to SMERSH Front Headquarters near Dresden, and from there by plane to Moscow.[43] Soviet prosecutors filled the interregnum between Vlasov's capture and trial with a mammoth effort aimed at documenting every point in the indictment sevenfold: "each episode of criminal activity of the accused was scrupulously investigated and confirmed by [eye] witness testimony and other evidence, by the gathering and examination [of evidence] in accordance with criminal procedure laws of the Soviet government." As a result this best known of all collaborators had to contend with the direct trial testimony of twenty-eight prosecution witnesses and the interrogation transcripts of an additional eighty-three accusers. The court found Vlasov guilty on every point of the indictment: (1) his voluntary surrender to the enemy; (2) his "verbal and written agitation" among POWs and forced laborers, "calling them to enter the German army for the struggle with Soviet power"; (3) his creation of the anti-Soviet Committee for the Liberation of the Peoples of Russia (KONR—Komitet Osvobozhdeniia Narodov Rossii) and the Russian Liberation Army (ROA—Russkaia Osvoboditel'naia Armiia); and (4) his sponsorship of KONR and ROA intelligence schools designed to train agents "for espionage, diversionary, and terroristic activities in the rear of the Soviet Army."[44]

Some points should be made for the record. First, Vlasov was not a willing POW. Twice he had escaped encirclement, and he continued resistance within the Volkhov pocket as long as was practicable. His capture was more Stalin's fault than his own (see ch. 1). Second, he did recruit Soviet POWs and Ostarbeiter for the Wehrmacht. Third, he did found the KONR and the ROA. Finally, as for intelligence activities, the rare Vlasov agent behind the Red Army lines neither had the means nor the inclination for sabotage or "terroristic activities."

Vlasov rode out the three-day trial with only one point of vigorous opposition: he had not, he said, taken part in nor sponsored terroristic activities. Predictably, the denial made not a shred of difference, Stalin's former favorite being convicted on all charges anyway. His capture, not his trial, sealed his doom. The Military Collegium of the Soviet Supreme Court handed down its guilty verdict against all eleven defendants on 1 August 1946. The sentence called for death by hanging, which was carried out the same day, or at the latest, by the press deadline for the 2 August edition of *Pravda*. Joining Vlasov on the scaffold were: Major General Vasilii F. Malyshkin, purge victim, former chief of staff of the Soviet Nineteenth Army, head of KONR's Organization Department; General D. E. Zakutnyi, head of KONR's Civilian Department; Major General Georgii N. Zhilenkov, former Moscow Communist party official, head of KONR's Propaganda Department; Major General Feodor I. Trukhin, former chief of staff in the Red Army's Baltic Military District, ROA chief of staff; Major General Sergei K. Buniachenko, former Red Army division commander and chief of staff to General Semën K. Timoshenko, commander of the ROA First Division; General G. A. Zverev, commander of the ROA's stillborn Second Division; Major General I. A. Blagoveshchenskii, instructor and one-time head of the ROA training school at Dabendorf, Germany; Colonel V. I. Mal'tsev, head of the ROA air force; and V. D. Korbukov and N. S. Shatov, aides to ROA Chief of Staff Trukhin.[45] The only other public announcement of the execution of repatriates came on 17 January 1947, when *Pravda* announced the trial and conviction of leaders of "White Guard detachments." Five of the six mentioned by name had never been Soviet citizens, were not subject to the Yalta agreement, but had been handed over to the NKVD by the British in Austria anyway. Moscow thus had the chance to settle old scores with General Petr Krasnov, novelist, Don Cossack Ataman and ex-tsarist and Civil War White commander; General Semën Krasnov, son of the celebrated warrior; General Kelech Ghirey, Caucasian chieftain; and General Andrei G. Shkuro, Kuban Cossack and Civil War White cavalry officer. Executed at Lefortovo Prison in Moscow along with the above were General Helmuth von Pannwitz, German head of the Wehrmacht's Cossack division, and ex–Red Army Colonel T. I. Domanov, the only one of those listed holding Soviet citizenship and therefore liable to repatriation under terms of the Yalta accord.[46]

Some have characterized the Vlasov affair as the work of a vile Quisling-like traitor; others have seen it as the handiwork of a Russian national hero.[47] Neither description fits the man behind the movement. Andrei Andreievich Vlasov, given to drink and fits of fatalism and inertia in captivity, lacked the sterling character deemed essential for a martyr. On the other hand, the ROA chief was anything but a Nazi—he caused his German supporters discomfort with his strong Russian nationalism and his refusal to lend his voice to the prevailing, official anti-Semitism. He possessed neither a Quisling's moral blindness to questions of patriotism nor a Joan of Arc's penchant for self-immolation. He came closer to the mean of most humans, aptly personifying the nightmarish predicament that confronted millions of the Eastern front's victims. Vlasov, like multitudes of other helpless Soviet citizens, was cruelly pulverized between the enormous and unfeeling mill stones of Nazism and Communism. Shuffled about Europe's wargame board, first by Stalin, then by Hitler, Vlasov was a pawn in the epic struggle, just like the lowliest POW or forced laborer. He fantasized a Russia minus Marx and, though it is not saying much, came closer than any other Russian since the Civil War to fulfilling that hope. Nothing better indicates the feebleness of opposition to Russia's Bolshevik regime than the knowledge that, after 1920, the politically ineffectual figure of Vlasov led the greatest native challenge to it to date. Products of the Soviet system like Vlasov and relics of tsarism like Krasnov were "creatures ground up in the gears of processes beyond their control or understanding."[48]

The trial and execution of key collaborators are known facts. The widespread employment of the death penalty against repatriated officers also is well documented. What is lacking are verifiable figures on the NKVD's overall use of capital punishment on returning Soviet citizens. Moscow never has advertised the number of executed repatriates, but an approximation can be had, based on Western estimates of all categories of returners and discriminating use of Russian statistics (total returnees minus those sent to prison and camps, those assigned to the armed forces, and those sent home or into exile). Out of 5.2 million repatriates, Soviet screening commissions dispatched 2.5 million (nearly one-half) to prisons or forced labor camps;[49] approximately 1.1 million (just over one-fifth) into military ranks;[50] and perhaps 1.3 million (one-quarter) to their homes or into exile.[51] Stalin apparently had the remainder, some 300,000 repatriates, executed for service in enemy ranks or simply for being captured alive by the Germans.[52]

Accepting the probability that approximately 300,000 repatriates did not survive the screening and vetting, then for each returner shot or hung, seventeen lived at least long enough to deteriorate or die in imprisonment or to start over in the armed services, in internal exile, or back home. Two and one-half million, or just about one out of every two retrieved from abroad, merely traded Nazi for Soviet imprisonment. The language of the guards changed from German to Russian, but the barbed wire remained constant. To hear Moscow's spokesmen, one would never guess the true size of the stream being channeled straight from imprisonment abroad to imprisonment back home. Solzhenitsyn has maintained that the flow of repatriates into the Gulag could be likened figuratively to the breadth of Siberia's mighty Yenisei River; yet Marshal Zhukov has recounted that "we did our best to return all those released to their homes which throughout the grim years of imprisonment they had all been longing for."[53]

American officials of the World War II period would agree readily that the Soviet Union had done all in its power to repatriate its displaced nationals. But from what they glimpsed of the reception committees, they could hardly accept the Soviet contention of a happy homecoming for repatriates. Only a fraction of the DPs and POWs Zhukov referred to were "released to their homes." Contemporary Soviet calculations did indicate that 4,491,403 persons formerly stranded in Europe had "arrived at their places of residence and employment" by 30 September 1945.[54] But nothing in the misleading statement excluded the possibility, indeed the probability, that a large percentage of those 4.5 million were "residing" in prison or were "employed" as forced laborers.

Soviet resources barely coped with the veritable flood of refugees. Careful screening in the prescribed, systematic way lapsed as the press of humanity forced Russian authorities into shortcuts and expedients. Not that this let any suspect person through the sieve unscathed: rather than take that chance, overloaded screening commissions mechanically slapped ten-year labor camp sentences on returners simply as a precautionary measure. In April 1945 General Filip Golikov claimed his organization was "capable of quickly and effectively dealing with its tasks."[55] But 10,000 Red Army men actively assisting the repatriation commission proved insufficient. The job took them and personnel from every branch of the Soviet security empire: from SMERSH, of course (Golikov's commission being basically a front for it), but also from every sector of the NKGB and NKVD, even guards and administrators from the Gulag itself. Still the penal system labored under the weight of the suspect masses returning from abroad.[56] Solzhenitsyn, himself an inmate at the end of the war, relates that the Gulag was "overstrained" from 1944 to 1946 because the number of repatriates funneled down the "sewer pipes" of the system "defied all imagination."[57]

In the early fall of 1945 *Pravda* quoted General Golikov as saying that in the period of 25 May to 1 September alone, more than 2 million Soviet citizens had returned to their homeland. That figures out to a staggering pace of some 150,000 persons per week.[58] U.S. officials in Germany reported to Washington that Moscow's representatives seemed "unable to cope" with the "traffic" due to "heavy congestion" in the Soviet zone of occupation.[59] General Dwight Eisenhower noted in July that Russian officials, normally adamant in their insistence upon repatriation post haste, had refused for the moment to accept some trainloads of DPs because of logistical problems. From 4 July to 14 July 1945, SHAEF repatriated 165,000 Soviet citizens, but in the next ten days, only 38,000, because of strains on transportation on both sides of the demarcation line.[60]

Repatriates garnered forced labor terms ranging from three to twenty-five years, ten being a favorite figure, less than ten, a fluke.[61] Neither rhyme nor reason seemed to play much of a part in the dispensing of sentences. Military collaborators frequently received longer terms of imprisonment than ex-POWs or Ostarbeiter, but the outcome often times remained the same: the amnesties that followed Stalin's death frequently applied to genuine war criminals as well as to the mass of innocent "tenners," those serving a decade just as a precautionary measure. B. V. Biazrov, a Red Army officer captured in 1942 who subsequently joined an Osttruppen legion, served ten years for military collaboration.[62] A Soviet court in Latvia convicted Oscars Recis of membership in the Germans' dread SD (the SS security service) and of participating in Jewish pogroms. He received an eighteen-year sentence but spent only eleven behind bars. Another repatriated Latvian collaborator, convicted of atrocities against the civilian population, received fifteen years of hard labor but served less than nine.[63] Old émigré Civil War veterans swept back to Russia in the mass tide of 1945, who had willingly fought in Wehrmacht ranks, as a rule spent ten years in Soviet labor camps.[64]

Strangely, however, punishments meted out for lesser crimes or no crimes at all differed little in severity.[65] Stalin's "filtration plants" frequently settled the fate of repatriates in cavalier fashion with innumerable instances of the war's innocent victims receiving the same "reward" as voluntary collaborators. One returner who later managed an escape to the West reported the manner of treatment Soviet screening teams afforded retrieved Ostarbeiter:

> In 1942 I was forcibly taken to Germany together with my wife and child and for three years on end I worked in one of the factories near Aachen. I left for Russia with one of the first groups of repatriants [sic]. . . . I appeared before three examination commissions . . . and as I was able to prove that for the whole time I had remained an "eastworker," I was given a certificate according to which I was allowed to proceed to my former place of residence in Russia. A formation of freight cars—one for every 60 persons—was made ready for all those who had received such a certificate and we started East under convoy of Red Army soldiers. On the way I got acquainted with one of the soldiers, who told me that he had already accompanied several similar groups of repatriants [sic] and knew for certain that none of us was going to get home.[66]

In *The First Circle* Solzhenitsyn aptly illustrates the arbitrariness of Soviet treatment of repatriates by setting former Soviet resistance fighters in France down to the same game of prison dominoes with Vlasovites assigned to antiguerrilla combat in France. This authentic novel of the postwar Soviet Gulag is stocked liberally with an array of unfortunate repatriates. Spiridon Yegorov, for one, was "guilty" of having been a German slave laborer. His family had convinced him that they should return home so his daughter could marry a Russian instead of a German and his two sons could get a Russian education. They received instruction, to be sure, but not in subjects they cared for. "At the border station the men and the women were separated right away and sent on in separate trains. The Yegorov family, which had kept together through the whole war, now fell apart." Spiridon's wife and daughter ended up in a Siberian lumber camp with the girl running a chain saw. The men each got ten years for treason. The elder son finished his upbringing in the Kolyma gold fields. Spiridon and his youngest boy at least landed in the same camp. "This was home. This was the daughter's husband and the sons' schooling."[67]

Andrei Potapov, the Dnieper power plant engineer convicted of sabotaging the project *after* its destruction, is another repatriate in *The First Circle* gallery of Stalin's victims. In German captivity Potapov had warded off a collaborator's attempt to secure his help in rebuilding the Dnieper plant. Because of his refusal this patriot had been returned to the POW death camps where men "ate bark from the trees, grass, and their dead comrades."[68] Potapov survived Nazi imprisonment and therefore had the chance to compare German and Soviet camps. That he got ten years for his trouble was bitter; that another engineer, who had agreed to help the Germans, got the same "tenner" was acid.

Model Soviet patriots returning from Nazi death camps consistently felt the same, indiscriminate, heavy hand of Stalin's justice, apparently for nothing more than their capture alive by the enemy. U.S. military archives preserve the testimony of one repatriated officer who later escaped to the West. Even with sterling credentials (twice wounded, Red Army decorations for bravery, two attempted escapes from German captivity, and two point blank refusals to join Vlasov's ranks), he came home not to a hero's welcome but to a Siberian labor camp.[69] Roy Medvedev reports other repatriates punished for nonexistent crimes: a Red Army major who had participated in the renowned, sacrificial defense of the Brest fortress back in 1941; and a poet, a lieutenant colonel, and a general who had all been members of Norway's anti-Fascist camp underground. Even for POWs who escaped Nazi captivity to join European resistance movements, liberation could serve merely as a prelude to further confinement. *The First Circle* reminds its readers: "That was Stalin's signature—that magnificent equating of friends and enemies which made him unique in all human history."[70]

The callous Soviet treatment of persons who, returning to other homelands, would have been welcomed as heroes, is no better documented than in the case of Lieutenant General Mikhail F. Lukin. Captured in the Viaz'ma encirclement of October 1941, along with 650,000 other soldiers, this luckless commander of the Soviet Nineteenth Army turned out to be the highest ranking prisoner out of a pocket that at one point included some forty-five divisions. Seriously wounded, Lukin survived, but Wehrmacht doctors had to amputate both his legs. The Germans' trouble was for nothing because the crippled general would have no part of their plans for him. At one point Vlasov personally met with Lukin in a vain attempt to recruit his services, but the invalid commander never gave in. A Soviet account says he called Vlasov a traitor to his face, but what it fails to relate is that Lukin's courageous stand counted not a whit to the screeners and vetters after the war. He underwent grueling interrogations just like any other repatriate, his condition notwithstanding. Unlike Vlasov or Krasnov, Lukin had nothing to hold back, for he had staunchly refused to collaborate. But no matter, the Kremlin still felt more comfortable giving him a prison term anyway.[71] One Gulag anecdote drives home the arbitrariness and senselessness of the punishments in a poignant manner that would be humorous but for the tragedy of so many million wrecked lives. In the Novosibirsk Transit Prison a curious guard asked one repatriate what he had done for a twenty-five-year sentence. "Nothing at all," the prisoner replied.

"You're lying," the jailer countered. *"The sentence for nothing at all is ten years."* [72]

One can only speculate what percentage of repatriates outlived their sentences. The odds were not very good. All but a few thousand of the hundreds of thousands of German POWs captured at Stalingrad perished in Soviet camps. And the keepers of the Gulag took an even dimmer view of collaborators than they did of Germans. The weather, the regimen, and the guards all proved harsh, and for many, lethal. Some despairing repatriates died by their own hands; some perished in impulsive escape attempts equivalent to suicide; some starved or froze to death; some forfeited their lives for no apparent reason save the whim of their escorts. Most of those who did not last to the amnesties of the post-Stalin era died due to the horrible conditions of confinement. Like all political inmates, repatriates were ill-fed, ill-clothed, overworked, poorly housed, terrorized by genuine criminals as well as guards, and subjected to the debilitating, deteriorating effect of the Russian winters. The first days of the ordeal went like this for an ex-POW and ex–Red Army officer: "After four days marching we were herded into box cars with nailed windows. Our box car had 62 inmates . . . and there was no question of one being able to lay [sic] down or even to sit down due to cramped quarters. The freight train consisted of about 50 cars and all were full of such as me. During the journey there were many suicides. Twice each day the box car doors were thrown open in order that we could witness in first instance two persons and on second three persons shot presumably for an attempt to escape." [73]

Nikolai Krasnov, Jr., grandson of Civil War White General P. N. Krasnov, lived to tell of the oddly differential handling at first afforded certain Civil War "celebrities" like his family. Far from a box car packed with over five dozen people, the Krasnovs rated a plane flight direct from Austria to Moscow. But their end mirrored that of countless other returners. Two of the four men of this famous family received the death penalty while standard Soviet mistreatment drove Nikolai's father to an early grave in 1947. Only the son, the youngest and the hardiest, outlasted Stalin to receive a 1955 amnesty, and because of his Yugoslav citizenship, a ticket out of Russia. Before that miracle, though, Nikolai endured his share of transports contrasting sharply to the speedy plane flight of 1945. The youngest Krasnov recalled in detail one agonizing shuffle, one bound to shorten the lifespan of even the healthiest prisoner: "Into a railroad compartment intended for six passengers they pushed two dozen. We could not even turn around, much less sit down. Crushed to the point of suffocation, dressed in heavy cotton quilted clothing, the prisoners fainted from the heat despite the heavy frost outside. Many were unable to control their functions, and the atmosphere grew so foul that people longed to die. Even now in thinking about this journey I become nauseated and experience again that frantic terror which cannot be compared with anything else."[74]

Given the available, gruesome evidence, Nicholas Bethell seems a thoroughly reasonable man in surmising that surely no more than half the repatriates could have survived ten years in Soviet camps—as Nikolai Krasnov did.[75] If that be the case, and roughly 2.5 million Soviet citizens returned from Europe directly to forced labor camps, then fatalities among these powerless victims of the war—taking no account of executions *prior* to entering the Gulag—may have approached 1.25 million persons. The staggering statistics merely hint at the load of human misery and suffering born by Soviet refugees and POWs, a load entailed by a homeland perverse in its expectations of patriotic sacrifices.

Is it any wonder Solzhenitsyn directs volley after volley at the Kremlin for its callousness towards its own flesh and blood returning from abroad? Again and again the now-exiled author has recounted the sorrowful tale of Soviet returners in a variety of published works. Nowhere, however, are the painful wounds and scars of the tragedy developed with better definition than in the pages of *The First Circle*. And perhaps no single episode of that novel is more laden with pathos—and with stinging satire on totalitarian bureaucracy—than the inmates' mock trial of Prince Igor.

"The concluding charge of the case under investigation, number five million slant three million six hundred fifty-one thousand nine hundred seventy-four, indicting Olgovich, Igor Svyatoslavich.

"Organs of State Security have arrested the accused in the said case, Olgovich, I.S. The investigation has established that Olgovich, who was a military leader of the brilliant Russian Army, with the rank of prince, in the post of troop commander, turned out to be a foul traitor to his country. His traitorous activities consisted of voluntarily surrendering and becoming a prisoner of the accursed enemy of our people, Khan Konchak. . . .

"Comrade judges," Rubin intoned gloomily, "I have but little to add to that chain of dreadful accusations, to that dirty jumble of crimes, which has been revealed before your eyes. In the first place, I would like to reject once and for all the widespread rotten opinion that a wounded man has the moral right to let himself be taken prisoner. That's basically not our view, comrades! And all the more so in the case of Prince Igor. They tell us that he was wounded on the battlefield. But who can prove this now, 765 years later? Has there been preserved any official evidence of a wound, signed by his divisional military surgeon? In any case, there is no such official attestation in the indictment file, comrade judges!"

Amantai Bulatov took off his glasses, and without their mischievous gleam his eyes were utterly sad.

He, Pryanchikov, Potapov, and many others among those present had been imprisoned for the very same "treason to the country": "voluntary" surrender.[76]

In war, if anything could be worse than millions suffering at the hands of a bestial enemy host, it would be punishment redoubled by a homeland that distrusted and automatically condemned millions of its citizens who survived the ordeal of captivity. Russia's repatriates experienced both.

If Soviet authorities did not execute or imprison returners, they inducted them into the armed services or released them to their homes or internal exile. According to Mikhail Semiriaga, author of a major Russian study on the wartime activities of displaced Soviet nationals, better than one million repatriates entered military ranks upon their return to Russia.[77] While not giving overall estimates, other sources, East and West, agree that the Red Army did bolster its manpower by this device. One Soviet account of ten Red Army POWs escaping Germany in a Luftwaffe aircraft has seven of them enrolling in a rifle regiment "after a month and a half's rest."[78] And all seven contributors in a Soviet memoir collection written by Buchenwald survivors indicate military service followed their repatriation.[79]

The Soviet press accused the Nazis of violating international law when German POWs repatriated by the British, presumably in an exchange of wounded, ended up fighting on the Eastern front. Moscow's mouthpieces did not specifically cite the Geneva POW Convention—Russia had not signed it—but must have been alluding to it, for Article 74 reads, "No repatriated person may be utilized in active military service."[80] That, however, did not hinder the Soviet armed forces from making wholesale use of POWs returning from German captivity, some, for sure, before the war's end.

U.S. intelligence knew at the time that military deployment in the Red Army awaited at least a portion of the former prisoners returning from abroad.[81] But it took postwar evidence gleaned from German sources and Soviet defectors to learn that suspect military recruits fared little better than prison inmates. Especially for those condemned to penal battalions, the rigors of Red Army ranks offered few discernible advantages over labor camps and, during the war, much greater danger of immediate death.[82] Seven of ten men were put into Red Army ranks from Mikhail Deviataev's party of POW escapees. They could not have spent more than a few months in combat between their February 1945 escape and the war's conclusion in early May. That six of the seven died in subsequent fighting strongly suggests that they landed in high-risk penal battalions.[83] Perhaps because of the physical risks involved, Moscow even assigned some repatriated ex-Osttruppen to closely watched punishment units of the Red Army rather than to forced labor.[84]

But whether the repatriates-turned-recruits had stains on their records or not, they definitely lived with stricter supervision than ordinary enlistees. One postwar defector, previously in a contingent of willing returners, remembered that the Red Army took charge of all the able-bodied in his group between the ages of eighteen and thirty, whether ex-POW or ex-Ostarbeiter. Guards escorted them to a training camp holding 5,000 draftees, all former German captives. Soviet authorities prolonged their basic training, probably, the Soviet defector suggested, "for the purpose of observing the political reliability of the trainees." Even after the conclusion of boot camp, the stigma of having been abroad constantly hurt his chances for advancement and permanently branded him as being unreliable.[85]

The same lingering, indelible distrust accompanied even the approximate 1.3 million repatriates allowed to go home, or at least given internal exile rather than terms of confinement, the draft, or the death penalty.[86] The "overt animosity" and "unfriendliness" with which Red Army troops greeted collaborators and POWs, an émigré reported, extended to all Soviet citizens abroad, including those forcibly removed to Germany as slave laborers.[87] Soviet screening commissions allowed Ostarbeiter to go home or into internal exile more than any other category of returner, but even these hapless refugees suffered rejection and persecution as outcasts. They faced years of effective isolation from the mainstream of Soviet society due to harassment and officially mandated restrictions. Stalin and his entourage, doubting Communism's hold on popular loyalty, regarded anyone who had had contact with the outside world, even if exclusively at the point of a German bayonet, to be suspect and infected with alien influences. Simply having been liberated by U.S. or British forces could cast an additional shadow on luckless Soviet refugees.[88] The blind, paranoid nativism of the postwar era grew so intense, a defector recalled, that it cast a threatening pall not only on the minority of repatriates at liberty but on all who simply had lived in German-occupied territory. In the darkened atmosphere of Stalin's last decade these people could not be counted as "full-fledged Soviet citizens."[89]

Moscow especially feared that those who had spent some part of the war in the Third Reich proper might come home with unwanted ideas and might "contaminate others with their admiration for the standard of living in Germany."[90] Consequently, the regime went to great lengths to quarantine released repatriates in order to check the spread of dread ideological infections and material aspirations. An NKVD defector estimated that his superiors had exiled to Siberia, for terms not less than six years, about 10 percent of the entire repatriate population (which would mean better than 500,000).[91] Regulations prohibited even the freest sort of returner from residing within 100 kilometers of Moscow, Leningrad, Kiev, Odessa, Khar'kov, or Minsk.[92]

Besides administrative exile and returner-free urban zones, the Soviet Union contained the presumed contagions of released repatriates through direct police supervision and surveillance. Local NKVD branches kept watchful eyes on all returners in their jurisdictions; and in peak years of antiforeign hysteria, the late 1940s and early 1950s, they oversaw new waves of arrests that engulfed many of the Ostarbeiter and POW remnants previously spared this, the most common fate of repatriates.[93]

For those miraculously spared execution, imprisonment, and military service, and for those who served out their terms of confinement, the lingering stigma of repatriate status measurably increased their personal hardships and poisoned all human relations. The regime chose to bar some returners from receiving further education; stood in the way of job advancement for others; and made servants of some Ostarbeiter girls for the benefit—and pleasure—of Red Army officers. The blemishes on the records of repatriates played havoc not only with their lives and livelihoods; the stains damaged the prospects of their relatives as well.[94]

In George Feifer's *Moscow Farewell*, a largely autobiographical account by an American exchange student in Russia in the early 1960s, readers get a fleeting but poignant glimpse of one of the repatriated untouchables, obviously still hurting from wounds inflicted first by Hitler, then by Stalin:

> I push off in the direction of Dobrininskaya peasant market. This section of the city, mostly untouched by rebuilding, has a small-town flavor. In a decrepit "snack room" I breakfast on kasha and gritty coffee. After eyeing me, the ragged man sharing my stand-up table volunteers that he spent the decade 1944-54 in concentration camps, mostly in the notorious Vorkuta complex. Fingers are missing on both hands—Vorkuta was above the Arctic Circle, he reminds me—and he has difficulty swallowing a bun; might I spare a few kopeks? His crime was to be taken prisoner by the Germans in 1942, when his unit disintegrated near Rostov. Worked and starved to a living skelton, he escaped, made his own way to his own lines, and was immediately sentenced because former POWs were regarderd as traitors. . . . I had no idea how badly off some still are.[95]

Whatever repatriates' specific destination—the gallows, the Gulag, penal battalions, exile, or home—none of the more than 5 million received invitations to the "victors' feast," and all, Solzhenitsyn declares, carried the "Brand of a flame that no atonement quenches."[96] So the toll of human destruction from Russia's boundless vindictiveness toward returners must encompass not only those killed outright and those who languished or perished in camps. It must also encompass the remainder of returner-pariahs, crippled physically and spiritually by malevolent, security-obsessed figures ensconced behind the Kremlin's ornate facade.

NOTES

1. Of these only the short story and *One Day* have been published in the Soviet Union. *From under the Rubble* (Boston, 1975) provides a fleeting yet caustic condemnation of Western participation in forced repatriation. See "Repentance and Self-Limitation in the Life of Nations," ibid., 112. The other works are cited below.

2. Solzhenitsyn, *Gulag*, I: 238. See also ibid., 164, 256-57.

3. Solzhenitsyn, *Prussian Nights* (New York, 1977), 75. Solzhenitsyn once thought of calling the piece *Victors' Feast*. Thomas Weiss, "An Analysis of Solzhenitsyn's 'Prussian Nights,' " 14 Feb. 1975, Radio Liberty Dispatch RL 63/75.

4. Erickson, *Stalingrad*, 176. See also Werth, *Russia at War*, 226, 395.

5. Solzhenitsyn, *Gulag*, I: 79.

6. Ibid., 237-76; Solzhenitsyn, *One Day in the Life of Ivan Denisovich* (New York, 1963), 71.

7. Fischer, *Thirteen*, 52, 76, 96; Solzhenitsyn, *Gulag*, I: 244; Petr P. Vershigora, *Men with a Clear Conscience* (Moscow, 1949), 262. See also George Feifer, *Moscow Farewell* (New York, 1976), 341; A. Furman, "Behind the Barbed Wire: Ukrainian-Russian Relations in the Concentration Camps from 1945-1955," *Ukrainian Review*, 8 (Spring 1961), 47-48; Luxenburg, "Solzhenitsyn," 2; Harrison Salisbury, *The Gates of Hell* (New York, 1975), 279; Varlam Shalamov, "Poslednii boi maiora Pugacheva," *Grani*, 76 (July 1970), 46; Simonov, *The Living*, 193-94; Steenberg, *Vlasov*, 172; Toppe, "Russian Methods," 14.

8. Kirk to Secretary of State, 13 Apr. 1945, NA RG 59, 740.00114 EW/4-1345.

9. Fischer, ed., *Thirteen*, 12. See also Kydd, *Over*, 294-95.

10. Edward J. Brown, *Russian Literature since the Revolution* (New York, 1963), 229.

11. Alliluyeva, *Only One Year*, 370; Amalrik, "Victims," 94. See also ibid., 91-92.

12. Deriabin and Gibney, *Secret World*, 66.

13. Krasnov, *Hidden Russia*, 70.

14. OSS, "Reichswehr," 24.

15. Solzhenitsyn, *Gulag*, I: 243. See also ibid., 82, 244-45; Dallin and Nikolaevskii, *Forced Labor*, 282; Ivan S. Lubachko, *Belorussia under Soviet Rule, 1917-1957* (Lexington, Ky., 1972), 168; Lyons, *Secret*, 266, 282-83; Simonov, *The Living*, 190. Edward Crankshaw incorrectly states that Vlasovites forcibly repa-

triated to the Soviet Union faced "certain death." *Khrushchev's Russia* (Baltimore, 1959), 158.

16. Harriman to Stettinius, 11 June 1945, *FR, 1945*, V: 1097-98. See also Alliluyeva, *Only One Year*, 268; Fischer, "New Emigration," 10; OSS, "Reichswehr," 20; Posdnjakoff, "German Counterintelligence," 182; Shub, *Choice*, 46-47; Werth, *Russia at War*, 709.

17. Lyons, *Secret*, 283.

18. "Repatriation," 533. See also Proudfoot, *European Refugees*, 218; and "Repatriation of DPs from Germany and Austria," 1 Mar. 1946, NAS RG 165, WDGSS, Military Intelligence Service Project File, Project No. 2897.

19. Quoted in Kennan to Hull, 11 Nov. 1944, *FR, 1944*, IV: 1264.

20. Kotov, "Stalin," 57.

21. Ibid.; Army Signal Corps film, no. 4928, NA RG 111; Bethell, *Secret*, 62-63; Coffin, *Once*, 76-77; Col. D. C. Howell to author, 2 Jan. 1978; Tolstoy, *Secret*, 403.

22. The Germans captured a copy of a Soviet order that detailed procedures to be used in handling Vlasovites. It came into the possession of the Western Allies at the end of the war. Dallin and Mavrogordato, "Soviet Reaction," 320-21. See also Blake, "Solzhenitsyn," 39; Michael Schatoff's introduction to Osokin, *Vlasov*, 7.

23. Dvinov, *Politics*, 365.

24. Ibid., 364; Solzhenitsyn, *Gulag*, I: 255. See also Dvinov, *Politics*, 110, 365; Romanov, *Nights*, 150; S. Swianiewicz, *Forced Labour and Economic Development, an Enquiry into the Experience of Soviet Industrialization* (London, 1965), 44; Tolstoy, *Secret*, 140, 295, 310.

25. Fischer, ed., *Thirteen*, 50; P. J. Juris, president of American Friends of Lithuania, to Gen. John H. Hilldring, WD, CAD, 3 Aug. 1947, enclosure received July 1947 from formerly repatriated Soviet officer, NA RG 165 WDGSS, WDSCA, 383.7, CAD, Sec. 20, pp. 5-7; Russian-American Union for Protection and Aid to Russians, Petitions Addendum, "Excerpts from Reports on Conditions in the Soviet Camps for Repatriated Russians," 21 Oct. 1945, NA RG 165, WDGSS, WDSCA, 383.7 Russia 25 Aug. 45–10 June 46; Solzhenitsyn, *First Circle*, 463; Tolstoy, *Secret*, 317. (The Juris to Hilldring communication enumerated segregated groups but, certainly by accident, omitted a separate category for collaborators.)

26. Harriman to Byrnes, 16 Aug. 1945, NA RG 59, 711.62114/8-1645; Proverochno-Fil'trovochnye Komissii: Romanov, *Nights*, 124. See also Dallin and Mavrogordato, "Soviet Reaction," 321; " 'Liberation'–And Life Thereafter," 7; "Repatriation of DPs from Germany and Austria," 1 Mar. 1946, NAS RG 165 WDGSS, Military Intelligence Service Project File, Project No. 2897; Solzhenitsyn, *Gulag*, I: 248-49.

27. Juris to Hilldring, 3 Aug. 1947, NA RG 165 WDGSS, WDSCA 383.7, CAD, Sec. 20, pp. 6-7. See also Solzhenitsyn, *Gulag*, I: 222-23.

28. Solzhenitsyn, *First Circle*, xii, 182-83.

29. "Minutes of Meeting with Soviet Liaison Officer," Mittenwald Camp, 28 Aug. 1947, NA RG 59, 800.4016 DP/10-1447, Enclosure to Dispatch 409, 14 Oct. 1947, p. 2; Chargé of USSR Kasputin to Secretary of State, 13 July 1944, *FR, 1944*, IV: 1242-43.

30. Juris to Hilldring, 3 Aug. 1947, NA RG 165, WDGSS, WDSCA 383.7, CAD, Sec. 20, p. 5. Various abridgements and translations of this same eyewit-

ness account have appeared over the years: Dallin and Nikolaevskii, *Forced Labor*, 286-89; Lyons, *Secret*, 266; Shub, *Choice*, 38-39. For similar episodes see " 'Liberation'—And Life Thereafter," 7-8; Lyons, *Secret*, 282-84, 290; Medvedev, *Let History Judge*, 467-68; and Shub, *Choice*, 40-43.

31. Solzhenitsyn, *Gulag*, I: 249; Solzhenitsyn, *First Circle*, 353. (The trial in this novel covers pp. 347-57.)

32. "Minutes of Meeting with Soviet Liaison Officer," Mittenwald Camp, 28 Aug. 1947, NA RG 59, 800.4016 DP/10-1447, p. 5.

33. Contained in Murphy to SD, 2 June 1945, NA RG 59, no decimal number, dispatch number 451. This is quoted almost verbatim in Shub, *Choice*, 15.

34. Dallin and Mavrogordato, "Soviet Reaction," 321; Georgii V. Yevstigneev, *Flight to Freedom* (Moscow, 1965), 23, 25.

35. Bethell, *Secret*, 204; Romanov, *Nights*, 173; Solzhenitsyn, *Gulag*, I: 249.

36. Miron I. Kochiashvili, "Uchastie sovetskikh grazhdan—gruzin v dvizhenii soprotivleniia v stranakh zapadnoi Evropy" in *Vtoraia mirovaia voina*, vol. 3, *Dvizhenie soprotivleniia v Evrope*, ed. by E. A. Boltin (Moscow, 1966), 128-29.

37. Solzhenitsyn, *Gulag*, I: 248-49; Juris to Hilldring, 3 Aug. 1947, NA RG 165, WDGSS, WDSCA, 383.7, CAD, Sec. 20, p. 5; Russian-American Union for Protection and Aid to Russians, Petition Addendum, "Excerpts from Reports [by escapees] on Conditions in the Soviet Camps for Repatriated Russians," 21 Oct. 1945, NA RG 165, WDGSS, WDSCA 383.7, Russia 25 Aug. 45–10 June 46.

38. Shub, *Choice*, 39-40.

39. Tolstoy, *Secret*, 319.

40. Shub, *Choice*, 39-40. See also Bethell, *Secret*, 101; Tolstoy, *Secret*, 185, 247, 350.

41. A full translation of the announcement can be found in Fischer, *Soviet Opposition*, 120.

42. Tishkov, "Predatel'," 90. I would like to credit Tolstoy (*Secret*, 302) with the very plausible suggestion that the article on Vlasov's trial was a deliberate anticipation of Solzhenitsyn's *Gulag*.

43. Romanov, *Nights*, 152.

44. Tishkov, "Predatel'," 90.

45. Ibid.; Randolph Boothby Best, "A Doctrine of Counterinsurgence" (Ph.D. diss., University of South Carolina, 1973), 191-92; Romanov, *Nights*, 126; Steenberg, *Vlasov*, 47, 226, Thorwald, *Illusion*, 90, 118, 221, 231; Tolstoy, *Secret*, 296, 301.

46. Bethell, *Secret*, 164; Bosse, "Cossack Corps," P-064, 25; Karmann, "Tragodie," 661; Krasnov, *Hidden Russia*, 76; Pronin, "Guerilla Warfare," 46-47; Reitlinger, *House Built on Sand*, 392; Romanov, *Nights*, 153-54; Solzhenitsyn, *Gulag*, I: 627; Tolstoy, *Secret*, 188, 196-97, 234; Toppe, "Political Indoctrination," 64. For additional information concerning the treatment of old émigré repatriates see: Walter Dushnyck, "The Importance of the Problem of Displaced Persons," *Ukrainian Review*, 2 (Spring 1946), 286; Grzybowski, *Soviet Public International Law*, 240; Koriakov, *I'll Never Go Back*, 216; Manning, "Significance," 20; Naumenko, *Velikoe predatel'stvo*, II: 297-317; Smith, "American Role," 69-70; Solzhenitsyn, *Gulag*, I: 84-85, 265; Steenberg, *Vlasov*, 220.

47. Negative: Taratuta, "Tell Me," 116; Tishkov, "Predatel'," 98; positive: Amalrik, "Victims," 92; Strik-Strikfeldt, *Against Stalin and Hitler*.

48. Stephan, *Russian Fascists*, 28.

49. Swianiewicz, *Forced Labour*, 44. Werth (*Russia: The Postwar Years*, 28) figured no more than 500,000 repatriates ended up in camps, a calculation so low as to lack credibility.

50. Semiriaga, *Sovetskie Liudi*, 327, states "more than one million."

51. Amalrik, "Victims," 94. The above figures may be compared with less precise but compatible calculations offered by an ex-NKVD agent: Deriabin and Gibney, *Secret World*, 99.

52. This estimate, useful as it is, nevertheless should be considered a conservative, partial total of casualties, since it takes into account neither Red Army frontline units' uncontrolled, unreported shootings of collaborators *before* repatriation nor the deaths in Soviet camps caused by mistreatment, malnourishment, unsanitary conditions, and exposure to the elements.

53. *Gulag*, I: 24; Zhukov, *Memoirs*, 665.

54. "Repatriation," 533.

55. Quoted in Kennan to Stettinius, 30 Apr. 1945, NA RG 334, USMMM-POWs, 25 Apr. 1945–15 June 1945.

56. "Repatriation," 533; Romanov, *Nights*, 172; Semiriaga, *Sovetskie liudi*, 326; Tolstoy, *Secret*, 405.

57. *First Circle*, 239; *Gulag*, I: 24. See also ibid., 10-11.

58. Naumenko, *Velikoe predatel'stvo*, II: 380.

59. Murphy to Secretary of State, 20 June 1945, NA RG 59, 800.4016 DP/6-2045.

60. Eisenhower to USMMM, 20 July 1945, microfilm reel 5 July 1945–18 July 1946, Clifford Papers; Proudfoot, *European Refugees*, 211.

61. Bethell, *Secret*, 204; Major Burnside in *Before Winter Comes*; Enquist, *The Legionnaires*, 439; Krasnov, *Hidden Russia*, 240-41; " 'Liberation'—And Life Thereafter," 8; Medvedev, *Let History Judge*, 468; Shub, *Choice*, 45; Solzhenitsyn, *First Circle*, 464; Solzhenitsyn, *Gulag*, I: 61, II: 498-99. The unique and most problematic source documenting the treatment of Soviet repatriates is Per Olav Enquist's *The Legionnaires*: unique because the author went to Soviet Latvia and interviewed many of the 146 Baltic military collaborators extradited by Sweden to Russia after the war; problematic because, as the author admits, such testimony presents "enormous problems of source criticism" (p. 424). This "documentary novel," which garnered two literary prizes and a film adaptation, maintains that the Soviet Union punished only about 24 percent of those extradited; that a legionnaire officer suffered no worse than a labor camp term; that a Baltic lieutenant in the notorious German SD security service, convicted of participation in Jewish genocide, served but eleven years for his crimes; and that in general these 146 men looked back on repatriation n.ore "as a troublesome episode in their lives than as a momentous tragedy" (pp. 508, 465-66, 469, 456-57, 500). *The Legionnaires*, read by itself, seems credible, but that military collaborators received such mild treatment does not square with abundant evidence to the contrary. One explanation is that Enquist was "set up" in a traditional Russian fashion (dating back to eighteenth-century stage set villages propped up along riverbanks by Empress Catherine's favorite, Potemkin, to impress visiting European monarchs). Solzhenitsyn's *First Circle* has a masterful chapter on the deception of American Quakers visiting Butyrskaya Prison in 1945 ("Buddha's Smile," pp. 378-90). But more precisely parallel is his account in the *Gulag* of a Potemkin-like encounter between visiting Swedish reporters and Soviet sailors repatriated following wartime internment in Sweden. Russia stilled Swedish rumors of rough handling of

the extradited by plying these gullible journalists with ex-sailor prisoners fattened and dressed up for the occasion. On cue the repatriates decried the slanders of the bourgeois press concerning their fate, which convinced the Swedes that earlier reports of their ill-treatment lacked substance. (I: 83. See also Tolstoy, *Secret*, 388.) Another possible explanation for Enquist's account being at odds with most of the evidence is that Moscow may have exercised more leniency in the case of the 146 extradited Balts, anticipating continued Western interest in their fate.

62. Eduard M. Bartoshevich and Evgenii I. Borisoglebskii, *Imenem bog iegovy* (Moscow, 1960), 109-10.

63. Enquist, *Legionnaires*, 439, 456-67.

64. Huxley-Blythe, *East*, 112, 203-10; Krasnov, *Hidden Years*, 240-41.

65. Bethell, *Secret*, 23; Enquist, *Legionnaires*, 464.

66. Russian-American Union for Protection and Aid to Russians, Petition Addendum, "Excerpts from Reports [by escapees] on Conditions in the Soviet Camps for Repatriated Russians," 21 Oct. 1945, NA RG 165, WDGSS, WDSCA 383.7, Russia 25 Aug. 45–10 June 46.

67. *First Circle*, 542-43, 463-64. See also ibid., xiii, 462.

68. Ibid., 183-84.

69. Juris to Hilldring, 3 Aug. 1947, NA RG 165, WDGSS, WDSCA 383.7, CAD, Sec. 20, pp. 1-6.

70. Medvedev, *Let History Judge*, 467-69; Solzhenitsyn, *First Circle*, 184.

71. Dallin, "Gallery," 79-80; Dallin, *German Rule*, 528; Mikhail F. Lukin, "My ne sdaemsia, tovarishch general!," *Ogonek*, no. 47 (Nov. 1964), 26-30. [Portions of this article are reprinted in M. V. Schatov, *Materialy i dokumenty osvoboditel'nogo dvizheniia narodov Rossii v gody vtoroi mirovoi voiny (1945-1965)* (New York, 1966), 2: 97-115.] Romanov, *Nights*, 81; Seaton, *Battle*, 107; Seaton, *Russo-German War*, 184; Strik-Strikfeldt, *Against Stalin and Hitler*, 35-36, 93-94; Tishkov, "Predatel'," 92, 95; Zhukov, *Memoirs*, 330.

72. Solzhenitsyn, *Gulag*, I: 293. See also ibid., 248; Robert Conquest, *Kolyma: The Arctic Death Camps* (New York, 1978), 228.

73. Juris to Hilldring, 3 Aug. 1947, NA RG 165, WDGSS, WDSCA 383.7, CAD, Sec. 20, p. 8. See also Koriakov, *I'll Never Go Back*, 216; Naumenko, *Velikoe predatel'stvo*, II: 307; Tolstoy, *Secret*, 407-8. *Before Winter Comes* contains a powerful portrayal of the bloody outcome of an escape attempt.

74. Krasnov, *Hidden Russia*, 128-29, 183.

75. Bethell, *Secret*, 163.

76. Solzhenitsyn, *First Circle*, 348-49, 352. Deming Brown appreciatively characterizes the heavy-laden spoof as one of the novel's "burlesque fantasies": *Soviet Russian Literature since Stalin* (Cambridge, 1970), 315-16.

77. Semiriaga, *Sovetskoe liudi*, 327.

78. Yevstigneev, *Flight to Freedom*, 74. One cannot help but speculate what percentage of those forty-five days was spent in recuperation and what percentage in interrogation, especially knowing that other POWs who fled in commandeered German aircraft received ten years in Soviet labor camps for their heroics: Medvedev, *Let History Judge*, 468.

79. Solasko, *War behind Barbed Wire*. Other Soviet accounts specifying this end for repatriates are: *Avengers: Reminiscences of Soviet Members of the Resistance Movement* (Moscow, 1965), 179; Sholokhov, *Fate*, 38-39; V. V. Zelenin, "Uchastie sovetskikh liudei v narodno-osvoboditel'noi voine v Iugoslavii" in *Vtoraia mirovaia voina*, vol. 3, *Dvizhenie soprotivleniia v Evrope*, ed. Boltin, 137; L.

S. Zhugarina, "Uchastie sovetskikh partizan v dvizhenii Soprotivleniia v raione Rima," in *Ob"edinenie Italii* (Moscow, 1936), 390.

80. OSS, "Russian Intentions to Punish War Criminals," 27 June 1944, NA RG 59, no. 1988.

81. OSS, "Reichswehr," 24. See also Tolstoy, *Secret*, 88-89.

82. Toppe, "Russian Methods," 14.

83. Yevstigneev, *Flight to Freedom*, 76.

84. Huxley-Blythe, *East*, 180-81.

85. U.S. Department of State, *Former Soviet Citizens*, 1-3.

86. Amalrik, "Victims," 94.

87. Fischer, "Defectors," 697.

88. Solzhenitsyn, *Gulag*, I: 249.

89. Fischer, ed., *Thirteen*, 151.

90. U.S. Department of State, *Former Soviet Citizens*, 1, 3.

91. Deriabin and Gibney, *Secret World*, 99. See also Solzhenitsyn, *Gulag*, III: 371.

92. " 'Liberation'—And Life Thereafter," 8. See also Harriman to Stettinius, 11 June 1945, *FR, 1945*, V: 1097.

93. Fischer, ed., *Thirteen*, 51; Vladimir K. Gerasimenko *et al., S chuzhogo golosa* (Simferopol', 1975), 26-27; Romanov, *Nights*, 173; Solzhenitsyn, *Gulag*, I: 249-50; Tolstoy, *Secret*, 406; U.S. Department of State, *Former Soviet Citizens*, 1, 3.

94. Deriabin and Gibney, *Secret World*, 99; Enquist, *Legionnaires*, 448-49; Romanov, *Nights*, 173.

95. Feifer, *Moscow Farewell*, 341.

96. *Prussian Nights*, 75.

9

THE PAWNS AND THE PARTY LINE:

"Traitors" Turned "Resistance Fighters"

THOUGH CLEARLY NOT ENOUGH TO REJUVENATE the likes of George Feifer's sad beggar in *Moscow Farewell*, the party line on repatriation and Soviet citizens abroad did evolve in the postwar era away from its original, rigidly Stalinist formulation. And the stages of reevaluation neatly paralleled the changes in Soviet leadership: in Stalin's last decade—obscure, infrequent references to displacement and military collaboration, and virtual silence on the reception afforded returners; with the dictator's death in 1953 and the rise of Nikita Khrushchev—substantial shifts in the handling of these subjects, including massive attention to Soviet resistance abroad and publicly acknowledged amnesties for repatriates in labor camps; and after Khrushchev's fall in 1964—less dramatic but nevertheless significant alterations in the handling of sensitive, refugee-related issues.

From the end of the war to 1953 practically nothing appeared in the Soviet Union for popular view that shed any real light on repatriation. In 1944 and 1945 Moscow did allow General Filip Golikov to recite statistics in public, but these declarations skirted sensitive issues such as punishment for returners.[1] The Kremlin also approved four pamphlets and books between 1945 and 1949 dealing directly with repatriation; however, they addressed not the home population but nonreturners in the West.[2] A volume of the second edition of *Bol'shaia sovetskaia entsiklopediia* published in 1953 made a passing reference to the subject in an article on the Crimean Conference but did not elaborate.[3] And, as detailed earlier, the Soviet Union under Stalin regularly denounced the West for noncompliance with the Yalta exchange accord and launched a barrage of unfounded stories about the United States and Britain holding Soviet citizens against their will.

Sergei Mikhalkov's 1949 play, *Ia khochu domoi!* [I Want to Go Home!], a perfect example of such fabrication, had the Western Allies forcibly restraining Soviet orphans from returning to their native land. In the final episode young Sasha Butuzov escaped his Western captors and dramatically gained Red Army lines in eastern Germany.[4] This fantastic story, which in maudlin fashion turned history squarely on its head, one Western writer labeled "crudely sentimental"; but in Moscow's view Mikhalkov's effort demonstrated "the greatness and power of our country which never forgets its children and is able to stick up for its own."[5]

While interpretations of the piece inevitably differ, all agree it received a great deal of attention in the Soviet Union, more, it appears, than any other work dealing with repatriation under Stalin. The play, a tortured, hopelessly distorted version of the predicament of Soviet citizens abroad, premiered in Moscow's Central Children's Theatre 22 March 1949. It played to large and approving audiences in the capital, while a later film adaptation, entitled *U nikh est' Rodinu* [They Have a Homeland], reached millions of viewers in Russia and, so a Soviet source claims, abroad as well.[6]

Apart from extremely circumscribed, even spurious approaches like Mikhalkov's, journalists, academicians, and literary artists avoided, or were told to avoid, the topics of displacement and repatriation lest they raise awkward and embarrassing issues—the extent of military collaboration and the punishment of millions of returners being chief among them. What went unexplored under Stalin is glaringly evident, sometimes in the footnotes and bibliographies of later works. For themes related to Soviet citizens abroad and their return, studies by E. A. Brodskii, Mikhail I. Semiriaga, and G. A. Kumanev illustrate the point. In 1965 Brodskii produced the first full-length academic monograph on the Soviet resistance movement outside Russia; yet this volume, which regularly includes in its documentation correspondence from participants to the author, cites no letter dated earlier than 1956, with the bulk dated 1957 or later.[7] The most nearly definitive study published in the U.S.S.R. on Soviet involvement in resistance movements throughout Europe is Mikhail Semiriaga's *Sovetskie liudi v evropeiskom soprotivlenii* [Soviet People in the European Resistance]. Still this volume, well researched considering the obstacles placed on historians by party guidelines, includes in its bibliography not a single Soviet title published prior to Stalin's death, while most of the works cited bear 1960s imprints.[8] And while a bibliographical essay on the same subject by G. A. Kumanev contains titles published under Stalin, the vast majority of these do not address the resistance activites of Soviet citizens but rather German crimes against the same. Kumanev even says, straight out, "Until recent times Soviet historiography did not have at its disposal research in which was reflected the liberation struggle of Soviet patriots in fascist Germany."[9]

Stalin excluded not just questions of displacement but a whole host of war-related issues from more than superficial examination. He rightly feared that thorough investigations might prove embarrassing to the regime and to himself, open discussions possibly triggering a volley of negative judgments of the party's, maybe even his own, war leadership. An old man eaten up with suspicions could see such permissiveness as leading only to disaster. Consequently, between 1945 and 1952 only two overall treatments of the Nazi-Soviet war appeared: one book and a seventy-one-page pamphlet. In the same period twenty-one monographs and tracts sufficed to cover individual military operations. Apart from the equally sparse serial literature, that accounted for the total output of eight years of Soviet academic publication concerning the most costly war in the history of the Russian state. As a result World War II historiography published in the U.S.S.R. has had to speak repeatedly of *maloissledovannyi*, "under-researched" topics, a euphemism for the myriad of longtime taboo subjects. [10]

A central theme bearing indirectly on repatriation that became enshrined even before the war's end stressed Red Army soldiers fighting to the last bullet and the last breath. The military codes, cited earlier, made it abundantly clear to the troops that capture by the enemy made them traitors no matter what the circumstances. And nothing during the war indicated any different. War correspondent Alexander Poliakov informed his readers, in a 1942 recounting of the Red Army's first twelve months of exploits, that *Russians Don't Surrender*. Although the book's major focus was a year's worth of encirclement and breakout, the uninitiated reader could hardly guess that the Wehrmacht was mauling Soviet forces at the time, so prominent and jaundiced are the nonstop heroics of Russian warriors. [11]

Poliakov briefly alluded to harsh punishment for cowards and deserters, but the Krasnodar and Khar'kov war crimes trials of July and December 1943 went further with the open acknowledgment that Soviet citizens were aiding and abetting the Germans in occupied territory. Embarrassing as it was to the party line on the undivided wartime solidarity of the Soviet peoples, the Kremlin nevertheless took the unusual step of advertising the hanging of eight convicted Soviet collaborators at Krasnodar and one at Khar'kov as a warning to all those still behind enemy lines. [12]

But the Soviet media did not dwell on treason trials long, what with their disconcerting evidence of disloyalty to the socialist motherland. More commonly they held up models of heroism for those in various sectors of the military effort. For patriots in enemy hands the expected behavior included nothing less than intense, perpetual resistance no matter what the odds or personal consequences. In Mikhail Romm's 1944 film, *Girl 217*, the heroine is a slave worker brutalized by a German household.

Tanya revolts and wreaks vengeance on the family by slaying its two soldier sons home on leave. The incident that best typifies the tale's compatibility with the party line and its incompatibility with historical probability is Girl 217's successful escape from Germany on a POW transport bound *for* Russia. [13]

Petr Vershigora's *Liudi s chistoi sovest'iu* [People with a Clear Conscience], which first appeared serially in *Znamia* [The Banner] in 1945-46, stands out as one of the few publications of Stalin's last decade to treat the theme of wartime disloyalty. This war reportage of partisan fighting in the Ukraine and Belorussia provides intermittent glimpses of turncoats, but each one portrayed is presented as an aberration definitely out of the mainstream. [14] In contrast, the usual literary fare in Stalinist renderings of the war perferred not to even hint at the possibility of disloyalty. The short novel *Zvezda* [Star] by Emmanuil Kazakevich, Stalin Prize winner in 1947, was more typical in portraying a surrounded Soviet reconnaissance patrol fighting to the death rather than surrendering. [15]

With the advent of Nikita Khrushchev, de-Stalinization, and somewhat less shackling censorship, questions of wartime displacement and repatriation began to receive more attention and to be viewed in a different light. In 1944 the Tatar poet Musa Dzhalil' had died in Nazi captivity uncompromised; but just after the war Moscow had branded him "an enemy of the people." Only in 1954, after Stalin's death, was he rehabilitated and his patriotic prison verse published. [16] Still, of all the postwar years, 1955, more than any other, witnessed demonstrable shifts in official attitudes and actions toward those who had seen the outside world. For one, a 1955 volume of *Bol'shaia sovetskaia entsiklopediia* differed in its definition of repatriation significantly from earlier formulations. It did follow the wording of a 1939 Soviet dictionary closely, but a seemingly minor amplification—to be underlined in the following quotation—heralded a genuine alteration in the Soviet regime's approach to the subject: "Repatriation 1) The return of emigrants to the country of their origin *with the restoration of their legal citizenship.* 2) The return home of prisoners of war and displaced persons who found themselves outside their countries as a result of the war." [17] The Soviet government during Stalin's lifetime made direct promises to DPs much more comprehensive than a mere restoration of legal citizenship. But this hint at accommodation, never before presented to the population at large, in effect signaled that returners no longer were to be regarded as pariahs. Moscow now began to go beyond empty assurances, demonstrating by concrete acts the reality of its less vindictive attitude toward repatriates.

In 1955 a repatriated POW, General Mikhailov, became the head of a new Soviet Committee for the Return to the Homeland, a development that would have been inconceivable under Stalin. Moreover, Mikhailov's organization reversed years of virulent Russian insistence upon unconditional, forced repatriation by vouchsafing at least its public support for the principle of voluntary return.[18]

Another change of policy in 1955, the Soviet Union's decision to extend diplomatic recognition to West Germany, related indirectly to repatriation. In the negotiations the Bonn government refused to consider seriously diplomatic relations without Moscow's agreement to return the remaining German POWs held in Soviet labor camps. For its part the Kremlin maintained that the German Federal Republic held 100,000 Soviet war refugees against their will. In September 1955, in talks with Chancellor Konrad Adenauer, the Soviet Union's titular prime minister, Nikolai Bulganin, failed to get a German commitment to repatriate Soviet citizens abroad; nor could he budge Adenauer from his insistence upon repatriation of German POWs. Despite Bonn's refusal to compromise on these specific issues the protocol of 13 September of the Adenauer-Bulganin talks announced that the two countries had agreed to exchange ambassadors. And without compromising the Soviet diaspora's right of political asylum, the West Germans secured the release of 10,000 Wehrmacht POWs still in the Soviet Union.[19]

On 17 September 1955, the U.S.S.R. declared an amnesty for Soviet citizens who, during the war years, had collaborated with "hostile occupation forces."[20] In explaining its rationale Moscow did not include what must have been one factor: its desire to dispense with the incongruity of Germans leaving Siberia while their Soviet collaborators stayed put with twenty- and twenty-five-year sentences.[21] The text of the amnesty, instead, stressed loftier considerations: "After the victorious conclusion of the Great Patriotic War Soviet people obtained large new successes in all areas of economic and cultural development and the further strengthening of the socialist state. Bearing this in mind, and also the cessation of the condition of war between the Soviet Union and Germany and the guiding principle of humanism, the Presidium of the Supreme Soviet of the U.S.S.R. grants an amnesty." Those to benefit were Soviet nationals who aided the Nazis "through weakness or thoughtlessness."[22] Article 3 specifically included Soviet citizens who had served in the German army. Article 7 promised amnesty to émigrés guilty of a variety of offenses, one of which, revealingly, was simply surrender to the enemy. More understandable as a crime, at any rate from Moscow's perspective, was expatriate involvement in anti-Soviet organizations. Even this, so the document read, no longer figured against those willing to return to their native land. In the same vein the amnesty promised a restoration of citizenship to all Soviet citizens abroad who agreed to come home, an identical fillip to that

laid out in the 1955 *Bol'shaia sovetskaia entsiklopediia* article on repatriation.[23]

As Nikolai Krasnov noted, the amnesty made no difference to the wary
Soviet diaspora unwilling to dispense with its healthy distrust of Kremlin
promises; but for persons like himself who thereby gained their freedom,
it was a restoration to life.[24] While this decree, which at the very least
ended the confinement of hundreds of thousands of repatriates, by no
means ended the regime's arbitrariness and oppressiveness, it did provide
the most indisputable sign of 1955 that the grossest injustices and excesses
of the Stalinist period would henceforth be the exception rather than the
rule.

Five months after the amnesty decree, Khrushchev made an even more
decisive break with the past in his famous "secret speech," delivered at
the Twentieth Congress of the Communist Party of the U.S.S.R. In the
last hour of 24 February 1956, and the wee hours of the 25th, he denounced Stalin's "cult of the individual," his purge of innocent party
members, and his inadequacy as a military leader. Freedom of speech did
not result because a new party secretary roundly condemned a hitherto
sacrosanct leader. It did, however, become easier after the pronouncements of the Twentieth Party Congress for the Soviet media, and individual academicians, to treat a whole range of topics previously off limits,
including many sensitive questions relating to World War II. Military historian Seweryn Bialer noted, "After Stalin's death in 1953 and, more
specifically after Khrushchev's disclosure in 1956 of Stalin's alleged wartime errors, there was a rapid increase and far-reaching qualitative improvement in Soviet writing on the war period." In 1958 a major Soviet
journal devoted exclusively to military history began publication. And
from its outset *Voenno-istoricheskii zhurnal* [Military-Historical
Journal] has seen the explication of the "Great Patriotic War" as a primary function. Also the publication of military memoirs and memoir ex-
tracts burgeoned under Stalin's successors. Only a smattering of war reminiscences appeared in 1956–57, but by 1967 the number had increased to
more than 150 books and hundreds of articles. And whereas less than 100
nonfiction works dealing with the war made their way into print in the
entire period from 1945 to Stalin's death, Soviet presses turned out over
750 titles on this subject in 1973 alone.[25]

The start of Khrushchev's de-Stalinization campaign also served as an
unmistakable watershed in Soviet attitudes toward displacement and repatriation. This showed itself in gestures like belated military decorations
for ex-POWs and public reunions of former Soviet participants in European partisan movements; in nonfiction accounts; and in novels and short
stories. After the war Moscow had condemned Musa Dzalil' as "an

enemy of the people" even though he had been killed in captivity by the Germans. However, in 1956 he received posthumously the nation's title of honor for wartime bravery, "Hero of the Soviet Union."[26] In 1957 Mikhail Deviataev, who had led a band of POWs out of captivity aboard a commandeered Nazi plane, received from the Soviet government not only the honorific "Hero of the Soviet Union" but the Order of Lenin, the Gold Star, and an invitation from the Soviet Committee of War Veterans to meet in Moscow with other ex-Sachsenhausen inmates.[27] As with honors and decorations, descriptions of public reunions of Nazi captives-turned-resistance fighters became a fixture in the U.S.S.R.'s historical literature only after the start of de-Stalinization.[28]

Soviet scholars found a politically acceptable way to explore in print the question of Soviet citizens abroad by downplaying or ignoring collaboration with the Nazis and stressing instead the participation of Soviet forced laborers and POWs in European resistance movements. Moscow found this approach perfectly acceptable, since it served to strengthen the myth of the wartime loyalty of all Soviet peoples. E. A. Brodskii set precedent in 1957 with an article in the leading Soviet historical journal, *Voprosy istorii*, entitled "The Struggle for Liberation among Soviet People in Fascist Germany (1939-1945)." The author rejected the Stalinist formula of automatic condemnation for persons falling into enemy hands and expressed sympathy for the plight and admiration for the fortitude of those who "found themselves" in German camps.[29]

Even Brodskii's grammatical structure—Soviet citizens abroad being the object rather than the agent of the action—seemed to point to his belief that displacement resulted from forces beyond the control of individual DPs or POWs. They had not willingly forsaken their native land, and therefore, he implied, they should not be held accountable for unavoidable surrender or forcible deportation to Germany. In praising the patriotic resistance of Soviet nationals in Nazi captivity, Brodskii thus contributed to the removal of the pall of suspicion that surrounded every repatriate since the end of the war. Making the most of the opportunity presented by his newly fashioned investigative niche, Brodskii has made a career out of the explication of the theme of Soviet patriotism in German captivity. He has lectured widely and written extensively on the subject, always sticking close to his original, publishable approach. He has developed the theme in articles printed in 1957, 1962, and 1966; in a 1965 monograph treating south Germany, derived from his 1964 doctoral dissertation; and in 1970 in an expanded, more comprehensive study of Soviet resistance throughout Germany.[30]

Many journals and researchers followed suit in the enterprise, indeed the industry, of *Soprotivleniia* [resistance] writing, with the incidental result of a refurbished image for at least a portion of repatriates. Besides Brodskii's groundbreaking work, 1957 also saw the publication of a collection of documents detailing the patriotic feats of the Russian underground in Buchenwald concentration camp,[31] and the first joint Soviet–East German historical conference on the European resistance movements met in Leningrad.[32]

Early post-Stalinist works on Soviet resistance activities in Europe provided academics and memoirists with the parameters for permissible approaches to the sensitive issues of displacement and repatriation, limits that held constant throughout Khrushchev's tenure with only slight modifications. To be sure, historical accounts continued to look past the hostile reception and punishment given returners: the collection of Buchenwald memoirs gave the current occupation of thirteen of sixteen resistance leaders but did not mention how they fared between 1945 and the 1955 amnesty.[33] But the investigation of questions like wartime displacement, even if under the awkward guise of Soviet participation in European anti-Fascist movements, did at least open up topics heretofore unexplored or "under-researched." The momentum of 1955-57 carried through Khrushchev's years in power. In 1958-59 journal articles appeared on patriotic Soviet activities in various Nazi camps; a provincial publishing house printed a compilation of revelations by German concentration camp survivors; and a major Moscow political press published the book-length memoirs of a former repatriation official.[34]

All these articles and books indicated, either explicitly or implicitly, a subtle softening of the party line on wartime displacement and repatriation. But, with the exception of Aleksei Bruikhanov's informative semi-memoir, semimonograph, none of these works demonstrated the shift away from unqualified denunciation of returners as clearly as a 1959 compilation, *War behind Barbed Wire, Reminiscences of Buchenwald Ex-Prisoners of War*. While the editor, F. Solasko, greatly understated the number of Soviet soldiers taken prisoner by the Germans—it was more like millions than hundreds of thousands—he did declare without reservation that these men "had requited themselves with honour on the battlefields" and had been "taken prisoner through no fault of their own." Furthermore, "it is not easy to be a hero at the front; it is more difficult still to be one in captivity. Many books and articles have been written about the horrors of Nazi POW camps. The horrible in these books has only too often eclipsed the heroic. We are now beginning to see these things in their proper perspective."[35] This compassion and sympathy for persevering Red Army POWs Stalin would have branded as pro-Fascist and treasonous. But under Khrushchev a somewhat more discriminating and positively less punitive approach toward repatriates became the norm.

The autobiographical sketches of Solasko's compilation also demonstrate that it had become standard practice by the end of the 1950s to portray Soviet citizens abroad as model freedom fighters, whose bravery and steadfastness heartened native resistance movements throughout occupied Europe. For example, *Voprosy istorii* published an article in March 1960, which boasted that the activities of POWs and civilians deported to France from Russia "exhibited to millions of Frenchmen the condition of man when educated by society and freed for good from exploitation and class oppression." Those men, misnamed *untermenschen* by the Germans, who did not escape and join the French partisans, were said to have devoted themselves to the task of sabotaging the Nazi war economy: "In each mine where there were only Soviet people, a diversionary group operated which put machines out of action" and carried out other "acts of mass sabotage." Undaunted by the risks, these fearless anti-Fascists somehow even managed to print underground newsheets such as "Return from the Camps" and "Soviet Patriot."[36]

Publications of the post-Stalinist era stereotyped Soviet citizens abroad as paragons of socialist virtue who, while the war lasted, had had thoughts for nothing other than rejoining their countrymen in the struggle against Nazism. One captured Red Army pilot, who regained Soviet territory by commandeering a German plane, wrote in 1960 what Stalin's successors accept as the typical attitude of a patriot in enemy hands. "Homeland: What is there that is dearer to a Soviet man or woman! During all the days and months in Nazi captivity, we lived only with one dream—to return to our own Soviet land, and we did our utmost to hasten the hour."[37] And again, "The Communist party which was with us, inspired us in the struggle with the enemy [and] pointed out the path to victory. Only because of this was it possible for us to fly from fascist captivity to our Homeland."[38]

These patriotic paeans served Kremlin propagandists not only by stressing supposed popular loyalty and gratitude to the Communist party for its leadership role in the struggle against Fascism but also by reiterating the spurious theme of common wartime devotion and solidarity among all Soviet nationalities: on board the commandeered German airship en route to Soviet lines were representatives of the Russian, Ukrainian, "Siberian," Belorussian, Kazakh, Tatar, Uzbek, and Georgian peoples. Many captive Soviet nationals did remain loyal to their country and did refuse to collaborate with the Germans—only to be thoroughly shocked at the hostile reception accorded repatriates. Warm approbation for escapees under Khrushchev and his successors, like that given the airmen of *Flight to Freedom*, hardly squares with Roy Medvedev's account of three other captured pilots who managed to regain Soviet lines. They came home not to bear hugs and decorations but to a typically Stalinist reception: arrest, interrogation, and ten-year prison terms.[39]

After 1953 historical studies and memoirs treating displacement and repatriation improved in some respects but, like their Stalinist predecessors, remained badly skewed overall. In contrast, various bits and pieces of fiction under Khrushchev made more headway. After Stalin's death, in war novels and short stories touching upon these themes, extenuating circumstances acceptable in the eyes of the new leaders began to surface: those who returned from abroad no longer had to be ignored or treated as scoundrels. In fact, with the party line adopting the notion that returners had been patriots in captivity and had been welcomed home as such, the more tolerant approach of Khrushchev's years was well served, but the facts of their brutal reception under Stalin were badly obscured. The resulting literary products thus combined greater truthfulness than Stalin had allowed on POWs' loyalty to their native land. Yet at the same time these pieces perpetrated gross distortions of the homecoming afforded repatriates, a subject so politically delicate that writers under Stalin usually had opted simply to pass over it in silence.

By far the best-known work illustrating these divergent trends ran in *Pravda* in 1957 under the title *Sud'ba cheloveka* [Fate of a Man].[40] The author, Mikhail Sholokhov, relates the poignant tale of a hard luck soldier from Voronezh. Andrei Sokolov lost to the German invaders not only his freedom but his home, his wife, and all his children. After the war this grieving ex-POW and ex-father took up with a homeless waif who had lost every bit as much. The well-told story is touching, perfectly consistent with the notion of millions of refugees caught between the likes of Hitler and Stalin: "Two orphans, two grains of sand swept into strange parts by the tremendous hurricane of war." In 1963 an American critic of Soviet literature praised the piece as "a powerful and tender treatment of the resilience of human love under adversity." "Utterly unpretentious in its manner," he added, "Sholokhov's story is one of the best things in recent Soviet writing."[41]

For all its sad beauty and flashes of truth *Fate of a Man* still bears the strong imprint of historical distortions imposed by the party line. Nothing demonstrates this better than the aftermath of the escape episode, where Sholokhov's rendering of the hero's welcome home is patently artificial. Upon reaching Red Army lines in German uniform, Sokolov quickly overcame initial confusion as to his identity and went on to a glorious reunion with his countrymen. All the first day he received food, a bath, a new uniform, handshakes from solicitous officers, a recommendation for a decoration, even a buss from a division commander! The closest the story comes to hinting that a man returning from behind enemy lines might not have it so easy is a vaguely worded but suggestive passage: "No, it's not an easy thing to understand, mate, it's not easy to understand that you've got taken prisoner through no fault of your own. And it takes time to explain to a fellow who's never felt it on his own hide, just what that thing means." Still, the reception Sholokhov constructs is unabashedly contrived from first to last. According to the author, Sokolov received his fine welcome even though he had served as a chauffeur for a German major overseeing road and defense construction.[42] Contrast that to the real fate of a Russian driver in service to the Nazis who was tried with three Germans in the Khar'kov war crimes trial of December 1943. Along with his co-defendants, he got the gallows.[43]

A short story in a Russian émigré journal comes closer to the mark than Sholokhov, at least on the subject of rewards for repatriates. The author, Varlam Shalamov, has another Russian POW chauffeur make a successful break for Red Army lines only to be arrested, charged with attempted espionage, and given a twenty-five-year term in Kolyma, Siberia. Considering the sensitivity of the subject, even twelve years after the war, Sholokhov's *Fate of a Man* had played it safe with only one hint of treason: the German camp commandant spoke excellent Russian with "a bit of a Volga accent, as if he'd been born and bred in those parts."[44] Sholokhov had increased his story's prospects for publication, if not its authenticity, by never baring the truth that in reality wartime Soviet authorities would have branded even his hero Sokolov a traitor.

As a rule, under Stalin fiction had bypassed the fact that repatriates underwent rough handling and sorting. Emmanuil Kazakevich published one such novel entitled *Vesna na Odere* [Spring on the Oder]. This Stalin Prize winner of 1949 had Soviet troops embracing liberated Ostarbeiter and POWs with kisses and tears all around. But the reunions carried not a hint of screening commissions, interrogations, or summary punishments for treason.[45] However, with de-Stalinization came the first hints in fictional literature that returners had not been dealt with in a reasonable manner. Konstantin Simonov's *Zhivye i mertvye* [The Living and the Dead], which first appeared serially in *Znamia* in 1959, gave cautious but clear signals that the inhospitable reception that hit Soviet citizens returning from abroad had been unwarranted. Although the novel deals only with the first seven months of the Nazi-Soviet conflict, its criticism of the oppressive suspiciousness of Stalin's Russia casts a direct light upon postwar repatriation. Against tremendous odds, Serpilin, one of the book's two major characters, leads a band of men out of German encirclement. Like the returners of 1945, Soviet authorities treat them not as heroes but as deserters or worse. They lose their weapons, and the secret police whisk them off to a special camp, where interrogators subject them to close screening.[46]

In a short story, also printed in 1959, Sergei Voronin made an even more daring venture into the dangerous terrain of wartime displacement and repatriation. "V rodnykh mestakh" [In His Native Village], published in the Leningrad literary magazine *Neva*, has a former soldier in Vlasov's army ensconced in his home town undetected and un-punished. What is worse—from the perspective of Soviet literary critics and party ideologues—Voronin is content to let the hero of the story, who knows the truth, pass over the crime and let sleeping dogs lie.[47] The chief editor of *Literaturnaia gazeta*, Sergei Smirnov, indignantly attacked this handling of a collaborator repatriate for its "saccharine tone of Christian all-forgiveness about the fortunes of an accomplice of the enemy" and its "attempt to slobber mawkishly over the 'affliction' of a 'Vlasovite.' "[48] The next year Vsevolod Kochetov's *Brat'ia Ershovy* [The Brothers Ershov] suggested circumspectly the possibility of a military col-laborator's rehabilitation. But in contrast to Voronin's unpunished Vla-sovite, Kochetov's turncoat at least redeemed himself by means of a term of imprisonment.[49]

From 1961 to 1964, the year of Khrushchev's fall, censors continued to permit statements on the themes of displacement and repatriation that would not have been tolerated under Stalin. In 1961 the premier of Gre-gory Chukrai's *Clear Skies* deeply touched Moscow moviegoers with its vivid contrast of "the honor and suffering of Soviet prisoners of war with the brutality of the system which suspected and humiliated them in the post-war period." James Billington, who penned this description of the film, reported the viewing public's response to be "an emotional demon-stration of approval." And a Belorussian, Vasilii Bykau, found room in *Alpine Ballad*, a 1964 escape thriller featuring a deeply patriotic Russian POW and his admiring Italian POW lover, to intone, "People . . . should not vent their spite on prisoners, whose capture is not their fault but their misfortune."[50]

In the same vein *Novyi mir* published a short story by Alexander Solzhenitsyn in 1963 that demonstrated the unreasonable harshness used in "processing" repatriates. Ex-actor Igor Dementyevich Tveritinov, who had escaped German encirclement only to end up on a transport bound for a Soviet detention camp, became separated from his train in this "Incident at Krechetovka Station." The story's railroad dispatcher, Lieutenant Vasil Vasilich Zotov, sympathized with this bedraggled stranger who asked him for help, but finally chose to arrest him rather than to take a chance on a man without papers. Zotov hoped the security police would go easy on the likeable Tveritinov, but he could take no comfort in the icy response he got to inquiries about the actor's fate: "Your Tverikin's been sorted out all right. We don't make mistakes."[51] In "Matryona's House," published by *Novyi mir* simultaneously with

"The Incident at Krechetovka Station," Solzhenitsyn even managed an allusion to voluntary nonreturners abroad, to this day a rarity in Soviet publications.[52]

But by far the best-known work of the Khrushchev period, with a kindly portrait of an imprisoned repatriate, was Solzhenitsyn's *One Day in the Life of Ivan Denisovich*, published serially in 1962, also in *Novyi mir*.[53] This short novel, upon which Khrushchev passed judgment personally, created a sensation with its frank portrayal of the institutionalized inhumanity of Stalinist concentration camps. One Moscow book dealer, allotted only ten copies, had a waiting list of 1,200 by the end of the first day's distribution. After only two days on the market 94,900 copies had been sold.[54] Again, the regime's boundless suspiciousness did its damage to the novel's hero, Ivan Denisovich Shukhov. Guilty of nothing except fighting his way out of German encirclement, he nevertheless was condemned to forced labor for treason: "And it's true he gave evidence against himself and said he'd surrendered to the enemy with the intention of betraying his country, and came back with instructions from the Germans. But just what he was supposed to do for the Germans neither Shukhov nor the interrogator could say. So they just left it at that and put down: 'On instructions from the Germans.' "[55]

It is doubtful that Khrushchev held any personal sympathy for the millions of repatriates undeservedly punished under Stalin; still, controlled revelations of his predecessor's mistakes and crimes, on this as well as a host of other issues, served a purpose. The reason for tolerating expressions of returners' grievances in the publications of Solzhenitsyn, as in those of Sholokhov, Simonov, Voronin, Kalinin, and Bykau, was to mollify volatile political undercurrents in the country by channeling criticism in ways that would spare the present leadership the responsibility for past excesses.

Fictional and nonfictional treatments of displacement and repatriation broke new ground under Leonid Brezhnev and Aleksei Kosygin, particularly several publications of 1965 and 1966. *"Political Refugees" Unmasked*, released in 1965 by the Latvian State Publishing House, hammered away at the reactionary nature of émigré political organizations, as would be expected; but it also took the unprecedented step of extending to nonreturners the forgive-and-forget attitude formulated under Khrushchev. Whereas it had been customary to brand all nonreturners as traitors to the motherland, this publication, instead, stated: "The majority of Latvians abroad, just like other peoples of good-will, struggle for a lasting peace. . . . The émigrés in various countries abroad endured hardship when they were in their homeland, due to the Nazi war of expansion. . . . They have surmounted . . . anti-Soviet propaganda, and now strengthen ties with their homeland. . . . They come as tourists, go back and tell their children all they saw, and teach them to love their native country."[56]

Thus, by 1965 the party line on wartime displacement had evolved to the point that not only ex-POWs and former forced laborers but also those who had consciously chosen not to return home could be treated with understanding. It was a marked contrast from the days when Stalin's overriding distrust of everyone adversely affected all returning POWs and war refugees.

By this point new variations also surfaced on the theme of Soviet captives' wholehearted, patriotic resistance to the enemy. In 1965 Moscow's approved writers outdid themselves elaborating this basically unhistorical notion. One author quoted poetry to the effect that escape had been forever uppermost in prisoners' minds:

> He for whom the battle is not ended,
> Will not say to the enemy "forgive,"
> In the most difficult situation,
> He will be able to find wings.[57]

One account claimed an incredible 24 to 28 percent of all Soviet citizens forcibly taken to France had managed to join the partisans.[58] Another historian indulged in patently untruthful glorification of the millions of POWs and Ostarbeiter abroad: "The Soviet people who found themselves in foreign countries during the grim years of the war displayed inextinguishable love for their socialist homeland and fathomless faith in the righteousness of their cause."[59]

But after Khrushchev's fall by far the most arresting new tack in the party line, as it touched on Soviet citizens formerly in German hands, came out of a 1965 historical conference in Moscow convened to discuss anti-Fascist resistance movements. Academician Miron I. Kochiashvili detailed, in approving terms, the resistance struggle of ex–Red Army Georgians, *who had fought in German ranks in Western Europe.* This altogether surprising address was the first high-profile public acknowledgment in the U.S.S.R. that even military collaborators—traitors by any Soviet definition—could have maintained their love for their homeland and deserved a sympathetic hearing.[60]

Kochiashvili, on an uncharted course fraught with danger for the incautious scholar, took great pains at every turn to justify the actions of his incongruous collaborator-resisters. He argued that the "Hitlerites" had used "violent means" to force Soviet Georgian POWs into Wehrmacht ranks. Furthermore, these allegedly unwilling turncoats had covertly aided the Polish underground; escaped in droves to the French and Italian partisans after their shipment westward; made contact with the Dutch Communist party after another transfer; and, finally, staged a full-fledged insurrection against the Germans on Holland's Texel island.[61]

Finally, in 1966 Iurii Piliar's memoir, *Liudi ostaiutsia liu'dmi* [People (Still) Remain People], presented not so much a departure from the precedents of the Khrushchev years as a reinforcement of a trend first encountered in the works of Simonov, Solzhenitsyn, and others published between 1959 and 1963—that of open discussion of the unjust punishment of repatriates. In this case the author had volunteered for active duty in December 1941, had been wounded and captured, and had participated actively in an international resistance organization in Mauthausen concentration camp. Moscow had rewarded Piliar for his model behavior in enemy hands with a ten-year term of forced labor in the Urals. The summary provided in the memoir's front note elliptically referred to his imprisonment following repatriation as one of his "new difficulties." However, in the text Piliar more bluntly refers to the homecoming given POWs like himself as a move "from German camps into Soviet camps."[62]

In literature the years since 1966 have seen the publication of additional material bearing upon displacement and repatriation. *Dve zimy i tri leta* [Two Winters and Three Summers], Fedor Abramov's 1968 novel of destitution in a remote, north Russian backwater, sees an ex-POW, Timofei Lobanov, return home to universal suspiciousness—until cancer arouses some sympathetic second thoughts among the villagers of Pekashino.[63] And Vladimir Bogomolov's "V Avguste sorok chetvertogo . . ." [In August 1944 . . .], a 1974 counterespionage adventure tale, has SMERSH units absolutely paranoid about the possibility of German spies filtering through their screening nets undetected.[64] But Soviet writers, for some time, had been sketching repatriation scenes quite similar to those of Abramov and Bogomolov.

Much the same lack of new ventures applies to post-1966 nonfiction bearing upon Soviet citizens abroad in World War II. Numerous articles and books expound on the topic of Soviet resistance activities in German-occupied Europe.[65] The only development on this front at all noteworthy has been the publication of two studies in 1970-71 that, from the Soviet point of view, provide the definitive treatments of the subject—Brodskii covering in detail Soviet anti-Fascist activities in Germany, and Semiriaga doing the same for all of Nazi-occupied Europe.[66]

The trouble with Moscow's abundant literature on Soviet aid to the European resistance movement, really from its 1957 watershed on, is not so much its factual errors and patent falsehoods—though these do abound; rather, the major fault lies in its nourishing the grossly misleading implication that Soviet POW and Ostarbeiter assistance to the anti-

Fascist cause made much difference. From a historian's perspective the results produced by the large Soviet research expenditure on this topic have been slight: the historical return simply has not merited the investment. But that is not the point. Moscow prizes Soviet resistance abroad as an ideologically acceptable schema that helps justify, by inference, the presence of millions of Russians, Ukrainians, and others outside the U.S.S.R. during the war and contributes to the myth of the Soviet peoples' solidarity in the face of Nazi aggression. The topic's explication in Soviet publications may not be objective history, but from the perspective of totalitarian mind-molders, it is objectively constructive propaganda.

To be sure, the European resistance movement proved to be a significant, debilitating force contributing to the Nazis' defeat. But the Soviet part in it, outside Russia's German-occupied territory, did lack substance. The statistics alone amply demonstrate how militarily inconsequential Soviet freedom fighters abroad really were. Kochiashvili has made much of an April 1945 uprising of impressed Soviet Georgians on the Dutch island of Texel: it involved all of 300 men.[67] Accounts published in the U.S.S.R. estimate 2,000 to 5,000 Soviet citizens joined the resistance movement in Italy—out of a total of 250,000 partisans there of all nationalities.[68] And Semiriaga's major study of European-wide Soviet resistance activity tallied no more than 40,000 partisans from the U.S.S.R. for the entire continent outside Russia.[69]

In strikingly dramatic contrast, approximately 1 million Soviet citizens fought in German ranks in World War II; and on that subject the Soviet Union is deathly silent. Adding to the huge disparity between the number of military collaborators and resistance participants is the fact that a great many, if not the majority, of Semiriaga's 40,000 Soviet partisans saw action only in the war's waning hours, after Germany's defeat was certain. A study by V. V. Zelenin, for instance, uncovered 2,000 Soviet resistance fighters in Yugoslavia as of March 1945, but only 400 Soviet partisans had been active there just the previous fall. And whatever modest damage Soviet citizens abroad were able to inflict upon their German persecutors, it amounted to very little compared to the tremendous boost captive labor provided the Axis war effort. There can be no denying that the use of millions of foreign workers and POWs (with Soviet citizens forming the largest single contingent) bolstered the German war economy significantly. Edward Homze, in his definitive study of this subject, noted that "by using foreigners in her factories and fields, Nazi Germany was able to draft thirteen million German men into the military services, which not only held out for years against overwhelming odds, but came very near to winning the war."[70]

As a result of the unwarranted emphasis placed on the resistance activity of Soviet citizens abroad, the literature on the subject from the U.S.S.R assists the Western researcher interested in wartime displacement and repatriation only indirectly and in ways unintended by its authors. It in no way proves the universality of active opposition among Soviet nationals in German hands; however, it does demonstrate amply that Moscow no longer tendered a blanket condemnation of the millions moved westward by irresistible forces. And Soviet war fiction occasionally has shifted even further by criticizing or implying criticism of the tragic plight of innocents who had managed to survive years of cruel German mistreatment only to return home to more of the same.

Thus modifications, usually subtle, have worked their way into Soviet historical and fictional accounts of wartime displacement and repatriation. And these shifts in the party line on Soviet citizens abroad have paralleled changes in Kremlin leadership rather closely. But Moscow's stance on two questions has not changed from Stalin's time down to the present: the Kremlin insists that the repatriation of war-displaced populations is an obligatory tenet of international law and that ex–Red Army General A. A. Vlasov was a despicable traitor. While the young Soviet state made numerous treaties specifying repatriation as an optional matter, since Stalin's time Moscow consistently has assumed the return home of POWs and refugees to be mandatory under international law.[71] A 1939 Soviet dictionary maintained that "prisoners, refugees, internees, and emigrants are subject to repatriation."[72] In 1953 a Russian legal reference work more forcefully and specifically declared that after a war's end "belligerent governments are obliged to carry out the unconditional repatriation of prisoners of war." The only exceptions were the seriously ill and those convicted of criminal offenses. Here it was contended that repatriation was obligatory, "according to the universally recognized norms of international law," a point reiterated in 1973 in the latest edition of the Soviet diplomatic dictionary.[73] Curiously, Soviet officials never saw these hallowed provisions as applicable to their own treatment of German and Japanese POWs. Whereas the United States and Britain repatriated the vast majority of Soviet citizens in the West, and most of these in a matter of months, the U.S.S.R. never released 1.5 to 2 million German POWs and 200,000 to 300,000 Japanese POWs (presumed dead) and took eleven years to repatriate those ex-Axis soldiers who did manage to survive the Gulag. Yet by not returning every last Soviet refugee the "detestable" Western Allies were said to be "trampling on their solemn international obligation" in an exhibition of "false humanitarianism."[74]

Moscow's virulent castigation of one specific repatriate, General Vlasov, also has remained rigidly and consistently firm to the present. On

Vlasovites, the expected condemnation occasionally has been tempered and diluted, but on Vlasov himself, never. From the moment the hero of the Battle of Moscow opted for active collaboration, Soviet propagandists painted him in the blackest of colors. It was said he had been a spy since 1936; had been a "Trotskyite"; and had deliberately engineered the destruction of his encircled Second Shock Army.[75]

Since the war Soviet publications have in no way altered this damning portrait of Stalin's former favorite. The one variation of any consequence has involved the degree of attention focused on Vlasov. For almost three decades, up to 1973, Moscow rarely permitted mention of the collaborator-general, even to blast him. In 1961 the second volume of a major history of the "Great Patriotic War" did blame the destruction of the Second Shock Army on his "cowardice and [criminal] negligence."[76] Occasionally, Soviet military memoirists have referred to Vlasov, in critical fashion of course.[77] And a very brief entry in a 1971 volume of *Bol'shaia sovetskaia entsiklopediia* did admit that Vlasov "went over to the Hitlerites after surrendering to the enemy in July 1942," for which, after repatriation, he paid with his life.[78]

Still, by far the most extended of the limited comments on Vlasov, up to 1973, came from the pen of Il'ia Ehrenburg. In his memoirs this Soviet writer recalled meeting the future collaborator in March 1942, just months before his capture in the Volkhov pocket. With the advantage of hindsight Ehrenburg dwelled on the general's faults, intermingling real ones with others he exaggerated or imagined. The memoirs read vanity into the general's fascination with the heroics of tsardom's General Suvorov. Furthermore, Ehrenburg deemed Vlasov theatrical to a fault and so ambitious as to be apolitical—not as much an ideological enemy of Soviet socialism as an irrepressible, conniving opportunist.[79]

Compared with other Soviet judgments of Vlasov published between 1945 and 1972, Ehrenburg's estimation of the general, in five pages no less, seems lengthy. But it pales in significance next to the flood of belated invective poured out on Vlasov in 1973-74. Undue attention to this ranking Red Army collaborator could have done extensive damage to the party line on wartime unity. Consequently, taking the dangerous course of publicizing his treason meant Moscow had perceived a serious threat to its monopoly on interpretations of Vlasov. In 1973 such a challenge did loom before the Kremlin in the person of Alexander Solzhenitsyn. The Nobel Prize winner published the first volume of his *Gulag Archipelago* that year, with one chapter devoted exclusively to the exorbitant, vengeful punishments meted out to repatriates, Vlasovites foremost.[80]

A. V. Tishkov's unprecedented, detailed recitation of Vlasov's trial, published in February 1973, preceded the release of the *Gulag* abroad.

However, the Kremlin probably knew of the manuscript before its publication and anticipated the bad publicity with this article entitled "A Traitor before the Soviet Court." Tishkov did not mention Solzhenitsyn by name but did roundly castigate "ideological opponents" of the U.S.S.R. who lauded the collaborator general as a "national hero" and his followers as " 'ideological warriors.' " Speaking openly and at length about the Soviet Union's premier traitor was such a novelty that Tishkov felt compelled to justify even a negative piece on the ex–Red Army commander: "in order to properly hate it is necessary to know the enemy."[81]

If any doubt lingers about the relationship of *The Gulag Archipelago* to the intensified vilification of Vlasov, it surely is dispelled by two 1974 polemics, *Solzhenitsyn's Archipelago of Lies* and *The Last Circle*. Here the *Gulag* is blasted as "one continuous chain of slander about our people, slander which has surpassed the wildest inventions of the Western Sovietologists."[82] In its counteroffensive against this expose of the Soviet penal system, Moscow has used Solzhenitsyn's sympathy for the plight of Vlasovites to declare him a traitor. The polemicists' reasoning is clear, if illogical, guilt by association: "Vlasov betrayed his people and his country. Solzhenitsyn has tried to glorify him and in doing so has also committed treason."[83] Soviet propagandists even invented a term for their newly manufactured brand of betrayal, calling Solzhenitsyn a "literary Vlasovite."[84]

The celebrated Russian writer made it easier for his enemies to defame him by not only decrying Soviet punishment of repatriated POWs, including Vlasovites, but by closely identifying with them; "beneath the domes of the brick-red Butyrki castle, I felt that the story of these several million Russian prisoners had got me in its grip once and for all, like a pin through a specimen beetle. My own story of landing in prison seemed insignificant. I stopped regretting my torn-off shoulder boards. It was mere chance that had kept me from ending up exactly where these contemporaries of mine had ended. I came to understand that it was my duty to take upon my shoulders a share of their common burden." As if that were not damaging enough, Soviet detractors could point out that Solzhenitsyn had even called these unfortunates "my own brothers."[85]

But it was not enough for these calumnies to equate sympathy for Vlasovites with treason; the wartime records of both Solzhenitsyn and Vlasov had to be rewritten to suit the party line. *Archipelago of Lies* attributes Captain Solzhenitsyn's arrest in February 1945 to "spreading slanderous rumours aimed at undermining the morale of Soviet troops." In fact his arrest and summary dispatch to the Gulag resulted from no more than a letter disparaging Stalin in veiled but identifiable terms. The same work blames the destruction of the Second Shock Army in 1942 on

Vlasov's "bungling," whereas in reality Stalin's refusal to permit a timely breakout and retreat had sealed the doom of Soviet troops in the Volkhov pocket.[86]

A Western audience might regard Soviet invectives leveled at Vlasov and Solzhenitsyn as ineffectual and unconvincing. But they strike Soviet readers, including even some opponents of the regime, differently. In Russia people commonly associate the term Vlasovite with military collaborators used by the Germans in merciless antipartisan warfare, a bloody role that in no way endeared those involved to the suffering population of occupied territories. Consequently, ordinary Soviet citizens consider Vlasovites and, by association, anyone the least bit sympathetic to them, to be the basest dregs of humankind. One defector who in time concluded that these collaborators had not always been perpetrators of atrocities nevertheless came to the West simultaneously hostile to the likes of Stalin and Vlasov.[87]

In conclusion, since Stalin's death Soviet leaders have permitted a reevaluation of displacement and repatriation, the emerging consensus being that the wartime Soviet dictator had been wrong in judging all POWs and DPs unreliable and had exacted too harsh a penalty on them. At the same time Moscow has tolerated no alterations in the accepted interpretation of General Andrei Vlasov, condemned to this day as a despicable traitor. Surprisingly, fictional accounts touching upon Vlasovites, as opposed to Vlasov, have stayed within the confines of what Kremlin censors will permit, yet have reached conclusions more lenient and generous toward repatriates than those accepted by the Soviet populace at large.

NOTES

1. Harriman to Secretary of State, 1 June 1945, NA RG 59, 740.00114EW/6-145.
2. Brychev, *Domoi, na rodinu*; R. Grygar'iants, *Vazhnaia dziarzhainaia zadacha* (Minsk, 1945); Nemirov, *Dorogi i vstrechi*; and *Otvety*. The second and fourth works were sponsored directly by the Soviet Repatriation Commission. Internal evidence makes it clear that the other two were also addressed to the émigré community.
3. "Krymskaia Konferentsiia, 1945," *Bol'shaia sovetskaia entsiklopediia*, 2nd ed., vol. 23 (1953), 547. The first edition did not carry an entry on repatriation and the publication of the second edition did not reach the R's until 1955. The 1953 volume may or may not have been released before the Soviet dictator's demise, but, at the very least, it is safe to say it passed Stalinist censorship.
4. G. Ershov and V. Tel'pugov, *Sergei Mikhalkov, Kritiko-biograficheskii ocherk* (Moscow, 1956), 89; Sergei Mikhalkov, *Sobranie sochinenii*, 2 (Moscow, 1963), 63-122.

5. Struve, *Russian Literature*, 369; Ershov and Tel'pugov, *Sergei Mikhalkov*, 90.

6. Ershov and Tel'pugov, *Sergei Mikhalkov*, 91; Bethell, *Secret*, 210.

7. *Zhivye boriutsia* (Moscow, 1965).

8. Moscow, 1970. In the same vein a 1959 article by N. F. Kiung and U. R. Talmant on Soviet resistance in German concentration camps cites no memoirs published before 1957: "Iz istorii dvizheniia soprotivleniia," 39-55.

9. "Sovetskaia istoriografiia," 267, 261-71. See also Andreas Hillgruber, "World War II" in *Marxism, Communism, and Western Society, a Comparative Encyclopedia*, ed. by C. D. Kernig (New York, 1973), VIII: 386; P. N. Pospelov *et al.*, *Istoriia velikoi otechestvennoi voiny sovetskogo soiuza, 1941-1945*, 6 (Moscow, 1965), 404.

10. Bialer, "Introduction, the Politics of Soviet War Literature," 16; Erickson, *Stalingrad*, 537.

11. New York, 1942. See also Struve, *Russian Literature*, 332.

12. Ginsburgs, "Laws of War," 263-64, 270; OSS, "Russian Intentions to Punish War Criminals," 27 June 1944, NA RG 59, R and A report no. 1988, p. 19.

13. Manvell, *Films*, 213-14.

14. *Znamia*, no. 8 (Aug. 1945), 21-108; no. 4 (Apr. 1946), 3-79; nos. 5-6 (May-June 1946), 24-97; no. 7 (July 1946), 7-62; no. 8 (Aug. 1946), 21-108. The hardback version was published in Moscow in 1946 while Moscow's Foreign Languages Publishing House released an English translation in 1949 under the title, *Men with a Clear Conscience*. For treatments of treason, see pp. 45-46, 92-93, 96-97, 213-21, 266-70. See also Struve, *Russian Literature*, 333-34. Vershigora was named a Hero of the Soviet Union and attained the rank of major general while his book earned a Stalin Prize in 1946.

15. Moscow, 1948. Moscow's Foreign Languages Publishing House produced an English translation in 1952.

16. Musa Dzhalil', *Iz Moabitskoi tetradi* (Moscow, 1954), 3; Medvedev, *Let History Judge*, 469.

17. B. M. Volin and D. N. Ushakov, *Tolkovyi slovar' russkogo iazyka*, 3 (Moscow, 1939), 1346; "Repatriatsiia," *Bol'shaia sovetskaia entsiklopediia*, 2nd ed., vol. 36 (1955), 394. See also ibid., 3rd ed., vol. 22 (1975), 34-35; "Repatriatsiia," *Diplomaticheskii slovar'*, 3 (Moscow, 1964), 53, and 3 (Moscow, 1973), 46.

18. Dallin and Mavrogordato, "Rodionov," 79; Ginsburgs, "Refugees," 359. For details of the moderately successful Armenian repatriation campaign of 1946-47, which may have served as a model for the 1955 drive, see Agasi A. Esaian, *Nekotorie voprosy sovetskogo grazhdanstva; voprosy naseleniia v praktike sovetskoi Armenii* (Erevan, 1966), 20; Ginsburgs, "Refugees," 347; SD to Soviet Embassy in Washington, 28 May 1947, *FR, 1947*, IV: 728-29; Walter Bedell Smith to Marshall, 1 July 1946, NA RG 59, 840.4016/ 7-146; Vernant, *Refugee*, 57.

19. Ivushkina, *Rodina*, 7; Keesing's, *Germany*, 114, 120.

20. Jane Perlberg Shapiro, "Rehabilitation Policy and Political Conflict in the Soviet Union, 1953-64" (Ph.D. diss., Columbia University, 1967), 61. See also Briukhanov, *Vot kak eto bylo*, 203; Dallin and Mavrogordato, "Soviet Reaction," 322; Zigurds L. Zile, "Amnesty and Pardon in the Soviet Union," *Soviet Union*, 3 (1976), 43. The complete text is printed in Ivushkina, *Rodina*, 3-6; and P. S. Romashkin, *Amnistiia i pomilivanie v SSSR* (Moscow, 1959), 75. Earlier amnesties in 1945 and 1953 did not measurably reduce the repatriate population of Soviet labor camps: Solzhenitsyn, *Gulag*, II: 188; Zile, "Amnesty," 43.

21. Solzhenitsyn, *Gulag*, III: 441-42.
22. Ivushkina, *Rodina*, 3. See also Romashkin, *Amnestiia*, 10.
23. Deriabin and Gibney, *Secret World*, 309; Ivushkina, *Rodina*, 3-6; V. S. Shevtsov, *Sovetskoe grazhdanstvo* (Moscow, 1965), 58.
24. Krasnov, *Hidden Russia*, 317. See also Bartoshevich and Borisoglebskii, *Imenem bog iegovy*, 110; Bauer, Inkeles, and Kluckhohn, *Soviet System*, 12; Bethell, *Secret*, 163; deWeerd, "Operation Keelhaul," 40; Enquist, *Legionnaires*, 471; Werth, *Russia at War*, 699.
25. Bialer, "Introduction, the Politics of Soviet War Literature," 16, 23; P. A. Zhilin, "Soviet Writings on Military History," *Social Sciences*, 6 (1975), 61.
26. Brodskii, "Geroicheskaia bor'ba," 141; Medvedev, *Let History Judge*, 469; N. A. Shokina *et al.*, *Geroi Velikoi Otechestvennoi Voiny. Rekomendatel'nyi ukazatel' literatury* (Moscow, 1970), 107-8; Solzhenitsyn, *First Circle*, 59. Shokina's annotated bibliography asserts that Lt. Gen. Dmitrii M. Karbyshev, who died in Mauthausen in 1945, received the same honor in 1946; however, none of the three books listed that treat this Hero appeared before 1961. If the 1946 date is indeed correct, then it is definitely out of keeping with Stalin's persistently negative attitude towards POWs. Shokina, *Geroi*, 106-7. In contrast, L'v Manevich, a Soviet partisan killed in action in Italy, lay in his grave twenty years before his belated designation as a "Hero of the Soviet Union": M. E. Kireeva *et al.*, *Velikaia pobeda; rekomendatel'nyi ukazatel' literatury o Velikoi Otechestvennoi Voine 1941-1945 gg* (Moscow, 1975), 176; Evgeniia Vorob'ev, *Zemlia, do vostrebovaniia* (Moscow, 1972), 748. See also the case of Vasilii V. Porik in Shokina, *Geroi*, 105.
27. Mikhail Deviataev, *Pobed iz ADA* (Saransk, 1963), 106, 110; Kireeva *et al.*, *Velikaia pobeda*, 113; Shokina, *Geroi*, 108; Yevstigneev, *Flight to Freedom*, 75, 81.
28. *Avengers*, 167; Deviataev, *Pobed*, 109; G. Nechaev, "Sovetskie liudi srazhalis' v Dordoni," *Voprosy istorii*, no. 10 (Oct. 1969), 197.
29. E. A. Brodskii, "Osvoboditel'naia bor'ba sovetskikh liudei v fashistskoi Germanii (1943-1945 gody)," *Voprosy istorii*, no. 3 (Mar. 1957), 85. Brodskii published another article that same year concentrating on organized Soviet resistance in south German POW and Ostarbeiter camps: "BSV," *Novyi mir*, no. 8 (Aug. 1957), 188-201. At least two earlier harbingers of this approach somehow managed to overcome Stalinist censors' aversion to war themes in general and Soviet citizens abroad in particular. But these exceptions to the rule enjoyed very limited exposure, one being an unpublished dissertation, and both originating in the provinces: Miron I. Kochiashvili, "Gruziny-partizany v Gollandii (Vosstanie na ostrove Teksel')," Candidate diss., Tbilisi University, 1949; and Nadezhda G. Tsvetkova, "900 dnei v fashistskikh zastenkakh," *Sovetskaia otchizna* (Minsk, 1949), no. 6. I was unable to locate copies of these studies for firsthand examination. Still, the approach of these authors may be evaluated in later, more readily accessible works: Kochiashvili, "Uchastie sovetskikh grazhdan-gruzin v dvizhenii soprotivleniia," 122-29; Nadezhda G. Tsvetkova, ed., *V fashistskikh zastenkakh; zapiski* (Minsk, 1958).
30. Brodskii, "BSV," 188-201; Brodskii, "Geroicheskaia bor'ba," 139-46; Brodskii, "Kommunisty vo glave osvoboditel'noi bor'by sovetskikh voennoplennykh v gitlerovskoi Germanii," *Voprosy istorii KPSS*, no. 3 (Mar. 1962), 79-93; Brodskii, "Osvoboditel'naia bor'ba," 85-99; Brodskii, *Vo imia*; Brodskii, *Zhivye boriutsia*; Kumanev, "Sovetskaia istoriografiia," 268.

31. "Bukhenval'dskoe soprotivlenie. (Dokumenty). Vvodnaia stat'ia I. F. Kiunga, T. A. Illeritskoi i B. G. Litvaka," *Istoricheskii arkhiv*, no. 4 (1957), 82-100; no. 6 (1957), 83-110.

32. Kumanev, "Sovetskaia istoriografiia," 265. Subsequent joint conferences met at Berlin in 1959 and 1969; with active Soviet participation, the first international conference on European resistance movements met in Milan in 1961. Ibid.; Brodskii, "Geroicheskaia bor'ba," 141. See Semiriaga, *Sovetskie liudi*, 328, for information on the Organization of Soviet Participants in the European Resistance and similar associations.

33. "Bukhenval'dskoe soprotivlenie," 106-9.

34. Valter' Bartel', "Sovmestnaia bor'ba Nemetskikh i sovetskikh bortsov soprotivleniia v Bukhenval'de," *Novaia i noveishaia istoriia*, no. 3 (May-June 1958), 139-54; Briukhanov, *Vot kak eto bylo*; Kiung and Talmant, "Iz istorii dvizheniia soprotivleniia," 39-55; Tsvetkova, *V fashistskikh zastenkakh*.

35. Solasko, *War behind Barbed Wire*, 5-6.

36. M. A. Kokorin and A. A. Strichkov, "O boevoi deiatel'nosti sovetskikh patriotov na territorii Frantsii v 1943-1944 godakh," *Voprosy istorii*, no. 3 (Mar. 1960), 101, 89, 100, 95. Further information concerning the newspapers can be found in "Russian Émigrés and Foreign Workers in France" (manuscript, Harry S. Truman Library, 1945), 9. Contributions in the 1960s to the hagiography of Western-based Soviet partisans also include A. I. Bruikhanov, M. K. Gavrilov, and N. A. Filatov, "Stranitsa istorii, zhdushchaia svoikh issledovatelei," *Voprosy istorii*, no. 2 (Feb. 1961), 209-12; A. Maslakov, "Soviet Fighters for the Liberation of Italy," *International Affairs*, no. 1 (Jan. 1960), 116-19; G. Nechaev, "Uchastie sovetskikh grazhdan v dvizhenii Soprotivleniia vo Frantsii v gody vtoroi mirovoi voiny," *Voenno-istoricheskii zhurnal*, no. 6 (June 1965), 37-50.

37. Yevstigneev, *Flight to Freedom*, 55. For an example of how this theme is presented to Soviet school children, see T. S. Golubeva and L. S. Gellershtein, *Rasskazy po istorii SSSR: dlia 4 klassa* (Moscow, 1972), 183-84.

38. Deviataev, *Pobed*, 112. See also M. P. Deviataev, *Polet k solntsu* (Moscow, 1972).

39. Deviataev, *Pobed*, 100; Medvedev, *Let History Judge*, 468.

40. Progress Publishers commissioned the English translation done by Robert Daglish. See also V. Borshchukov, "Voina v tvorchestve Sholokhova" in *Literatura velikogo podviga; Velikaia Otechestvennaia voina v sovetskoi literature*, ed. by A. Kogan and G. Solov'ev (Moscow, 1970), 370-71; Brown, *Soviet Russian Literature*, 173; S. Lochtin, "The War in the Soviet Novel. From the Heroic to the Prosaic," *Soviet Survey*, no. 33 (1960), 69; Luxenburg, "Solzhenitsyn," 1; Lev A. Plotkin, *Literatura i voina. Velikaia otechestvennaia voina v russkoi sovetskoi proze* (Leningrad, 1967), 156-63. Solzhenitsyn (*Gulag*, I: 244) blasts this short story unmercifully. His belief that Sholokhov did not write *The Quiet Don* seems to have prejudiced him against finding anything of value in any works this author penned.

41. *Fate*, 50; Brown, *Russian Literature*, 189. Sergei Bondarchuk directed and starred in the 1959 film adaptation, also entitled *Fate of a Man*. It won the Grand Prize at the 1960 Moscow Film Festival. In 1979 Corinth Films secured the American distribution rights previously held by Audio Brandon. Audio Brandon Films, *Collection of International Cinema*, 1 (1975), 410; Lev G. Iakimenko, *Tvorchestvo M. A. Sholokhova* (Moscow, 1977), 613; Manvell, *Films*, 337, 347.

42. *Fate*, 38-39, 19, 35.

43. Ginsburgs, "Laws of War," 263-64.

44. Shalamov, "Poslednii boi," 46; Sholokhov, *Fate*, 29-30.

45. English translation by Foreign Languages Publishing House, 1953. See pp. 18, 194. See also Struve, *Russian Literature*, 384.

46. *The Living*, 188-200. *Znamia* published the novel serially in no. 4 (Apr. 1959), 3-96; no. 10 (Oct. 1959), 10-55; no. 11 (Nov. 1959), 56-124; and no. 12 (Dec. 1959), 3-107. See also Reuben Ainsztein, "The Soviet Russian War Novel since Stalin's Death," *Twentieth Century*, 167 (Apr. 1960), 335-36; I. Kuz'michev, "Zametki o sovremennom voennom romane," *Oktiabr'*, no. 3 (Mar. 1965), 185-97; L. Lazarev, "Voennye romany K. Simonova," *Novyi mir*, no. 8 (Aug. 1964), 238-52; Lochtin, "Novel," 65-67; Plotkin, *Literatura*, 173-218.

47. *Neva*, no. 9 (Sept. 1959), 15-22. Translated in *Current Digest of the Soviet Press*, 11 (6 Jan. 1960), 3-6.

48. Sergei S. Smirnov, "In Behalf of Soldiers," *Current Digest of the Soviet Press*, 11 (6 Jan. 1960), 8. Translated from *Literaturnaia gazeta* (27 Oct. 1959), 3. *Current Digest of the Soviet Press*, 11 (6 Jan. 1960), 7. See also Lochtin, "Novel," 68-69; Harold Swayze, *Political Control of Literature in the USSR: 1946-1959* (Cambridge, Mass., 1962), 220.

49. (Moscow, 1960), 24-27, 84-89, 105-13, 139, 394-95. See also Luxenburg, "Solzhenitsyn," 2; Alexander Werth, *Russia under Khrushchev* (New York, 1961), 198, 245.

50. James H. Billington, *The Icon and the Axe, an Interpretive History of Russian Culture* (New York, 1966), 577; *Alpine Ballad* (Moscow, 1966), 41. The original work, *Al'piiskaia ballada*, appeared in 1964. Progress Publishers issued an English translation in 1966. Russian language editions of this Belorussian author's works spell his name Bykov.

51. The number was 193 in Michael Glenny's translation. This story, "Sluchai na stantsii Krechetovka," originally appeared in *Novyi mir*, no. 1 (Jan. 1963), 9-42.

52. Pp. 19-20 in Glenny's translation. "Matrënin dvor" first appeared in *Novyi mir*, no. 1 (Jan. 1963), 42-63.

53. "Odin den' Ivana Denisovicha," *Novyi mir*, no. 11 (Nov. 1962), 8-74.

54. Marc Slonim, *Soviet Russian Literature: Writers and Problems, 1917-1977*, 2nd ed. (New York, 1977), 363.

55. Solzhenitsyn, *One Day*, 76. A Radio Liberty study contends that censors excised much of what the novel had to say about poor treatment of World War II repatriates. Thomas Weiss, "How the Censors Changed 'Ivan Denisovich' and 'Matrëna's Home,' " 7 Mar. 1975, Radio Liberty Dispatch RL 96/75.

56. Silabriedas and Arklans, *"Political Refugees" Unmasked*, 210-11. In 1964 Moscow had created the "Soviet Committee for Cultural Relations with Compatriots [!] Abroad." Shevtsov, *Sovetskoe grazhdantsvo*, 61. Times indeed were changing.

57. Yevstigneev, *Flight to Freedom*, 82.

58. Nechaev, "Uchastie sovetskikh grazhdan," 37, 46, 48.

59. *Avengers*, 5.

60. "Uchastie sovetskikh grazhdan-gruzin v dvizhenii soprotivleniia," 122-29; Kumanev, "Sovetskaia istoriografiia," 269. An article by Col. P. Z. Kalinin published in 1962 openly treated German antipartisan units consisting of former Soviet POWs, but it is ambivalent in its evaluation of even those collaborators who redefected to Soviet partisan formations: Kalinin, "Uchastie," 32-37. Also,

a 1963 article by I. N. Kulikov touched upon Soviet POWs in German antipartisan units who, it was said, lived for the chance to fulfill their "fixed goal" of turning their arms against the Fascists. ("Ob uchastii sovetskikh grazhdan v ital'ianskom Soprotivlenii [1943-45 gg.]" in *Ob"edinenie Italii* [Moscow, 1963], 350.) But the piece did not document effectual, coordinated resistance among collaborators as did Kochiashvili. In addition, the Kulikov article had a very limited circulation: the collection in which it appeared managed a printing of only 3,000. In contrast, Kochiashvili's detailed 1965 examination of the Georgian uprising on Texel took place at a major historical meeting in the Soviet capital and appeared the next year in a publication of conference proceedings that had a print run of 18,300. As mentioned earlier, Kochiashvili's 1949 thesis has not been located. It may or may not have been as candid about the military collaborator origins of the miniscule Georgian resistance movement in the West. But even if the earlier work matched the 1965 address in its direct, favorable assessment of collaborators-turned-patriots, which seems improbable, it undoubtedly had an extremely restricted circulation and thus should not be considered the first positive *public* discussion of Soviet troops in German uniform.

61. Kochiashvili, "Uchastie," 122, 125-28. Two less innovatively daring, but still useful, studies of Soviet resistance abroad, presented at the 1965 historical conference in Moscow, are: Brodskii, "Geroicheskaia bor'ba," 139-46; and Zelenin, "Uchastie sovetskikh liudei," 130-38.

62. (Moscow, 1966), 2, 319, 307. Two years earlier General Lukin had mentioned briefly his harsh treatment and imprisonment following repatriation in an autobiographical piece published in late 1964: "My ne sdaemsia," 29.

63. (Leningrad, 1969), 258, 273-74, 308, 371. The novel first appeared serially in *Novyi mir* in 1968: no. 1 (Jan. 1968), 3-67; no. 2 (Feb. 1968), 10-69; no. 3 (Mar. 1968), 68-132. Both Brown (*Soviet Russian Literature*, 233) and Werth (*Russia: Post-War*, 19-22) rate this novel very highly. See also Lily Daetz, "The Portrayal of War in the Latest Soviet Literature," *Bulletin of the Institute for the Study of the USSR*, 18 (Oct. 1971), 36.

64. *Novyi mir*, no. 12 (Dec. 1974), 212-16.

65. A sampling follows: Nechaev, "Sovetskie liudi," 193-97; Nechaev, "V lesakh Lotaringii," *Voenno-istoricheskii zhurnal*, no. 4 (Apr. 1971): 86-90; Pospelov, ed., *Great Patriotic War*, 224, 460. Several aids enumerate many more recent titles on Soviet resistance abroad: Kireeva, *Velikaia pobeda*; Kumanev, "Sovetskaia istoriografiia"; Shokina, *Geroi*.

66. Brodskii, *Vo imia*; Semiriaga, *Sovetskie liudi*. For comments on these works see: Kireeva, *Velikaia pobeda*, 111-12; Zhilin, "Soviet Writings," 67.

67. Kochiashvili, "Uchastie," 128.

68. Mauro Galleni, *I patrigiani sovietici nella Resistenza italiana* (Rome, 1967), 239. (A Russian translation, *Sovetskie partizany v ital'ianskom dvizhenii Soprotivleniia*, appeared in 1970.) Kulikov, "Ob uchastii sovetskikh," 375; Semiriaga, *Sovetskie liudi*, 7.

69. Semiriaga, *Sovetskie liudi*, 7. His incomplete breakdown indicates: 18,000 Soviet partisans in Poland; 5,000 in Italy; 3,000 in Czechoslovakia; nearly 3,000 in France; 2,900 in Yugoslavia; 800 in Belgium; and hundreds in various other countries.

70. Zelenin, "Uchastie," 132; Homze, *Foreign Labor*, 308.

71. Dean Acheson, "The Truce Talks in Korea: A Full Report to the United Nations," *Harper's*, 206 (Jan. 1953), 28; Ginsburgs, "Refugees," 351-52, 354,

361. The support for voluntary repatriation declared in 1955 by the Soviet Committee for Return to the Homeland should be considered a public relations gambit. Ginsburgs, "Laws of War," 259.

72. Volin and Ushakov, *Tolkvyi slovar'*, 3: 1340.

73. Bratus', "Repatriatsiia," 573; "Repatriatsiia," *Diplomaticheskii slovar'*, 3 (1973), 46.

74. The quote is from Briukhanov, *Vot kak eto bylo*, 2. The figures are based on: Aidan Crawley, *The Spoils of War; the Rise of Western Germany since 1945* (Indianapolis, Ind., 1973), 68; *New York Times*, 28 Aug. 1952, p. 6; Rodger Swearingen, *The Soviet Union and Postwar Japan* (Stanford, Calif., 1978), 42.

75. Vought, "Soviet Partisan Movement," 176.

76. Pospelov *et al.*, *Istoriia velikoi otechestvennoi voiny*, 2: 470.

77. Marshal K. A. Meretskov, *Na sluzhbe narodu: stranitsy vospominanii* (Moscow, 1968), 275; Col. Gen. Leonid M. Sandalov, *Na Moskovskom napravlenii* (Moscow, 1970), 263-64.

78. "Vlasovtsy," V: 151. See also Erickson, *Stalingrad*, 537; Seaton, *Russo-German War*, 207.

79. *The War, 1941-45* (London, 1964) 47-50. This is part of Ehrenburg's multivolume *Liudi, gody, zhizn*. See also Thorwald, *Illusion*, xxii. Werth (*Russia: Post-War*, 25) has no reservations about accepting the above judgment; yet it is as self-serving as Ehrenburg claims Vlasov was. Before the general's capture this Soviet writer had been embarrassingly uncritical in sizing him up, perhaps explaining why the 1964 war memoirs squirm with: "Of course I did meet informers, mercenary turncoats and careerists, but they did not become my friends." (*The War, 1941-45*, 47.) For Ehrenburg's favorable 1942 sketch of Vlasov, see his collection of war reportage, *The Tempering of Russia* (New York, 1944), 153-54.

80. One Soviet tract called "That Spring," the chapter devoted to returning POWs, "an ode to treachery and betrayal." Zhilin, "How A. Solzhenitsyn Sang," 105.

81. "Predatel'," 89.

82. Nikolai N. Iakovlev, *Solzhenitsyn's Archipelago of Lies* (Moscow, 1974), 36.

83. Taratuta, "Tell Me," 117.

84. Zhilin, "How A. Solzhenitsyn Sang," 105. See also Blake, "Solzhenitsyn," 39.

85. Solzhenitsyn, *Gulag*, I: 239, 549.

86. Iakovlev, *Archipelago*, 23, 35. See also the following articles from *The Last Circle* (1974): Bondarev, "A Russian View," 65-67; Aleksandr Rekemchuk, "The Catechism of the Provocateur," 36; and Galina Serebryakova, "Bankruptcy," 56. The émigré press responded to the intensified attacks on Vlasov with returning salvos defending his wartime record. See for example: I. I. Novosil'tsev, "Andrei Andreevich Vlasov," *Novyi zhurnal*, no. 129 (1977), 183-90.

87. Dvinov, *Politics*, 367; Tishkov, "Predatel'," 89. Dvinov noted, "Every single piece of testimony from recent refugees in the present writer's files gives further evidence of the universal hatred engendered by the Vlasovites" (*Politics*, 366). See also Werth, *Russia under Khrushchev*, 69.

CONCLUSION

The West—Inept   The East—Vindictive

As a segment of a larger picture, repatriation formed an integral part of two important developments of the 1944-47 period: a massive demographic upheaval in which millions of European refugees were shuffled and reshuffled, and the disintegration of the Grand Alliance against Hitler leading to the onset of the Cold War. The European phase of World War II resulted in the displacement of 30 million persons from their native countries, not to mention millions of additional refugees who were dislocated within the borders of their homelands.[1] The 5.5 million Soviet citizens abroad at the end of the war easily formed the largest contingent of displaced persons from any one nation.[2]

The cumulative effect of Europe's wartime demographic rearrangements was not the accentuation of minority problems, as had been the case after World War I, but rather the ethnographic simplification of the continent.[3] Toward the end of the war Hitler started the process by permitting the withdrawal of ethnic Germans to Germany, and after VE-Day the victorious Allies continued his policy by making such movement mandatory. Nazi extermination of Jews, gypsies, and other peoples deemed inferior also "simplified" the ethnic picture of Europe, although at a hideous cost in human lives. Finally, postwar bilateral agreements eliminated several minority problems. These provided for population exchanges between Poland and Russia, Russia and Czechoslovakia, and Czechoslovakia and Rumania.[4] Relating the trend of ethnographic simplification to repatriation, World War II not only "solved" many of Europe's longstanding minority problems in frightful fashion, it avoided a new one because of Russian insistence on and Western compliance with a policy of forced repatriation. Only 500,000 former Soviet citizens escaped the sieve of the Yalta accord. These few constituted the living remains of the "tidal wave of war" that had swept Europe, the "sloughs and rivulets of humanity isolated amid the wreckage of a continent."[5] But their number amounted to little compared to what it might have been if displaced Soviet nationals had been free to choose between returning home and settling abroad permanently.

Besides the correlation between repatriation and other contemporary population movements, Soviet-American handling of the DP-POW problem conforms in important respects to the diplomatic trend from 1944 to 1947, characterized by the erosion of the Grand Alliance and the advent of the Cold War. During World War II U.S. officials publicly tended to give the Soviet system the benefit of the doubt, glossing over the Allies' fundamental differences. This conciliatory approach and the nagging fear of a German military renaissance caused Washington to regard the maintenance of Soviet friendship as an important safeguard to world peace. Roosevelt believed that all covenants had to be strictly fulfilled in order to convince the Kremlin of American trustworthiness. Thus, initially, Washington manifested careful propriety in its dealings with Moscow concerning Lend-Lease, German reparations, Austrian and German zonal boundaries, the policy of unconditional surrender, and repatriation. For example, in addition to the forced return of Soviet citizens, the United States at first agreed to Soviet dismantling of German factories in the Western zones of occupation and followed through on a military pullback from territory prearranged to be part of the Soviet zone.

However, as Washington gradually became disillusioned with its Eastern partner, it eased away from the punctilious fulfillment of all agreements. Specific sources of American disenchantment included the Sovietization of Eastern Europe and dissatisfaction with Soviet treatment of stranded American servicemen. But of more fundamental importance was the ideological gulf separating the Allies. In reality, the defeat of Nazi Germany, the cement of the anti-Hitler coalition, brought an end to the wartime coalition. This break should not have come as a surprise, since alliances based solely upon military expedience seldom have outlasted a common enemy. In *Before Winter Comes* the British Major Burnside reminded his Red Army counterpart, "We are allies." But the Russian, determined to fight for the repatriation of every Soviet citizen hiding in Burnside's camp, replied, "For the moment. And only against the Germans."[6] For many months after the German surrender ideological differences did not complicate reciprocal repatriation only because the United States and Britain acquiesced in the Soviet interpretation of the Yalta agreement.[7]

Prior to the Yalta agreement the United States forcibly repatriated the few claimants to Soviet nationality in its custody without clearly recognizing the possible ramifications of this precedent. In a cogently argued critique of Cold War revisionism, J. L. Richardson contends that Washington's overall approach to the Soviet Union in the mid-1940s fits this pattern of ignorance of, or inattention to, the probable long-range results of specific policies. He believes that recent diplomatic studies are unconvincing because they take for granted a consistency and certainty of purpose in Washington's dealings with Moscow that simply did not exist. Objecting to the contrary arguments of revisionists and cold warriors alike, he maintains that from 1944 to 1947 American policy toward the Soviet Union evidenced no "overriding strategy or design." Sounding the same chord, American diplomatic historian Gaddis Smith also argues that Washington's foreign policy during World War II "was not monolithic"; rather, "it was an extension of American society in all its complexity. . . . Americans in their wartime diplomacy were seeking to create not one rigid world on a single model, either idealistic or reactionary, but many."[8]

This less dogmatic approach serves as a reasonable alternative to both New Left and conservative critiques of American diplomacy of the mid-1940s. According to Richardson, the revisionist model of a rapacious United States seeking world hegemony breaks down simply because it "postulates a degree of consistency and clearsightedness not characteristic of American policy at the time."[9] The same argument serves to counter the accusations of indiscriminate Russophobes. In this case the shibboleth of single-mindedness in foreign policy underlies an equally fatuous notion that the postwar era witnessed repeated, unconscionable appeasement of Stalin and that the blame lay with Moscow's supporters within the American government.[10]

Whether one wishes to accept or reject Richardson's thesis that officials in Washington were not of one mind in their approach to the Soviet Union and did not operate according to any master plan, this description does fit the handling of repatriation perfectly. Here U.S. policy lacked both coherence and consistency. Especially before the war ended, American officials had little appreciation for the long-range consequences of early precedents in processing Soviet refugees. For example, SHAEF from the start went out of its way to assist Red Army officers working among Soviet nationals in the West without making that aid contingent upon comparable treatment of British and American citizens. On 23 September 1944, Soviet Ambassador Andrei Gromyko told Secretary of State Cordell Hull in great detail what his government expected of America repatriation authorities. Well before the Yalta conference the United States had complied with most of Gromyko's demands. Just one month after the ambassador's admonitions, JCS advised Eisenhower to regard Soviet citizens captured in German uniform as POWs "for disciplinary purposes"; otherwise not only DPs and POWs but even military collaborators were to be treated like any other liberated Allied nationals.[11]

The United States squandered its negotiating assets without even ver-

bal guarantees of reciprocity. The more help U.S. repatriation officials
afforded Moscow, the less cooperation Western authorities seemed to get
in expediting the return of American POWs in Eastern Europe. Furthermore, Washington's compliance with the demands of Soviet officials
prior to the conclusion of a repatriation accord weakened the American
bargaining position on the POW question. Unilateral concessions did not
make the Russians more accommodating, for they continued adamantly
to insist upon total, forced repatriation. The imbalance in levels of
cooperation continued as long as there were refugees to send home.
Whereas the Western Allies admitted hundreds of Soviet repatriation
officials into their zones of occupied Germany, the most Moscow ever allowed Washington in its portion of the defeated Reich was one American
contact team making one limited excursion. [12] (Granted, there were more
Soviet than American citizens to repatriate, but the French with hundreds of thousands of their nationals in Eastern Europe received no better cooperation from the Russians. Thus, even if there had been more
English-speaking POWs in Red Army hands, there is no reason to believe
Moscow would have been any less indifferent to their plight.)

SHAEF's ascendancy over the State Department in fashioning the final
form of the repatriation agreement demonstrated another shortcoming in
American repatriation policy. Representatives of the armed services received exclusive responsibility for formulating an accord with Soviet representatives at Yalta. Neither the State Department nor SWNCC had any
influence upon the deliberations; these two offices were not even posted
regularly concerning the exchange agreement being made at Yalta. Apparently no specific command from Roosevelt excluded these bodies
from the negotiations. Rather, the president passed over them because it
was the natural order of things in wartime Washington for a host of civil
and political questions, even if only partially related to military affairs, to
be resolved according to the wishes of the generals.

Some State Department and SWNCC staff members had studied repatriation in depth and were much more aware of what was at stake than was
SHAEF or JCS. In particular, they knew that Moscow would be seeking
the total—and thus forced—repatriation of Soviet DPs and POWs. In
contrast, U.S. Army negotiators were apparently unaware until after the
signing of the Yalta agreement that coercion would be necessary to effect
the return of all Soviet citizens abroad.

SHAEF headquarters as well as USMMM favored rapid repatriation
of Soviet nationals because these bodies suspected that proper treatment
of Americans in Red Army custody was contingent upon it. Also Western
military officials wished to reduce the number of mouths to feed, since
they would be responsible for the care of any unrepatriated refugees in

the winter of 1945-46. They gave almost no consideration to the predicament of DPs and POWs who dreaded repatriation. Indeed, initially, military authorities did not seem to be aware that large numbers might opt to remain outside the Soviet Union if given the chance. Granted, the question of stranded Americans and logistical considerations demanded attention. But the solution of these problems should not have entailed an utter disregard for the plight of millions of hapless Soviet refugees.

The overpowering impression gained from a study of repatriation negotiations is Western ineptitude. Few responsible parties within the U.S. government realized beforehand how heartrending forced repatriation would be or what the vindictive Soviet government had in store for reluctant returners. Outstanding exceptions were Alexander Kirk, Joseph Grew, Robert Murphy, and Dean Acheson, State Department officials who were more experienced diplomats than either of the two secretaries of state during the years 1945-46, Edward Stettinius or James F. Byrnes. These second-echelon men had an accurate understanding of what repatriation involved long before Stettinius or Byrnes, who came to their high posts as novices in foreign affairs. Kirk, Grew, Murphy, and Acheson offered discerning criticism and advice that went unheeded by their superiors for nearly a year. Not until military authorities began to chafe under a policy for which they were responsible in the first place did the use of coercion come under serious review. By this time repatriation was practically complete. The subsequent policy revision in December 1945 was of little comfort to the more than 2 million Soviet citizens already repatriated from Western occupation zones.

Even upon the basis of strict national self-interest, the United States probably could have secured a more effective guarantee of safe, speedy repatriation for American POWs. In terms of hard bargaining points, the Soviet Union had a great deal more to lose than the West in the event the Allies could not agree upon a repatriation accord. Had 2 million Soviet nationals remained in the West, the Soviet Union would have been dealt a serious economic and demographic blow, and Soviet prestige abroad would have been severely damaged. The Kremlin also imagined that a large, hostile émigré community in the West would be a threat to the Soviet Union's national security. If the United States had recognized what the Soviet Union had to lose and had seen to repatriation on a strictly *quid pro quo* basis, the Russians might have been more accommodating and considerate in their care for and repatriation of American POWs.

Malcolm Proudfoot, a Western repatriation official, spoke from experience when he characterized the Yalta settlement as "a tightly drawn contract serving Soviet convenience." As he and many others discovered, the accord confirmed existing concessions to the Russians but failed to make sufficient provision for Soviet reciprocity.[13] Considering the Red Army's casual if not negligent treatment of 23,500 liberated U.S. POWs, and bearing in mind SHAEF's tremendous efforts to repatriate speedily 2 million Soviet nationals, it is no wonder that General John Deane and Averell Harriman eventually recommended that Washington adopt a *quid pro quo* approach to the Russians.[14]

Robert C. Williams, in an article on European political émigrés and their defeated dreams, correctly notes, "Historians generally dislike lost causes. They seek to explain what happened, rather than what might have happened."[15] Normally it is so difficult to determine what did occur that few researchers care to expend much energy on what might have been. Nevertheless, as an illustration that alternatives to massive forced repatriation did exist, consider for a moment that American officials approaching Yalta never contemplated possible compromise positions between the extremes of an extraordinarily large and cumbersome Soviet political diaspora and total repatriation. One seemingly tenable middle ground would have been for the United States to return by force only those Soviet citizens who were proven war criminals or who had joined Wehrmacht units of their own accord. Even if, of the latter group, Washington had repatriated just those admitting willing service in German ranks, the number in all likelihood would have far surpassed the sum of American and British POWs in Eastern Europe.

To be sure, this policy still would have dealt a blow to America's reputation as a protector of political exiles—but not nearly so much as the damage actually done through roughshod implementation of the Yalta repatriation accord. A selective approach might have spared many hundreds of thousands of these pawns of war their dreaded reunion with a vengeful homeland, especially if Washington had informed Moscow in firm language that any attempt to use American POWs in Eastern Europe as hostages would bring a halt to the forced repatriation of all Soviet citizens regardless of offense. Given Stalin's paranoia about Vlasovites spearheading a Western attack on Russia, and given his well-documented vindictiveness, chances are he would have repatriated the relative handful of Allied POWs in order to insure receiving those abroad whom he most loathed and feared. Even if the trade of Vlasovites for American and British POWs had not worked, the West still could have repatriated all Soviet citizens to secure its own and have done nothing worse than it finally did anyway.

Some may argue that the United States entered the Yalta exchange accord naively but, once a signator, was obligated under international law to fulfill it. But by complying with this bilateral agreement Washington simultaneously was breaking a separate international treaty. Before the

German surrender the United States recognized its obligation under the 1929 Geneva Prisoner of War Convention to treat its POWs "on the basis of the uniforms worn at the time of capture." This meant American forces did "not look, without [the POWs'] consent, behind the uniforms to determine ultimate questions of citizenship or nationality."[16] But after VE-Day, with the fear of Nazi reprisal past, the United States proceeded to repatriate its German POWs according to nationality, in this case Soviet citizens to Russia, in direct and conscious violation of the Geneva Convention.[17]

And what is one to make of the West's general concurrence in Moscow's designation of Vlasov as a traitor? Stalin's former favorite surely may be defined as one—but no more so than Vladimir Lenin, Walter Ulbricht, or Klaus von Stauffenberg. Each of these, unlike Vlasov, represented causes that prevailed, and as a result none today is thought of as a traitor. Vlasov is one precisely because victors, as a rule, name traitors. In the cases of Lenin and Vlasov, both did everything in their power to see Germany defeat a tyrannical regime in Russia; yet Moscow designates Lenin saint and Vlasov sinner. Or take the case of the German Communist, Walter Ulbricht. He sat in Moscow decrying Hitler in the same years that Vlasov sat in Berlin decrying Stalin. However, no one, not even writers in the West, accuses him of being a traitor for opposing the Nazis. What one person calls patriotism another can call treason. Vlasov's interpreter, Strik-Strikfeldt, remarked: "If it be true that those are no traitors whose aim is to serve, not to harm their country, then the German Claus Graf von Stauffenberg [leader in the abortive July 1944 coup against Hitler] and the Russian General A. A. Vlasov were not traitors."[18]

Vlasov and his followers were anti-Communists but, in the main, not Fascists. Tragically for these disaffected Soviet nationals, that proved to be too fine a distinction for U.S. authorities. On the eve of his homegoing one of Vlasov's lieutenants wrote, "We are called German mercenaries. It may look so, on a superficial level, for we had to arm ourselves in the enemy's camp. But no one who knows the true spirit of Bolshevism can honestly maintain such a charge."[19]

The enormous tragedy of forced repatriation was, in large measure, a product of expediency. Some might argue that the United States had no choice but to cooperate with the Soviet Union in repatriation if liberated American servicemen stranded in Eastern Europe were to arrive home quickly and safely. However, as events developed, the journey home for these GIs was hazardous, harrowing, and prolonged despite Washington's attempts to satisfy Moscow. The Yalta repatriation agreement proved regrettable not only because it failed to secure better treatment of

American ex-POWs in Soviet-occupied territory or to expedite their return home; what was worse, it necessitated the coercion of helpless refugees fearful of a hostile reception back home. Both the United States and the Soviet Union formulated their repatriation policies in heartless fashion. The factors weighed most heavily in the capitals of both countries were invariably reasons of state: prestige, domestic politics, economics, and national security. Even when a humanitarian consideration did enter into the calculations, as with America's interest in the well-being of its stranded ex-POWs, it was a stringently compartmentalized compassion. Washington, with its sights trained so closely upon the retrieval of its own POWs, seemed oblivious to the cruel plight of millions of other refugees.

General Deane, chief of USMMM, signed the Yalta repatriation accord without realizing the sentence he was imposing upon millions of Soviet nationals. It is tragic that they were forcibly returned, but it is damning, as well, that the overall humanitarian aspects of the situation were never seriously considered by either Soviet or American authorities. The prospect of mass political defections haunted Soviet leaders; fear for the safety of a comparatively small number of American servicemen obsessed U.S. authorities. If any thought for the personal wishes of the millions of war-weary Soviet refugees ever surfaced, in the East or in the West, the wielders of power in Moscow and Washington dismissed that thought from consideration—at least until the effective completion of forced repatriation rendered the question academic.

It is possible that an American policy of mandatory but carefully selective repatriation of war criminals and voluntary collaborators might have succeeded better in satisfying the ideal of human treatment of refugees and POWs and still have retrieved American servicemen in Red Army hands. But U.S. policy makers, during the time when their decisions could have made a difference, thought their choices were limited to the return of all Soviet citizens or none; they opted for all.

Even though the great majority of displaced Allied nationals did return home, both Washington and Moscow came to view the Yalta DP-POW accord as a failure. The United States eventually realized that the Kremlin did not appreciate the tremendous effort it expended in repatriating Soviet nationals. What was worse, Washington concluded that the Soviet Union, even though a party to the convention, had made only a token effort to expedite the repatriation of American POWs and, in some cases, had hindered it. For its part, Moscow viewed the Yalta agreement as something less than a complete success because the document did not secure the total recovery of all Soviet nationals abroad. Considering the reluctance of many repatriates, a 90 percent rate of return might appear to be a substantial accomplishment. But the Kremlin, smarting from the jabs of the small but virulently anti-Communist Soviet diaspora, did not see it that way and for years denounced the Western powers for their alleged noncompliance with the Yalta accord.

The reciprocal exchange agreement also failed in other ways. It failed to ameliorate East-West tensions; instead, disagreements over the proper interpretation of the accord further strained Soviet-American relations and thereby contributed to the dangerous tensions of the Cold War era. And finally, it failed the test of basic human decency that Americans in 1945 automatically but naively assumed to be the only way the United States operated. But for the vindictive nature of Soviet power, millions of homesick Soviet citizens would have had no reason to fear repatriation and most probably would have returned home willingly. Likewise, but for Western acquiescence in forced repatriation, this massive affront to civilized behavior could have been avoided. But Moscow was vindictive, and Washington did acquiesce. The sad truth is that both the Soviet Union and the United States managed repatriation in glaring disregard of what today would be called fundamental human rights.

NOTES

1. Fried, *Exploitation*, i.
2. EUCOM, "Displaced Persons," 58.
3. Wright, *Ordeal*, 264.
4. Kulischer, *Europe on the Move*, 274-311.
5. John McCormac in *New York Times*, 24 June 1945.
6. Windward Productions.
7. Conway, "Intellectual Origins," 93-94; Gaddis, *Origins*, 42, 105, 359.
8. J. L. Richardson, "Cold-War Revisionism: A Critique," *World Politics*, 24 (July 1972), 607; Gaddis Smith, "Rewriting the History of American Diplomacy during the Second World War" in *The National Archives and Foreign Relations Research*, ed. by Milton O. Gustafson (Athens, Ohio, 1974), 146.
9. Richardson, "Cold-War Revisionism," 592. Richardson, for example, takes Gar Alperovitz to task for his characterization of U.S. policymakers as reckless gunslingers bent on a showdown with their Soviet ally-turned-adversary. *Atomic Diplomacy: Hiroshima and Potsdam* (New York, 1965), 239-40.
10. Martin, "Not 'Displaced Persons,' " 109; Perlmutter, "Dean Acheson," 897.
11. Gromyko to Hull, 23 Sept. 1944, NA RG 218, CCS 383.6 (7-4-44) Sec. 1, Part 2 (reprinted in *FR, 1944*, IV: 1252-53); JCS to Eisenhower, 22 Nov. 1944, NA RG 218, CCS 383.6 (7-4-44) Sec. 1, Part 2.
12. OCH, EUCOM, *Survey*, 274.
13. Proudfoot, *European Refugees*, 155.
14. Gaddis, *Origins*, 81.

15. Robert C. Williams, "European Political Emigrations: A Lost Subject," *Comparative Studies in Society and History*, 12 (Apr. 1970), 140.

16. Bernard Gufler to G. R. Ranken, British Embassy, 28 Apr. 1945, NA RG 59, 740.00114 EW/4-945.

17. Contrast Grew to Novikov, 5 May 1945, *FR, 1945*, V: 1094-95, with Grew to Forrestal, 12 May 1945, *FR, 1945*, V: 1095-96.

18. Strik-Strikfeldt, *Against Stalin and Hitler*, 248. See also Elliott, "Vlasov"; Epstein, *Operation Keelhaul*, 114; Fisher, "New Emigration," 11-12.

19. Thorwald, *Illusion*, 315, quoting Col. M. Meandrov.

Bibliography

BIBLIOGRAPHICAL AIDS

Armstrong, John A. "Recent Soviet Publications on World War II." *Slavic Review*, 21 (Sept. 1962): 508-19.

Boltine, E. "L'Union Sovietique et la Resistance en Europe," *European Resistance Movements, 1939-45. Proceedings of the Second International Conference on the History of the Resistance Movements, Held at Milan, 26-29 March 1961*. New York: Macmillan, 1964.

Bray, Mayfield S., and William T. Murphy. "Audiovisual Records in the National Archives Relating to World War II." Washington, D.C.: National Archives, 1971.

Butler, William E. *Writings on Soviet Law and Soviet International Law*. Cambridge, Mass.: Harvard Law School Library, 1966.

Civil-Military Relations: An Annotated Bibliography, 1940-1952. New York: Columbia University Press, 1954.

Dallin, Alexander. *The German Occupation of the U.S.S.R. in World War II: A Bibliography*. Washington, D.C.: Department of State, External Research Staff, 1955.

Dexter, Byron. *The Foreign Affairs 50-Year Bibliography: New Evaluations of Significant Books on International Relations, 1920-1970*. New York: Bowker, 1972.

Displaced Persons: A Selected Bibliography, 1939-1947. New York: Russell Sage Foundation, 1948.

Egorov, V. N. *Mezhdunarodnye otnosheniia (bibliograficheskii spravochnik. 1945-1960 gg.)*. Moscow: Izdatel'stvo Instituta Mezhdunarodnikh Otnoshenii, 1961.

Enser, A. G. S. *A Subject Bibliography of the Second World War: Books in English, 1939-1974*. Boulder, Colo.: Westview, 1977.

Erickson, John. "The Soviet Union at War (1941-1945): An Essay on Sources and Studies." *Soviet Studies*, 14 (Jan. 1963): 249-74.

Faxon, Frederick *et al. Cumulated Magazine Subject Index 1907-1949*, 2 volumes. Boston: G. K. Hall, 1964.

Funk, Arthur L. *The Second World War: A Bibliography; a Select List of Publications Appearing since 1968*. Gainesville, Fla.: American Committee on the History of the Second World War, 1972.

Golovanova, L. G. *et al. Rekomendatel'nii ukazatel' literatury o velikoi otechestvennoi voine sovetskogo soiuza*. Moscow: Kniga, 1970.

Gustafson, Milton O., ed. *The National Archives and Foreign Relations Research*. Athens: Ohio University Press, 1974.

Harold, John E. "An Annotated Bibliography: The American Military Occupation of Germany, 1945-1949." Carlisle Barracks, Pa.: Military History Research Collection, 1971.

Hersch, Gisela. *A Bibliography of German Studies, 1945-1971: Germany under Allied Occupation, Federal Republic of Germany, German Democratic Republic.* Bloomington: Indiana University Press, 1972.

Higham, Robin. *A Guide to the Sources of United States Military History.* Hamden, Conn.: Archon, 1975.

————. *Official Histories: Essays and Bibliographies from All over the World.* Manhattan: Kansas State University Library, 1970.

Kandel', Boris L. *Istoriia zarubezhnikh stran; bibliografiia russkikh bibliografii, opublikovannikh s 1857 po 1965 god.* Moscow: Kniga, 1960.

Kireev, V. P. *et al. Antifashistskoe dvizhenie soprotivleniia v stranakh Evropy v gody vtoroi mirovoi voiny (1939-1945). Informatsionno—bibliograficheskii ukazatel' sovetskikh i zarubezhnikh bibliografii.* Moscow: Vsesoiuznaia Gosudarstvennaia Ordena Trudovogo Krasnogo Znameni Biblioteka Inostrannoi Literatury, 1973.

Kireeva, M. E. *et al. Velikaia Otechestvennaia Voina sovetskogo soiuza (1941-1945 gg.), rekomendatel'nyi ukazetel' literatury.* Moscow: Kniga, 1965.

————. *Velikaia pobeda; rekomendatel'nyi ukazatel' literatury o Velikoi Otechestvennoi Voine 1941-1945 gg.* Moscow: Kniga, 1975.

Kumanev, G. A. "Sovetskaia istoriografiia ob uchastii grazhdan SSSR v antifashistskom dvizhenii soprotivleniia v Evrope" in *Vtoraia mirovaia voina i sovremenost',* ed. by P. A. Zhilin. Moscow: Izdatel'stvo "Nauka," 1972.

————. *Velikaia otechestvennaia voina sovetskogo soiuza (1941-1945 gg.); bibliografiia sovetskoi istoricheskoi literatury za 1946-1959 gg.* Moscow: Izdatel'stvo Akademii Nauk SSSR, 1960.

———— *et al. SSSR v period velikoi otechestvennoi voiny, 1941-1945; ukazatel' dissertatsii i avtoreferatov.* Moscow: Izdatel'stvo Akademii Nauk SSSR, 1961.

Mangalam, J. J. *Human Migration: A Guide to Migration Literature in English, 1955-1962.* Lexington: University of Kentucky Press, 1968.

Meyer, Klaus. *Bibliographie der Arbeiten zur Osteuropäischen Geschichte aus den Deutschsprachigen Fachzeitschriften 1858-1964.* Berlin: Osteuropa Institut an der Freien Universität Berlin, 1966.

————. *Bibliographie zur Osteuropäischen Geschichte. Verzeichnis der zwischen 1939 und 1964 veröffentlichten Literatur im Westeuropäischen Sprachen zur Osteuropäischen Geschichte bis 1945.* Berlin: Osteuropa Institut an der Freien Universität Berlin, 1972.

Millett, Allan R., and B. Franklin Cooling III. *Doctoral Dissertations in Military Affairs: A Bibliography.* Manhattan: Kansas State University Library, 1972.

Morton, Louis. "Sources for the History of World War II." *World Politics,* 13 (Apr. 1961), 435-53.

Munden, Kenneth W. "Analytical Guide to the Combined British-American Records of the Mediterranean Theatre of Operations in World War II." Rome: Allied Force Records Administration, 1948.

O'Neill, James E., and Robert W. Krauskopf, eds. *World War II, an Account of Its Documents.* Washington, D.C.: Howard University Press, 1976.

Parrish, Michael, comp. *Soviet Armed Forces: Books in English, 1950-1967.* Stanford, Calif.: Hoover Institution Press, 1970.

Prisoners of War and Political Hostages, a Select Bibliography. Springfield, Va.: Monroe Corporation, 1973.

"Publications of the Harvard Project on the Soviet Social System" in *Ten-Year Report and Current Projects 1948-1958*. Cambridge, Mass.: Russian Research Center, Harvard University, 1958.

Schatoff [Shatov], Michael. *Bibliografiia osvoboditel'nogo dvizheniia narodov Rossii v gody vtoroi mirovoi voiny (1941-1945)*. New York: All-Slavic Publishing House, 1961.

Shokina, N. A. *et al. Geroi Velikoi Otechestvennoi Voiny. Rekomendatel'nyi ukazatel' literatury*. Moscow: Kniga, 1970.

Smith, Solomon C. "Prisoners of War—Selected Writings." New Haven, Conn.: Yale Law Library, 1973.

Stewart, William J. *The Era of Franklin D. Roosevelt: A Selected Bibliography of Periodical, Essay, and Dissertation Literature, 1945-1971*, 2nd ed. Hyde Park, N.Y.: National Archives and Records Service, 1967.

U.S. Army. European Command. Historical Division. *Guide to Foreign Military Studies 1945-54*. Headquarters, U.S. Army, Europe, 1954.

U.S. Congress. House of Representatives. *The Displaced Persons Analytical Bibliography*. H. R. 1687, 81st Cong., 2d sess., 1950.

U.S. Department of the Army. Army Library, Law Section. "Bibliography on Repatriation of Prisoners of War." Typescript. 1960.

Victor Kamkin Bookstore. *Emigrantskie i zarubezhnie izdaniia*. Rockville, Md.: Victor Kamkin Bookstore, 1973.

Zhilin, P. A. "Sovetskaia voenno-istoricheskaia literatura" in *Razvitie sovetskoi istoricheskoi nauki 1970-1974*. Moscow: Izdatel'stvo "Nauka," 1975.

———. "Soviet Writings on Military History." *Social Sciences*, 6 (1975): 56-69.

Ziegler, Janet. *World War II: Books in English, 1945-65*. Stanford, Calif.: Hoover Institution Press, 1971.

U.S. GOVERNMENT RECORDS: NATIONAL ARCHIVES, WASHINGTON, D.C. (NA), AND WASHINGTON NATIONAL RECORDS CENTER, SUITLAND, MARYLAND (NAS)

NO.	TITLE
43	Records of United States Participation in International Conferences, Commissions, and Expositions
59	General Records of the Department of State
107	Records of the Office of the Secretary of War
111	Records of the Office of the Chief Signal Officer
165	Records of the War Department General Staff
208	Records of the Office of War Information
218	Records of the United States Joint Chiefs of Staff
226	Records of the Office of Strategic Services
306	Records of the United States Information Agency
319	Records of the Army Staff
331	Records of Allied Operational and Occupational Headquarters, World War II
334	Records of Interservice Agencies
338	Records of United States Army Commands, 1942–. Captured Records Division
353	Records of Interdepartmental and Intradepartmental Committees (State Department)

MANUSCRIPT COLLECTIONS

American Council for Nationalities Service. Immigration History Research Center. University of Minnesota. Minneapolis.
Clifford, Clark. Harry S. Truman Library. Independence, Mo.
Eisenhower, Dwight D. Dwight D. Eisenhower Library, Abilene, Kans.
Elsey, George M. Harry S. Truman Library. Independence, Mo.
Harmon, Ernest N. Military History Research Collection. Carlisle Barracks, Pa.
Harvard Project on the Soviet Social System. Russian Research Center. Cambridge, Mass.
Marshall, George C. George C. Marshall Research Foundation. Lexington, Va.
Mosely, Philip. University of Illinois Archives. Urbana.
Panchuk, John. Immigration History Research Center. University of Minnesota. Minneapolis.
Roosevelt, Franklin D. Franklin D. Roosevelt Library. Hyde Park, N.Y.
Stettinius, Edward R., Jr. University of Virginia Library. Charlottesville.
Stimson, Henry L. Yale University Library. New Haven, Conn.
United Ukrainian American Relief Committee. Immigration History Research Center. University of Minnesota. Minneapolis.

FEATURE FILMS AND DOCUMENTARIES

Army of the Damned. CBS. 1962.
Before Winter Comes. Windward Film Productions. 1969.
Orders from Above. BBC. 1975.
Vstrecha o rodinoi [Encounter with the Homeland]. Soviet Embassy, Washington, D.C.

UNPUBLISHED SOURCES

Dissertations, Theses, and Papers

Albrecht, Ambassador Dr. "The Legal Situation Existing between Germany and the Soviet Union." Appendix of "German Camps for Russian and Polish War Prisoners" by Adolph Westhoff. NA RG 338, Captured Records Division. Foreign Military Studies.
Baird, Jay Warren. "German Home Propaganda, 1941-1945, and the Russian Front." Ph.D. diss., University of Colorado, 1966.
Bauer, Alice H. "A Guide for Interviewing Soviet Escapees." 1953. Harvard Project on the Soviet Social System, Cambridge, Mass.
Beier, Helen. "Responses to the Rorschach Test of Former Soviet Citizens." 1954. Harvard Project on the Soviet Social System, Cambridge, Mass.
Best, Randolph Boothby. "A Doctrine of Counterinsurgence." Ph.D. diss., University of South Carolina, 1973.
Bland, Larry Irvin. "W. Averell Harriman: Businessman and Diplomat, 1891-1945." Ph.D. diss., University of Wisconsin, 1972.
Bosse, Alexander von. "The Cossack Corps." P-064. 1950. NA RG 338, Captured Records Division. Foreign Military Studies.
Buchsbaum, John. "German Psychological Warfare on the Eastern Front: 1941-1945." Ph.D. diss., Georgetown University, 1960.

Burton, Robert B. "The Vlasov Movement of World War II: An Appraisal." Ph.D. diss., American University, 1963.

Chyz, Yaroslav J. "Russians in America." 1951. American Council for Nationalities Service files. Immigration History Research Center, University of Minnesota, Minneapolis.

―――. "Statistical Data on the Number of Persons in the U.S. Born in the U.S.S.R. or Pre-War Russia and Their Descendants." 1951. American Council for Nationalities Service files. Immigration History Research Center, University of Minnesota, Minneapolis.

―――. "Ukrainians in America, Political Attitudes and Activities." 1953. American Council for Nationalities Service files. Immigration History Research Center, University of Minnesota, Minneapolis.

Clifford, Clark. "American Relations with the Soviet Union; a Report to the President by the Special Counsel to the President." 24 Sept. 1946. George M. Elsey Papers, Harry S. Truman Library, Independence, Mo.

Conway, Maurice Bernard. "The Intellectual Origins of the Cold War: American Policy Makers and Policy, 1933-1945." Ph.D. diss., University of California, Santa Barbara, 1974.

Dallin, Alexander, and Sylvia Gilliam. "Aspects of the German Occupation of the Soviet Union." No date. Harvard Project on the Soviet Social System, Cambridge, Mass.

Elliott, Mark. "The Greco-Turkish Compulsory Exchange of Populations of 1923." In author's possession, 1970.

―――. "The Repatriation Issue in Soviet-American Relations, 1944-1947." Ph.D. diss., University of Kentucky, 1974.

EUCOM. Historical Division. "Displaced Persons." 1947. Military History Research Collection, Carlisle Barracks, Pa.

―――. "International Aspects of the Occupation." 1947. Military History Research Collection, Carlisle Barracks, Pa.

―――. "RAMP's: The Recovery and Repatriation of Liberated Prisoners of War." Frankfurt-am-Main: 1947. Military History Research Collection, Carlisle Barracks, Pa.

"Forcible Repatriation of Displaced Soviet Citizens—Operation Keelhaul." 3 vols. NAS RG 331, AFHQ, G-5 file 383.7-14.1, Reel 17-L.

"General Board Report on Displaced Persons, Refugees, and Recovered Allied Military." NA RG 165 WDGSS, OPD, Study No. 35.

Goodwin, James E. "Repatriation of Prisoners of War—Forcible and Non-Forcible." Thesis, Army War College, 1960.

Gordon, Gary Howard. "Soviet Partisan Warfare, 1941-1944: The German Perspective." Ph.D. diss., University of Iowa, 1972.

Gottlieb, Margaret R. "Repatriation in Theory and in Practice throughout the First World War." Thesis, Bryn Mawr College, 1945.

Griswold, Gillett. "The Recovery and Repatriation of Liberated Prisoners of War, Occupation Forces in Europe, 1945-1946." 1947. Military History Research Collection, Carlisle Barracks, Pa.

" 'Haunted Forests': Enemy Partisans behind the Front." C-037. 1948. NA RG 338 Captured Records Division. Foreign Military Studies.

Heim, Keith M. "Hope without Power: Truman and the Russians, 1945." Ph.D. diss., University of North Carolina, 1973.

Herwarth, Hans von, with S. Frederick Starr. "Memoirs: 1904-1945." In possession of S. Frederick Starr, Tulane University, New Orleans, La.

"History of the United States Military Mission to Moscow." 30 Oct. 1945. NA RG 165 OPD, Case 233.

Holowka, Orest. "Development of U.S. Policy Regarding Repatriation of Soviet Nationals during and after World War II." 10 May 1977. In possession of author.

Hupp, Alfred R., Jr. "The Technique of Soviet Diplomatic Negotiation." National Technical Information Service, AD728773, 1971.

Inkeles, Alex, and Raymond A. Bauer. "Patterns of Life Experience and Attitudes under the Soviet System (Composite Survey)." 1954. Harvard Project on the Soviet Social System, Cambridge, Mass.

Jefferson, Charles J. "Bureaucracy, Diplomacy, and the Origins of the Cold War." Ph.D. diss., Claremont Graduate School, 1975.

Keck, Daniel Newton. "Designs for the Postwar World: Anglo-American Diplomacy, 1941-1945." Ph.D. diss., University of Connecticut, 1967.

Koestring, Ernst. "Commentary on the Report of Dr. Seraphim Concerning Turkic Units." Appendix of "Eastern Nationals as Volunteers in the German Army" by Hans Seraphim. C-043. 1952. NA RG 338 Captured Records Division. Foreign Military Studies.

———. Interrogation Report. 30-31 Aug. 1945. NA RG 165 WDGSS, Shuster Mission.

———. "The People of the Soviet Union." C-035. 1948. NA RG 338 Captured Records Division. Foreign Military Studies.

Lorimer, Sister M. Madeline. "America's Response to Europe's Displaced Persons, 1945-1952: A Preliminary Report." Ph.D. diss., St. Louis University, 1964.

Luxenburg, Norman. "Solzhenitsyn, Soviet Literature and the Returned P.O.W.'s Issue." Cleveland State University, Midwest Slavic Conference, 2 May 1975.

Messer, Robert Louis. "The Making of a Cold Warrior: James F. Byrnes and American-Soviet Relations, 1945-1946." Ph.D. diss., University of California, Berkeley, 1975.

Office of the Chief of Military History. "The Exchange with the Soviet Forces of Liberated Personnel—World War II." Washington, D.C. OCMH, no date.

Office of Strategic Services. Research and Analysis Branch. "An Estimate of Russian Workers Removed to Axis Europe (Based upon Russian Charges)." No. 2173. 12 June 1944. NA RG 59 State Department.

———. "Russian Intentions to Punish War Criminals." No. 1988. 27 June 1944. NA RG 59 State Department.

———. "Use of Soviet Citizens in the Reichswehr." No. 2297. 13 Dec. 1944. NA RG 59 State Department.

Petelchuk, Paul. "The National Alliance of Russian Solidarists—A Study of a Russian Freedom Movement Group." Ph.D. diss., Syracuse University, 1970.

Pluth, Edward John. "The Administration and Operation of German Prisoner of War Camps in the United States during World War II." Ph.D. diss., Ball State University, 1970.

Posdnjakoff, Wladimir W. "German Counterintelligence Activities in Occupied

Russia 1941-45." P-122. 1953. NA RG 338 Captured Records Division. Foreign Military Studies.

Pronin, Alexander. "Guerilla Warfare in the German-Occupied Soviet Territories, 1941-44." Ph.D. diss., Georgetown University, 1965.

Raymond, Edward A. "The Juridical Status of Persons Displaced from Soviet and Soviet-dominated Territory." Ph.D. diss., American University, 1952.

Ruddy, Thomas M. "Charles E. Bohlen and the Soviet Union, 1929-1969." Ph.D. diss., Kent State University, 1973.

"Russian Émigrés and Foreign Workers in France." 1945. Harry S. Truman Library, Independence, Mo.

Seraphim, Hans. "Eastern Nationals as Volunteers in the German Army." C-043. 1952. NA RG 338 Captured Records Division. Foreign Military Studies.

Shapiro, Jane Perlberg. "Rehabilitation Policy and Political Conflict in the Soviet Union, 1953-64." Ph.D. diss., Columbia University, 1967.

Smith, Frederic N. "The American Role in the Repatriation of Certain Soviet Citizens, Forcible and Otherwise, to the USSR Following World War II." Ph.D. diss., Georgetown University, 1970.

Tomasziwskyj, Jaroslaw. " 'Vozrozhdenie': A Russian Periodical Abroad and Its Contributors." Ph.D. diss., Vanderbilt University, 1974.

Toppe, Alfred. "Russian Methods of Interrogating War Prisoners." P-0l8b. 1949. NA RG 338 Captured Records Division. Foreign Military Studies.

——— *et al.* "Political Indoctrination of War Prisoners." P-0l8d. 1949. NA RG 338 Captured Records Division. Foreign Military Studies.

U.S. Department of State. "Memorandum: Legal Considerations Underlying the Position of the United Nations Command Regarding the Issue of Forced Repatriation of Prisoners of War." 24 Oct. 1952. Pentagon Library, Washington, D.C.

Vizzard, William Raymond. "Prisoners of War Policy in Relation to Changing Concepts of War." Ph.D. diss., University of California, Berkeley, 1961.

Volzhanin, V. "Zuyev's Republic." P-124. 1951. NA RG 338 Captured Records Division. Foreign Military Studies.

Vought, Donald B. "An Inquiry into Certain Aspects of the Soviet Partisan Movement 1941-1944." M.A. thesis, University of Louisville, 1963.

Weiss, Thomas. "An Analysis of Solzhenitsyn's 'Prussian Nights.' " Radio Liberty Research. 14 Feb. 1975. RL 63/75.

———. "How the Censors Changed 'Ivan Denisovich' and 'Matrena's Home.' " Radio Liberty Research. 7 Mar. 1975. RL 96/75.

Westhoff, Adolf. "German Camps for Russian and Polish War Prisoners." NA RG 338 Captured Records Division. Foreign Military Studies.

Wyle, Frederick. "Memorandum on Statistical Data on Soviet Displaced Persons." 1952. Harvard Project on the Soviet Social System.

Interviews

Anonymous. Former displaced person. Lexington, Ky. Jan. 1971.

———. Former State Department official. Washington, D.C. 29 July 1977.

———. Former U.S. Army private. Slippery Rock, Pa. 8 Aug. 1977.

Durbrow, Elbridge. Washington, D.C. 6 July 1977.

Elliott, Mark. On *As It Happens*, Canadian Broadcasting Corporation. 18 Apr. 1978.
Shimkin, Demitrii. University of Illinois, Urbana. 28 July 1976.

Letters

Anonymous. Retired U.S. Army sergeant to author, 28 Dec. 1977.
Eugene Kulischer to Robert Feldmesser, 13 Aug. 1953. Harvard Project on the Social System, Cambridge, Mass.
Col. D. C. Howell to author, 2 Jan. 1978.
Angelo Montella to author, 17 Jan. 1979.
Demitrii Shimkin to author, 17 Aug. 1976.
Paul W. Titman to author, 14 Apr. 1979.

BOOKS

Abramov, Fedor A. *Dve zimy i tri leta*. Leningrad: "Sovetskii pisatel'," 1969.
Alliluyeva, Svetlana. *Only One Year*. New York: Harper and Row, 1969.
———. *Twenty Letters to a Friend*. New York: Harper and Row, 1967.
Alperovitz, Gar. *Atomic Diplomacy: Hiroshima and Potsdam*. New York: Simon and Schuster, 1965.
Animisov, Oleg. *The German Occupation in Northern Russia during World War II: Political and Administrative Aspects*. New York: Research Program on the U.S.S.R., 1954.
Avengers: Reminiscences of Soviet Members of the Resistance Movement. Moscow: Progress, 1965.
Barker, Carol M., and Matthew H. Fox. *Classified Files: The Yellowing Pages; a Report on Scholars' Access to Government Documents*. New York: Twentieth Century Fund, 1972.
Bartoshevich, Eduard M., and Evgenii I. Borisoglebskii. *Imenem bog iegovy*. Moscow: Gosudarstvennoe Izdatel'stvo Politicheskoi Literatury, 1960.
Bauer, Raymond A., Alex Inkeles, and Clyde Kluckhohn. *How the Soviet System Works: Cultural, Psychological and Social Themes*. Cambridge, Mass.: Harvard University Press, 1956.
Berman, Harold J., and Miroslav Kerner. *Soviet Military Law and Administration*. Cambridge, Mass.: Harvard University Press, 1955.
Bethell, Lord Nicholas. *The Last Secret: The Delivery to Stalin of over Two Million Russians by Britain and the United States*. New York: Basic Books, 1974.
Billington, James H. *The Icon and the Axe, an Interpretive History of Russian Culture*. New York: Random House, 1966.
Boder, David Pablo. *I Did Not Interview the Dead*. Urbana: University of Illinois Press, 1949.
Bohlen, Charles E. *Witness to History 1929-1969*. New York: Norton, 1973.
Bouscaren, Anthony J. *International Migrations since 1945*. New York: Praeger, 1963.
Brereton, Lt. Gen. Lewis H. *The Brereton Diaries*. New York: Morrow, 1946.
Brezhnev, Leonid I. *The Great Victory of the Soviet People*. Moscow: Novosti, 1965.
Briukhanov, Aleksei I. *Vot kak eto bylo; o rabote misii po repatriatsii sovetskikh grazhdan; vospominaniia sovetskogo ofitsera*. Moscow: Gosudarstvennoe Izdatel'stvo Politicheskoi Literatury, 1958.

Brodskii, E. A. *Vo imia pobedy nad fashizmom: antifashistskaia bor'ba sov-
etskikh liudei v gitlerovskoi Germanii (1941-1945)*. Moscow: Nauka, 1970.
————. *Zhivye boriutsia*. Moscow. Voenizdat, 1965.
Brown, Deming. *Soviet Russian Literature since Stalin*. Cambridge: University
Press, 1978.
Brown, Edward J. *Russian Literature since the Revolution*. New York: Collier,
1963.
Brychev, Nikolai F. *Domoi, na rodinu!* 2nd ed. Moscow: Voennoe Izdatel'stvo,
1945.
Burns, James MacGregor. *Roosevelt: The Soldier of Freedom*. New York: Har-
court Brace, 1970.
Bykau [Bykov], Vasilii U. *Al'piiskaia ballada*. Moscow: "Sovetskii pisatel',"
1964. *Alpine Ballad*. Moscow: Progress, 1966.
Byrnes, James F. *Speaking Frankly*. New York: Harper, 1947.
Carrell, Paul. *Hitler Moves East 1941-1943*. London: Harrap, 1964.
Chandler, Alfred D., ed. *The Papers of Dwight David Eisenhower; the War
Years*. Vol. IV. Baltimore: Johns Hopkins University Press, 1970.
Chkhikvadze, Viktor M. *Sovetskoe voenno-ugolovnoe pravo*. Moscow: Iuridi-
cheskoe Izdatel'stvo Ministerstva Iustitsii SSSR, 1948.
Clark, Alan. *Barbarossa. The Russian-German Conflict, 1941-45*. New York:
Morrow, 1965.
Clark, Mark W. *Calculated Risk*. New York: Harper, 1950.
Clemens, Diane. *Yalta*. New York: Oxford University Press, 1970.
Coakley, Robert W., and Richard M. Leighton. *Global Logistics and Strategy,
1943-1945*. Washington, D.C.: Office of Chief of Military History, 1968.
Coffin, William Sloane, Jr. *Once to Every Man: A Memoir*. New York: Athe-
neum, 1977.
Coles, Harry L., and Albert K. Weinberg. *Civil Affairs: Soldiers Become Gov-
ernors*. Washington, D.C.: Government Printing Office, 1964.
Commission for the Publication of Diplomatic Documents. Ministry of Foreign
Affairs of the U.S.S.R. *Correspondence between the Chairman of the Coun-
cil of Ministers of the U.S.S.R. and the Presidents of the U.S.A. and the Prime
Ministers of Great Britain during the Great Patriotic War of 1941-1945*. Vol.
II: *Correspondence with Franklin D. Roosevelt and Harry S. Truman
(August 1941–December 1945)*. New York: Dutton, 1958.
Conquest, Robert. *Kolyma: The Arctic Death Camps*. New York: Viking, 1978.
Crankshaw, Edward. *Khrushchev's Russia*. Baltimore: Penguin, 1959.
Crawley, Aidan. *The Spoils of War; the Rise of Western Germany since 1945*. In-
dianapolis: Bobbs-Merrill, 1973.
Crowley, Edward L., ed. *The Soviet Diplomatic Corps, 1917-1967*. Metuchen,
N.J.: Scarecrow Press, 1970.
Crowley, Edward L., Andrew I. Lebed, and Heinrich E. Schulz. *Prominent Per-
sonalities in the USSR, a Biographic Directory Containing 6,015 Biographies
of Prominent Personalities in the Soviet Union*. Metuchen, N.J.: Scarecrow
Press, 1968.
Curry, George. *James F. Byrnes*. New York: Cooper Square, 1965.
Dallin, Alexander. *German Rule in Russia, 1941-1945*. New York: St. Martin's
Press, 1957.
Dallin, David, and Boris Nikolaevskii. *Forced Labor in Soviet Russia*. New
Haven, Conn.: Yale University Press, 1947.

Deane, John R. *The Strange Alliance: The Story of Our Efforts at Wartime Co-operation with Russia.* New York: Viking Press, 1947.

Dennett, Raymond, and Joseph E. Johnson, eds. *Negotiating with the Russians.* Boston: World Peace Foundation, 1951.

Deriabin, Peter, and Frank Gibney. *The Secret World.* Garden City, N.Y.: Doubleday, 1959.

Deviataev, Mikhail. *Pobed iz ADA.* Saransk: Mordovskoe Knizhnoe Izdatel'stvo, 1963.

———. *Polet k solntsu.* Moscow: Izdatel'stvo DOSAAF, 1972.

Divine, Robert. *American Immigration Policy, 1924-1952.* New Haven, Conn: Yale University Press, 1957

Donnison, F. S. V. *Civil Affairs and Military Government Central Organization and Planning.* London: Her Majesty's Stationery Office, 1966.

———. *Civil Affairs and Military Government, North-West Europe, 1944-45.* London: Her Majesty's Stationery Office, 1961.

Dushnyck, Walter, and William J. Gibbons. *Refugees Are People: The Plight of Europe's Displaced Persons.* New York: America Press, 1947.

Dvinov, Boris L. *Politics of the Russian Emigration.* Santa Monica, Calif.: Rand Corporation, 1955.

Dzhalil', Musa. *Iz moabitskoi tetradi.* Moscow: Sovetskii pisatel', 1954.

Ehrenburg, Il'ia. *The Tempering of Russia.* New York: Knopf, 1944.

———. *The War, 1941-45.* London: MacGibbon and Kee, 1964.

Eisenhower, Dwight D. *Crusade in Europe.* Garden City, N.Y.: Doubleday, 1948.

Enquist, Per Olov. *The Legionnaires; a Documentary Novel.* New York: Delacorte, 1973.

Epstein, Julius. *Operation Keelhaul.* Old Greenwich, Conn.: Devin-Adair, 1973.

Erickson, John. *The Road to Stalingard: Stalin's War with Germany.* New York: Harper and Row, 1975.

Ershov, G., and T. Tel'pugov. *Sergei Mikhalkov, Kritiko-biograficheskii ocherk.* Moscow: Sovetskii Pisatel', 1956.

Esaian, Agasi A. *Nekotorie voprosy sovetskogo grazhdanstva; voprosy naseleniia v praktike sovetskoi Armenii.* Erevan: Izdatel'stvo "Mitk," 1966.

Eubank, Nancy. *The Russians in America.* Minneapolis: Lerner, 1973.

Feifer, George. *Moscow Farewell.* New York: Viking, 1976.

Feis, Herbert. *Churchill, Roosevelt, and Stalin: The War They Waged and the Peace They Sought.* Princeton, N.J.: Princeton University Press, 1967.

Fischer, George. *Soviet Opposition to Stalin: A Case Study in World War II.* Cambridge, Mass.: Harvard University Press, 1952.

———, ed. *Russian Émigré Politics.* New York: Free Russia Fund, 1951.

Fischer, Louis, ed. *Thirteen Who Fled.* New York: Harper and Brothers, 1949.

Fried, John E. *Exploitation of Foreign Labour in Germany.* Montreal: International Labour Office, 1945.

Friedrich, Carl J. *et al. American Experiences in Military Government in World War II.* New York: Rinehart, 1948.

Gaddis, John Lewis. *The United States and the Origins of the Cold War 1941-1947.* New York: Columbia University Press, 1972.

Galleni, Mauro. *I partigiami sovietici nella Resistenza italiana.* Rome: Editori riuniti, 1967. Russian translation: *Sovetskie partizamy v ital'ianskom dvizhenii Soprotivleniia.* Moscow: Progress, 1970.

Gehlen, Reinhard. *The Service: The Memoirs of Reinhard Gehlen.* New York: World Publishing, 1972.

Gerasimenko, Vladimir K. *et al. S chuzhogo golosa.* Simferopol': Izdatel'stvo "Tavriia," 1975.

Golikov, F. I. *V Moskovskoi bitve, zapiski komandarma.* Moscow: "Nauka," 1967.

Golubeva, T. S., and L. S. Gellershtein. *Rasskazy po istorii SSSR: dlia 4 klassa.* Moscow: Izdatel'stvo "Prosveshchenie," 1972.

Grahl-Madsen, Atle. *The Status of Refugees in International Law.* Vol. I. *Refugee Character.* Leyden: Sijthoff, 1966.

Grygar'iants, R. *Vazhnaia dziarzhainaia zadacha.* Minsk: Dzhairzhainae Vidavetztva BSSR, 1945.

Grygier, Tadeusz. *Oppression; a Study in Social and Criminal Psychology.* Westport, Conn.: Greenwood, 1973.

Grzybowski, Kazimierz. *Soviet Public International Law; Doctrines and Diplomatic Practice.* Leyden: Sijthoff, 1970.

Gsovski, Vladimir. *Soviet Civil Law; Private Rights and Their Background under the Soviet Regime.* 2 volumes. Ann Arbor: University of Michigan Law School, 1948-49.

Gustafson, Milton O., ed. *The National Archives and Foreign Relations Research.* Athens: Ohio University Press, 1974.

Hanfmann, Eugenia, and Helen Beier. *Six Russian Men: Lives in Turmoil.* North Quincy, Mass.: Christopher Publishing House, 1976.

Harmon, Ernest. *Combat Commander: Autobiography of a Soldier.* Englewood Cliffs, N.J.: Prentice-Hall, 1970.

Harriman, W. Averell. *America and Russia in a Changing World, a Half Century of Personal Observation.* Garden City, N.Y.: Doubleday, 1971.

——— and Elie Abel. *Special Envoy to Churchill and Stalin 1941-1946.* New York: Random House, 1975.

Hazard, John N. *Law and Social Change in the U.S.S.R.* Toronto: Carswell, 1953.

Herring, George C., Jr. *Aid to Russia 1941-1946: Strategy, Diplomacy, the Origins of the Cold War.* New York: Columbia University Press, 1973.

Hoess, Rudolf. *Commandant of Auschwitz, the Autobiography of Rudolf Hoess.* Cleveland: World Publishing Company, 1959.

Holborn, Louise W. *The International Refugee Organization, a Specialized Agency of the United Nations: Its History and Work, 1946-1952.* London: Oxford University Press, 1956.

Homze, Edward L. *Foreign Labor in Nazi Germany.* Princeton, N.J.: Princeton University Press, 1967.

Hulme, Kathryn. *The Wild Place.* Boston: Little, Brown, 1953.

Huxley-Blythe, Peter J. *The East Came West.* Caldwell, Idaho: Caxton Printers, 1964.

Iakimenko, Lev G. *Tvorchestvo M. A. Sholokhova.* Moscow: Sovetskii pisatel', 1977.

Iakovlev, Nikolai N. *Solzhenitsyn's Archipelago of Lies.* Moscow: Novosti Press Agency Publishing House, 1974.

Il'nytz'kyi, Roman. *The Free Press of the Suppressed Nations.* Augsburg: Association of the Free Press of Central and Eastern Europe, Baltic and Balkan States in Germany, 1950.

Infield, Glenn B. *The Poltava Affair: A Russian Warning, an American Tragedy.* New York: Macmillan, 1973.

Inkeles, Alex, and Raymond A. Bauer. *The Soviet Citizen.* Cambridge, Mass.: Harvard University Press, 1959.

Institute for the Study of the USSR. *Who Was Who in the USSR.* Metuchen, N.J.: Scarecrow, 1972.

International Military Tribunal. *Trial of the Major War Criminals.* Vols. 29 and 41. Nuremberg: International Military Tribunal, 1949.

International Refugee Organization. *The Facts about Refugees.* N.p., 1948.

————. *Statistical Report with 51 Months Summary.* Geneva: International Refugee Organization, 1951.

In the Name of the Lithuanian People. Wolfberg, Germany: "Perkunas," 1945.

Ivushkina, A. P. *Rodina zovet! Sbornik. (Po materialam gazety "Za vozvrashchenie na rodinu.")*. Berlin: Komitet "Za vozvrashchenie na rodinu," 1955.

Kazakevich, Emmanuil G. *Vesna na Odere.* Moscow: Sovetskii pisatel', 1950. *Spring on the Oder.* Moscow: Foreign Languages Publishing House, 1953.

————. *Zvezda; povest'.* Moscow: Moskovskii rabochii, 1948. *Star; a Story.* Moscow: Foreign Languages Publishing House, 1950.

Keesing's Research Report. *Germany and Eastern Europe since 1945: From the Potsdam Agreement to Chancellor Brandt's "Ostpolitik."* New York: Scribner's, 1973.

Khrushchev, Nikita. *Khrushchev Remembers.* Boston: Little, Brown, 1970.

Kochetov, Vsevelod. *Brat'ia Ershovy.* Moscow: Sovetskii pisatel', 1960.

Koestring, Ernst. *General Ernst Koestring.* Frankfurt am Main: Mittler, 1966.

Kolarz, Walter. *Russia and Her Colonies.* New York: Praeger, 1952.

Kolko, Gabriel. *The Politics of War: The World and United States Foreign Policy, 1943-1945.* New York: Random House, 1968.

Koriakov, Mikhail M. *I'll Never Go Back: A Red Army Officer Talks.* New York: Dutton, 1948.

Krasnov, Nikolai N., Jr. *The Hidden Russia; My Ten Years as a Slave Laborer.* New York: Holt, 1960.

Kravchenko, Viktor. *I Chose Freedom.* New York: Scribner's, 1946.

Krock, Arthur. *Memoirs: Sixty Years on the Firing Line.* New York: Funk and Wagnalls, 1968.

Kubijovych, Volodymyr, ed. *Ukraine: A Concise Encyclopedia,* 2 volumes. Toronto: University of Toronto Press, 1963-71.

Kulischer, Eugene. *The Displacement of Population in Europe.* Montreal: International Labour Office, 1943.

————. *Europe on the Move: War and Population Changes, 1917-47.* New York: Columbia University Press, 1948.

Kuznetsov, B. M., comp. *V ugodu Stalinu; gody 1945-1946,* 2 volumes. New York: Voennii Vestnik, 1958.

Kydd, Sam. *for You the War is Over.* London: Bachman and Turner, 1973.

Ladas, Stephen P. *The Exchange of Minorities; Bulgaria, Greece, and Turkey.* New York: Macmillan, 1932.

The Last Circle. Moscow: Novosti Press, 1974.

Leahy, William D. *I Was There.* New York: Whittlesey House, 1950.

Lerner, Daniel. *Sykewar. Psychological Warfare against Nazi Germany, D-Day to VE-Day.* New York: George W. Stewart, 1949.

Levering, Ralph B. *American Opinion and the Russian Alliance, 1939-1945.* Chapel Hill: University of North Carolina Press, 1976.

Levytsky, Borys. *The Soviet Political Elite.* Munich: Hoover Institution, 1969.

Lewis, George C., and John Mewha. *History of Prisoner of War Utilization by the United States Army, 1776-1945.* Washington, D.C.: Department of the Army, 1955.

Lorimer, Frank. *The Population of the Soviet Union: History and Prospects.* Geneva: League of Nations, 1946.

Lototskii, S. S., ed. *Armiia sovetskaia.* Moscow: Izdatel'stvo Politicheskoi Literatury, 1969.

Lubachko, Ivan S. *Belorussia under Soviet Rule, 1917-1957.* Lexington: University of Kentucky Press, 1972.

Lukas, Richard C. *Eagles East: The Army Air Forces and the Soviet Union, 1941-1945.* Tallahassee: Florida State University Press, 1970.

Lyons, Eugene. *Our Secret Allies, the Peoples of Russia.* New York: Duell, Sloan and Pearce, 1953.

McNeill, William Hardy. *America, Britain, and Russia: Their Cooperation and Conflict, 1941-1946.* London: Oxford University Press, 1953.

Mair, John. *Austria* in *Four-Power Control in Germany and Austria, 1945-1946.* London: Oxford University Press, 1956.

Maisky, Ivan. *Memoirs of a Soviet Ambassador. The War: 1939-43.* New York: Scribner's, 1967.

Mandryka, M. I. *Ukrainian Refugees.* Winnipeg: Ukrainian Canadian Committee, 1946.

Manning, Clarence A. *Twentieth Century Ukraine.* New York: Bookman Associates, 1951.

Manvell, Roger. *Films and the Second World War.* New York: A. S. Barnes, 1974.

Marshall, Bruce. *Vespers in Vienna.* Boston: Houghton Mifflin, 1947.

Medvedev, Roy A. *Let History Judge: The Origins and Consequences of Stalinism.* New York: Knopf, 1971.

Meretskov, Marshal K. A. *Na sluzhbe narodu: stranitsy vospominamii.* Moscow: Izdatel'stvo Politicheskoi Literatury, 1968.

Mikhalkov, Sergei. *Sobranie sochinenii.* 2 volumes. Moscow: Gosudarstvennoe Izdatel'stvo Khudozhestvennoi Literatury, 1963.

Naumenko, Viacheslav. *Velikoe predatel'stvo: vydacha Kazakov v Lientze i drugikh mestakh (1945-1947).* 2 volumes. New York: Vseslavianskoe Izdatel'stvo, 1962-70.

Nemirov, A. *Dorogi i vstrechi.* Munich: Ekho, 1947.

Nicholson, Harold. *The War Years, 1939-1945.* New York: Atheneum, 1967.

Notestein, Frank W. *et al. The Future Population of Europe and the Soviet Union, Population Projections, 1940-1970.* Geneva: League of Nations, 1944.

Notter, Harley, ed. *Postwar Foreign Policy Preparation, 1939-1945.* Washington, D.C.: Government Printing Office, 1949.

Office of the Chief Historian, European Command. *Survey of Soviet Aims, Policies and Tactics.* Frankfurt: European Command, 1948.

Osnovy sovetskogo voyennogo zakonodatel'stva. Moscow: Military Publishing House, 1966. JPRS 36,420, Soviet Military Translations No. 286. *Principles of Soviet Military Legislation.*

Osokin, B. *Andrei Andreevich Vlasov, kratkaia biografiia.* New York: All-Slavic Publishing House, 1966.

Otvety na volnuiushchie voprosy sovetskikh grazhdan nakhodiashchikhsia za granitsei na polozhenii peremeshchennykh lits. Moscow: Upravlenie Upolnomochennogo Soveta Ministrov Souiza SSR Po Delam Repatriatsii, 1949.

Pašlaitis, Juozas. *Hearken Then Judge, Sidelights on Lithuanian DPs.* Tubingen: "Patria," 1950.

Patton, George S. *War As I Knew It.* Boston: Houghton Mifflin, 1947.

Petrov, Vladimir. *My Retreat from Russia.* New Haven, Conn.: Yale University Press, 1950.

Pickard, Bertram. *Europe's Uprooted People: The Relocation of Displaced Population.* Washington, D.C.: National Planning Associate, 1944.

Piliar, Iurii E. *Liudi ostaiutsia liud'mi.* Moscow: Izdatel'stvo "Sovetskaia Rossiia," 1966.

Plotkin, Lev A. *Literatura i voina. Velikaia otechestvennaia vioina v russkoi sovetskoi proze.* Leningrad: Sovetskii pisatel', 1967.

Pogue, Forrest C. *The Supreme Command.* Washington, D.C.: Government Printing Office, 1954.

Poliakov, Aleksandr F. *Russians Don't Surrender.* New York: Dutton, 1942.

Pospelov, P. N., ed. *Great Patriotic War of the Soviet Union, 1941-1945, a General Outline.* Moscow: Progress, 1974.

——— *et al. Istoriia velikoi otechestvennoi voiny sovetskogo soiuza, 1941-1945,* vols. 2 and 6. Moscow: Voennoe Izdatel'stvo, 1961, 1965.

Proudfoot, Malcolm. *European Refugees, 1939-52.* Evanston, Ill.: Northwestern University Press, 1956.

Reitlinger, Gerald. *The House Built on Sand: The Conflict of German Policy in Russia, 1939-1945.* New York: Viking Press, 1960.

"Romanov, A. I." *Nights Are Longest There: Smersh from the Inside.* Boston: Little, Brown, 1972.

Romashkin, P. S. *Amnistiia i pomilovanie v SSSR.* Moscow: Gosudarstvennoe Izdatel'stvo Iuridicheskoi Literatury, 1959.

Salisbury, Harrison. *The Gates of Hell.* New York: New American Library, 1975.

Samarin, Vladimir D. *Civilian Life under the German Occupation, 1942-1944.* New York: Research Program on the U.S.S.R., 1954.

Sanakoev, Sh. P., and B. L. Tsibulevskii. *Tegeran. Ialta. Potsdam. Sbornik dokumentov.* Moscow: "Mezhdunarodnie Otnosheniia," 1970.

Sandalov, Col. Gen. Leonid M. *Na Moskovskom napravlenii.* Moscow: Nauka, 1970.

Sawczuk, Janusz. *Hitlerowski Obozy Jenieckie W Lambinowicach W Latach 1939-1945.* Cieszyn: Instytut Slaski W Opolu, 1974.

Schatoff [Shatov], Michael. *Materialy i dokumenty osvoboditel'nogo dvizheniia narodov Rossii v gody vtoroi mirovoi voiny (1941-1965).* New York: All-Slavic Publishing House, 1966.

Seaton, Albert. *The Battle for Moscow, 1941-1942.* New York: Stein and Day, 1971.

———. *The Russo-German War, 1941-45.* London: Barker, 1971.

Sehn, Jan. *Oswiecim-Brzezinka (Auschwitz-Birkenau) Concentration Camp.* Warsaw: Wydawnictwo Prawnicze, 1961.

Semiriaga, Mikhail I. *Sovetskie liudi v evropeiskom soprotivlenii.* Moscow: Nauka, 1970.

Seydewitz, Max. *Civil Life in Wartime Germany.* New York: Viking, 1945.
Shevtsov, V. S. *Sovetskoe grazhdanstvo.* Moscow: Iuridicheskaia literatura, 1965.
Sholokhov, Mikhail. *The Fate of a Man.* Moscow: Progress, 1974 [1957].
Shtemenko, Gen. S. M. *The Last Six Months: Russia's Final Battles with Hitler's Armies in World War II.* Garden City, N.Y.: Doubleday, 1977.
Shub, Boris. *The Choice.* New York: Duell, Sloan and Pearce, 1950.
Silabriedis, J., and B. Arklans. *"Political Refugees" Unmasked.* Riga: Latvian State Publishing House, 1965.
Simonov, Konstantin. *The Living and the Dead.* Garden City, N.Y.: Doubleday, 1962.
Slonim, Marc. *Soviet Russian Literature: Writers and Problems, 1917-1977.* 2nd ed. New York: Oxford University Press, 1977.
Smith, Jessica, ed. *The Molotov Note on the Abduction of Soviet Citizens into German Slavery. Hitler's Slave Markets.* New York: Soviet Russia Today, 1943.
Smith, Perry M. *The Air Force Plans for Peace, 1943-1945.* Baltimore: Johns Hopkins University Press, 1970.
Smith, Walter Bedell. *My Three Years in Moscow.* Philadelphia: Lippincott, 1950.
Solasko, F., ed. *War behind Barbed Wire; Reminiscences of Buchenwald Ex-Prisoners of War.* Moscow: Foreign Languages Publishing House, 1959.
Solzhenitsyn, Alexander. *The First Circle.* New York: Harper and Row, 1968.
———. *The Gulag Archipelago.* 3 volumes. New York: Harper and Row, 1973-78.
———. *One Day in the Life of Ivan Denisovich.* New York: Dutton, 1963.
———. *Prussian Nights, A Poem.* New York: Farrar, Straus and Giroux, 1977.
Steenberg, Sven. *Vlasov.* New York: Knopf, 1970.
Stephan, John J. *The Russian Fascists: Tragedy and Farce in Exile, 1925-1945.* New York: Harper and Row, 1978.
Stettinius, Edward R., Jr. *Roosevelt and the Russians: The Yalta Conference.* New York: Doubleday, 1949.
Strik-Strikfeldt, Wilfried. *Against Stalin and Hitler: Memoir of the Russian Liberation Movement, 1941-5.* London: Macmillan, 1970.
Struve, Gleb. *Russian Literature under Lenin and Stalin 1917-1953.* Norman: University of Oklahoma Press, 1971.
Swayze, Harold. *Political Control of Literature in the USSR: 1946-1959.* Cambridge, Mass.: Harvard University Press, 1962.
Swearingen, Rodger. *The Soviet Union and Postwar Japan.* Stanford, Calif.: Stanford University Press, 1978.
Swianiewicz, S. *Forced Labour and Economic Development, an Enquiry into the Experience of Soviet Industrialization.* London: Oxford University Press, 1965.
Taft, Donald R., and Richard Robbins. *International Migrations, the Immigrant in the Modern World.* New York: Ronald Press, 1955.
Thorwald, Juergen. *Flight in the Winter.* New York: Pantheon, 1951.
———. *The Illusion: Soviet Soldiers in Hitler's Army.* New York: Harcourt, Brace, Jovanovich, 1975.
Tolstoy, Nikolai. *The Secret Betrayal: 1944-1947.* New York: Scribner's, 1978.
Trainin, Aron N. *Hitlerite Responsibility under Criminal Law.* London: Hutchinson, n.d. [1945].

Treadgold, Donald. *Twentieth Century Russia.* 3rd ed. Chicago: Rand McNally, 1972.

Triska, Jan F., and Robert M. Slusser. *The Theory, Law, and Policy of Soviet Treaties.* Stanford, Calif.: Stanford University Press, 1962.

Tsvetkova, Nadezhda G., ed. *V fashistskikh zastenkakh; zapiski.* Minsk: Gosudarstvennoe Izdatel'stvo BSSR, 1958.

Ulam, Adam B. *Expansion and Coexistence: The History of Soviet Foreign Policy, 1917-1967.* New York: Praeger, 1968.

Ullmann, Walter. *The United States in Prague, 1945-1948.* Boulder, Colo.: *East European Quarterly*, 1978.

Umiastowski, Roman. *Poland, Russia, and Great Britain, 1941-1945: A Study of the Evidence.* London: Hollis and Curler, 1946.

U.S.S.R. Commissar of Foreign Affairs. *Note Submitted by V. Molotov, People's Commissar of Foreign Affairs of the U.S.S.R., Concerning the Wholesale Forcible Transportation of Soviet Citizens to German Fascist Slavery and the Responsibility Borne for This Crime by the German Authorities and by Private Persons Who Exploit the Forced Labor of Soviet Citizens in Germany.* Moscow: Foreign Languages Publishing House, 1943.

U.S. Congress. House of Representatives. Committee on Military Affairs. *Investigations of the National War Effort.* H. R. 2740. 79th Cong., 2d sess., 1947.

U.S. Congress. Senate. Committee on Foreign Relations. *Nomination of Charles E. Bohlen. Hearings before the Committee of Foreign Relations, Senate.* 83d Cong., 1st sess., 1953.

U.S. Department of State. *Foreign Relations of the United States: Diplomatic Papers. The Conference at Berlin (Potsdam), 1945.* 2 volumes. Washington, D.C.: Government Printing Office, 1960.

———. *Foreign Relations of the United States: Diplomatic Papers. The Conferences at Malta and Yalta, 1945.* Washington, D.C.: Government Printing Office, 1955.

———. *Foreign Relations of the United States: Diplomatic Papers, 1944.* Vol. IV: *Europe.* Washington, D.C.: Government Printing Office, 1966.

———. *Foreign Relations of the United States: Diplomatic Papers, 1945.* Vol. II: *General: Political and Economic Matters.* Washington, D.C.: Government Printing Office, 1967.

———. *Foreign Relations of the United States: Diplomatic Papers, 1945.* Vol. V: *Europe.* Washington, D.C.: Government Printing Office, 1967.

———. *Foreign Relations of the United States: Diplomatic Papers, 1946.* Vol. V: *The British Commonwealth, Western and Central Europe.* Washington, D.C.: Government Printing Office, 1969.

———. *Foreign Relations of the United States: Diplomatic Papers, 1947.* Vol. II: *Council of Foreign Ministers; Germany and Austria.* Washington, D.C.: Government Printing Office, 1972.

———. *Foreign Relations of the United States: Diplomatic Papers, 1947.* Vol. IV: *Eastern Europe; the Soviet Union.* Washington, D.C.: Government Printing Office, 1972.

———. *Foreign Relations of the United States: Diplomatic Papers, 1948.* Vol. IV: *Eastern Europe; the Soviet Union.* Washington, D.C.: Government Printing Office, 1974.

———. *Germany, 1947-1949; the Story in Documents.* Washington, D.C.: Department of State, 1950.

————. *Occupation of Germany, Policy and Progress, 1945-46.* Washington, D.C.: Government Printing Office, 1947.

————. *Liberated Prisoners of War and Civilians, Agreement between United States and Union of Soviet Socialist Republics, Signed at Crimea February 11, 1945.* Executive Agreement Series 505, Pubn. No. 2530 (1946).

————. Intelligence Research Office. *The Soviet Union as Reported by Former Soviet Citizens; Interview Report[s].* Washington, D.C.: Department of State, 1952–.

U.S. Forces European Theater. Military Government. *Weekly Field Report*, 14 (Oct. 1945).

U.S. Office of the Director. Office of Military Government (U.S. zone). U.S. Forces European Theater. Reports and Information Branch. "Soviet Repatriation." *Weekly Information Bulletin*, 19 (1 Dec. 1945), 27.

U.S. Office of the U.S. Chief of Counsel for the Prosecution of Axis Criminality. *Nazi Conspiracy and Aggression*, vols. 1, 6, and 8. Washington, D.C.: Government Printing Office, 1946.

Urlanis, Boris. *Wars and Population.* Moscow: Progress, 1971.

Val'kov, Vasilii A. *SSSR i SSha. Ikh politicheskie i ekonomicheskie otnosheniia.* Moscow: Nauka, 1965.

Vernant, Jacques. *The Refugee in the Post-war World.* New Haven, Conn.: Yale University Press, 1953.

Vershigora, Petr Petrovich. *Liudi s chistoi sovest'iu.* Moscow: Moskovskii rabochii, 1946. *Men with a Clear Conscience.* Moscow: Foreign Languages Publishing House, 1949.

Volin, B. M., and D. N. Ushakov. *Tolkovyi slovar' russkogo iazyka.* Vol. 3. Moscow: Gosudarstvennoe Izdatel'stvo Inostrannykh i Natsional'nykh Slovarei, 1939.

Vorob'ev, Evgeniia. *Zemlia, do vostrebovaniia.* Moscow: Sovetskii pisatel', 1972.

Voropai, Oleksii I. *V dorozi na zakhid; shchodennik utikacha.* London: Ukrains'ka Vidavnicha Spilka, 1970.

Vyshinski, Andrei Y. *Speech Delivered by A. Y. Vyshinski . . . in the General Assembly—November 6, 1946.* Washington, D.C.: Embassy of the U.S.S.R., 1946.

Walker, Richard L. *E. R. Stettinius, Jr.* New York: Cooper Square, 1965.

Werth, Alexander. *Russia at War, 1941-1945.* New York: Dutton, 1964.

————. *Russia: The Post-War Years.* New York: Taplinger, 1971.

————. *Russia under Khrushchev.* New York: Hill and Wang, 1961.

Williams, William A. *American-Russian Relations, 1781-1947.* New York: Rinehart, 1952.

Willis, Edward F. *Herbert Hoover and the Russian Prisoners of World War I; a Study in Diplomacy and Relief, 1918-1919.* Stanford, Calif.: Stanford University Press, 1951.

Wolfe, Bertram D. *Three Who Made a Revolution.* rev. ed. New York: Dell, 1964.

Woodbridge, George. *UNRRA: The History of the United Nations Relief and Rehabilitation Administration.* Vols. 2 and 3. New York: Columbia University Press, 1950.

Wright, Gordon. *The Ordeal of Total War, 1939-1945.* New York: Harper and Row, 1968.

Yevstigneev, Georgii V. *Flight to Freedom.* Moscow: Progress Publishers, 1965.
Zagorul'ko, M. M., and A. F. Iugenkov, *Krakh ekonomicheskikh planov fashistskoi Germanii na vremenno okkupirovannoi territorii SSSR.* Moscow: Izdatel'stvo "Ekonomika," 1970.
Zenushkina, I. *Soviet Nationalities Policy and Bourgeois Historians.* Moscow: Progress, 1975.
Zhukov, Georgii I. *The Memoirs of Marshal Zhukov.* New York: Delacorte, 1971.

ARTICLES AND CONTRIBUTIONS TO EDITED WORKS

Acheson, Dean. "The Truce Talks in Korea: A Full Report to the United Nations." *Harper's,* 206 (Jan. 1953): 21-31.
"Agreement Relating to Prisoners of War and Civilians Liberated by Forces Operating under Soviet Command and Forces Operating under United States of America Command. Signed in the Crimea, on 11 February 1945." *Treaties and International Agreements Registered or Filed and Recorded with the Secretariat of the United Nations,* 68 (1950): 175-78.
Ainsztein, Reuben. "The Soviet Russian War Novel since Stalin's Death." *Twentieth Century,* 167 (Apr. 1960): 328-38.
Amalrik, Andrei. "Victims of Yalta." *Harper's,* 258 (May 1979): 91-94.
Ansbacher, Heinz L. "The Problem of Interpreting Attitude Survey Data: A Case Study of the Attitude of Russian Workers in Wartime Germany." *Public Opinion Quarterly,* 14 (Spring 1950): 126-38.
Artiemev, V. P. "Crime and Punishment in the Soviet Armed Forces." *Military Review,* 42 (Nov. 1962): 68-74.
Audio Brandon Films. "Fate of a Man." *Collection of International Cinema,* 1 (1975): 410.
Bahryany, Ivan. "Why I Do Not Want to Go 'Home.' " *Ukrainian Quarterly,* 2 (Winter 1946): 236-51.
Bakis, Eduard. " 'D. P. Apathy' " in *Flight and Resettlement,* edited by Henry B. M. Murphy. Paris: UNESCO, 1955.
Bartel', Valter'. "Sovmestnaia bor'ba Nemetskikh i sovetskikh bortsov soprotivleniia v Bukhenval'de." *Novaia i noveishaia istoriia,* no. 3 (May-June 1958): 139-54.
Bauer, Raymond A. "Some Trends in Sources of Alienation from the Soviet System." *Public Opinion Quarterly,* 19 (Fall 1955): 279-91.
Before Winter Comes. American Film Institute Catalogue, Feature Films, 1961-70.
Beier, Helen, and Eugenia Hanfmann. "Emotional Attitudes of Former Soviet Citizens as Studied by the Technique of Projective Questions." *Journal of Abnormal and Social Psychology,* 53 (Sept. 1956): 143-53.
Berman, Harold J., and Miroslav Kerner. "Soviet Military Crimes." *Military Review,* 32 (July 1952): 3-15.
"Bezhentsy i peremeshchenny litsa." *Bol'shaia sovetskaia entsiklopediia.* 3rd ed. Vol. 3, 1970.
Bialer, Seweryn. "Introduction, the Politics of Soviet War Literature" and "Biographical Index" in *Stalin and His Generals; Soviet Military Memoirs of World War II,* edited by Seweryn Bialer. New York: Pegasus, 1969.
Blake, Patricia. "Solzhenitsyn: An Artist Becomes an Exile." *Time,* 103 (25 Feb. 1974): 34-40.

Bogomolov, Vladimir. "V Avguste sorok chetvertogo. . . ." *Novyi mir*, no. 10 (Oct. 1974): 3-109; no. 11 (Nov. 1974): 5-95; no. 12 (Dec. 1974): 161-232.

Bondarev, Yuri. "A Russian View." *The Last Circle*. Moscow: Novosti Press, 1974.

Borisov, Alexander, "Recent Anglo–U.S. Bourgeois Historiography of the Soviet Union's Great Patriotic War" in *Soviet Studies on the Second World War*, edited by M. Goncharuk. Moscow: Social Sciences Today, U.S.S.R. Academy of Sciences, 1976.

Borshchukov, V. "Voina v tvorchestve Sholokhova" in *Literatura velikogo podviga; Velikaia Otechestvennaia voina v sovetskoi literature*, edited by A. Kogan and G. Solov'ev. Moscow: Izdatel'stvo "Khudozhestvennaia Literatura," 1970.

Bratus', S. N. *et al*. "Repatriatsiia" in *Iuridicheskii slovar'*. Moscow: Gosudarstvennoe Izdatel'stvo Iuridicheskoi Literatury, 1953.

Brodskii, E. A. "BSV." *Novyi mir*, no. 8 (Aug. 1957): 188-201.

———. "Geroicheskaia bor'ba sovetskikh patriotov v fashistskoi Germanii" in *Vtoraia mirovaia Voina*, vol. 3: *Dvizhenie soprotivleniia v Evrope*, edited by E. A. Boltin. Moscow: Nauka, 1966.

———. "Kommunisty vo glave osvoboditel'noi bor'by sovetskikh voennoplennykh v gitlerovskoi Germanii." *Voprosy istorii KPSS*, no. 3 (Mar. 1962): 79-93.

———. "Osvoboditel'naia bor'ba sovetskikh liudei v fashistskoi Germanii (1943-1945 gody)." *Voprosy istorii*, no. 3 (Mar. 1957): 85-99.

Bruikhanov, A. I., M. K. Gavrilov, and N. A. Filatov. "Stranitsa istorii, zhdushchaia svoikh issledovatelei." *Voprosy istorii*, no. 2 (Feb. 1961): 209-12.

Buhite, Russell D. "Soviet-American Relations and the Repatriation of Prisoners of War, 1945." *The Historian*, 35 (May 1973): 384-97.

"Bukhenval'dskoe soprotivlenie. (Dokumenty). Vvodnaia stat'ia I. F. Kiunga, T. A. Illeritskoi and B. G. Litvaka." *Istoricheskii arkhiv*, no. 4 (1957), 82-100; no. 6 (1957): 82-110.

Cook, Don. "On Revealing the 'Last Secret.' " *Encounter*, 45 (July 1975): 80-86.

Craig, Gordon A. "Techniques of Negotiation" in *Russian Foreign Policy: Essays in Historical Perspective*, edited by Ivo J. Lederer. New Haven, Conn.: Yale University Press, 1962.

Daetz, Lily. "The Portrayal of War in the Latest Soviet Literature." *Bulletin of the Institute for the Study of the USSR*, 18 (Oct. 1971): 34-50.

Dallin, Alexander. "From the Gallery of Wartime Disaffection." *Russian Review*, 21 (Jan. 1962): 75-80.

———. "The Kaminsky Brigade: A Case-Study of Soviet Disaffection " in *Revolution and Politics in Russia: Essays in Memory of B. I. Nicolaevsky*, edited by Alexander and Janet Rabinowitch. Bloomington: Indiana University Press, 1972.

———. "Portrait of a Collaborator: Oktan." *Survey: A Journal of Soviet and East European Studies*, no. 35 (Jan.-Mar. 1961): 114-19.

Dallin, Alexander, and Ralph Mavrogordato. "Rodionov: A Case-Study of Wartime Redefection." *American Slavic and East European Review*, 18 (Feb. 1959): 25-33.

———. "The Soviet Reaction to Vlasov." *World Politics*, 8 (Apr. 1956): 307-22.

Darbinian, Reuben. "The Proposed Second Repatriation by the Government of Soviet Armenia: What Does Moscow Want from Its Armenian Collaborators of the Armenian Diaspora?" *Armenian Review*, 15 (Apr. 1962): 3-10.

David, Vaclav. "The Truth about Who Saved Prague in May 1945" in *The Last Circle*. Moscow: Novosti, 1974.

Delzell, Charles F. "Russian Power in Central-Eastern Europe" in *The Meaning of Yalta: Big Three Diplomacy and the New Balance of Power*, edited by John L. Snell. Baton Rouge: Louisiana State University Press, 1956.

Deutscher, Isaac. "Strange World of Russian 'Non-Returners.' " *New York Times Magazine* (24 July 1949): 9, 19.

deWeerd, Hans. "Operation Keelhaul." *Ukrainian Review*, 2 (Dec. 1955): 25-40.

Dickson, Alec. "Displaced Persons." *National Review*, 129 (Nov. 1947): 382-92; (Dec. 1947): 490-93.

"Document Tells Allied Part in Deaths of Thousands." *Sunday Oklahoman* (21 Jan. 1973).

Dohnanyi, Ernst von. "Combatting Soviet Guerillas" in *Modern Guerilla Warfare; Fighting Communist Guerilla Movements, 1941-1961*, edited by Franklin M. Osanka. New York: Glencoe, 1962.

Dushnyck, Walter. "The Importance of the Problem of Displaced Persons." *Ukrainian Review*, 2 (Spring 1946): 285-88.

Eason, Warren W. "Demography" in *Handbook of Soviet Social Science Data*, edited by Ellen Mickiewicz. New York: Free Press, 1973.

———. "Population and Labor Force" in *Soviet Economic Growth, Conditions and Perspectives*, edited by Abram Bergson. Evanston, Ill.: Row, Peterson, 1953.

Elliott, Mark. "Andei Vlasov: Red Army General in Hitler's Service." *Military Affairs* (in press).

———. Review of *Operation Keelhaul* by Julius Epstein. *Canadian American Slavic Studies*, 9 (Spring 1975): 125-26.

———. "The United States and Forced Repatriation of Soviet Citizens, 1944-47." *Political Science Quarterly*, 88 (June 1973): 253-75.

Epstein, Julius. "An American Crime." *National Review*, 1 (21 Dec. 1955): 19-21.

———. "American Forced Repatriation." *Ukrainian Quarterly*, 10 (Autumn 1954): 354-66.

———. "Forced Repatriation: Some Unanswered Questions." *Russian Review*, 29 (Apr. 1970): 209-10.

———. Review of *Wlassow, Verrater oder Patriot*, by Sven Steenberg. *Russian Review*, 28 (July 1969): 367-68.

Erickson, John. "The Soviet Union at War (1941-1945): An Essay on Sources and Studies." *Soviet Studies*, 14 (Jan. 1963): 249-74.

Fainsod, Merle. "Controls and Tensions in the Soviet System." *American Political Science Review*, 44 (June 1950): 266-82.

Fischer, Alfred Joachim. "A Russian Quisling." *Contemporary Review*, 167 (Feb. 1945): 118-21.

Fischer, George. "General Vlasov's Official Biography." *Russian Review*, 8 (Oct. 1949): 284-301.

———. "The New Soviet Emigration." *Russian Review*, 8 (Jan. 1949): 6-19.

———. "The Soviet 'Non-Returners.' " *New Republic*, 120 (13 June 1949): 13-15.

Fisher, Ralph T., Jr. Review of *Operation Keelhaul* by Julius Epstein and *The Last Secret* by Nicholas Bethell. *Slavic Review*, 34 (Dec. 1975): 823-25.

"Forcible Repatriation of the Soviet Citizens." *Lithuanian Bulletin*, 5 (Jan.-Feb. 1945): 8-9.

Furman, A. "Behind the Barbed Wire; Ukrainian-Russian Relations in the Concentration Camps from 1945-1955." *Ukrainian Review*, 8 (Spring 1961): 45-51.

Garthoff, Raymond L. "The Marshals and the Party: Soviet Civil-Military Relations in the Postwar Period" in *Total War and Cold War: Problems in Civilian Control of the Military*, edited by Harry L. Coles. Columbus: Ohio State University Press, 1962.

Ginsburgs, George. "Displaced Persons" in *Encyclopedia of Soviet Law*, vol. I, edited by F. J. M. Feldbrugge. Leiden: Sijthoff, 1973.

————. "Laws of War and War Crimes on the Russian Front during World War II: The Soviet View." *Soviet Studies*, 11 (Jan. 1960): 253-85.

————. "Soviet Union and the Problem of Refugees and Displaced Persons, 1917-1956." *American Journal of International Law*, 51 (Apr. 1957): 325-61.

Guerney, Bernard Guilbert, ed. "A Quota of Soviet Saws and Sayings" in *An Anthology of Russian Literature in the Soviet Period from Gorki to Pasternak*. New York: Vintage, 1960.

Gutteridge, J. A. C. "The Repatriation of Prisoners of War." *International and Comparative Law Quarterly*, 2 (Apr. 1953): 207-16.

Hale, Oron J. "World War II Documents and Interrogations." *Social Science*, 47 (Spring 1972): 75-81.

Hanfmann, Eugenia, and Jacob W. Getzels. "Inter-personal Attitudes of Former Soviet Citizens as Studied by a Semi-Projective Method." *Psychological Monographs*, 69 (no. 4, 1955): 1-37.

Hilldring, John H. "Position on Resettlement of Displaced Persons." *Department of State Bulletin*, 16 (15 June 1947): 1162-66.

Hillgruber, Andreas. "World War II" in *Marxism, Communism, and Western Society, a Comparative Encyclopedia*, vol. 8, edited by C. D. Kernig. New York: Herder and Herder, 1973.

Hlynka, Anthony. "On Behalf of Ukrainian Displaced Persons." *Ukrainian Review*, 2 (Winter 1946): 167-81.

Inkeles, Alex, Eugenia Hanfmann, and Helen Beier. "Modal Personality and Adjustment to the Soviet Sociopolitical System" in *Social Change in Soviet Russia*, edited by Alex Inkeles. Cambridge, Mass.: Harvard University Press, 1968.

Iskrin, M. "V bor'be protiv gitlerovskikh okkupantov Norvegii." *Novaia i noveishaia istoriia*, no. 6 (Nov.-Dec. 1962): 125-34.

Kaasik, J. N. "The Baltic Refugee in Sweden: A Successful Experiment." *Baltic Review*, 2 (Dec. 1947): 55-61.

————. "The Legal Status of Baltic Refugees." *Baltic Review*, 1 (Dec. 1945): 21-26.

Kalinin, Col. P. Z. "Uchastie sovetskikh voinov v partizanskom dvizhenii Belorussii." *Voenno-istoricheskii zhurnal*, no. 10 (Oct. 1962): 24-40.

Karmann, Rudolf. "Die Tragödie der Kosaken." *Neues Abendland*, 9 (1954): 661-68.

Keefe, Frederick L. "The Interpreter." *New Yorker*, 62 (10 Dec. 1966): 178-96.

Kertesz, Stephen D. "Reflections on Soviet and American Negotiating Behavior." *Review of Politics*, 19 (Jan. 1957): 3-36.

Kiung, N. F., and U. R. Talmant. "Iz istorii dvizheniia soprotivleniia sovetskikh liudei v lageriakh gitlerovskoi Germanii (1941-1945gg.)." *Istoriia SSSR*, no. 5 (Sept.-Oct. 1959): 39-55.

Kochiashvili, Miron I. "Uchastie sovetskikh grazhdan-gruzin v dvizhenii soprotivleniia v stranakh zapadnoi Evropy" in *Vtoraia mirovaia voina*, vol. 3: *Dvizhenie soprotivleniia v Evrope*, edited by E. A. Boltin. Moscow: Nauka, 1966.

Kokorin, M. A., and A. A. Strichkov. "O boevoi deiatel'nosti sovetskikh patriotov na territorii Frantsii v 1943-1944 godakh." *Voprosy istorii*, no. 3 (Mar. 1960): 88-101.

Kotov, Vasili. "Stalin Thinks I'm Dead." *Saturday Evening Post*, 220 (17 Jan. 1948): 18-19, 114-18; (24 Jan. 1948): 28, 109-10; (31 Jan. 1948): 28, 57-60.

Kotschnig, Walter M. "Problems of the Resettlement Program." *Department of State Bulletin*, 20 (13 Mar. 1949): 307-8.

"Krymskaia Konferentsiia 1945." *Bol'shaia sovetskaia entsiklopediia*. 2nd ed. Vol. 23. 1953.

Kulikov, I. N. "Ob uchastii sovetskikh grazhdan v ital'ianskom Soprotivlenii (1943-1945 gg.)" in *Ob"edinenie Italii*. Moscow: Izdatel'stvo Akademii Nauk SSSR, 1963.

Kulikov, V. G. "Internatsional'naia pomoshch' sovetskikh vooruzhennykh sil narodam Evropy." *Novaia i noveishaia istoriia*, no. 1 (Jan.-Feb. 1974): 22-47.

Kulischer, Eugene M. "Displaced Persons in the Modern World." *Annals of the American Academy of Political and Social Science*, 262 (Mar. 1949): 166-77.

Kuz'michev, I. "Zametki o sovremennom voennom romane." *Oktiabr'*, no. 3 (Mar. 1965): 185-97.

Lazarev, L. "Voennye romany K. Simonova." *Novyi mir*, no. 8 (Aug. 1964): 238-52.

Lebedev, N. "The Truth about the Second World War." *International Affairs*, no. 1 (Jan. 1974): 101-3.

" 'Liberation'—And Life Thereafter. . . ." *Lithuanian Bulletin*, 5 (May-June 1947): 5-10.

Lochtin, S. "The War in the Soviet Novel. From the Heroic to the Prosaic." *Soviet Survey*, no. 33 (1960): 62-69.

Lukin, Lt. Gen. Mikhail F. "My ne sdaemsia, tovarishch general!" *Ogonek*, no. 47 (Nov. 1964): 26-30.

Lyons, Eugene. "Orphans of Tyranny." *Plain Talk*, 2 (Mar. 1948): 41-46.

Manning, Clarence A. "Significance of the Soviet Refugees." *Ukrainian Quarterly*, 2 (Autumn 1945): 14-24.

Marshall, George C. "Concern Expressed on Resettlement of Displaced Persons." *Department of State Bulletin*, 17 (27 July 1947): 194-97.

———. "Policy on Repatriation of Displaced Persons." *Department of State Bulletin*, 16 (1 June 1947): 1085.

Martin, David. "Not 'Displaced Persons'—But Refugees." *Ukrainian Quarterly*, 4 (Spring 1948): 109-14.

Maslakov, A. "Soviet Fighters for the Liberation of Italy." *International Affairs*, no. 1 (Jan. 1960): 116-19.

Nechaev, G. "Sovetskie liudi srazhalis' v Dordoni." *Voprosy istorii*, no. 10 (Oct. 1969): 193-97.

———. "Uchastie sovetskikh grazhdan v dvizhenii Soprotivleniia vo Frantsii v gody vtoroi mirovoi voiny." *Voenno-istoricheskii zhurnal*, no. 6 (June 1965): 37-50.

———. "V lesakh Lotaringii." *Voenno-istoricheskii zhurnal*, no. 4 (Apr. 1971): 86-90.

Novosil'tsev, I. I. "Andrei Andreevich Vlasov." *Novyi zhurnal*, no. 129 (Dec. 1977): 183-90.

Oberbeck, S. K. "Their Unfinest Hour." Review of *The Last Secret* by Nicholas Bethell. *Newsweek*, 85 (20 Jan. 1975): 76, 78.

Osers, Ewald. "The Liberation of Prague: Fact and Fiction." *Survey: A Journal of Soviet and East European Studies*, no. 76 (Summer 1970): 99-111.

"The Peoples of the U.S.S.R." *Life*, 14 (29 Mar. 1943): 23-26.

Perlmutter, Oscar William. "Dean Acheson and the Diplomacy of World War II." *Western Political Quarterly*, 14 (Dec. 1961): 896-911.

Proudfoot, Malcolm J. "Anglo-American Displaced Persons Program for Germany and Austria." *American Journal of Economics and Sociology*, 6 (Oct. 1946): 33-54.

"Red Leaders: They Are Tough, Loyal, Capable Administrators." *Life*, 14 (29 Mar. 1943): 38-42.

"Refugees and Displaced Persons." *Great Soviet Encyclopedia*. 3rd ed. 1973 [c1970].

Rekemchuk, Aleksandr. "The Catechism of the Provocateur" in *The Last Circle*. Moscow: Novosti, 1974.

"Repatriation of Soviet Citizens." *International Labour Review*, 52 (Nov. 1945): 533-34.

"Repatriatsiia." *Bol'shaia sovetskaia entsiklopediia*. 2nd ed. Vol. 36. 1955.

―――. *Bol'shaia sovetskaia entsiklopediia*. 3rd. ed. Vol. 22. 1975.

―――. *Diplomaticheskii slovar'*. Vol. 3. Moscow: Gosudarstvennoe Izdatel'stvo Politicheskoi Literatury, 1964.

―――. *Diplomaticheskii slovar'*. Vol. 3. Moscow: Izdatel'stvo Politicheskoi Literatury, 1973.

―――. *Politicheskii slovar'*. 2nd ed. Moscow: Gosudarstvennoe Izdatel'stvo Politicheskoi Literatury, 1958.

Richardson, J. L. "Cold-War Revisionism: A Critique." *World Politics*, 24 (July 1972): 579-612.

Roof, Michael K., and Frederick A. Leedy. "Population Redistribution in the Soviet Union, 1939-1956." *Geographical Review*, 49 (Apr. 1959): 208-21.

Sage, Jerry M. "The Future of DP's in Europe." *Department of State Bulletin*, 17 (13 July 1947): 86-95.

Sampson, Francis. "Paratrooper Padre." *American Ecclesiastical Review*, 116 (Feb. 1947): 109-23; (Mar. 1947): 199-209.

Sauvy, Alfred. "Psycho-Social Aspects of Migration" in *Economics of International Migration*, edited by Brimley Thomas. London: Macmillan, 1958.

Scott, John. "Interview with a Russian D. P." *Fortune*, 39 (Apr. 1949): 81-84.

"The Search." *New York Times Film Reviews (1939-1948)*, 3 (24 Mar. 1948): 2242-43.

Serebryakova, Galina. "Bankruptcy" in *The Last Circle*. Moscow: Novosti, 1974.

Shalamov, Varlam. "Poslednii boi maiora Pugacheva." *Grani*, 76 (July 1970): 40-52.

Shils, Edward A. "Social and Psychological Aspects of Displacement and Repatriation." *Journal of Social Issues*, 2 (Aug. 1946): 3-18.

Shmel'tser, Ia. "Soprotivlenie inostrannykh rabochikh, ugnannykh v gitlerovskuiu Germaniiu." *Novaia i noveishaia istoriia*, no. 2 (Mar.-Apr. 1962): 130-39.

"Skonchalsia Dzhulius Epstein." *Novoe Russkoe Slovo* (10 July 1975): 10.
Small, Melvin. "Buffoons and Brave Hearts: Hollywood Portrays the Russians, 1939-1944." *California Historical Quarterly*, 52 (Winter 1973): 326-37.
————. "How We Learned to Love the Russians: American Media and the Soviet Union during World War II." *The Historian*, 36 (May 1974): 455-78.
Smirnov, Sergei S. "In Behalf of Soldiers." *Current Digest of the Soviet Press*, 11 (6 Jan. 1960): 6-8. Translated from *Literaturnaia gazeta* (27 Oct. 1959): 3.
Smith, Gaddis. "Rewriting the History of American Diplomacy during the Second World War" in *The National Archives and Foreign Relations Research*, edited by Milton O. Gustafson. Athens: Ohio University Press, 1974.
Smith, T. L. "Refugee Orthodox Congregations in Western Europe, 1945-1948." *Church History*, 38 (Sept. 1969): 312-26.
Solzhenitsyn, Alexander. "An Incident at Krechetovka Station" in *Stories and Prose Poems*, translated by Michael Glenny. New York: Farrar, Straus, and Giroux, 1971.
————. "Matryona's House" in *Stories and Prose Poems*, translated by Michael Glenny. New York: Farrar, Straus and Giroux, 1971.
————. "Repentance and Self-Limitation in the Life of Nations" in *From under the Rubble*, edited by Alexander Solzhenitsyn. Boston: Little, Brown, 1975 [c1974].
"Soviet Citizenship Law." *Soviet Statutes and Decisions*, 7 (Fall 1970): 10-116; (Winter 1970-71): 131-224; (Summer 1971): 457-66.
Stars and Stripes (several editions).
Swingler, Randall. "The Right to Free Expression (Annotated by George Orwell)." *Polemic*, 5 (Sept.-Oct. 1946): 45-53.
Taratuta, Jean. "Tell Me Who Your Friend Is. . . ." in *The Last Circle*. Moscow: Novosti, 1974.
Theoharis, Athan. "James F. Byrnes: Unwitting Yalta Myth Maker." *Political Science Quarterly*, 81 (Dec. 1966): 581-92.
Tishkov, A. V. "Predatel' pered sovetskim sudom." *Sovetskoe gosudarstvo i pravo*, no. 2 (Feb. 1973): 89-98.
Tolstoy, Alexandra. "The Russian DPs." *Russian Review*, 9 (Jan. 1950): 53-58.
Twohey, James S. "U. S. Opinion on Russia." *Fortune*, 32 (Sept. 1945): 233-43.
United States Forces European Theater. "Soviet Repatriation." *Weekly Information Bulletin*, 19 (1 Dec. 1945): 27.
"U.S. Requests Withdrawal of Soviet Repatriation Mission from American Zone in Germany." *Department of State Bulletin*, 20 (13 Mar. 1949): 320-22.
Utechin, Sergej. "Refugees." *Everyman's Concise Encyclopedia of Russia*. New York: Dutton, 1964.
Vagts, Alfred. "Battle and Other Combatant Casualties in the Second World War." *Journal of Politics*, 7 (Sept. 1945): 411-38.
"Vlasovtsy." *Bol'shaia sovetskaia entsiklopediia*. 3rd ed. Vol. 5. 1971.
Voronin, Sergei. "V rodnykh mestakh." *Neva*, no. 9 (Sept. 1959): 15-22, translated in *Current Digest of the Soviet Press*, 11 (6 Jan. 1960): 3-6.
Walsh, Warren B. "What the American People Think of Russia." *Public Opinion Quarterly*, 8 (Winter 1944): 513-22.
Williams, Robert C. "European Political Emigrations: A Lost Subject." *Comparative Studies in Society and History*, 12 (Apr. 1970): 140-48.
Zelenin, V. V. "Uchastie sovetskikh liudei v narodno-osvoboditel'noi voine v

Iugoslavii" in *Vtoraia mirovaia voina*, vol. 3: *Dvizhenie soprotivleniia v Evrope*, edited by E. A. Boltin. Moscow: Nauka, 1966.

Zhilin, P. A. "How A. Solzhenitsyn Sang of the Vlasovites' Betrayal" in *The Last Circle*. Moscow: Novosti, 1974.

——. "O problemakh istorii vtoroi mirovoi voiny." *Novaia i noveishaia istoriia*, no. 2 (Mar.-Apr. 1973): 3-19.

Zhugarina, L. S. "Uchastie sovetskikh partizan v dvizhenii Soprotivleniia v raione Rima" in *Ob"edinenie Italii*. Moscow: Izdatel'stvo Akademii Nauk S.S.S.R., 1963.

Zile, Zigurds L. "Amnesty and Pardon in the Soviet Union." *Soviet Union*, 3 (part 1, 1976): 37-49.

Zink, Harold. "American Civil-Military Relations in the Occupation of Germany" in *Total War and Cold War: Problems in Civilian Control of the Military*, edited by Harry L. Coles. Columbus: Ohio State University, 1962.

Index

*r = repatriation.

A Note on the Author

MARK R. ELLIOTT is an associate professor of history at Asbury College, Wilmore, Kentucky. Born in Stearns, Kentucky, and reared in Atlanta, Georgia, he received his B.A. from Asbury College (1969) and his M.A. and Ph.D. from the University of Kentucky (1971 and 1974, respectively). His publications include articles for *Military Affairs*, the *Modern Encyclopedia of Russian and Soviet History*, and *Political Science Quarterly*.